RADIO MASTER

THE LIFE AND TIMES OF
SPORTS BROADCASTING GREAT

TED HUSING

RADIO MASTER

THE LIFE AND TIMES OF
SPORTS BROADCASTING GREAT
TED HUSING

JOHN LEWIS

LANGDON STREET PRESS

Minneapolis

Langdon Street Press

212 3rd Avenue North, Suite 290

Minneapolis, MN 55401

612.455.2293

www.langdonstreetpress.com

ISBN - 978-1-936183-24-1

ISBN - 1-936183-24-2

LCCN - 2010936395

Cover Design & Typeset by Kristeen Wegner

Printed in the United States of America

LANGDON STREET PRESS

For Edie Britt Lewis.

Always remain uplifted by your name.

CONTENTS

PRELUDE

Dark circles blotched his eyes. A wooden cane helped keep his thin, brittle frame from collapsing. Cancer filled his brain, depression ravaged his once mighty spirit. When he died, Ted Husing resembled a decrepit, ancient man, but in reality he was just sixty years of age. During more vibrant times, he was eloquent, endearing, and loquacious—essential traits for a radio announcer. He breathed direction and command into a business that had before him flapped recklessly around the dial. He didn't just speak into a microphone, Ted informed a nation.

Whether he was covering breaking news or doing political convention coverage, Ted could deliver a spew of words like popcorn from a hot pan. At night he prowled the club scene looking for the next "big thing" in music, unafraid to put his reputation on the line and give unknown artists exposure through a national radio audience. But it was on the mantel of sports play-by-play that the "Master" hung his star.

Ask any fan to fill a list of all-time great sports announcers, and it will by and large be sprinkled with the iconic names of Barber, Allen, Nelson, McKay, Costas, Cosell, and Buck, each one possessing awesome talents, rightfully taking their place in broadcasting history. Regrettably, the name Husing will almost always be absent, off to the side, shamefully overlooked. The reason? Ted made his mark during the Golden Age of radio, single-handedly creating the ins and outs of a modern profession, but he was unable to transfer his work to the enduring images of televison. However, if not for Ted Husing, all the great sports broadcasting names that followed him would have been lost behind their microphones. My hope is that this book will not only help reinstate Mr. Husing to the honored lists, but also place him near the top where he most certainly belongs. Trust me when I say, Ted Husing was so much more than just some "sports announcer."

He would be called many things throughout his existence: roughneck, arrogant, kind, chump, punk, big shot, pioneer, hero, doughboy, playboy, go-to man, forgotten man. At different times in his life, all the labels fit. But no one ever called him boring. No one dared to call him subtle. They knew better. Ted's approach to living mirrored his approach to broadcasting, accurate and true—no beating around the bush. The man teetered precariously on moments of irony. He could be irascible and profane one minute, thoughtful and charming the next. At worst, Ted was a son-of-a-bitch. But at his best, he was a star, light among the darkness, inspiring the throngs who followed him and worshipped the ground he walked on.

By the time I got to Husing he was simply a name, a broadcast voice of another time, spinning records and calling football games, track events, and political conventions. I heard of the man, yes, but knew little about him. And if one must know, I cared even less. So like any good writer worth his words, I began asking questions. I figured a good place to start was those aging sports announcers, retired and bustling with tales of their youth, who actually knew Ted, heard Ted's work, and remembered his broadcasts: network stars like Chris Schenkel and local legends Ernie Harwell, Les Keiter, Bill Mazer, Chuck Thompson, and Marty Glickman. To my surprise, these great talents answered my queries with patience and kindness.

But, I wasn't so much struck by the fact that they responded to my questions, but how. Some smiled, some laughed, some squawked, some breathed a little heavier; some lost their ability to speak at all, a voice cracking with emotion.

My journey to Husing started along Boylston Street in Boston on a warm Indian summer afternoon, October 9, 1999. Blood rushed to my head. The moisture on my palms spread as the pulse quickened. I was meeting one of my childhood heroes. I took a deep breath, gathered my nerve, and pressed firmly on the buzzer. The door opened and there stood a man I did not recognize. His shoulders folded inward. The face was wrinkled and pocked with patches of blazing sun. His hair was snowflake white. The orange shirt and tan slippers he sported were unfamiliar as well. Yet, the sound of his voice I knew. It was the voice of a "Cowboy" named Gowdy.

Curt Gowdy called every big sporting event of my boyhood over the NBC Television airwaves: Super Bowls, World Series, NCAA Final Fours, and Rose Bowls. I even watched the "American Sportsman" on ABC just to get another fix of my guy Gowdy when God knows I never enjoyed fishing and the only gun I ever fired was a BB rifle at a neighborhood dog, popping it on the ass purely by accident. The man made me love sports and those who called the action. Curt Gowdy is dead now, but even in his waning years, to me, Gowdy was special and I felt lucky to have known him.

As Gowdy was my guy, Ted was his. Listening from his tiny home in Cheyenne, Wyoming, young Curt grew up lionizing the great CBS announcer with the captivating voice. When I asked him about Ted Husing what followed was a Niagara of words that seemed to flow faster than my ability to feed blank tapes into my flimsy handheld recorder. His annoying silver-furred dog Feefe nibbled forever at my heels, barking incessantly. However, she wasn't the only one in the room excited, feeling the energy. I held my ground and stayed focused because I knew I had the "Cowboy" where I wanted him—story time.

"I remember going up there (New York) in 1946 to do the North Carolina versus Oklahoma A&M basketball game. My station: KMOA in Oklahoma City—we were a CBS affiliate. My boss called up there and got a hold of Husing and said this kid really looks up to you and while he's in New York, would he have a chance to meet with you and talk? Husing said, 'Yes, send him up to the office.' I wasn't feeling well when I got there. I was coming down with a cold. So I was up there talking to Ted. He was always on the phone, very brusque guy. Then he said, 'What the fuck's the matter with you? Jeez, your head is full of snot. Do you have a cold?' I said, 'I've got a terrible head cold.' He said, 'Get your coat on, let's go.' I said, 'where are we going?' 'Shut up!' he said. That's the way he talked. I didn't say anything. I was in awe of him. I got in the car with him and drove up to upper Manhattan, I remember. We got out and went in. There was a doctor's office. They were old friends. He said, 'I want you to take a look at this kid, he's got a broadcast tonight.' So I sat in the chair and he (the doctor) sprayed my nose and opened it up. So I said, 'Are you Mr. Husing's doctor?' He said, 'You know what? He had an appointment with me today but gave it up so I could see you.' See, the guy had a lot of good sides. That's my first relations with Ted Husing. . . . A lot of guys didn't like him because he was sort of uppity. I liked him. He was always good to me."[1]

Gowdy's story of Ted had me laughing. Perhaps it was the fact that my idol, Curt Gowdy, was becoming more human to me by the minute, cursing and chewing the fat like long lost friends on a weekend bender. But, the laughter soon stopped. I looked in Gowdy's eyes and saw how much the man he spoke of had meant— that one moment of kindness from his hero still fresh in his mind like it happened only hours before. I was moved. I was beginning to understand that this man Husing went beyond just a voice calling sports over a hot radio mike. He was flesh and blood. Complex. Proud. Vulnerable. Strange. I craved for more, and I still do.

I have spent nearly ten years researching this book, interviewing hundreds of people, streaming through countless reels of microfilm, listening to recorded broadcasts, entering stadium booths, clicking on search engines, climbing library steps, and traveling thousands of miles to undercover the truth. Unfortunately, that bold quest sometimes eluded me, lost to time, defeated by circumstances. In lieu of the truth, I have been left to rely on my own fertile imagination of what may have been. Any artistic liberties taken were done with the sole purpose of enhancing the facts. I leaned heavily on this potent mix of resources to create the scenes and dialogue you are about to discover.

My goal from the very beginning of this project was to give the reader a vivid look at a unique, untold history with the sound and feel of a novel. Ted Husing fought many battles in his life, some real, others imagined. I felt compelled within these pages to fight many of those battles with him. This is the story of the greatest sports broadcaster who ever lived, not so much a stagnant biography as it is a living, breathing, human testimony of the times in which he lived, worked, and loved. Every person mentioned is real. Every human emotion is heart-felt. The details of his life are far too impossible to be considered untrue.

* For reasons of clarity to the reader, actual quotes and recorded broadcasts will be either footnoted or sourced through out the book. Any dialoug created by the author will not.

CHAPTER ONE

A NIGHT OF REDEMPTION

It was cold outside, a cloudy, gray sky packed tight with moisture. The smell of snow made him think of boyhood pranks, toboggan rides, and late-season football games played by grown men. Ted filled his lungs with the raw surroundings of the last day in January, 1957. He let it go with a deep bilious groan. Arching his back, he tried to straighten himself up by leaning against the car. In the light he could gently make out the shadows of his breath. "Sounds like the old feisty Ted," the good father said. "I feel good Ben," he remarked to the priest. "I'm really glad you're with me." For Ted Husing the patient, the past five months at Burke Rehabilitation Hospital was more a chamber of horrors than home sweet home. And he felt grateful for a change of scenery, whatever the reason.

As the drive progressed, Ted trembled with nervous anticipation. What was in store for the evening, he only wondered. From Ted the questions were many, but the priest would not budge, tight-lipped about what lay ahead. "All in good time, my friend," Fr. Dudley suggested. "All in good time." From the car radio played an upbeat melody vaguely familiar. A pretty singer named Doris Day sang the story, the lyrics profound, cruel and equally prophetic.

Que Sera, Sera
Whatever will be, will be
The Future's not ours to see
Que Sera, Sera[2]

Ted could barely see, but his ears worked fine. Forced to play detective, the broadcaster searched for clues, anything that might reveal where they were headed. From the sound of water kicking off the tires, he knew it was precipitating. Thick ghostly flakes, meteors disguised as snow, blanked the streets and sidewalks. Soon he heard the rumblings of a multitude of automobiles, horns, and other assorted traffic. He felt the light rhythms, a distinctive pace pulling him further upward like the chic riffs of cool Harlem Jazz. It could be only one place—Manhattan. Father Dudley said nothing, keeping Ted in the dark. He maneuvered the car along 42nd Street, passed the United Nations building and veered uptown four blocks on Vanderbilt Avenue. A line of red brake lights crawled bumper to bumper. The rubber-lipped wipers scraped back and forth against the windshield.

Ten more minutes passed before the duo reached their final destination. The time had come to reveal the secret. The priest stopped the car along 46th and spoke. "Mel and the rest of the SBA boys thought it was time they threw you a little party." This night, Mel Allen had nothing to do with broadcasting the New York Yankees or a World Series game. This night, he was a friend, a disciple, really—one of the many Ted helped along the way. Surprisingly, Ted had thought little of the Sports Broadcasters Association since the surgeon's scalpels intervened, but his mind retreated to finer days. He thought of his home away from home, comfortable among those he trusted the most. "Oh God! 21?" he guessed. He guessed wrong. Fr. Dudley countered, temporarily bursting his friend's bubble. "No, I don't think the 21 Club is big enough for what's in store tonight, my boy. How does the Roosevelt grab you?" Ted's eyes, still sightless, opened wider. He knew the hotel of high rollers and businessmen travelers very well.

He thought of Guy Lombardo, who booked a lengthy engagement at the hotel in 1929 after Ted gave him a spot on the CBS chain. Playing "Auld Lang Syne" at the stroke of midnight turned into a staple of New Year's Eve gayety. The world might have never known of the famous bandleader if it wasn't for Ted Husing.

Dudley continued to speak, jarring his friend back to the present. "They're doing this for you. They're honoring you tonight." A smile crept across Ted's face, something that had seldom happened in recent months. He was happy to be alive. He was blind, his voice almost unrecognizable, but he was happy nonetheless. "I should have known I couldn't trust a man of the cloth," he said with a laugh. Dudley smiled back saying, "I'll go to the confessional tomorrow. Let's go have a few drinks so I can really have something to talk about. Stick with me fella, I'll make a good Catholic of you yet."

The priest played one more trump card, leaving the best surprise for last. "Oh, and by the way. They thought that you should receive The Graham McNamee Award." It was a special piece of hardware, a prize honoring the dead sports announcer, bestowed upon a living member for his own accomplishments behind the microphone. Ted's jovial mood instantly changed. He sat silent with a hand inside his mouth. He was shocked, suddenly filled with terror. The valet rapped on the window ready to park the car. The windshield wipers continued their metrical dance against the glass. "You can do this, Ted. You're ready," the priest reassured him. "They're waiting for you. Shall we go inside and say hello?" Calling a football game on a Saturday afternoon, a World Series game from Sportsman's Park, a savage Joe Louis right hook to millions of network listeners was easy compared to facing a room full of eager sports announcers. What would they think? Husing, the man many called the "Master," for better or worse, was about to find out. One thing was for sure, if not for Ted Husing, there wouldn't be a Sports Broadcasters Association.

In the early days, radio was seen as the ugly stepchild to print media. The public devoured newspapers, preferring noisy headlines and a cup of joe in the morning. New York and Brooklyn alone printed some fifteen daily newspapers in 1925.[3] But, where newspapers could reach thousands of eyes in advertising, radio could reach millions of ears. Radio offered the immediacy of news and information. No longer did the public have to wait until morning papers hit the streets for details and descriptions. A click of the dial equaled instant access. Better yet, it was free.

Publishers and their sales staffs, threatened by the cut in profits, tried blocking the networks from wire service use. Some newspapers during the early 1930s refused even to print area radio logs and program notes. A.A. Schechter, then NBC news chief, summed up the feud saying, "They don't speak to us and we don't answer."[4] None felt more bullied by radio than writers, dependent on the hungry eyes of readers for their bread and butter. "This was an era when the newspaper reporter was an earthbound deity," wrote historian Robert Smith. "Gathering free hats, suits of clothes, meals without charge, and even more fleshly tributes for printing, under any pretext whatever, the name of some stage or screen actor or of a store, restaurant, petty crook, big politician, or professional athlete."[5]

The perks were good for newspapermen. With the new medium, they got better. As it were, writers recognized the changing tide, the force of radio, clearer than anyone. Many gifted newspapermen jumped ship to talk instead from a microphone, renowned journalist Lowell Thomas and gossip moll Walter Winchell among them. On the air came preferable fame, superior access, and fatter paychecks than a weekly column could provide. Over time, the two mediums learned to live together. Yet, not all agreed. Among a few scribes, namely sportswriters, bitterness lingered. Hard-liners and war hawks held onto the past. Below all the civility boiled an undertow of jealousy and tension on the verge of eruption. The World Series of 1941 hosted not only a showdown for baseball supremacy, but would settle, once and for all, the battle of the booth.

As the month of September closed that year, New York burned with pennant fever. Not because Joe DiMaggio slapped a base hit in fifty-six straight games. Not because Red Sox left fielder Ted Williams batted over .400. It was because the Dodgers had won first place in the National League, a feat not witnessed in twenty-one seasons. The people of Brooklyn collectively jumped for joy and threw a parade down Flatbush Avenue. Could the championship be within reach? One very imposing obstacle blocked their way—the hated Yankees across town. Showcased throughout the '41 campaign were the singular talents of DiMaggio, the Yankee Clipper. War raged in Europe. But, the fight for baseball supremacy would happen stateside between the white lines, New York style. Yankee pinstripes versus Dodger blue, Game 1 in the Bronx at Yankee Stadium, October 1, 1941.

While October approached, interest soared. School kids played hooky. Hotel rooms from Montague Street to Broadway sold out.[6] As for tickets, like the locals would say, "fawget about it!" List price for Ebbets Field box seats was a bulky $16.50,[7] yet cost didn't seem to matter. Scalpers found fans willing to pay five times that much.[8] For those who couldn't gain admittance to the '41 Series, there was always the radio. Dodger's voice Walter "Red" Barber alongside Chicago broadcaster Bob Elson would call the action over the Mutual Broadcasting System.[9]

Besides MBS, the other network fat-cat sports announcers from NBC and CBS figured on gaining press credentials, not wanting to miss the sports event of the year. They, too, were working members of the media. Or so they thought. Of course, one of those expecting press credentials was the best-known sports announcer in America, Ted Husing. Surprisingly, Ted and his comrades met resistance—the boys at the newspapers, and none more powerful than the Baseball Writers Association of America.

Perhaps no group of writers and columnists wielded more influence: Baseball was king, the national past time. American-born, made of hallowed records, played by mythic figures, and promoted by the motto of its most talented wordsmiths, such as Shirley Povich of the *Washington Post*, Damon Runyand, *Sporting News* Editor J.G. Taylor Spink, and Grantland Rice, the greatest of them all.

The World Series always doubled up the press box. Everybody wanted in. Local writers from every Major League city were welcomed, as well as syndicated columnists and PR suits from the Commissioner's office. For the 1941 Series, the need grew stronger. Stadiums dressed in red, white, and blue banners. Commemorative press pins were made and special programs were printed. Even the Yankee Stadium press box received a quick overhaul prior to the first pitch. "The press box is being equipped with plush seats with gold trimming," announced the *New York Daily News*. "Probably borrowed from some undertaker."[10] In the end, they alone—the writers—decided who gained entrance to the press box. Surrendering valuable workspace, not to mention plush gold seats to the hacks of radio, was unthinkable. The decision was made—no additional mike men.

Anger and resentment torched the radio ranks. Ted spoke for them all. "Fuck those newspaper pricks," he cursed. "There'd be enough room in that press box if some writers I know stopped hitting the food buffet harder than they thump their typewriters. We'll get organized. We know a few people in high places." Ted wasn't so much concerned about himself. Few men garnered more respect in a press box than he. Besides, some of his closest friends were sports writers, covering the same events and sharing the same dining car on trains over the years. But Ted saw the future of solidarity.

He phoned a few of the veteran members of the BWAA[11] hoping cooler heads might prevail. Ironically, joining Barber and Elson in the Mutual booth was *New York Herald* writer and Husing drinking buddy Bill Corum who got an ear full.[12] Still no change. Some of the more vocal gatekeepers were Charley Segar of the *New York Daily Mirror* and *New York Herald* baseball beat writer Arthur "Red" Patterson, who refused to budge.[13] Ted wasn't finished yet. He quickly gathered the troops and assigned a task force. The strategy: if the writers wouldn't grant permission to the press box, maybe the ball clubs would. Hall of Fame boxing announcer Don Dunphy was a constituent on that committee. "We called on Larry McPhail (Dodgers) and Ed Barrow, the general manager of the Yankees and told them our thoughts," he recalled. "They were very sympathetic to us but replied that at the moment their hands were tied. . . ."[14] McPhail and Barrow countered with the next best thing, free tickets to all the games. The group accepted the seats in quiet defeat. Ted sat alongside his brethren except Game 3, absent due to work, calling the Southern Methodist versus Fordham football clash on the network from the Polo Grounds.[15] No one despised losing and hated consolation more than Ted.

After the Series, Husing took action and formed the Sports Broadcasters Association. Not surprisingly, he was unanimously voted its first president. "Never Again" became the rallying cry. The 1941 World Series taught the group a valuable lesson. There was power in numbers. Writers as well as radio sports announcers could benefit from an alliance of sanctioned authority. The SBA quickly grew. Members came from small markets and large, Boston, Chicago, Philly, D.C., Pittsburgh, Cleveland. New York, as always, never stood overshadowed. The hub of decision-making, the city juiced with 50,000 watts of network power and was now home to the most formidable union of sports announcers in America.

The Sports Broadcasters Association's Annual Gala was born in 1947. Classy affairs, VIP guest lists, sponsors, and an open bar became the norm, a far cry from the usual weekly luncheons of networking and broadcast business. Some of the biggest names in sports, news, and entertainment graced the dais. Even some of the not-so-famous appeared. "One year we had an Irish rabbi from some synagogue in Rhode Island do the benediction," recalled Mel Allen's younger brother Larry. "I don't know how they found him. He had everybody doubled-up laughing."

But as memorable as the past SBA dinners had been, January 31, 1957, would be remembered above any other. With the Roosevelt came the perfect setting. The hotel's grand ballroom captured the majestic tradition of the SBA dinner: high ceilings; rectangle windows stretching from floor to roof; round, bold pillars topped off by a series of glimmering chandeliers. All came hoping to catch a glimpse of the one they called the "Master." Outside, Dudley led Ted from the car to the hotel lobby. Anticipation swelled. Heads turned. The giant catering hall was filled to capacity.

The room held a litany of Who's Who in the business of broadcasting and sports: CBS broadcast legend Edward R. Murrow, who served as toast master; NBC president Robert Sarnoff, son of the famous General who gave Ted his first radio job; former assistants Les Quailey, Jimmy Dolan, and Walter Kennedy; Corum and other prominent sportswriters such as Jimmy Cannon and Red Smith; restaurateurs Toots Shor and Pete Kriendler; fellow sports mike men such as Red Barber, Al Helfer, and Clem McCarthy; Yankee greats Yogi Berra and Whitey Ford; and *Sports Magazine's* Man of the Year, Mickey Mantle. Ted's mother sat at a table near the front. Accompanying her was the friend he never knew he had, Sandy Simon.

At his best, few loved an adoring crowd more than Ted. Gravitating to the attention, he was strong and confident. He was none of those things now, thin, sickly, the sound of his voice soft and difficult to understand. He endured the generous heaping of well-wishers and vigorous handshakes. "Glad to see you, Ted. You look great." His friends tried to lie well. Ted, as always, remained the most honest man in the room. He knew the truth.

Rounding out the room was the new wave of sports announcing stars: Curt Gowdy, Marty Glickman, Lindsey Nelson, Chris Schenkel, and Mel Allen were among others who owed a debt of gratitude to the Master for teaching them the ropes. First as youngsters, they sat by their radios in awe as they listened. Now as men, they worshiped the ground he walked, following in his footsteps. "If only McNamee was here, alive—it would be perfect," Ted thought.

The outpouring of love and respect clearly humbled the great announcer. Surprisingly, another man attended the SBA gala, more unprepared than Ted, to face the onslaught of unbridled affection: a 22-year-old pole-vaulter from Oklahoma named Jim Graham. Because of an injured ankle, Graham had willingly given up his spot on the 1956 Olympic track team to another pole-vaulter, Bob Gutkowski of Occidental College. Gutkowski won a silver medal at Melbourne and went on to grace the cover of *Sports Illustrated* as one of the most distinguished amateur athletes of the decade. But, that night at the Roosevelt, Jim Graham was awarded the first ever Ted Husing Award for sportsmanship.

Honoring the accomplishments of a collegiate pole-vaulter was nice. But, a thousand guests inside the Roosevelt battled the harsh wintry New York elements outside for one reason—Husing. His loyal friends Jimmy Dolan, Les Quailey, and the big man with the hearty laugh, Toots Shor, rushed to the microphone and told stories. They poked fun, reminisced about younger days, and wished to God he never left them. His old boss William Paley paid tribute to a talent, thanking him for his tireless service. Nervous laughter and polite applause bounced from one end of the banquet room to the other. The proverbial roasting finally done, Murrow again took charge and returned to the podium. In his customary urgent, profound voice, he presented Ted with the Graham McNamee Award. The mention of the name—GRAHAM MCNAMEE—gave Ted pause. He missed the man dearly. A friend. An enemy. A mentor. A rival. Hated and loved simultaneously.

Then the moment came. It was time for the Master to

speak. Could he speak? What would he say? Fr. Dudley and Mel Allen delicately led him to the microphone. He looked weak and felt even weaker. Fear bit hard as sweat poured down his armpits. He held firm to the podium with both hands. For the first time since his operation, Ted thanked God he was blind. At least he wouldn't have to see their disappointment.

But in front of the mike, the broadcaster gained strength. Here, as so many times before, he was at home—safe. Power surged. He was invincible. Ted gasped for air and spoke. "Perhaps you don't know it, gentlemen," he began. "But not very long ago they operated on me for a brain tumor. And when they did that they disturbed my eyesight, so I can no longer see, but I can hear and sometimes I can feel, and what I hear today and what I feel today in the world of sports broadcasting by television or radio thrills me . . .gives me one of the greatest feelings I've ever had."[16]

Ted's voice began to crack. Emotions swelled. He stopped to gain his composure. The room sat riveted, still as midnight. Ted dipped his head down to his chest and lifted it again, biting his lower lip. "Tonight I don't need eyes in my head, such as those eyes that used to see all the sports . . . or the mouth which interpreted whatever the eyes saw, and passed it on. Tonight, my eyes are in my heart. And because you people have shown up here tonight, the things which have been said about me, which are consummate lies to the nth degree . . . although I'm most appreciative . . . do not have to be seen with these eyes, just felt inside."[17]

Ted paused again, looked out into the massive audience of dark figures and clasped his hands in prayer. He thanked them and stepped back from the microphone. The room exploded in wild applause. The sound was deafening. They loved him so much. How the man ever forgot that, only he knew. Flashbulbs popped. He felt the grips of their hands. No one wanted to leave. They yearned to touch him, to say hello, to thank him one last time. The crowd of giddy men rushed around him. Robert Sarnoff grabbed the award and placed it inside his hands. If Ted could read the words, all of the words, he might have died right there. Engraved on the gold plaque was:

To Ted Husing

Dean of Sportscasting and Architect of Our Profession[18]

Murrow returned to the microphone one last time and ended the program. The crowd was spent and begged to regain their composure, preferably outside in the cold, wintry air. A fresh cigarette, a moment to digest everything the evening fed them.

"God, he gave a great talk. It almost brought tears to your eyes," remembered Curt Gowdy years later. "It was a hell of a tribute." Mr. Gowdy was not the only one who left that evening with emotions swelling the throat. Ted's impassioned words, the presence of greatness, reduced many to tears. "Some who listened feared Ted might break up before he got to the mike," wrote Red Smith in his column a few days later. "He is a sentimental guy and he was visibly moved. Some of those who feared he wouldn't make it before he finished talking, it was they who were bawling."[19] Jim Graham, the honored Oklahoma A&M pole-vaulter was also amazed by Ted's sudden eloquence. "He had a very commanding voice. And it seemed to me like the volume and projection of his voice surprised me given how frail he looked. The delivery had a lot of strength to it."[20]

Even the stoic taskmaster of the profession, Red Barber, was moved. "He looked good, and his voice was the old Husing voice when he spoke," he said. "That was Husing's last great moment, maybe his pinnacle moment."[21] Don Dunphy and fellow sports mike man Win Elliot missed the dinner trying to return from Florida were they covered a boxing match, their planes grounded by the bad weather. Dunphy would say later, "It's always been a regret of mine that I couldn't be there to honor Ted."[22]

It was still snowing outside. The city covered in a blanket

11

of white. It was quiet, serene—ideal. As Father Dudley cautiously drove his friend back to White Plains, not a word passed between them. Dudley knew, like the Confessional, there was something sacred, gratifying in the silence. From the passenger seat, Ted rocked with quiet satisfaction. The radioman felt free. He could fly. Ted had purged his soul to the world that night. Instead of the damnation he feared, they stood in applause to support him. Ted dressed himself for bed that night. He didn't need help from the night nurse. He laid his head on the white pillow and gently crossed his arms. The broadcaster closed his eyes and felt his heart beat—strong. Ted was back—born again—among the living.

CHAPTER TWO

BLACK SHEEP, GERMAN SALOONS

Mmm! Something delicious wafted in the air unimpeded. An ice-blue sky behind a thousand barren trees rose above the hard frozen ground, making all the senses come alive. Turkey it was, or maybe goose. The aroma seeped through the walls of not just the Husing apartment but all those homes within smelling distance. On this day, it probably meant the entire Bronx borough. On this day, November 27, 1901, the neighborhood was getting ready to eat and pray. The next day would be Thanksgiving.

Bertha Husing was perhaps the only one not cooking. The young German-born woman lay with her immediate future in the hands of a midwife, the pain of childbirth digging into the belly, pushing at the back. Her 32-year-old husband Henry, also of German blood, having been born and raised in Hanover, could only wait. He was a hardworking man possessing a suave, diplomatic personality. Hanover was a bustling, modern city erected off the edge of the River Leine. Kingly estates, marble statues, and outlandish gardens covered the city from riverbank to hillside. It gained a reputation as a place where they spoke "the true German."[23] Henry had waited on tables there, earning a decent wage. But, he like many young minds, dreamed of success in the New World. He heard the

13

stories of Germans in places like Milwaukee and St. Louis building empires out of beer, making piles of cash with the aid of a knife and fork. If Hanover was once the city of dukes, in America he might be king. Then again, there were other reasons to get away.

When Henry Husing and Bertha Hecht entered the Old Barge Office on Manhattan's lower tip, they did not come like the typical immigrant, meek, humble, or clueless. They came striding with purpose, a man and woman on a mission.

Bertha grew-up in the city of Bielefeld, placed on the north-central lowlands and formed as a guard post during the Dark Age. When Henry Husing met Bertha Hecht she was one of less than 600 Jews residing in Bielefeld.[24] Lutherans, however, were a dime a dozen—teachers, bureaucrats, blacksmiths, soldiers, and farmers. Two-thirds of the German population called themselves Lutheran, including Henry.[25] Neither Henry nor Bertha were particularly religious souls. For Bertha, the inside of a synagogue was just as exotic as stained-glass windows were for Henry. Their courtship developed like most, innocent, natural, and untamed—traveling in common circles, visiting the same small villages, sharing likes and dislikes. Once Henry and Bertha fell in love, however, everything about their relationship became uncommon. The two made their intentions to marry public and were met with scorn and ridicule from the most unlikely source—family.

Henry and Bertha, intentional or not, were mavericks. Their relationship stirred the pot of insecurities and social norms. Henry's parents Louis and Sophie immediately ordered the love affair stopped. The rule of thumb, stick to your own kind. A Gentile marrying a Jew wasn't just a step down. It was an insult. "In those days it mattered," said Bertha's great nephew Stanley Wertheim. "In Germany at that time if you were Catholic and married a Protestant, or vise versa, you'd get the same reaction. All the schools were sectarian. People tended to stay within their bounds."[26]

However, the most vocal dissatisfaction came from the

Hecht's. A legacy of wealthy merchants combined with a sprinkling of past high-ranking government posts developed in many on Bertha's side of the family a sense of prestige and entitlement. To them, marrying a man of little means, little potential, and even less formal education equaled disaster. "It wouldn't have mattered if he was Christian if she had married a Von something or other, or a well-to-do physician," laughed Wertheim. "That would have been perfectly fine. No one would have said a peep then. They considered him a common peasant."

In spite of everything, Henry and Bertha stayed determined. Who needed family when they had each other? Within their own homeland, they were refugees, strangers in a strange land. Out of options, Henry and Bertha made plans for a fresh start, a new home—a land where no one knew them, a place with fleeting expectations, and better yet, no family history. That place was New York City.

Henry came first, arriving on the afternoon of October 15, 1891.[27] Two years later, Bertha's steamship sailed from Hamburg through the North Sea. First stop, Amsterdam; then Southampton, where new cargo and fresh passengers filled with similar yearnings boarded. Last stop: Lady Liberty and New York Harbor.

A simple ceremony made Henry and Bertha Mr. and Mrs. Husing. With marriage came a new residence and with marriage came children. According to conventional law, if a woman of Jewish blood gives birth, then the children she brings forth are considered Jews. For Bertha Husing, it would never be an issue. Being Jewish was simply an ethnic reality, at best, an afterthought for the gritty lady from Bielefeld. Then again, Bertha was aware enough to know that assimilation equaled the road of less resistance, even in the States.

The insults and digs followed most from the old country. Slurs liberally cast about like the tried and true, "Shylock! Shylock!" However, a new one caught her attention, "Rubenstein," reference to a Jew who rotted in New York's infamous Tombs Prison for murder.[28] "Rubenstein" or "Christ Killer," the implications were obvious. Bertha's English was crude at best, but she understood all too well. Yesterday, the past, was gone, a distant memory.

"She never talked about her past," remembered her great-granddaughter Kate Lacey. "She was always in the moment. She would only talk about the present and the future."[29] Even years later, when she was overheard speaking Yiddish to an acquaintance, people reacted in disbelief, with dropped jaws and eyes popping the size of ping-pong balls.[30] "Bertha—Jewish? No way!" Her response was one of casual indifference, unimportant, not even worth two minutes of her time. "That wasn't her being dismissive," Stanley Wertheim insisted. "It was simply true."

Home was the South Bronx. Jagged hills north of the Harlem River cut into a thriving migrant neighborhood. The Husings chose the section known as Melrose for good reason. Germans and Irish workers first arrived in the Bronx around 1840, helping to swing picks and hammers of the New York and Harlem Railroad.[31] By the close of the nineteenth century, miles and miles of fresh winding tracks were being laid for the bold completion of a new underground rail system. The subway connected every corner of the city from the Bronx through Manhattan, even latching onto the distant city of Brooklyn. Groundworks were dug and corner stone laid for municipal buildings and churches the size of palaces.

Many of the surrounding streets and avenues of Melrose honored the heroes of America's first one hundred years. Names like Sherman, Sheridan, Grant, Webster, Clay, and Washington stood proudly, unfamiliar to most settlers fresh into New York harbor.[32] It was a constant reminder that they were in a new world; new ideas, new customs, new language, and a new attitude.

Like almost every untried arrival, Henry came to the States speaking some English and carrying little money. But, the one functional thing he did pack was a trade. Henry knew how to wait on tables. Those skills could be exploited right away. Before he left for the States, Henry was told to visit an entrepreneur in New York named August Luchow. The man was German and owned a restaurant. Maybe he was looking for a good waiter. What Henry found was more than just a restaurant, but a way of life.

Located on the street level of East Fourteenth Street near Irving Place, the name "LUCHOWS" was nailed boldly on the front of a picturesque three-story building with wide, intricately carved brickwork.[33] Sprinkled throughout the Union Square district were a variety of recital halls and Vaudeville theaters—some large, some small; the centerpiece attraction being the American Academy of Music. The main drag of Broadway, one block west, coiled downtown where pedestrians and slow-hoofed horses tried to dodge the speeding trolley car traffic. Sometimes, they didn't make it. The infamous corner gained an appropriate moniker—"Dead Man's Curve." If high society wasn't at the theater, they were shopping at the area's finest stores like Tiffany's, Hearn's, and Macy's.[34] What was outside may have been culturally strapping; yet, inside dazzled the eyes and filled the stomach.

When Henry first met Guido August Luchow, he knew he had a friend. The man was also from Hanover.[35] Luchow enjoyed the pleasures of life, especially food. He was an imposing figure with a protruding stomach and handlebar moustache that seemed to delight everyone's fancy.

Luchow's was the place to go. Giant, tall ship models graced the main dinning room. Twelve-piece orchestras played into the night. A wine list thicker than a family bible was thumped down at the table of every lunch or dinner party. Barrels of hops and barley, packed in ice, stacked to the ceiling showcased Germany's best-kept secret, Wurzburger beer.[36] The finest chefs prepared rich Bavarian delicacies. Henry Husing was one of the lucky waiters who rushed from kitchen line to counter top with trays piled hot with knockwurst, Schnitzel, sauerbraten, and beef stroganoff. There was no such thing as a quick bite at Luchow's. Dining was often times an all-day affair.

High-end regulars like American business tycoon Diamond Jim Brady and opera star Lillian Russell helped establish the restaurant as upper crusty. But, the atmosphere remained warm, large, and festive. Christmas time sparkled as the high water mark, hanging lights, decorated trees in tinseled glow and a generous piece of stollen cake for everyone.

Henry soon established himself inside the busy restaurant. A graceful manner welcomed the most stubborn patron. [37] With a firm handshake, a guiding push of a chair, Henry became known as "the mayor."[38] His reputation quickly spread. Soon Luchow received several requests a week—not for special food items, but special service. "We'd like to be seated in Henry's section if possible," they pleaded. Often the requests had to be denied. Henry's section was usually filled with satisfied customers.

Inspired by August Luchow, Henry entertained visions of opening his own establishment. Around 1897, he purchased a three-story building at Brooke Avenue and 170th Street and set up shop. The apartment above was where the family called home. On the street level was Henry's establishment. A sturdy L-shaped bar made of oak cuddled one end of the room. Above hung a variety of polished beer steins hoping to be filled. Scattered about were four or five tables with chairs. In the corner was a piano, often out of tune, that happily provided entertainment when anyone played it and drunk enough to listen. Directly across, was Henry's pride and joy —the kitchen. The space wasn't big enough to boil water much less make a meal. The menu suffered little, offering plentiful shanks of cured beef and steamed vegetables. Inside, an angry chef sweated and chain-smoked while Henry worked the bar outside. He often did double duty. Smack dab in the middle for good luck sat the fixture of a tall wooden ship model, sails and all. Henry did his best to make the place reflect Luchow's tastes and high standards. But he quickly found out the only thing missing was a wealthy clientele. Cash registers coughed more than sang. The Bronx stayed a long way from Union Square. He realized things might be different when some of his regulars asked to have spittoon buckets placed on the floor of the bar. It would be more saloon than stylish restaurant.

He took care of all the bills, ice, oil, coal, and livery expenses, providing for his family with the mark of dedicated husband and father. Henry lived the challenges of running his own business. It didn't take long before his mind filled with second thoughts. He learned the duties of being boss were far greater than just another hired hand. Bertha helped when she could, but she had responsibilities outside the family business—children.

The plan: start small, then expand. Elsie was the couple's first child, born in June of 1898. Fourteen months later, they added a boy, naming him Albert. But, within a year their once bustling home quieted. Albert was dead of tuberculosis.[39] They were not the only grieving parents. For every 1,000 kids born in America at the time, 100 never celebrated a second birthday. Infant mortality in some cities peaked to a staggering thirty percent.[40] Henry and Bertha pushed forward, determined to try again and start fresh. Wiser, Stronger, Better.

By late November of 1901, Bertha was ready to deliver her third child. He finally arrived kicking and screaming—a boy. Proud and overjoyed, Henry went downstairs and unlocked the doors to his saloon. Drinks were on the house. Bertha and Henry could both give thanks. They had been blessed with a healthy new son. For the parents, instinct took over. The boy needed a name. His mother suggested Edmund.[41] His father, however, had other ideas.

CHAPTER THREE

SIR EDWARD

James Edward Britt was a 22-year-old boxer from San Francisco. Packed inside a pint-sized body, 5–6' and around 135 pounds, were hands made of bricks, throwing punches that jolted the human skin.[42] Lightening bolts came to mind. Where the power came from, no one knew. With narrow eyes and a weather-beaten face, he looked like an overgrown horse jockey. His mug may not have been the most attractive, but Jimmy Britt's voice was something to marvel. Vibrant. Confident. Clear.

The man loved to talk more than anything it seemed. His singsong cadence and affected Irish lilt was unmistakable. If the sound of the voice didn't turn heads, his wardrobe did. Britt adopted a cultured, chic way of existence. He strolled among the public rarely seen without a Prince Albert-style coat, top hat, and walking cane. High-end leather gloves dripped from his breast pocket.[43] Friends and foes alike were greeted with a quick one-liner and expensive cigar. He saw himself as more entertainer than boxer. Around the Bay Area, he was known as "Our Boy Jim," "Dapper Jimmy" to others.[44] Across America, he became known as "Sir Edward."[45]

Britt learned the fight game from his older brother Willis, who enjoyed a brief career as an amateur bantamweight. He learned his speaking skills, however, observing San Francisco's beatnik actors and poets. Britt became aware of the power in a well-crafted limerick. His favorite was a piece entitled *The Kid's Last Fight* about a washed-up boxer who takes one last tragic shot at glory by fighting his best friend. The rhyme became Britt's calling card, barking it out before fights, working the heavy bag or packing local theaters for what he called "house money."[46] He quoted the lines form memory, as if he wrote it himself.

> *Next month I fought with Brooklyn Mike;*
> *As tough a boy who hit the pike;*
> *Then Frisco Jim and Battlin' Ben,*
> *And knocked them all inside of ten.*
> *I done some trainin' and the night*
> *Set for the battle sure was right;*
> *The crowd was wild, for this here bout*
> *Was set to last till one was out.*[47]

He backed up the talk and hip walk with wins. Jimmy Britt jabbed his way from California to Oregon beginning in 1901. Yet, it didn't take long before he contended for title fights. His bouts against the likes of Joe Gans, Young Corbett, and "Battling" Nelson were epic. Henry Husing proudly admitted to being one of Britt's more ardent followers. He loved the sports of his new adopted country: baseball, horseracing, and tackle football. Following the fight game, however, gave the German a special thrill.

Boxing personified the immigrant plight like no other. From the ghettos of poverty, it was "come as you are." One had to punch their way to the top of society. No man could hide. Anyone who dared to enter the ring was asked to bring the appropriate accoutrements—bare chest, bare knuckles, a determination to fight, enough anger to kill. Pugilism offered hope and opportunity to any outsider—acceptance in its rawest form. The stakes were high. A bashed, bloodied loser limped back to alien status—a monster, a beast, a freak. A conqueror, a champion, could not only win the hearts and respect of an adoring crowd, but even a nation. If those watching still saw an animal, he was top dog.

Britt's expectant, unabashed style awed Henry, made him wonder how so much ability, so much influence emanated from one single man. From afar, through the telegraph and sports pages, he felt drawn to the boxer. Whatever the reasons, whatever the touch, Henry wanted to pay his young hero homage. How? Staring into the eyes of his new son, the answer came flying at him like wild thoroughbreds. The name was perfect. It fit like a glove—a boxing glove. Edward Britt Husing became the boy's name. Everyone called the young scrapper Eddie for short.

Eddie Husing pushed the limits; living up to his namesake, well-mannered one day, brat-like the next. His sister Elsie reluctantly took on the role of big sister. Rag dolls with spaghetti hair, rhyming songs (some in English, others in German), and make-believe fantasies were constantly interrupted by responsibility. She liked it at first, mother's little helper, a protector attentive to every sound and movement, including those of the bowels. "Ed hat seine hose wieder voll gemacht!" or "Mama! Ed's got stinky again!"

Once older, the novelty wore off. He was cute no more, a demon gnawing at her patience. Dressing up in mother's clothes and acting grownup didn't necessarily make her want to be one. "Where is your brother? Take care of your brother! You the big one now. He just a little boy!" In her mind, Eddie got away with everything. If not for fate, it would have been Albert escaping blame. There was a typical side to the rambunctious boy in his early years. Needs and wants and an endless array of questions worked his brain. What's this? Why is that? Bertha always had an answer. She caressed and encouraged him like only a mother could.[48]

"Momma, my hand itches," Eddie often whined. "Well, go ahead and scratch then," answered Bertha with a heavy German accent. "It means you will be rich."[49]

His response never wavered. The boy looked down with wide-eyed excitement at his hand as if it were a gold shiny coin. At his mother again, then back down at the hand. He tore into the skin surface, matching a cat to ear mites. With a smile on her face and a twinkle in her eye, Bertha walked away. A silly superstition or old German wives' tale, it did not matter. Her boy had an itch; Bertha gave it purpose—meaning.

If mother couldn't provoke thought, there were other sources. Books fed Eddie's savage thirst for knowledge. Hours in a library sparked imagination.[50] Bertha kept her son thumbing through the bible. But, his favorite books were those of adventure. *Huckleberry Finn* and *The Call of the Wild* were always on the top of the pile by his night table. Writers like Horatio Alger and Stephen Crane nourished bravado in an impressionable mind. From the beginning, young Eddie felt uninhibited. He would go to bed at night dreaming of what the next day would bring. There was a sense of destiny about the boy. Raw and untested, he felt it within himself.

Eddie had plenty of reasons to feel alive. All he had to do was go outside and join the sultry melting pot. Like most of his friends, he was the child of immigrants. And like most of his friends, there developed a sense of superiority over their parents, especially in the art of communication. Mother and father might have been German. He and sister Elsie were American-born and raised. Henry spoke English well enough. Bertha, however, had trouble grasping the new language. As all kids of immigrant parents, Eddie was the family go between, interpreting at local stores, with the cop on the corner, and the teachers at school.[51] Among the different languages, cultures, and customs, there was one common denominator—the streets. The boy quickly learned the rules of survival. Eddie could fight. There were plenty of late afternoons that he walked home with a black eye or bruised lip. But, the mean streets were the least of his problems. Elsie was sick.

Typically, parties were fun, especially the children's. Cakes layered thick with chocolate cream icing. On the outside, coconut sprinkles, a chewy crunch in every bite. Apple cider was served in thin glass mugs topped with a hint of cinnamon and tart green mint leaf. The cider tasted better cold. Henry always had a block of ice to shave, left over from beer cooling. This day, however, the cider was piping hot. Steaming, therapeutic. It took on a direct medicinal purpose. Elsie tried to enjoy the beverage, swallowing hard. Her throat raw, cutting like razor blades with every sip. Bertha sat on the edge of the bed pushing her daughter's burning head against her bosom. "No not again! Not her, too!" This was no way to celebrate a birthday. The party guests never came. The cake was never served. The girl's appetite non-existent. Eddie watched from the doorway, curious to know why his sister was covered by blankets in the middle of summer. A deep syrupy fluid filled her lungs. Her breathing was labored, shallow, weak. Doctors climbed the stairs to the Husing apartment for several days. They would all descend, blinking eyes, heads hung low, wondering if it best to call a minister.

Life expectancy in the early years of the twentieth century rarely ventured past the age of fifty.[52] Life expectation for the children of Bertha and Henry Husing was considerably less. Albert was gone at the age of one. Elsie, the couple's second child and only daughter, faired little better. She died of pneumonia just after her eighth birthday.[53] Henry and Bertha wondered if Eddie would be next. For the boy Husing, he did not quite understand death. He did, however, see the pain of Henry and Bertha. A quiet concern, a lost stare into the distance. Before he knew the difference, Eddie Husing was an only child.

Minus sibling rivalries, Eddie ruled the household. Bertha and Henry became doting parents, pampering, indulging. Whatever the boy wanted, he got. He begged for an animal to run the streets. The next day, Henry walked into the bar with an Irish setter, the dog's shinning red hair matching the color on his father's head. A slight cough, a sniffling nose, even a toothache prompted more activity than a three-bell fire alarm. When Eddie came down with measles, Bertha hovered over him like a guardian angel, barely sleeping for three days until the fever passed.

Henry was a mild-mannered man—a thinker, rarely expressing raw emotion, channeling his pain and frustrations through work. Leisure time was about sports in America. Henry planted the early seeds of interest in his son, frequenting baseball games at the Polo Grounds with the hometown Giants. Hilltop Park also was frequented, a thin stadium crunched into four corners of Upper Manhattan that another pro baseball team, the Highlanders, called home. A racetrack in Queens known as Aqueduct ate a few of Henry's dollars. Winnings didn't matter. Making memories with his son did. And on May 28, 1906, father and son bonded like never before. At a building called Madison Square Garden, they witnessed a ten-round championship boxing match together. Three preliminary fights, then the main event: "Terrible" Terry McGovern versus "Sir Edward."

Throughout the evening, the Husing men cheered wildly. They bobbed and weaved, dancing in unison up then down. With the conviction of a pious monk they believed that if they stopped, their man Jimmy might actually loose. He did not. The boxing match ended in a draw.[54] Perhaps the real winner that night was little Eddie Husing. The stamina he showed was impressive for such a young child. He blended into the crowded arena unnoticed, just one of the other boys selling programs and dusting seats.[55] Henry held firmly to his son as their train rumbled back to the Bronx from Manhattan. It was a memorable evening, one they would never forget. Both slept soundly that night—satisfied, believers. Life was often cruel. Watching Jimmy Britt box showed them just how beautiful life could be, even for a little while. A gray sky woke them in the morning. They spoke of Madison Square Garden and "Sir Edward" James Britt for the rest of the day.

Hope for the future blossomed. The boy understood the

unspoken boundaries. He learned a valuable lesson about hero worship. Jimmy Britt was not the man to emulate. It was Dad. It would always be Dad. Eddie adored his father, hoping to be like him in so many ways. However, following in one's footsteps was another matter. The boy watched and learned. Empty tables and a silent cash register was not the formula for a successful saloon. The entrepreneurial spirit of Henry Husing eventually gave way to practicality. The hardworking dreamer proved to be without business savvy. Patrons came and went, dwindling in numbers. So did the flow of steady income. Being the man in charge cut into the fun of his real talents—conversation. But, even that went away when Elsie died. A gloom hung about the place, blessed by the kiss of death.

As the summer of 1907 faded, HENRY'S was no longer. Doors locked. The tall ship models sold to friends with dreams of opening up a place. Whatever beer was left over, given away free of charge to whomever wanted to drink. Not surprising, on that day, the people showed up en masse. Henry was never worried, relieved a more appropriate word. He could always go home, return to papa. Luchow told him before he left, "I welcome you as if you were my own." Henry was not only given his old shifts back on 14th Street, but was promoted to headwaiter.

Eddie never wanted to be a waiter. He heard dad's stories about powerful men, those with a snarled face and brusque voice who sometimes chose to talk down to the person who served them. Such guests never asked the waiter anything. They usually summoned them like house slaves with a snap of the finger and an outrageous request from the kitchen. Five martini businessmen and temperamental actors were common culprits. Even in his youth, Eddie saw such pompous behavior as unforgivable. It made him angry. He was proud of his father. But, even at a young age, he couldn't understand for the life of him why or even how father took so much lip from another man.

By 1910, Luchow's was well established. Tables filled, music soared, and beer flowed. As good as it looked, changes peeked around the corner. The neighborhood was in for an uprooting. "Dead Man's Curve" and its bloody reputation increased with the advent of cars. New York's theater district was moving uptown where rent was cheaper. As Manhattan migrated north, most of Union Square went with it. Gone was the glitz and glitter. Sweatshops, penny pinchers, and bargain shops moved in. Trade remained steady inside Luchow's, but clearly something was lost in the shift. The beer wasn't quite as cold, the music not quite as sparkling, and parties broke up before midnight. The overflow of excess and carefree living faded into the past.

Also, a cold-blooded killer ran among the homes of the northeast fast and hard, leaving the streak of death behind. There was little distinction between class and color when it came to victims. The killer's name was Typhoid. What the origins of the disease were no one could say for certain. Some tried to blame an Irish cook named Mary Mallon who worked the kitchens of New York's well-to-do. The disease claimed hundreds of lives. Friends died. Neighbors suffered. Bertha and Henry Husing decided that for the safety of their one remaining child they would fight. To them, New York was cursed, dirty, and diseased. If they stayed, Eddie, too, would die. Tall trees, open space, and fresh mountain air was the answer. There, in the coolness of the forest, they prayed for life.

CHAPTER FOUR

GLOVERSVILLE

The first thing they noticed was how quiet it got, especially at night. One of the few sounds, the only sound, came from the winter winds bouncing off a loose shutter or half-open gate. In the summer months came more of a ruckus. Invisible choirs of frogs and crickets played a nightly lullaby. Fireflies danced in the shadows, flickering on then off. When they looked up, the night sky glowed with stars. Things were certainly different in the country.

Henry had stripped his Bronx apartment and headed north. The chill of late autumn and snow lie just ahead for the year 1910. Wide-open spaces, sycamore trees, and lungs filled high with clean, fresh air. Henry never heard of the place before. A new job and what they hoped to be a new life awaited the Husings. Another small but thriving German community was taking hold thirty miles south of Albany. Protecting the little town in every direction were the Adirondacks. Henry found work at a place called the Elks Club. Society men and locals put trust in a kitchen that prepared everything from a light soup and sandwich fare to a robust banquet for 800 guests. Of course, it wasn't Luchow's, but a job, nonetheless. Then again, they no longer lived in New York City. A much different town surrounded them—Gloversville.

By 1828, glove manufacturing was the town's main industry. The world took notice. Scores of European transplants made
Gloversville their new home.[56] Trains shipped out hundreds of pairs
of silk and leather gloves each week. What remained was the pride
of individual craftsmen. Mass production never developed. Instead,
companies, big and small, bonded to their cutters, keeping Gloversville's small town feel in tact. Work was steady. Fortunes were made.
By the turn of the century, "the glove town" prospered like never
before.[57]

Gloversville embodied a new immigrant spirit, hardwork-
ing, blue collar to the core, yet at the same time, progressive thinkers,
cultured in the arts and science. The same German pride put forth
in the making of gloves or the serving of food was instilled in the
promotion of quality taste, education, and music. The great com-
posers, all German, Beethoven, Wagner, Schubert, and Bach played
endlessly on family phonograph players. On a spring day, one could
walk from house to house for several blocks and never miss a note.
Italian arias packed the Kasson Opera House;[58] Men and woman
dressed in their Sunday best. A rare German opera more so ignited
an indescribable passion. Walls of the theater stuck with the sweat
of those standing in the back. Aisles overflowed with bodies hoping
to hear and see a taste of the Old Country. The only ones not enjoying the music seemed to be a mob of growing boys beginning to feel
their oats. They had other ideas of fun and entertainment, the kind
that usually involved breaking the law.

Double, double toil and trouble, a witch's brew of mischief
came from a handful of delinquents, including Eddie Husing. Fear-
some. Resourceful. Unpredictable. They tested authority, assessed
boundaries, and leaned toward the edge. [59]

The city morgue purchased a motorized vehicle to pick up
dead bodies. At night, the gang of devilish boys stole the black wagon, joy riding the dark streets of town. The shenanigans soon ended
once the real coroner noticed an empty gas tank every morning. At

the age of twelve, the growing Eddie met his first love—Fire. He was captivated, obsessed. Everything burned: matches, candles, tree stumps, autumn leaves, even worn-out shoes. Live insects perished under a hot magnified glare provided by a pair of Henry's old eyeglasses. Eddie had no malicious intent when it came to fire, but his mood changed after the town's mayor called him a "pyromaniac."[60] He became angry. Eddie decided to get even with the government boss. If the mayor wanted a pyromaniac, he would get one burning City Hall to the ground. By the time firefighters controlled the blaze, half the building was smoldering ash. Unfortunately for Eddie, he was seen running from the fiery scene. Soon, the authorities arrived at the Husings's door and quickly obtained a confession.

Screaming in his native tongue, Henry folded a thick belt around his hand and tore into Eddie's bottom, whipping and slashing. He kicked the boy behind the knee and leveled him to the ground. Then he bent down to meet his son, now crying, and said with a pointed finger, this time in English. "If you ever do like zat again, you'll be in a box lying next to Albert and Elsie! Do you understand me? DO YOU UNDERSTAND ME!" Eddie nodded his head yes, begging for mercy. Bertha watched in horror, thinking her husband might seriously hurt him. Henry straightened his back then ordered the boy to his room.

Just the mention of Albert and Elsie touched a nerve. Not a day escaped without thinking of both. His ears burned for Elsie's sisterly complaints, long-braided hair, and candy-cane striped stockings. Eddie would have done anything to bring her back. He profoundly missed Albert, odd feelings for someone he never met, imagining the shape of his brother's face, the muscles in his arms.

For the next twelve months, Eddie's mood wavered back and forth in sullen moments of detachment to searing aggression that kept schoolmasters, mother, and father baffled. Everyone said he would grow out of it, a phase every developing kid experienced. Henry and Bertha weren't so sure. It was clear that something was eating at the boy.[61]

The calendar of Eddie's boyhood revolved around sports. Amongst the growing discontent, he still found time to play. The taste of crisp, burning leaves and snow-frosted icicles on the tongue meant football. The smell of freshly cut grass could mean only one thing—baseball. Day and night, freezing rain or fiery sun, fists flew during a good boxing match. Many a schoolyard fisticuffs sprang from an impressionable boy's desire to emulate champion fighters, to capture the power of a solid right hook. Eddie, like every other boy, had his favorites: John McGraw, Connie Mack, and, of course, Jimmy Britt. Young Husing wondered if the same blissful fate of a star athlete awaited him as a man. As all boys do, he dreamed.

By 1914, Husing was becoming a teenager. His waist thickened, his legs stretched. His high-pitched mousy voice cracked with irregular layers of deep, bassy resonance. Husing was still thin, but resembled the look of his father, strong, hallow cheekbones and a tall lanky frame. His vocabulary grew. Words like "bullshit" and "piss off" slipped off his tongue with pesky regularity. He also began to smoke. A cigarette dangling from Husing's mouth brought a look of maturity.

Eddie liked girls. They were at times annoying and complicated creatures always saying something confusing with a glimmer of joviality in the eye, but he fancied the way they looked. He loved the way they smelled. And their mystery made him want to be around them even more. One girl in particular who caught his eye was Mildred Cooper. The Coopers were friends of Henry and Bertha's from Boston. During one summer visit to Gloversville, they brought their daughter. She had a freckled face and cute smile. Mildred also had something else that almost every teenaged boy noticed—round lips and developing breasts.

Mildred liked Eddie so the feeling was mutual. Her ideas of love and romance came from an infatuation of society novels. In those hormone-bursting pages, a name was everything. To her, Eddie was the name of a kid who played with bugs, set fires, and skipped rocks into lakes. A modern, mature label was needed—something male, something strong for someone who knew how to treat a lady, hold hands, kiss. She dubbed him "Ted."[62]

Suddenly "Eddie" was part of the past. The man-child took on a new attitude. He was infatuated with the new name, insisting on it, ignoring anyone who refused to change. Proud. Confident. Even former presidents used it. Was there a greater living American than Teddy Roosevelt? Around Gloversville, not many boys named "Ted" seemingly existed. He drew strength from the knowledge, a mystical pull leading him in a new, more mature direction. Names like John, Anthony, Billy, Tom, even Eddie, jumped off the class roll call at school with pesky regularity. When the name "Ted" was called, only one head turned to claim it—his.

CHAPTER FIVE

HOME

They were small in number, but a hearty group. Henry began to notice a party of worldly men frequenting the club in August of that year. He was impressed with their knowledge of food preparations and wines. They said they were alumni from Columbia University in New York. Henry, of course, knew of the school's stellar reputation. He was less familiar with a social club on campus that they spoke of called Deutsches Haus, a German Catholic club owned and operated by the college. The men were round, distinctly German with a New York attitude, aggressive, pushy, and not inclined to take no for an answer. They gave grand detail of the club's unique architecture, impressive cliental, and large food portions. Henry's curiosity was piqued. Over a two-week period, Henry also noticed the men eating daily meals, observing staff and asking ample questions. They seemed to focus their attention on him.

Since 1911, many colleges and universities in America had established foreign language houses. Deutsches Haus was the first. And Columbia was the first college to offer German language studies to their students.[63] The mission of the club was to promote everything German—not just it's language, but cultural achievements in the arts and science. Deutsches Haus was located in a stately mannered building on West 116th Street. On the ground floor was the club. Above stood six stories of apartment units housing faculty members.

It was an odd mix of artists and intellectuals. Speaking engagements, musical performances, and poetry readings were sandwiched between professors, lawyers, and scientists. They had little in common but a desire to share everything German. Philosopher Edmund Husserl, playwrights Gerhart Hauptmann and Hugo von Hofmannsthal, and future Nobel Prize winner Max Planck were among those who spoke at the club.[64] Their words and presence gave all in attendance inspiration. Everyone from guest to staff left the club with a bulging sense of pride. The club had its fill of German pride, but was still without a steward to run the place. "We're looking for someone like you, Husing," explained one of the men. "Someone with polish, someone we can trust. I guarantee to make it worth your while." Henry gazed at the man taking in his words. He was never very fond of the glove town. The money at the Elks Club was fine, but he missed New York, and he sensed his wife and son did as well. That's all they seem to talk about. This group of traveling men before him was offering a job. And it did not take long for him to accept.

During the fall of 1914, Henry moved the family a block away from the Columbia campus at 410 West115th Street. It was a large rectangular building that ran a quarter way down the road from 408 to 414. A healthy pocket of Germans and Poles lived in the area, giving the Husing's a sense of familiarity. Bertha found fast friends from the local Lutheran house of worship, Trinity Church, on West 100th. Ted even sang as a soloist in the boys choir and performed with the group at Madison Square Garden, the same arena where he witnessed "Sir Edward" fight Terry McGowan a few years earlier.

Business at Deutsches Haus thrived. And so did the fortunes of the Husing household. Henry began investing in real estate with his steady income. Running the floors of a restaurant was known to be wearing on the body. It was a profession that Henry realized could not last forever. He started purchasing small apartment buildings around the city, mostly in upper Manhattan, and taking on the role of landlord. In some cases, he had units renovated and sold again, this time for a profit. While living upstate, Henry even noticed a few choice plots and bought property in places like Stamford, New York. It would take time before Henry collected a solid return on his initial investments. The restaurant remained the family's main source of income. Henry Husing was by no means becoming a land baron. They were good investments, simple and plain. The more pressing issue on the mind of Henry and Bertha was finding a good school for their son to attend.

Stuyvesant High School on Eeast 15th Street looked more like a palace of lords. Giant, bold pillars stretched the facade one full city block long, four stories high. It could have passed for a federal municipal building in Washington. Stuyvesant reflected society's mores of early twentieth-century America. Education was important. [65] From student to teacher to custodian, everyone was reminded of this every day as walking through the spacious hallowed halls of the buildings. Ted was a bright child with a promising head on his shoulders. He would have to be if he attended Stuyvesant, which admitted no one before passing the rigors of various tests and entrance examinations. [66]

Ted was, perhaps, getting a better education right in his own backyard. Steps from home were the academic structures of Columbia University. The steady patronage of students and faculty kept a smile on his father's face. However, Ted was not drawn to the school's reputation of professors. The attraction was in sports. He saw the track team run by his window. He heard the cracks of baseball bats and roar of fans from South Field tucked behind a big brick dorm building one block over. The smell of athletic competition was alluring for the growing boy. His face was as visible as the library rotunda in the middle of campus. Soon, Ted found himself a most attentive student, soaking up a textbook of sports knowledge, taught by a willing group of coaches.

Ted was aware of sports like baseball and boxing. That came from his father. He soon took near fanatical interest in unfamiliar sports like swimming and basketball. The growing teenager asked a thousand and one questions, never satisfied, always wanting more. He begged baseball coach Andy Coakley to show him how to throw a curve ball. Ted sat poolside watching Ed Kennedy slice the water while teaching the perfect breaststroke. Track coach Carl Merner often gave Ted the stopwatch at practice and let him call out split times as the runners darted down the straight-aways. He mimicked Harry Fisher's textbook body position on rebounding a basketball. During autumn months, young Ted was especially attentive, feeling the jolts of head coach T. Nelson Metcalf rebuild the football program after a ten-year hiatus. Whistles blew, bodies crunched. More stimulating than the game's raw, physical emotion was watching Metcalf draw up plays outside his office. Thin, aggressive lines, Xs and Os etched in bold white chalk on a rickety, tired blackboard had players and formations moving in every direction. Metcalf dug into the board so hard with the chalk that shadows of the plays remained after they were erased. To the naked eye, the board was one big mess of confusion. However, if the play ran correctly, chaos transformed into a timeless ballet of beauty on the field.

More than the coaches, Ted's heroes were the student athletes themselves. They were gods, gladiators bulging with muscles. He wanted to be in their shoes, by their lockers, in their head. In return, they found the kid's infectious laugh, slicing wit, and unbending loyalty equally charming. They made him the official school mascot, a good-luck charm for victory. Bertha Husing saw the strapping young men of Columbia as the perfect role models for her boy. She was especially glad her son was under the watchful eye of the Lion's coaching staff—an advantage that kept him out of trouble and off the streets.

By January of 1917, Gloversville was a distant memory. Three years seemed like a lifetime away from New York. Henry, Bertha, and Ted thanked their lucky stars that the town had not deserted them. The brief time away had taught them that they were no longer some immigrant clan from a far-off world. They belonged to the city. Life again for the Husing's was running like a well-oiled machine. Ted was off to school, then sports mascot duties at the college; Bertha to her church activities and social groups; Henry guiding a full day of food service at the club. The only thing that seemed not to be cooperating for the Husings was the kitchen boiler at Deutsches Haus.

"That damn boiler" is how the staff affectionately referred to the considerable piece of metal. What loomed equally as large was its annoying tendency to break down. By late February, the spring semester at the college was half over. The food and service at Deutsches Haus had an impeccable reputation. But, as talented as Henry was at his post, as gifted as any chef or bartender may have been, the key to success was an efficient boiler. Cold plates and uncooked food was bad for business. The boiler was a faded copper color and made of thick cast iron. It was powered on very delicate but very potent steam. Forceful enough to make the kitchen run, hot enough to sear the hair off even the quickest cat. A series of pipe fixtures ran throughout the room, heating various ovens and stove tops. On this particular winter morning, the temperamental boiler was found again on the fritz. Fixing such machinery, unfortunately, was put into someone else's hands. Mr. Husing had telephoned a maintenance crew to come out and look at the failing yet all-important system. Still, everyone knew how that could be. Experience told him he could be waiting for some time. If the kitchen were to be opened on this day, the head steward would have to become a plumber.

Peering down on the cast iron, Henry wondered where to start. With a hammer and wrench in hand, his tools were large, his knowledge little. Humor perhaps would be the most useful means of fixing it. "A good swift kick should do za trick," he laughed. The crew joined in on the joke hoping he could salvage the day. After the lighthearted high jinks, everyone went back to their daily chores of dicing vegetables, prepping meat, and polishing silverware. Henry continued his struggle alone. As he poked at the thick steel structure, he noticed an oddity. He felt heat.

Unbeknownst to Henry, the pipes were somehow blocked. But, a massive pot of trapped, blinding steam continued to cook in the main boiler compartment. It was, if released, a bomb waiting to explode.[67] Innocent of the lurking danger, Henry was determined to find the problem. People's salaries, not to mention stomachs, depended so. He saw the name "Mills" engraved on the fickle hardware just above a small door on the main compartment. Henry decided to open the flap and look inside. Perhaps there an adjustment was needed. He grabbed a thick rag and pulled the handle toward him. It was a decision he would regret for the rest of his life. At once, the head steward's body shot back. Water and steam, scalding like hot molten lava, sprayed everywhere. His voice screamed in agony. Taking most of the blow was Henry's arms, face, and torso. He was burned badly. Knives dropped and dishes shattered as everyone rushed to help their fallen leader. The only service given that horrible day at Deutsches Haus was one of prayer. No one knew if Henry Husing would live or die.

While Henry lay in a hospital bed, Ted grew old with worry by the minute. For the high schooler, the future had become now. If father went, it would be he who was the man of the house, working, providing, caring—responsibility. His mind labored.

"A job doing what, shoveling shit, bagging groceries, working the railroad like the other German migrants? A waiter?"

He was too young to be a cowboy, a ball player. Or was he? His morbid thoughts skipped to mother.

"How much death could one woman endure?" he wondered. "First her children—now her husband?"

Ted Husing's future career prospects were held at bay. Henry survived, but not before thirty-one plastic surgeries were performed to repair his mangled features. Waiting on tables was something he could no longer do. Charm, confidence, and a ready smile were the most useful tools of the trade. And at present, with barely a recognizable face, Henry did not have any of that. A sadness changed the man. He saw people stare, all eyes saying one thing—ugly! He became a recluse, sitting in his favorite chair for hours alone in the dark. [68]

In reality, there was plenty to hide from other than just a distorted face in the year of 1917. What lurked around the corner for many German Americans was the ugly face of prejudice.

CHAPTER SIX

GET THE KRAUT

The rainy day that Henry had keenly, fervently saved for was now upon him. But it was not just raining—it was pouring in heavy doses. Something else would have to be done. Living in Morningside Heights no longer made sense. There was no job to go to and worst of all, no money coming in to the house. For the foreseeable future, Henry would have to tap into his reserves to make ends meet. Henry hated to relocate the family. It would be their third move in four years. The steady, homey surrounding of Columbia had been the perfect fit. He was left with little choice under the circumstances. The constant uprooting was taking its toll, building a psychological complex in them all, especially Ted.

Henry decided to move the family into one of his own buildings, 235 West 69th Street, near the corner of Amsterdam Avenue and Broadway. It was a clean, well-kept structure, six stories high with an inviting, light blue atrium outside two glass front doors. He had thirty-two apartments inside. Keeping the units filled with tenants was paramount. Yet, the best part for Henry's decision to move further downtown was the cheap mortgage payments. Henry knew he had a solid chance at holding his end of the bargain with the bank until he owned it outright. The building at 235 was in good shape.[69]

The neighborhood, however, needed some work. It was in stark contrast to Morningside Heights. Gone were the elite, booksmart professors and quiet college campus. What appeared were working class people, a blue-collar toughness and an edge that cut frozen blocks of ice down to tiny cubes.

Two parallel worlds, one good, one evil, seemed to co-exist. In almost every direction of the Husing apartment, there was a paradox. Two blocks east was the sprawling beauty of Central Park. Just above 72nd Street was the luxurious Ansonia Hotel, where the rich and famous like vaudeville producer Florence Zeigfield called home. If one were to walk southwest toward the river, they might have considered bringing a cop. A stubborn history of gangs, riots, and fires dotted the area for over a hundred years. Row houses and black-smoked factories along 10th Avenue filled the sky. It smelled of drunks and unemployment. There weren't many German faces sprinkled about either. The new neighbors had names like Murphy, Dwyer, and O'Farrell. Time Square, the heart of the city, playground to the world, was nearby. The neighborhood was called "Hell's Kitchen."

Ted didn't know what to make of his father's changing medical condition much less of his new surroundings. One week, Henry was fine, on the telephone dealing with tenants and unpacking crates of personal belongings. The next, he was back in a hospital bed only to return a week later torn, bruised, and bandaged. His mood bounced high and low like the yarn of a child's yo-yo. Ted searched for an anchor. He poured his energies into the four remaining months of the semester at Stuyvesant. His attitude became more studious. He stayed late after school. He took on an interest in all things mechanical—tinkering with automobile engines, pulling out the nuts and bolts of the phonograph player and reassembling before anyone noticed. But, like everything else in Ted's world lately, this, too, changed. He again would be on the run, a fugitive in his own backyard.

With twisting world events, well-earned German–American pride and ingenuity turned into the face of dread. An assassin's bullet ended the life of King Ferdinand in Bosnia and sparked the guns of the first World War. The Kaiser and his German army were on the march across Europe, shouting war at Russia, France, and Britain. For nearly two years, the States watched and wondered. Once the Lusitanian sank, paranoia from New York to California kicked in like a crazed mule to the back of a barn. Nationalism blazed as "Old Glory" waved from every flag poll and window ledge. Anyone with a German sounding name or accent became enemy #1, viewed as conspiring with the Kaiser. If none of those labels fit, they were smelly, evil foreigners. Suddenly, to the sprawling millions of German immigrants, the American dream became a nightmare.

They all heard the stories. Property burned, businesses closed. A relative, missing. Some were savagely killed, dragged through the streets and beaten, even hung; unjust victims of hate. Many changed names to conceal their identity. Some relocated to less conspicuous environments. Keeping a low profile and saluting the American flag became a priority. Stay out of trouble. Keep your mouth shut. Suddenly, Henry's many hospital stays and recuperations indoors became a blessing. In retrospect, the timing of his accident could not have been more ideal. Attendance at the club dropped off considerably in the last year he was employed. Functions became infrequent. No one wanted to admit it, but they all knew what was happening. No one was interested in singing the praises of the German culture once boatloads of American troops sailed across the Atlantic.

Henry never saw the end of his beloved Deutsches Haus. The college severed ties with the club, asking them to leave.[70] Henry and Bertha were never truly affected by anti-German sentiment. They were the exception, well established and trusted with solid reputations. Ted, however, was not so lucky. The narrow streets of adolescence played by a different rule. He was razzed endlessly in school. Every name from "Kraut" to "Boxhead Fucker," a reference to the notion that all Germans had square-shaped heads, was hurled in his direction.[71]

Ted was stalked through his own neighborhood by packs of older boys, beaten, battered, and bloodied. A few of the more hostile girls even threw rocks. Ted became isolated, denied his friends, his freedom, denied a fair shake, all because his name was Husing. An edge crept up his spine. A chip the size of mountains dug into his shoulder. He began to hate everything about his German heritage. He refused to speak it around the house, or even acknowledge he understood it. The terse sound of its language, the vowel-ridden surnames and strange customs all made him sick. Ted's resentment focused directly at the source, Henry and Bertha. It was they who brought such wrath upon him. They carried the seed of dirty Germany and placed it upon him.

School quickly turned from fun to torture. Anger colored his actions from first bell in the morning to the afternoon's last class. He acted out everywhere. Ted was not only belligerent with classmates, but instructors as well. Stuyvesant finally had enough, expelling him before the school year ended. Ted wondered what he had done to deserve such a fate. He was once a normal teenage boy with a life of endless wonder that somehow felt closer to hell than heaven. Yet, amongst all the confusion, a crystallizing moment appeared. Something caught his eye. Posted on the side of countless city buildings were signs supporting the war movement. The signs read, "Wake Up America! Civilization Calls Every Man, Woman and Child!" Ted saw the words and knew he had to act. No one would call him a coward. No one was going to call him yellow. His parents were tinted German. Ted was American, red, white, and blue. At sixteen years old, his honor, his pride, his life were at stake. There was only one thing left to do—Fight!

Ted decided to join the Army National Guard in June of 1917. It made perfect sense: Three square meals a day, money to help the family while Henry lay dormant, and above all a chance to prove them all wrong. From street corners and megaphones blared the sounds of George M. Cohan's "Over There." The popular song became the driving anthem, not just for Ted, but thousands of others compelled to enlist.

> *Johnnie get your gun, get your gun, get your gun,*
> *Johnnie show the Hun, you're a Son-of-a-Gun,*
> *Hoist the flag and let her fly*
> *Like true heroes do or die*
> *Over There, Over There*
> *Send the word, send the word,*
> *Over There*
> *That the Yanks are coming,*
> *The Yanks are coming,*
> *The drums rum tumming everywhere!*[72]

He liked to hum the catchy little tune. In an odd way, it gave him comfort. Arriving at the recruiting office on Governor's Island was one thing, getting accepted would be more of a challenge. Ted had two large obstacles to climb before suiting up. His name might raise suspicion—German, the enemy. His date of birth undoubtedly would. He was underage. Worse for Ted, his youthful, pimple-ridden face looked it. He told the Irish-lilted sergeant sitting at the desk that his name was Hastings.

"O.K. How old are you, Mr. Hastings?" asked the burly officer. Ted answered with a lie. "Eighteen, sir."

If that didn't suffice, he pulled out a fake birth certificate to back his story. Unsure, the sergeant kept in pursuit.

"Are you sure you're old enough to fight there, son? You look kind of young to me." Ted cleared his throat and deepened his voice before responding.

"Well, sir, eighteen makes me old enough to join this man's

army and that's my age."

"Ever shoot anybody?" the sergeant asked with a hearty laugh.

Some of the other veteran soldiers circled the young recruit and joined in the humor. Ted was in no mood for jokes. No school and no future, everything that brought him to this place, his father lying weak in a hospital bed with half his face torn off, made for a very serious demeanor. He barked back at the sergeant with an undeniable determination.

"The more we sit around asking these silly questions, sir, the Germans could be attacking us right now." Ted still saw doubt in the man's eyes but pressed his case more. "I'm an American. Born and raised right here in this city. Just like the paper says. New York is my home, sir. If it means me killing some Hun to protect my home, well then, that's just what I'll have to do."

"You're pretty sure about your self aren't you lad?"

"I am now, sir," he answered with confidence.

A few days later, the new soldier reported to Ft. Smith on the banks of the Hudson near Peekskill and began basic training. After six weeks of crawling in dirt and stabbing sand bags with a bayonet, he graduated as an elite member of the first Provisional New York Guard, 71st Regiment, Company B. He was given high marks of "good character" and declared fit to serve.[73] Ted waited for deployment overseas. Instead, he was assigned border patrol stationed along the docks on the western shore of Manhattan.

"Watch for anything suspicious," his commanding officer charged.

Among the murky, brown waters in between could live almost anything dangerous from sea monsters to a fleet of German submarines. His imagination ran wild. Visions of military fame and valor jumped around his mind. Ted kept his gun cocked and eyes peeled. He was so overzealous about his duties that on one memorable night patrol he mistook a floating beer bottle for a rising U-Boat periscope.[74] He was soon reassigned to supply duty.

After the Armistice was signed on November 11, 1918, Ted was discharged and sent back to civilian life. Gone were the slurs, the dirty looks, and back-street brawls. Suddenly, it was good to be German again, as if nothing happened. Young Husing once more embraced the blood of his parents and looked forward to those special things that gave him a sense of what it meant to be German, especially Christmas dinner at Luchows. He was two weeks shy of seventeen and still a year short of a high school diploma. Ted enrolled at Commerce High School only a few blocks away from the Husing apartment on West 69th Street for his senior year. The classrooms of Commerce were in a tall, stark building that climbed eight stories above street level on the corner of 62nd Street and 10th Avenue.[75]

One of the more brawny boys at the school was another son of German immigrants by the name of Lou Gerhig.[76] Just sixteen, he already showcased the powerful legs and a quiet inner strength that would help make him famous. Though Ted was nearly two years older, the boys did share a common experience. They both had older siblings who died young. Left as only children, an over-protective attitude by their parents prevailed, especially by their mothers. The similarities stopped there. The two friends loved sports, but Ted was no athlete compared to Gerhig. They played on the school's football and baseball teams together, at least for awhile. Ted eventually quit after being chewed out by head coach Harry Kane for not hustling.[77] Gerhig stayed on, winning, achieving, attending Columbia University, playing for the New York Yankees in 2,130 consecutive games, and earning the immortal nickname "The Iron Horse." What awaited Ted Husing, no one knew. For the moment, Ted was simply "Ted," war veteran and street survivor. Dealing with the pain. Keeping a stiff upper lip.

"He talked about growing up in Hell's Kitchen, like every other kid swimming in the river," recalled his son David Husing. "But, he really didn't discuss it a lot. He didn't romanticise it. He said it was a tough neighborhood and you had to take care of yourself."[78]

In the last weeks of spring 1919, Ted graduated from Commerce High School. He was glad to be finished. He was anxious to move on. There was a single question bouncing from end to end in Ted's expanding mind, "What's next?"

CHAPTER SEVEN

ON THE LAMB

The diploma hung haphazard, crooked, already beginning to fray around the edges. Ted's feelings about the piece of Manila-colored paper reflected the way he felt about the past two years, unattached yet disconcerted, wanting to forget every horrible injustice suffered. Bertha had different feelings. She was proud of her boy and wanted to display it prominently, a hopeful reminder of her son's determination and self-worth. She placed the credential in a glass-encased frame and mounted it like a trophy high above his bedroom door. There it would be, the first thing he saw in the morning and last thing before retiring to bed. Ted, however, had other ideas about where to rest his laurels.

Ted's love of books never wavered. Trips to the public library continued. His list of favorite authors matured and expanded with every book checked out and returned—Homer, Shakespeare, and Kipling. The idea of higher learning intrigued him. The country was filled with colleges, small and large. More than a dozen stood in New York City alone. For a fleeting moment a working career as a technical engineer was spoken about. However, he understood that stuff was more romance than reality. Four more years of school, Ted would be up to his eyeballs in stuffy shirts, haughty professors, and arduous study. What would the Irish neighborhood at West 69th Street think of him then? If he thought he got an ass whipping before. . . . Little, if any of it, appealed to him. Then again, Ted never gave much pause to another's opinion. He was always up for trying something at least once.

Columbia was the only college he knew anything about. So, Columbia it would be. In the autumn of 1919, Ted hoofed the train uptown to his old stomping grounds. Standing on the corner of 115th Street and Broadway, he burned a half-stoked cigarette into the sole of his shoe and walked toward the administration building. Filling out an application and spying girls was the agenda. He ended up doing neither. Looking across the street, something stopped him. Inside the campus, South Field stretched north near Amsterdam Avenue. Small brown sections of wooden seats spiraled above a twelve-foot-high wire fence. Ted had not seen the sports ground in a while and it looked good. It was not so much what he saw that focused his attention, but what he heard. Muffled voices and sounds of whistles were distant in the wind. The noticeable slaps of crunching shoulderpads and lunging flesh was loud and clear—football practice. None of the heroes he had worshipped as the team's official mascot were present. Time and graduation had taken them away. Coach Nelson Metcalf was gone, but Fred Dawson remained. An assistant under Metcalf, Dawson had risen to take over the helm of Columbia's varsity eleven.

Two hours and half a pack of cigarettes later, Ted never once thought of libraries or classes or erecting buildings of the next great city. There were other things to do like explore the neighborhood he once called home. As Ted walked, nostalgia did not flood his mind. Instead, disappointment, rage, and regret filled him. A few short years before, the view from the old apartment on West 115th sparkled clean compared to the broken glass outside West 69th Street. No one ever chased him up here. Up here he gladly ran for his Columbia heroes, fetching towels, water ladle, and a clean jersey. Ted passed Deutsches Haus, its doors still closed, and thought of his father's scarred features. He worked saliva around his mouth and spit harshly on the ground. The city left a bad taste. Leaving the big town behind made better sense than staying to earn another worthless degree. "Fuck You! Who needs it?" he thought. Ted was finished with college in the old neighborhood before ever earning one credit.

What Ted needed was an outlet to exercise his frustrations. He found it among the open fields of Central Park playing center for a semi-professional football squad called the Prescotts.[79] Not the ideal position for the wiry kid fresh out of high school, but he saw plenty of action, usually in the way of bruised ribs, sprained knees, and losses. Ted brought much of the punishment on himself, payback from much larger opponents irked by his sassy mouth and endless trash talking.[80] In between, he registered for classes at Pace Institute near Chambers Street in hopes of gaining some business know-how. He picked-up work as a payroll clerk for the New York Steam Corporation. Ted dropped both before the spring of 1920; then he tried his hand selling life insurance. Ted soon quit that as well.[81]

Nothing about New York appealed to him anymore. He wanted a new experience. A fresh start where no one knew him, nothing was expected. The feelings of an outsider looking in remained strong. The sounds of "get the kraut" still echoed inside his protruding ears. The wounds of German prejudice crippled his confidence, played tricks with his mind. No doubt in his solitary hours of reading, Ted came across Horace Greeley's imploring sentence "Go west, young man." Perhaps the answers lay out there, on the prairies and plains, high in the peaks of the Rocky Mountians. Nothing remained in New York except bad memories.

Of course, Henry and Bertha preferred more schooling. But, if their son wanted a real education, a real life lesson, they were willing to help him learn it. Henry remembered his own urges as a young man. The same wild oats, in part, that led him to America. Luckily for Ted, jumping into the unknown came with a life-line—relatives. The Husing's extended family reached halfway across the United States. Henry was not the only Husing who emigrated from Germany. Cousins, aunts, and other assorted relatives came to America and settled into a life of farming.[82]

That fall, Ted announced his plans of moving west and tackling life as a ranch hand. With such a fun journey ahead, he needed a traveling companion. Julius "Jay" Werner and Ted Husing could have been twins. Like Ted, Jay's father made a living in the food industry running a butcher shop near the Lower Eastside. Both teenagers were gangly and tall, hopelessly nearsighted, German, and filled with enough good humor to play vaudeville. But nothing else made these two fast friends more than a shared penchant for trouble. Ted and Jay met while at Stuyvesant, cutting class, smoking cigarettes, and running from the Irish bullies. Watching each other's back formed a trust. Jay, too, itched for an adventure, to lose himself in an environment other than New York. Hitching the nation's dusty back roads and jumping railway boxcars seemed the perfect escapade.

Before leaving, mother and father tested their son's will to take flight. "I'll keep your diploma on the wall of your room . . . just in case," Bertha assured. Henry reached into his pocket and handed Ted twenty-five dollars. "That's the best I do for you," he said to his son cautiously. "Send us letter now and then. Let us know how you are doing." Ted did not flinch. He kissed mother on the forehead, tucked the bills into his breast pocket and walked past 10th Avenue to meet his buddy.

The climate in the Midwest can be described in one word—extreme. The summers are brutally hot, followed by a bracing autumn. Just as the boys arrived in Tarkio, Missouri, winter arrived, early. Howling winds, eight-foot snow squalls and single-digit temperatures met them, and it wasn't even December. On the way out, Ted celebrated his 19th birthday in the back of a truck filled with rotting tomatoes and oil spilling from three large lawn mowers. Asking strangers for rides or chasing a moving freight train was a thrill. Ted's kinsfolk welcomed the two thrill seekers, keeping them in the dark of the duties that lie ahead.

Back east, they were used to sleeping late and venturing outside at will. They soon learned that the only existing will on a farm is the will of work. Grabbing cow titties made for a few good laughs. Finding gardener snakes in their bed did not. Sunday, the one off day, they looked forward to extended rest. Instead they were dragged to church with the rest of the locals. Of course, Ted hadn't the heart to tell them his friend was Jewish. Neither did Jay. They attended every week wearing a bowtie and carrying a King James Bible. There wasn't a synagogue in sight.

It didn't take six months to figure out farming was serious work. Ted and Jay were too young to take anything very seriously. The boys took to the west looking for a fresh start. What they really wanted was adventure and fun. The Missouri farm life offered little. Adding to the disappointment was lack of money and scarcity of young ladies. Bad habits of sleeping late, unfinished chores and latenight card games fed their apathy. Besides, the boys felt as if they did their best work not during the day, but at night.

Off they went, this time Emporia, Kansas. More Husing relatives were called upon to provide food and lodging. On route, they found the fun they hoped to find, the carnival. Cutting across the state were trucks filled with Ferris wheels, jugglers, pretty ladies in cowboy hats, and funny mirrors, the carnival set up shop for a few days before moving on. Much like the circus, carnivals employed a large assortment of gypsies, ex-cons, and runaways who showed a certain flair. Attracting curious on-lookers was one thing. Getting them to spend a few dollars was where the talent lay. The two vagabond New Yorkers easily fit the job description, especially Ted.[83] He seemed too young for the job of barker, thin and physically unassuming. However, they liked the way he used words. There was a strength about the lad, a presence that held people's attention. Like his football days, he showed a certain toughness. And in the big top, that was everything.

His friend, however, was offered less fulfilling employment, cleaning horse trailers, selling popcorn, and the most terrifying duty, climbing the big wheel when it got stuck, which was often. Kansas City to Iowa City, they saw townships big and small. The novelty soon wore off once the cold weather returned. Both learned the romantic notions of farming and carnival work wasn't everything they thought. Empty pockets combined with an empty stomach made the prospects of the old life much more desirable. By Christmas, Ted and Jay were back on a train headed east.

Back sitting at Bertha's kitchen table, he dug into a hardy meal of red cabbage and herring salad, a special treat always around the holidays. After a few minutes, Ted looked embarrassingly at his empty plate. He wondered why he had ever left home. He was glad to be back in New York, at least for a while. Working farm fields and pitching circus tents added muscle to his growing physique. Many of the same faces sprinkled the old neighborhood, ex-thugs, rock throwers. They passed him now with a rye smile, a nod of respect. The urges of revenge, to fight, bash teeth, murder in ways so unforgiving pulled hard at him stronger than ever. He chose to ignore them, focusing on the bright spots of Hell's Kitchen, mooching off mom and dad, three squares a day, a lit cig, and hanging out on a cold night trying desperately to get lucky.

His next stab at employment teetered on lunacy. Some thought he might have a death wish. Shifting wind currents made a smooth ride impossible. Wheels bounced on the landing strip like a pogo stick. The only protection in the open cockpit came from a thick pair of goggles across the eyes. An airplane ride in 1922 usually brought two things: a thrill story and stinging pain to the buttock. No one offered a chair for more than an hour after landing unless padded with a thick pillow and jelly. Ted was no exception. He was hired by New York City's finest to assist officers in aviation training.[84] The small squadron of single-engine airplanes called themselves the *Flying Jennies*. Ted was more observer than instructor, recording data and taking pictures. His co-pilot skills were less than desirable, crashing often, miraculously escaping the wreckage each time unharmed. [85] After ramming into shallow water off New Jersey, the department grounded him for good.

His near-death experience did not change him. Ted remained cocky and full of ideas. Like always, he proved to be a quick learner. But Ted wasn't' interested in working for a living. He was hoping to get rich quick. By 1923, Florida was turning out to be more than desolate swamps, depleted Indian reservations, and hot beaches. The weather was nice and the soil was lush with opportunity. Feeding pelicans, shopping on Central Avenue, and watching ceiling fans rotate at Hotel Detroit was all the rage in St. Petersburg. Western Florida, like much of the state, was booming with prime, available real estate.

Ted again recruited his old partner in crime Jay Werner, exiting the island of Manhattan and entering the world of entrepreneurship. The plan was to purchase land, develop it, and then sell for a high profit. They did not come empty-handed. Henrybelieved his son was on to something, knowing a thing or two about real estate, and gave Ted five hundred dollars to invest.[86] Instead, Ted and Jay blew the money on cute girls and slow ponies. Within three months, Ted wired his father for more money, money to come home.

Humbled once more, he returned to more familiar employment. He was hired again as payroll clerk for a silk stocking manufacturer. One of the few fringe benefits included free samples. But, without a female companion, it did him little good. Ted purposely stayed away from the action. He spent his evenings listening to the radio, fascinated by what he heard. Ted was not the only one falling in love with the new talking box called "radio." But as much as the man enjoyed it, what he really wanted was a girl.

CHAPTER EIGHT

THRILL OF THE CHASE

The red brick building on Westchester Avenue looked like an old livery, minus the smell of horse manure. It took them a while to find it from the remote subway stop. Barings got lost. Left turns taken when they should have gone right. The wintry chill of February 1924 did not help, streets layered in ice and leftover snow. Finally, music bellowed in the distance, sounds of mingling voices rose above the glowing streetlights. The sign outside told Ted and Jay that their search was over. *Dance Contest Tonight. Whitey Kaufman's Original Pennsylvania Serenaders play all your favorites!* Ted was back in the old borough where his life began—the Bronx.

The '20s were all about fun. The call for a good time came from the top. The war was over, the economy was strong, and to the victor goes the spoils. It was boom time. The sky was the limit in everything from business to pleasure. Boundaries faded away, resembling discreet lines on the palm of a human hand. Women won the right to vote, then raised their skirts, cut their hair, smoked cigarettes, and insisted they be called "flappers." The weird and the wacky was promoted, from catching cannon balls to sitting atop flag poles—anything to sell tickets, anything to make a buck. Dance competitions took hold in towns from east to west. The Charleston was the rage. Whispering in the ear of your partner or a good kick in the shin, whatever it took to keep dancing. This night in the Bronx was like many across America, young people looking for a thrill. Ted and Jules decided to take their chances. The last couple standing won twenty bucks. The boys saw it as a win-win opportunity. The money was nice. The girls were even better.

They came complete with all the proper accoutrements for an evening of fun and frolic, a sharp tailored suit, an empty dance card, and hip flask topped with gin the size of a human fist. If the girls didn't keep them warm, the booze would. The room had many females of various shapes and sizes, some with dark curls, some blond or Irish red. All were worth meeting. Playing the field was what every guy had in mind at such social occasions, including Ted. Yet, the moment he saw her, there were no others.

Her hair was gold, her features thin and Anglo. She didn't look like an American Indian, but drops of the Cherokee Nation had leaked into her veins through the blood of her half-breed mother May Cook. Her father Fred Giffords, however, looked more Caucasian, Swiss and German. Together, they named their daughter Helen. Born and raised in Newark, her father had changed the family name away from the more ethnic sounding *Gelderman* due to the anti-German attitudes during World War I. Helen chose to keep the original family name of Gelderman, an unashamed sign of her German heritage. She made her way into Manhattan looking for work. Thousands applied, only a few were accepted by Florence Zeigfeld to dance in his review. Helen was one of them. She picked the name "Bubbles" as her stage name, but everyone called her "Bubs" for short. She called Flatbush, Brooklyn, home.

When Ted first saw her, she stood alone by a large eight-foot table filled with cookie plates and a large punch bowl. Helen and her girlfriends laughed, sipped, and gossiped. Finely tweaked eyebrows and easy complexion gave her the look of a silent film star, a sophistication and maturity well beyond her years. No one could have guessed she was only seventeen. "She reminded me of a soft, creamy, delicious piece of French pastry," he once said. "The kind that someone else always chooses just before the tray is passed to you."[87]

Young Husing decided to take a chance. "Hey, Doll! Want to dance?" he asked. "First of all my name's not Doll. Its Bubs," the petite girl shot back. She wasn't usually that bold. "Bubs! What kind of name is that?" Ted mocked. "It's short for Bubbles, if you must know. My real name's Helen. My friends call me Bubs. You're not my friend!" Ted stood stunned at the girl's attitude. The way she carried herself—firm, womanly—might have scared off another admirer. But even at twenty-two, Ted had already shown the resilience of an elder statesman. "So if you want this conversation to continue, mister, I guess you'll just have to do a little better." Ted continued unmoved. He was falling in love. "I know that may not sound very ladylike," Helen continued. "But that's the way it is. Besides, you haven't passed on any references."

If Ted's cleverness was getting him in trouble, perhaps it could get him out. "Don't worry about that Ms. Helen, or is it Mrs.?" he said. "Married! You must be crazy!" she laughed. Ted pushed on. "I know just the fellow who can, as you say, pass on references. He's reliable, honest, and can vouch for my character."[88] "What's his name?" Helen asked. "Ted Husing," he answered. Whitey Kaufman's boys added to the scene, playing a soft interlude in the background as Ted maintained a fixed posture. Frustrated, she finally blurted out, "Well! . . . Are you going to bring him over?" It was a well-matched game of cat and mouse. "Won't be necessary. He's already here. . . . I'm Ted Husing, and I'm prepared to furnish any references you want."[89]

Something about Ted's rap caught her fancy. His boyish charm was refreshing compared to the older men that usually hit on her. "You're rather sure of yourself, aren't you?"[90] she said as her green eyes sparkled off his. Ted lifted his head back and smiled, still standing, taking her in again and again. He had never been more patient in his young life.[91] This girl in front of him clearly was different. He had known a few gals in his day, but Helen wasn't just another pretty face, but a real lady. Ted's mood became much more serious after she dropped the Ziegfeld bomb. Smitten changed to unbridled admiration. It all made perfect sense. He saw Helen as a woman of the world. Experienced in ways he only heard about. Keeping up with her on the dance floor would be easy compared to the rest of the night. He had to have her. Not just for one night, but for a lifetime.

A Ziegfeld girl was the envy of every woman from convent nun to street whore. They were the cornerstone of the show's success. A mile-long line of female hoofers, dressed in priceless gowns stuffed with precious stones, ribbons, and fresh flowers. Eye-popping costumes set fashion trends and had dressmakers rushing to copy the designs. A sizzling combination of youth, beauty, and a risqué spirit is what all the girls who graced the Ziegfeld stage possessed, some starting as early as thirteen years of age. Secretly, every woman wished to be one. Every man wanted to call one his own. Sex appeal sold tickets. Ziegfeld knew what his core audience coveted.

Ted himself caught the show, lusting from the back row, on occasion. "For in their heyday they were considered the most desirable women in town," wrote *New York Times* columnist Judy Klemesrud. "And their suitors included princes, barons, counts, famous actors, and the captains of industry."[92] In 1924, Ted Husing was far from a powerful man. He was a boring payroll clerk, low man on the totem pole of corporate America. Winning a girl like Bubs would take real work. Intrigue, insecurity prodded him further. *What was a glamorous queen like her doing among the lowlifes in a Bronx dance hall?* he wondered. As Ted pursued a trophy wife, Helen just happened to be searching for an average Joe.

She, too, heard the stories. "Enjoy it now, honey. It don't last forever," the old-timers warned. The old-timers were ex-Zigs, washed-up at thirty, out of fashion, out of work, and lonely. "Sometimes I wish my grandmother would have bought me a typewriter instead of toe shoes," said aging former Ziegfeld girl Harriett Fowler in a 1975 interview. "I wish I'd stayed in Philadelphia and married the boy next door and had lots of kids."[93] Few professions embraced the dreams of a career-minded women in the early 1920s. Outside of a showgirl, maybe one could sit behind a desk as a secretary, switch-board operator, or walk the halls of infirmaries dressed as a nurse. With few prospects for the working type, settling down to the role of housewife and mother was a welcome alternative. Harriett Fowler mouthed the fears of most of the Follies, including young Helen. "Unless you were a Ziegfeld girl who married well, you don't have anything. Look at me—I don't know how to do anything. It's even hard for me to open a jar."[94]

Helen knew how to look pretty. The rest she was willing to give her man no matter what his lot in life. Not all showgirls fit the gold-digger persona. Many resented being lumped in with the negative stereotype. In a 1997 *New York Times* letter to the editor, Joel Raphaelson gave the woman who raised him as proof. "My mother, a former Ziegfeld girl, is too soft-bitten to rise up in protest of that unkind generalization. I will do it for her. At twenty-three she married—not a broker, or a banker, or a sugar daddy—of all things, a playwright. Some gold-digger."[95] Helen, even at a young age, understood that money can't buy you love.

They continued to talk, sharing cookies and punch spiked with gin. Husing was a difficult man, but around this particular woman he had become soft. All he could do was lose himself and stare. Suddenly, the booming voice of the master of ceremonies returned him to the present. "Ladies and gentlemen, our contest is about to begin. All participants on to the dance floor, please, for the first number!" She grabbed his hand and ran him to the center of the floorboards.

For the next ninety minutes, the eight-piece band played

the best-known songs and foxtrots in their repertoire. "Ain't We Got Fun" and "Saxophobia" to the ever popular silly song "Barney Google." Goose feathers from the girls' cheap shoulder shawls and neckties littered the dance floor, giving the urban look of a hay barn. "Nola" did the most damage, playing four times throughout the evening, eliminating the weak couples while fueling the strong. Ted and Helen twirled and glided as they sang the words in unison, sweat pouring off their bodies.

> *Walking along the thoroughfare,*
> *She always draws attention,*
> *All the fellas stop to stare,*
> *She's called the fourth dimension.*
> *But if they think she'd ever care,*
> *It's mere misapprehension;*
> *Wait'll you see the angel with me,*
> *It's Nola.*[96]

Some sixty couples packed the dance floor at first, twenty, then ten, five, down to two. Finally, there was one. The team of Husing and Gelderman danced the final song alone, winners.[97] Ted offered to give her his half of the prize money. A momentary act of gallantry. "No, you need the money," she joked poking fun of his already receding hairline. "Get a trim will ya. I can't be seen around town with a Bowery boy." Helen smiled and coyly mopped the last beads of perspiration from his forehead with a napkin.

Ted was hooked under the spell of this girl. He thought of her day and night and nothing else. Always the big reader, Ted turned to the poets to try and deal with his feelings. He knew the pastoral rhymes of Whitman, the flowery prose of a Shakespeare sonnet. Outside of a few school assignments, Ted had never written anything before in his life. Worse, he knew little about love, even in the throes of it. The great epic tales of romance and devotion were always told with heightened language. Ted was convinced that Helen and he were made for each other. He begged her to marry him, promised to lavish her in diamonds. She laughed thinking it was a joke. He suggested they elope. "And disappoint mother?" she said. "Never." He answered by quitting his payroll job, devoting every waking hour to her. Ted loved a challenge. If she were to be convinced of his soulful intentions, then no rock would be left unturned.

She sat alone with curly blond hair
She was beautiful, succulent, and ripe as a summertime pear.

Ted dropped the pen and looked down at his creation. He liked the words, finding them heartfelt and honest. But he wasn't sure if Bubs would enjoy being compared to a piece of fruit. "She'd probably think I was calling her fat," the budding author thought. He tore the document into halves and threw it in the corner. Ted had experienced his first rewrite. With a fresh piece of paper in front of him, he started once again.

Winter snow, falling time in a breath of endless loving
She calls me with her eyes. Frozen, Frozen!
Can I survive, will I thrive?
Let me stay here in her gaze forever.

He signed it, "Your loving protector, Ted." He gave the poem one last look of review. Satisfied with his making, Ted folded the letter into an envelope and bolted for the post office. He would repeat the process countless times over the next several weeks. "I'd sit up far into the night composing poems, which I'd mail to her the next morning," he said in retrospect. "They were probably pretty bad. But, my heart was flowing into them."[98] Between frequent visits to her Brooklyn home, surprise visits to the Follie's stage door, latenight coffees, and his ceaseless run of written words, Helen was breaking.

Within four months, they were married, surrounded by the solemn bricks of the Episcopal Church of the Nativity in Flatbush. Family and friends gathered. On June 8, 1924, Helen Gelderman became Mrs. Ted Husing.[99] She was two days short of her eighteenth birthday. Among those who witnessed, the groom's best man, closest pal, and partner-in-crime Jay Werner. Ted and his new bride had grown up fast. They streaked across the sky, prepared to settle down to a life of reminded bliss. At night, they shared the same bed as honeymooners. Ted still had questions, not of his choice as a lifemate, but of himself. How did he find such perfect beauty? Had his words of poetry, his fervent passion been that persuasive? What intangible did he possess that a rich man couldn't buy, pulling the rug from under this dream and sending him back to the Bronx alone? He looked over to the woman by his side sleeping so peacefully. Ted knew her name, where she came from, every curve and birthmark on her body. He knew he loved her. In an infinite world of endless possibilities, Helen Maude Gelderman had chosen him.

CHAPTER NINE

WANTED: RADIO ANNOUNCER

Husing loved adventure, that much was clear. The Damon Runyon characters off the pages he read swam with life inside his head. The rustic words of Horace Greeley still called his restless spirit. Helen had become his partner. Whatever dreams he thought of, she lived with him. His visions were wild, unkempt—sordid. In his real life game of Cowboys and Indians, it was easy to figure out who was who. He had conquered his woman—for the time being. Yet, she was the only win in a landscape filled with losses.

With no job and little money, the newlyweds headed out on an open-ended honeymoon. Ted figured another stab at real estate couldn't hurt, hopping a train for St. Petersburg. Jay Werner stayed behind this time, as did his father's money. The couple stayed with friends, soaking up the West Florida sun and unsuccessfully searching for prospects. A lethargic attitude took over. Happy, in love, and tan, they had the rest of their lives to find the future. Everything changed with a message from mother.

FATHER GRAVELY ILL (Stop). COME HOME AT ONCE. (Stop)

Ted and his bride jumped the first rail back to New York.

Bertha's telegram, minus much detail, sounded ominous. Gravely ill—What did those words mean exactly? A layover in the Nation's capitol added more anxiety. Looking for a taste of home and an hour to kill before re-boarding, Ted purchased a copy of the *New York Times*. He glanced at the front page, then peeled the sections back for his first love—sports. For the moment, nothing could be done sitting in a railway station but wait. He devoured the big names and pounding stories of athletics in no time. As much as Ted tried to make light of a difficult situation, he was also unemployed. Finding work was quickly becoming top priority. He looked down at the tan line above his watch and decided to try his luck, the want ads.

The pages were not thick, five in all. Economic times were good and jobs plenty. But Ted just didn't want any occupation. He was searching for something invigorating, different, anything that possessed a sharp enough point to sew his wild oats. A few remedial positions, a few sun-baked adventures had yet to really test him. Ted understood that a man was measured by success. But, with the world looking down upon him, what chance did he have? Immigrant. Kraut. Bottom feeder. The pains of teenage intolerance remained fresh, rocks thrown by mobs.

Scanning across the page, a few large black font letters caught his roving eye. Wanted—Radio Announcer. He thought of the hours spent listening to the mysterious voices on the crystal set in his room. Might he now be one of them? Applicants needed to be young, married, proficient in music terminology, and college educated. College? Ted barely finished high school. Something about the promise of radio work stimulated his imagination. Why disqualify himself based on the minor details of education? If they wanted a college graduate, then a college graduate they would get. With a gallant flare that said everything about the man, Ted scratched in a name that was sure to grab attention—Harvard. He ran for the telegraph window to respond before their train pushed onto New York. "Of all colleges, Harvard made me feel my inadequacies the most," he wrote in retrospect. "And when I felt inadequate, I did not shrink. That is when I grew bold—sometimes too bold."[100]

Four hours later they entered the apartment on West 69th Street to encouraging news. Henry's conditioned improved, nothing that a short hospital stay couldn't cure. Better yet, there was a response to his cable, an interview for a radio job. The next day, Ted and Helen moved into an unoccupied apartment on the fourth floor. Looking after dad and helping mother made perfect sense, if not a break in rent on a New York City flat. He was surrounded by all his worldly possessions: a new wife, devoted parents, and a few dollars in his pocket. In every way, Ted was assured that there was no place like home.

The Aelian Building on West 42nd Street was a beehive of activity. Along cramped hallways, nervous want-to-be announcers paced, gnawed on fingernails, and mumbled to themselves, hoping to fill one on-air position for the Radio Corporation of America. For the next three weeks, 607 applicants, Ted Husing included, were tested with tongue twisters, the pronunciation of composer names, and ad libbing topical news stories. Among the observers listening was RCA general manager David Sarnoff, the same David Sarnoff who in 1912 sat at a wireless telegraph machine and relayed the gory details of a shipwreck off Nova Scotia. The ship was called Titanic.

Also judging the fresh pool of talent was Major Andrew White, adding to the stress of every man trying out. Anyone who clicked on a radio in New York knew the voice. Following his days as a gunner during World War I, White saw the future of radio as a moneymaker. He sold parts, wrote for trade magazines, and spoke often into the microphone. His early broadcast of political conventions, football games and boxing matches, most notably the Jack Dempsey versus Georges Carpentier heavyweight title fight of 1921, made him a pioneer, not to mention famous.[101] White's popularity extended off the air, frequenting Broadway nightclubs and enjoying a brief marriage to showgirl Katherine Titus.[102] His outlandish wardrobe and eagerness to drive expensive cars added to his celebrity. [103]

Sarnoff and White were about as qualified at picking radio talent as anyone living. Through the endless testing process, Ted emerged the winner. Poise, deep voice quality, and sports reports got the panel's attention. What impressed them most, however, was his stamina and speed, speaking for over a half-hour the details of a plane crash he picked up in a morning newspaper. Smart, well read, articulate—he certainly carried himself like a Harvard man. Then again, the question of college never came up. Oddly, Ted saw the unchecked, uninterrupted rambling of the airplane story as a rejection and left the studio crushed. Sarnoff called him at home, apologized for the misunderstanding and offered him a job at one of the company's two stations, WJZ, staring at forty-five dollars a week. Ted accepted. The following day, September 13, 1924, he began his new career as a radio announcer. [104]

The chances of on-air assignments were few in the beginning and often unsolicited. A fellow announcer early on asked him to read a pile of stock reports. "How was that?" the inexperienced announcer blurted out when finished. Ted was discreetly hushed having no idea the microphone was still open. [105] Andrew White didn't wait long to tap Ted's sports knowledge. In October, he used his help as statistician on the World Series broadcast, recreated live in the studio. [106] On-air opportunities came soon enough, fourteen-hour days, reading more stock reports, public service announcements, and introducing dance bands. In between, he answered phones, swept floors, and stayed close to the more seasoned announcers at the station, hoping to pick up a few useful tricks.

Programming expanded to meet the needs of the growing public, as did more radio stations. By the spring of 1925, twelve radio stations had budded across New York City. More were on their way. The future of the industry looked bright, as did Ted's first six months. Unlike past employments, he had not felt a compulsion to quit or been asked to vacate the building. Then came the rare recognition, rewards of the long hours in a broadcast studio. A piece of fan mail. A face on a crowded lunch line or subway platform might turn and say, "Hey, I know that voice. Aren't you on the radio?" An advertisement in an industry trade that year read, "The opportunities in radio have just begun. Are you sharing in them?"[107] If Ted Husing saw the question on the page, his answer would have been a resounding YES! Still, he wanted more, unsatisfied with his progress. Already aware of the radio announcer's unmerciful adage, "You're only as good as your next broadcast."

Helen shared in the passion of her husband's new career. She listened to his broadcasts, making suggestions, asking endless questions, and stroking his often broken ego. But she also had work on her mind, labor of a different kind. Ted had been far too busy to notice. Finally, a certain look among them during a rare quiet moment brought a sobering awareness. "What is it, doll? Got a bug on me or something," he gently asked. "Come here, daddy, and give me a kiss," she ordered. As he bent down to reach, her words struck. "Daddy? What do you mean daddy?" Helen was pregnant.

He anticipated impending fatherhood with great joy—at first. Things were looking up. Life was more full and exciting than it had ever been. He had a stunning young wife who was showing with each passing month. At the same time, he watched with fear and fascination the life growing inside her. His eyes no longer saw a baby, but a monster trying to devour his soul. Each kick, each ripple of movement from her rounded stomach dug him deeper into a hole of doubt and anxiety. Being a good father meant more than just bringing home the bacon. The sacrifices one had to make were something he was not sure he was ready for. Not when a world of possibilities exploded around him. The buzz he got on a daily basis from radio was more potent than a shot of whiskey. Did fatherhood mean letting go just when he was getting a grip?

In the early morning hours of April 17, 1925, Helen felt the first striking stings of childbirth. Bertha escorted her to nearby St.

Clair's hospital to assist her baby into the world. Henry called the station and told his son the moment was near. While Helen pushed, Ted chewed Wrigley's gum and smoked in an outside waiting room. Seven hours later, she gave birth to a girl, Peggemae. Slapped, cleaned, and fed, the newborn was displayed in the nursery window for the new father to view. Seeing the tiny child that he helped create stirred his emotions like nothing else. Ted cried openly. He looked into his daughter's eyes and all was right with the world—for the moment.

The next day, Ted bounced into the station like a stick ball from the streets. A happy kick, toothy smile, and high-end cigar was given to every man in sight. "This is for you Andy," he said passing Major White a stogie. "You've got a girl. Now my daughter has somebody to show her the ropes that her old man won't dare." White merrily grabbed Ted and wrapped his large arms around his back. He then whispered. "Congratulations, kid. You'll make a great father. I just know it." Ted took a deep breath and caught a glimpse of his reflection in the mirror. Panic shot back, nearly breaking the glass. A fragile, innocent life was totally dependent on him for the provisions of life. *I'm too young for all this shit*, he thought. *I can barely take care of a wife, much less myself. Now a child?* Fatherhood was upon him. At twenty-three years of age, Ted Husing was very much grown up.

The ceiling fans ran long and hard during the summer months. New York temperatures soared into the '90s like they usually did. The humidity was so thick some days that opening the icebox offered a rare breath of cool air. Ted stayed patient, glad to be around the house, spending time with Helen and baby Pegge. Once autumn broke, so did Ted, back at the yeoman hours in the studio and tugging at White for a crack at the one assignment he'd yet to try, sports. Occasionally, he released Ted to assist him on regatta races or boxing matches. Ted wasn't ready for airtime, but he did the next best thing, he listened. He learned. Ted heard White use direct, straightforward language. It was a simple approach and it worked.

"The one thing my father believed in most was respect for the listener," remembered White's son Blair. "He taught that some people who have tuned you in don't necessarily know what your talking about and you need to make it clear. Husing took what my father did and made it better."[108]

If he ever got the chance, the one sport Ted craved to do above any other was football. An opportunity finally arose on Thanksgiving, a game between Cornell and the University of Pennsylvania in Philadelphia. Instead of carving turkey at home, Ted opted for sitting next to White. He arrived at Franklin Field early and eager to help. Most announcers usually worked alone, including the Major, but had no quarrel in delegating his authority and lightening his load. A damp, steady rain matted the stadium and everyone in it. Ted and an engineer assembled equipment and checked sound. White, on the other hand, hobnobbed with relatives far from the broadcast location. As the teams took the field for kick-off, the Major was nowhere to be found, airtime only seconds away. Ted's wet hands grabbed the microphone and welcomed the audience to the broadcast. A small hook-up of stations, New York, Boston, D.C., and Schenectady carried his words. Instinct and adrenaline kept his mouth moving simultaneously searching the crowd. *Where was White?* A few minutes later, he reappeared, calmly reclaimed the mike and tore into his game description unfazed. "I'll never forget his broadcast," Ted recalled. "He just marched in cold, and a river of words began flowing"[109] Ted received a harsh, first lesson in preparation. The Major gave his helper another shot letting him talk in between quarters. The holiday contest brought the end of the football season. Ted, however, couldn't wait until next fall.

White recognized Ted's talent, but knew the young announcer needed more seasoning. White suggested another season of football with the Prescotts to help rekindle what he called "the feel."[110] Ted submitted himself to the trenches once more in 1926, bleeding lips and sore shoulders, determined to make football a staple of his work. The Major also advised he have his nose broken, a common practice among announcers. A widened atrium gave Ted's voice a richer more resonate sound. It was the start of an unleashing for the rising radioman. He would soon separate himself from the throngs of talking heads. It would not be the only separation, however. Family soon lagged behind, a wife and young child fading in the distance.

CHAPTER TEN

PUNCHING IN, GOING OUT
AND PAYING DUES

In the business world numbers usually tell the story, and it was clear that commercial radio was a booming trade. By the end of 1926, the Department of Commerce figured the radio industry generated a staggering $588 million, an increase of some $150 million from the previous year. [111] Better than five million receiving sets were wired across the country powered by large, cumbersome batteries, often leaking acid that could burn a hole through the thickest of floorboards.[112] Plugging into a wall socket was less than a year away. Soon enough, every convenience of the modern household was centered around the radio. Still, for most company executives and government officials, many questions remained. Who and what to say on the radio were already being answered. How to say it, nonetheless, still had the jury's attention.

Every market, every city big or small, had at least one talking head. Some preached, some sang, some told jokes. Some blathered radical politics while others called themselves strange names,[113] "The Little Colonel" and "Gloomy Gus" among them.[114] All spoke to loyal listeners, mesmerized by their rousing voices emanating from the radio. Regular folks with regular jobs and regular lives became celebrities. "Radio announcers are becoming American idols," one

Chicago radio executive A.J. Carter told a writer. "Women are falling in love with the pleasing voices of our announcers and falling out of love with faces of some of the screen stars."[115] There was little discrimination of programming in those early days. Whatever was on—music, comedy, sports or just a voice talking in the night—all received equal attention from the listeners. "Radio shocked people," explained former radio producer Gary Stevens. "It was a brand new medium. So immediately these people became part of your family." Ted was far from a household word, but people were beginning to notice. Newspapers listed his name. Radio critics wrote about his crisp baritone.[116] He found the sound intoxicating even to himself. "I knew that my voice was going into thousands of homes, but I wanted it to linger in the minds of the listeners."[117]

RCA owned several stations, none more important than D.C. affiliate WRC. At that point, Washington was not yet the glowing crown jewel of political posturing and crowded streets filled with tour buses. It was a sleepy metropolis on the Potomac amid stifling hot summers with the airless smell of fertilizer from nearby Virginia and Maryland farms. But, it was the nation's capital. Dome buildings, presidents, senators, and plenty of chances to place a microphone in front of them. The company believed in rotating their New York announcers down south to gain some political experience. Ted's turn came in April. He was told to report to station manager F.B. Guthrie. A four-month tour awaited.

Ted and Helen celebrated Pegge's first birthday from their modest apartment on the corner of 14th Street and Park Road in the Northwest section.[118] Not a mile south was the White House. Even closer were places like Piney Greek Park and the National Zoo. While Helen watched the baby, Ted chased his subjects through various government offices and restaurant bathrooms. The fourteen-hour days he had put in in the past were nothing compared to his grueling Washington schedule. Diplomat remarks, convention coverage, Marine Band remotes to train arrivals were all grist for the

WRC mill.[119] His introduction of President Calvin Coolidge twice in one day gave Ted ample press coverage.[120] By August, he was summoned back to New York to resume his duties at WJZ. No one was happier to hear the news than Helen. She looked forward to moving back to West 69th Street for one reason: Bertha. With a click of the heel on the floor or a tap on the pipe, Bertha could again be summoned to assist with the baby.

When Ted returned he found the station's sound had improved dramatically. A booming 50,000 watts carried the WJZ signal well beyond the tri-state. Ted was chosen to anchor the virgin broadcast. He was fast gaining a reputation for tenacity and creative intuition, whether he was forewarning listeners of a hurricane off the coast of Miami or hiding a microphone inside a flowerbed in order to air an unauthorized speech by the Queen of Romania. White also made him a weekly fixture on football games, allowing him to solo play-by-play for the first time. The radio played often at the Husing house, with Pegge, upon hearing her father's voice, pointing wildly at the giant speaker.

Then came a new word—"network!" The changes in radio were coming fast and furious. New York's most listened-to stations WJZ and WEAF, linked with stations from Boston to Kansas City, becoming the National Broadcasting Company. There was power in numbers, twenty-five stations in all.[121] Ted now worked for NBC. He didn't care who signed his paycheck as long as he stayed on the payroll. The result of a year-end, nationwide listeners poll gave every indication that work would remain plentiful. Of the top ten names, Ted had placed at number seven. Ted buzzed with excitement. They were talking about him. "Seventh in the United States kept skipping through my mind," he would write. "Hard work and intensive study of mike techniques had paid off."[122] He continued to review the list, searching for the one name he coveted most. Toward the bottom, placing at #9, he finally saw it, Graham McNamee.

He had met the man once or twice. He heard his work

countless times, coating the broadcast map. Ted was young and hungry but far from the only prodigy who emulated McNamee. He was the envy of every radioman, especially those who covered sports. As much as Ted respected White, he knew the Major fell short of McNamee's reach. The broadcaster stood about 5'–8", with thinning brown hair and a gangly look.[123] Crooked teeth and a seminal overbite filled his mouth. In the radio business, looks meant nothing. His sound shook the earth. Mac saw radio work as a performance, rooted in his days as a concert singer. The dullest events, the most rudimentary plays echoed with excitement, his lungs panting out of breath, a technique he perfected by running up and down steps, dashing through studio hallways.[124] He might not have been the most popular announcer in America, but Graham McNamee certainly was the most celebrated.

"No argument . . . no contest, the greatest sports announcer we ever had was Graham McNamee," believed Red Barber. "How he did, what he did, when he did . . . is to me a miracle."[125] No one ever described White in those terms. White kept his distance, a natural enemy. The press played up their rivalry, pitting one against the other.[126] But once NBC formed, the choice was clear. Mac was given top billing, covering all the big events—championship fights, World Series, and sent out to California to call the Rose Bowl clash New Year's Day of 1927. The game represented an historic first. Never before had there been a coast-to-coast broadcast.[127]

McNamee was not limited to just sports. After Charles Lindberg arrived from France on the second leg of his death-defying trans-Atlantic flight, millions lined Broadway to welcome their hero. But Americans were probably more familiar with the man who interviewed the pilot on the radio that day, the man named McNamee.[128] "On my desk, each day, lie batches of letters," he boasted. "And after big events, the mail is so heavy that it takes a large force of clerks to handle it."[129] Brand new NBC president Merlin H. Ayelsworth was asked by a reporter to name radio's greatest asset. He answered without hesitation, "Graham McNamee!"[130]

Ted felt confident in his sports know-how. No bigger fan walked the planet. Given the same platform, he questioned ever matching the heights reached by the one they called, "the voice with a smile."

"You know, this Graham McNamee is a god to me," Ted confessed to *New York Daily News* critic Ben Gross. "I'll be happy if I can be only half as good as he is."[131] Deep down Ted understood that listener polls were fun, subjective opinions taken with a grain of salt and an antacid before bed. The industry was new and the fans fickle. Still, the numbers did not lie. He studied the list again and again, the smile plastered hard to his face, #7, #7, #7 . . .

Ted also found his name sprinkled about New York's social guest lists. He had new fans and, better yet, new friends, none more loyal than *Daily News* columnist Mark Hellinger. His gutsy stories of urban life included Broadway stars, acerbic cops, and gaudy gangsters, making him a highly paid, trusted confidante to the "in" crowd. Hellinger knew how to party. He also knew how to dress, black shirts, pastel-colored ties, and expensive suede shoes. In Ted, he saw a man eager to learn the ways of sin. Mark Hellinger became his personal chaperone, introducing him to influential types, the best tailors, and best watering holes in Manhattan. If Hellinger said you belonged, then the doors opened. The writer had a reputation for staying awake into the wee hours of the morning, then sleeping late into the day. Saturday's were different. Hellinger loved football, rising before noon and listening often to games on the radio, Ted's accounts among them.[132]

At first, Ted had the look of an overworked coal miner in a closet full of clean white shirts. Back rooms, speakeasies, nightclubs, all of them were illegal and every patron subject to arrest. Walking into upscale places like Billy LaHiff's or the 300 Club, his jaw dropped. In one corner sat actress Jeanne Eagles. In the other was heavyweight champ Jack Dempsey. "Pretty amazing, isn't it, all these convicts in one cell," joked Hellinger. "Come on over here, there's somebody I want you to meet." A moment later Ted was shaking hands with the mayor of New York, Jimmy Walker.

The elegance and sophistication of carousing with the Broadway elite seemed equal to his maturing on-air persona—authoritative, classy, and a cut above the rest. More than that, he began to notice how people treated him. Ted was reminded of the simple lessons of appearance and respect his father had shown him when he was a boy. Helen shared the sparkling nights with him initially, eager to reconnect with the past, manicured fingernails glowing in lavender, hair curled, dressed with purpose. Ted had forgotten how stunning his wife could be. She, too, made friends, enjoying the lively conversation and dry martinis. Among her more familiar chums was fellow Ziegfeld showgirl Gladys Glad, who just happened to be Hellinger's fiancée. "I don't have an understanding of Helen as a person who stayed home much," said Ted's granddaughter Kim Lacey. "She clearly had the same instincts as a socialite."

The number seven still resonated come the new year. An upgrade on clothes were needed. A pair of Mary Jane pumps for Bubs. Maybe a new car. Life was getting better and more expensive. Ted didn't mind spending money. He simply wanted more at his disposal. The radioman noticed the wad of cash Hellinger pulled out of his pocket on a nightly base.[133] Ted began to wonder if the seventh most popular radio announcer in America was properly compensated. He wanted a raise, feeling confident his boss Charles Popenoe would agree. However, the network's GM denied his request. If a bump in pay was out of the question, then Popenoe did the next best thing, offering the disgruntled employee a sales position.[134] Ted had no interest operating behind the scenes, a stiff suit working the phones and schmoozing clients. The best salesmen in America didn't get fan mail. They didn't drink black-market booze with the mayor. And they most certainly didn't call football games in stadiums packed with stellar athletes and pretty girls.

"Look Charles, I want a raise. I deserve one," Ted said emphatically. "Can you count? The listeners like me. Where's Mc-Namee on that list, hah? You guys are doing swell thanks to me." Popenoe was glad that the public listened to his announcers. But, before anything he was a businessman concerned about the bottom line. "Come on Husing," he said. "NBC can't give you a pay increase just because some broad likes the sound of your voice. Hell, my wife's a big fan. Would you consider taking her off my hands instead?" The general manager roared with laughter. Biting the end of his thumbnail, Ted sat stone-faced with his eyes peering forward. The two were at an impasse. Popenoe tried to sooth the tension and buy some time. "You're doing a solid job Ted and Mr. Ayelsworth appreciates it, he really does. Let's wait until the end of the year and we'll talk about money then." Ted came back with a ready response. He quit.[135]

The man loved radio announcing, but had no desire to compromise himself. There would be other opportunities, he believed, better, more lucrative. He was now famous . . . almost. Fellow announcer Milton J. Cross waved through the studio glass as Ted passed, rewriting copy, checking mikes before an afternoon broadcast. He didn't know it was a wave goodbye. The list of America's most popular radio announcers exercised no leverage as a bargaining chip, at least in Ted's case. He wondered how others, if they had his guts, might fare. Cross happened to sit on top at #1. Ted grabbed his coat, shook his head, and left WJZ and NBC for the last time.

Ted walked along 69th Street with a bouquet of yellow and red flowers in his hand. The cold winter day needed a tangible mark of warm sunshine. The neighborhood thugs chuckled under their breath. He didn't care. The flowers weren't for them anyway. Helen was shocked to see him home at such an early hour. Ted gazed into her eyes, needing her now more than ever. "Get dressed baby, we're going out," he said to his wife. Tonight he wanted to celebrate freedom. Tomorrow he would contemplate the binding questions of life. What next? Helen assured him that whatever came next, they would endure it together.

CHAPTER ELEVEN

THIS GUY HUSING

The fight didn't last long, but it did get heated. "You are NOT going back to work, Bubs! Put it OUT of your head!" The idea wasn't completely unwarranted. With Ted unemployed, Pegge still in diapers, someone had to be the breadwinner. And why not Helen, temporarily? Chorus girls earned thirty-five dollars a week.[136] At 19 and wearing a size five, she still looked the part, young mother or not. But, for Ted, it was simply a matter of pride. " . . . and get nagged by mommy all evening while you're hoof'n it behind Hellinger's girl? Not to mention the tongue wagers trying to cop a feel? NO WAY!" Helen turned sassy "Well, it worked on you, didn't it?" The crass joke made them laugh, ending the hostility. "Stop worrying," he said caressing her face. "I've got some calls out. Something'll come." It was settled. They would wait it out.

Ted had no job and no microphone to speak into. He took advantage of the odd hours with a laissez-faire approach. Helen might have thought Ted was on holiday. He slept in several mornings, sometimes until noon, ignoring the desperate pleas from Pegge screaming from the next room. Instead, Helen rose from the bed and dragged their daughter outside or downstairs to Henry and Bertha's place. The vacation lasted about a week. From New England, came a job offer. *The Boston Evening Transcript* owned and operated a brand new radio station out of their offices on Federal Street. The station was appropriately given the call letters WBET. The suits at the *Transcript* liked Ted's confidence and energy. They knew he wasn't exactly Milton Cross or Graham McNamee, but coming from the Big Apple, he did have star quality—#7. He was hired with the title of Station Director. In late January of 1927, the Husings moved for the fifth time in three years.

Ted's boss was none other than the paper's tough-minded radio critic Richard Grant. Like many reviewers of the new medium, he was often merciless in his assessment and respected by his peers for word usage. "Dick was a dynamic customer who whacked the hell out of every bum program that came on the air," remembered Ted in later years. "All of New York's radio editors read him and took their opinions from him."[137] Despite his reputation, Grant wasn't interested in running the virgin station. He looked at the door keys and tossed them to his new hire. Ted would run the store —a virtual one-man show—free to pursue programming of his choice and grow without constraint.

Ted set up the family shop on 5 York Street in the quaint section of Brighton.[138] Along the short boulevard stretched green-leafed elms and three-floor apartments. Two-year-old Pegge played in nearby Franklin Park. They were prepared to make Boston home, but the Husings were definitely not in New York anymore. Instead of carousing the scene, Ted spent his after hours at home. It was no doubt a change of pace. "I'll give Boston full credit for one thing: my reformation," Ted admitted. "The city made me a better family man. At night there was no place to go but home."[139] Ted or Helen did not readily embrace the alteration of lifestyle. Catholic Churches and picnics on Boston Commons were nice. Beantowners also broke laws in speakeasies. But nothing equaled the lure of walking into a club filled with movie stars, business tycoons, and sports-page heroes.

Ted felt isolated, 190 miles away from the action and, worst of all, his friends. He noticed the multitude of Irish faces that swarmed the streets. In Boston, St. Patrick himself wouldn't have stood a chance with these roughnecks. If Ted had lived in Brighton ten years earlier, he might be dead. Helen worked the phone, begging Susan Stringer, her friend and maid of honor, to visit on occasion. She did bringing bagels from Lower East Side bakeries or the latest fashion catalogue from Gimbals. Ted poured his frustration into work and appreciated the salvation, being away from the ears of New York critics. He was totally free to experiment before the microphone. He voiced the usual shows, openings, sign-offs, dance band remotes, commercials, and sports with a twist. It was summer and that meant baseball.

Forty-two-year-old Fred Hoey was well established in Boston, calling both Red Sox and Braves games on station WNAC.[140] Games were mostly recreated. Ted figured it was time to give the old man some competition. He convinced Braves owner Emil Fuchs to not only air home games but air them live. Fuchs expressed trepidation at first, wondering if fans might decide to not pay for a ticket and listen to a Husing broadcast for free. Ted had never called baseball before. At times his work came off uneven and sloppy, much like the team he broadcasted. His bold experiment failed. Attendance at Braves Field dipped for the second year in a row. Mr. Fuchs could hardly blame Ted's broadcasts for the demise at the gate. The Braves finished the '27 season where they usually did, near the bottom in the standings and near the bottom in box office.[141] Ted, however, jettisoned his perch long before Boston's humdrum season closed. He was on a train in July, wife and child in tow, headed back to New York and a new position.

Major White never officially made the move to NBC. White focused more and more on radio behind the scenes, editing *Wireless Age* magazine and writing. His on-air assignments, mostly football, deliberately dwindled, booked on a freelance basis.[142] In the end, he saw himself as an administrator not a broadcaster. What he really wanted was his own network. The task would be daunting. Long hours, sleepless nights, and at best a long shot to succeed. If it was to be successful, White had to surround himself with good people. A staff made of driven souls and pit-bull ferocity. One man, one voice rushed immediately to mind—Ted Husing. Not much of a salary was offered at first, but White promised the one thing money could never buy—opportunity.

Ted still burned over NBC's refusal to give him a pay raise. He would make them wish they'd offered stock options. He loved White and felt indebted to the father figure who showed him the ropes that first year in radio. Henry and Bertha had kept the upstairs apartment vacant, knowing someday he would come back. There existed, then again, a hundred other reasons why the vagabond announcer returned to New York, none more strident than another shot at the big-time, and a chance to out dual the man, Graham McNamee.

At times it seemed there existed two Graham McNamees. For many listeners, there were. When WEAF hired him in 1923, across the hall, inside an adjoining studio talked Phillips Carlin, over weight, college educated, and wire glasses. He looked more like an AT&T board member than radio announcer. Before long, they shared the microphone on assignments big and small. NBC showcased them together on every event, especially sports. McNamee usually handled the play-by-play while Carlin filled in with color.[143] The press dubbed them "The Radio Twins." Audiences loved them. Soon, resentment soured their relationship, feeling one took away from the other or, worse, stole the other's broadcast style.[144] Neither realized the significance of their teaming, history's first two-man broadcast crew.

White's new network venture staggered out of the blocks. He joined forces with concert manager Arthur Judson to form a chain of radio stations. Judson simply wanted a vehicle to showcase his performers. White, on the other hand, preferred supplemental programming such as sports. The two partners signed contracts in January of 1927, calling themselves the United Independent Broadcasters. United in spirit, yes, but they had yet to raise any capital. For the next ten months, a baffling mix of sponsors and underwriters tried to keep UIB afloat. The Columbia Phonograph Company tried first, followed by Philadelphia millionaire Jerome Louchheim.[145] Affiliate problems, poor cash flow, and general mismanagement kept the network delayed. Ted sat helpless on the sidelines, chomping to get behind the microphone.

White was determined to see the network fly and asked his anxious talent to exercise patience. Ted hit the streets looking for temporary work. Station WHN hired him, filling two positions in one paycheck, announcer and assistant program director. With the football season fast approaching, Ted worked quickly, keeping his eye on the prize. He rustled up old contacts at Columbia University asking if they wanted their football games broadcast citywide. The school jumped at the chance. He convinced daily newspaper *The New York American* to sponsor the broadcasts.

The American gave Ted's game broadcast ample publicity throughout the season. Listenership was strong and so was his play-by-play descriptions. Once Columbia concluded their season, Ted broadcast the high-profile Army versus Navy and Army versus Notre Dame games from Yankee Stadium.[146] Critics at the *New York Herald Tribune* favored the newcomer's work over that of the "Twins." "Mr. Husing is likely to become radio's most appreciated football describer, unless, of course, Mr. McNamee and Mr. Carlin come to realize that the primary purpose of a football broadcast is not to furnish verbal entertainment but to provide immediate news of what the twenty-two football players are doing."[147]

Ted's voice quickly gained additional notice. Metro-Goldwyn-Mayer in partnership with station WPAR hired him to narrate a special showing of their upcoming silent film entitled *Love*. The movie was based on the classic tale *Anna Karenina* and starred a sultry German actress named Greta Garbo. On December 20, from the Embassy Theater in midtown, Ted addressed a packed house and, better yet, a national audience—a rare opportunity. He stood in front of the microphone wowing the audience with what one historian called "a dramatic, blow-by-blow account."[148] Again, Ted exhibited his speed and accuracy, mouthing 155 words a minute.[149]

On December 25, Ted was enjoying Christmas with his family. When the phone rang he figured it was a friend calling to spread some cheer. On the other end talked White, inviting himself over for a visit and to take care of some business that just couldn't wait. The Major entered an hour later bearing gifts, a bottle of perfume for Bubs, a doll for the little one, and a fresh contract for Ted to sign. Shortly before Thanksgiving, Columbia Phonograph had eagerly sold off its interest in the failing UIB experiment in exchange for free advertising. The Columbia Broadcasting System was on the air and picked J. Andrew White as their first president. Ted took a pen from his new boss and wrote his name on the paper in bold, cursive letters: Edward B. Husing. It was official, he now worked for CBS. White gave him the job title of "Assistant to the President."

The first few months on the job simmered. Not much on-air work and chasing White around the office left him frustrated. He described it as "losing much of my identity as a radio announcer, much to my regret."[150] CBS continued in the red, spending almost three times as much as it earned.[151] Come spring, 1928, things improved, as did Ted's airtime. Floyd Bennett, the hero pilot of Admiral Richard Byrd's North Pole expedition in 1926, had died of pneumonia after attempting to rescue a downed aircraft along the Gulf of St. Lawrence. President Coolidge insisted he be buried at Arlington National Cemetery in full regale. CBS seized the opportunity.

Ted hustled to Washington, secured communication lines and an all-important waver from Bennett's grieving widow to broadcast the funeral. A crew from NBC ascended on Arlington for the same purpose, only they didn't secure the release from Mrs. Bennett.

Ted's diligence had guaranteed CBS an exclusive. His on-air descriptions lasted nearly two hours, speaking in whispered tones, braving a heavy rain. The somber broadcast helped the network gain national attention and much-needed commercial accounts.[152] Ted was just warming up. He traveled to Houston in June to cover the Democratic National Convention. On October 15, he covered the landing of the German airship Graf Zeppelin from Lakehurst, New Jersey. He again showed his improvisational skills, speaking to the pilot in his native German language and coyly asking him to place his cap on the NBC microphone. Columbia had another exclusive.[153]

To say the new network struggled would be an understatement. Outside of the odd special event, only one program secured a regular spot on the weekly schedule, *Night Club Romances*. The premise of the show was simple: sappy love stories, broken hearts underscored by a fictitious nightclub setting, a precursor to soap opera dramas that flooded the radio and television market years later. Ted narrated the stories drafted by staff writer Dick Clark and showcased a number of orchestras during the run of the show, none more famous than the *Connecticut Yankees* lead by a recent red-haired Yale graduate named Rudy Valee. The network hooked into Vallee and his *Yankees* a few more times, giving them additional exposure, Valee singing in a high-pitched voice and swinging his baton freely. Soon a nationwide vaudeville tour followed, then a recording contract and a radio show of his own.

The Major had not fully abandoned sports announcing. He took the CBS mikes to the World Series that fall, splitting the play-by-play with Hal Totten from their Chicago affiliate WBBM. Ted worked commentary in between innings and post game. Across the way sat the "Radio Twins," calling the games on NBC.[154] Ted got the ultimate chance a few weeks later to prove his durability on the night of Tuesday, November 4, 1928. It was election night. An eager nation waited to know the results. He situated himself amongst a pool of curious writers in the newsroom of the *New York World*. He went on the air at 8 PM, as precincts reported and ballots were tallied. For the next ten hours, his mouth kept moving. He received an occasional break when there was nothing to report, throwing it back to the studio. It was a night of no sleep and black coffee for many. The brass at NBC didn't see the need to post a man at the microphone and read the results. They figured people would wait until the morning like they always had and read it in the newspapers. Republican Herbert Hoover won. The eastern half of the nation rose from a sound slumber to the voice of Ted Husing telling them who the next president would be.[155]

The *World* never thought twice of having a radio announcer in their midst. He utilized the full resources of the paper to his advantage—AP wire, reporters, and common sense. Perhaps for the first time, radio trumped the age-old print media at breaking a major news story. A shot heard across the bow. The beginning of war. "By using his own arithmetic and logic he scooped the paper by reporting Hoover's election by a whole hour."[156] Ted's work received some 12,000 telegrams.[157] Each day, each week, another sign that CBS had no plan to back down from NBC. White's instincts about Ted had been vindicated. He might have been president of the network. But, Ted was in charge. "He called him 'This guy Husing.' He called him that way a number of times," recalled Blair White about his father. "There was a number of times that they had to face people who weren't too happy to have them there or didn't know why they were there. And somebody had to stand up for the cause. Husing was usually that guy. My dad said you could practically throw him into a hornet's nest and come out without a scratch"[158]

Despite the hard work, CBS still lagged behind. NBC just wasn't one network, but two, known as the Red and Blue—which meant more affiliates, more revenue, and more respect. Somehow, someway, CBS still breathed with life. The agile feat and fast-talking lips of Ted Husing had helped save the network, for the moment. However, radio could not live on announcers alone. Sooner or later,

Columbia needed a new direction and more resources if they were to survive.

Jerome Louchheim had enough. He wanted out of the radio business and offered his friend, Philadelphia cigar mogul, Samuel Paley a crack at it. Paley wasn't interested, but his 26-year-old son was. William Paley was a man of privilege: boarding schools, fraternity parties, and trips abroad. However, he didn't mind hard work jumping into the family business known as Congress Cigars after graduating from the University of Chicago. As a junior executive, he witnessed first hand the influence of radio buying ad time on the new UIB network. The cigar company sponsored a half-hour show called *The La Palina Smoker*. The brand became a best seller due in large part to the exposure, sparking Paley's interest in the network. By the fall of 1928, CBS had a new boss. "I became tremendously excited at the prospects and the network's shaky condition did not deter me," he later wrote.[159]

Paley, at first, took on the role of "Mr. Nice Guy," young, inexperienced, simply trying to navigate his way around the world of network radio. He extended himself to the National Broadcast Company as a courtesy. He tried to arrange a meeting with NBC president Merlin Aylesworth, a chance to exchange pleasantries and discuss common interest, namely, the future of radio. A curt response soon arrived, one Paley did not expect—NO! Aylesworth ran his network with a closed door and iron fist. Of course, Ted could have told him that. "NBC did not recognize CBS, just as an established nation might not recognize a newly formed state," explained Paley years later. "He wanted to keep it that way. Aylesworth said we were too small. It made me wonder."[160]

Paley embraced a more human approach to business. And his initial order of business was to get to know the employees. The early years at CBS resembled a close-knit family. One for all and all for one. Paley was the leader, setting the tone. But the contributions of everyone—from announcers, secretaries, engineers, and even

Mike Donavan, the office doorman—had a stake in the network's success. "William Paley was a very prideful man," noticed Gary Stevens. "He was so different from NBC. They were stoic and stayed and conservative. Paley ran his network as one of the boys. He told me that he wanted to know everyone who works for him, what their problems are. To me, he represented style and class. CBS was like a friendly club and NBC was stiff."[161]

Then again, success also depended on efficiency. Paley came in with fresh ideas, overturning flawed policy and put everyone in the right place. One employee, an office manager, he thought was particularly misplaced. The man annoyed, tried patience, and made Paley wonder exactly why he had a job in the first place. Obviously, he was unfamiliar with his pool of announcers. "One day soon after I arrived, Major White was ill and unable to broadcast a football game. So with my fingers crossed, I sent the inept office manager to Chicago to substitute for White. He told me he had some experience broadcasting local sporting events. As a result I lost an impossible office manager and gained the best and most famous sportscaster in the country—Ted Husing.[162] William Paley was not the only one who enjoyed Ted's football work. *Life Magazine* radio critic Agnes Smith wrote, "It's a treat to find a boy who realizes that he is broadcasting a sporting event and not making a speech at the Annual Banquet of the Realtor's Boosters Club."[163]

That same year, Ted began making Harlem a nightly stop. He wasn't alone. Whites ventured uptown looking to experience culture shock and exotic entertainment. They found it at the corner of 142nd Street and Lenox Avenue. The Cotton Club showcased some of the most glamorous dancers, sublime singers, and gifted musicians in New York. All were black. Front and center lead was a tall, good looking piano player named Edward Kennedy Ellington. Everyone called him "Duke." His "jungle style jazz" was all the rage, the nightly floor shows had standing room only.[164] Ted, like most, became a fan.

Owney Madden and his partner Big Frenchy De Mange, ran the Cotton Club like the majority of underworld figures, deep pockets, well-placed bribes, and heavy muscle intimidation. They enforced a strict "whites only" policy when it came to patronage, adding to the club's allure and shameless exclusivity. They also enjoyed publicity. Mob figures of the prohibition era were some of the most famed men in America, simultaneously feared, loathed, and at the least observed with a large dose of intrigue. Madden earned the nickname "Killer" the old fashion way. Radio announcers and newspaper men were good for business, better yet, good for the ego. A chosen few, Mark Hellinger, in particular, became confidants, building friendships, protecting secrets. Hellinger biographer Jim Bishop saw the paradox such relationships created, "The columnist's affection for the racketeers cost him a lot of good stories which, as a pal of the punks, he couldn't use."[165]

For Ted, the Hellinger connection worked again. He just wasn't another customer sitting at a table in the Cotton Club. He could be trusted. Then again, Ted and the gang of wise guys had more in common than friends. They had 10th Avenue. Madden and De Mange were once sworn enemies, leaders of the fabled Gopher Gang and Hudson Dusters in their younger days.[166] Hell's Kitchen was a blood bath, knife fights, gun battles, and fisticuffs. The radio announcer was well familiar with the gangs' penchant for busting heads of people they didn't like.

Ted quickly convinced his new boss of the monumental opportunity facing them, broadcasting "The Duke" nationwide. Paley dispatched Ted back to the club to negotiate a deal. He feared the gangsters who ran the joint might put on the squeeze. To his surprise, Ted returned holding gold. The club agreed to let CBS broadcast at no cost. In exchange, they wanted what general manager Herman Stark called "a first class air check."[167] Ted provided that and more, opening a door to history.

The broadcasts were magical: Unrehearsed, long form; announcer and musician coolly bantering back and forth in between numbers. Ellington enjoyed their on-air rapport, calling Ted "a beautiful cat with an up-to-the minute awareness then known as hip."[168] It did not take long before Duke Ellington became a national sensation. Fan letters poured in all throughout the land. His records sold through the roof. In smaller towns, theaters packed them in to hear the CBS broadcasts from the wild place called Harlem. It was also the first time a person of color was heard consistently on network radio. "Here was the real springboard because we were on the radio from the Cotton Club practically every night," Ellington recalled. [169] "He (Husing) did a great deal for us."[170] Oftentimes, Ted broadcast two shows a night, one for the East Coast listeners, a second midnight show for the West. [171]

Ellington became so popular that he asked Madden and De Mange to loosen the "whites only" rule. The syndicate eventually obliged, opening admission to wealthy, light-skinned blacks and seating them in back tables.[172] By no means did Ted take on the role of activist. His motives for putting anyone on the air were much simpler. They had little to do with race, socioeconomics, or political ideology. Ted never really saw the big picture in anything he did. His radio career was no exception. If someone had talent, no matter what skin color, he did what he could to get them airtime. Then again, no white man felt the pangs of intolerance, prejudice, or discrimination more than Ted Husing.

Paley tapped into every asset he could those first few months, hell bent on giving NBC a run for their money. From Philadelphia, he brought along his personal secretary Larry Lowman, taking care of Paley on the social scene, booking theater tickets, restaurant reservations, and a table at the city's hottest speakeasies. Once inside, public relations guru Edward Bernays coached him who to talk with and how to milk every drop of media exposure for the network.[173] He took full advantage of his status as young, rich, and single. Showing up at the same clubs often was Ted, young, wanting, and married. A wink, a nod, a knowing smile, partners now with a common purpose and common enemy.

One man he no longer needed was Andrew White. The ship belonged to Paley—no room on the deck for two commanders. He envisioned the former president returning to the microphone, nurturing Ted and other on-air talent, but clashing egos would not allow such plans to unfold. "He definitely set my dad aside and told him where he thought he ought to be," remembered Blair White. "And within a year my dad said, 'I'm out of here. I can't do this.'" White tried to smile, telling his friends, "I'm off to play polo." Leaving was more difficult than he let on. Wounded and eager to put the past behind, the Major sold all his stock in the fledgling CBS network and looked forward to his new life outside of radio. A shoddy 1930 investment would in time become worth millions. "Boy, I wish he hadn't sold it," chuckled Blair White. "My butler would have answered the phone when you called."[174]

On January 8, 1929, Ted introduced Paley to the radio audience for the first time. He shared the news of his growing radio empire. CBS stretched coast-to-coast, forty-nine stations deep and broadcasting in forty-two separate markets. The cramped offices of home station WABC inside Steinway Hall did not reflect the company's true size. It was the largest radio network in the world. [175] A new year was upon them. And things were looking up for CBS. Still, a nagging insecurity pulled at Ted's soul. Never satisfied, never content, work remained the mission, far from accomplished.

CHAPTER TWELVE

CLYDE VAN HUSING

It was easily the most popular sporting event of the calendar year, outside of the World Series, Rose Bowl, or championship fight. Half the people who attended the Kentucky Derby didn't know the difference between a horseshoe and a hockey puck. They went to be seen. High society from New York, as far west as St. Louis, and south to Miami Beach chartered special Pullman's. The more adventurous started flying to the annual party. U.S. senators, captains of industry, and the occasional heiress converged on Lexington to exchange stock tips or brag about summer travel plans. The race itself fell a furlong behind to sipping mint juleps and smiling for the camera along millionaire row. The women wore large, fluorescent-colored hats and enough diamonds to make the west coast of Africa blink. The men dressed in duck-tailed tuxedos, including a pink carnation stabbed through their lapels. Win or lose, it was a rite of passage for the rich and famous. They didn't call it the "sport of kings" for nothing. William Paley wanted a man at the horse racing show of the year, one with a live microphone.

On May 10, 1929, the National Broadcasting Company announced their intention to broadcast the famous horse race. Paley was not altogether surprised, but, the expected news needed a response, a quick decision. Allowing NBC an exclusive would be unforgiveable. The young CEO spent the afteroon eating knockwurst and formulated a counter move.[176] The Derby would run in a little more than a week. What did NBC have planned? Who were they sending? Details were sketchy, but one thing was sure, the Kentucky Derby was virgin territory for the network, any network.

Two local radio stations, one from Louisville, the other Chicago's WGN, had broadcast the big race in the past. But their reach was limited, regional. The full-size New York networks stayed away for one simple reason—Fear. No one really knew what to do. Tote boards, photo finishes, and track announcers were part of the future. So much acreage at a racetrack to cover, sight lines, logistics, where to place announcers, how to run cable, where to string telephone wires, and perhaps the most important uncertainty, what to say. Paley needed to find a man who was up for the test, bound with energy, unafraid to confront uncharted on-air land.

It didn't take long for Ted to hear the news about NBC's plans. Reports traveled fast. He figured Paley might send someone down to cover it. Ted hardly figured that someone to be him. "Ted, I'd like for you to call the Derby for us," the boss firmly stated. "We can't let Aylesworth have all the fun," referring to NBC's big chief Merlin Aylesworth. "Are you up for it?" Paley knew the answer before he asked. Ted stood tall trying not to fidget, trying to squelch what he really thought. "Wherever you need me, Bill," the talented broadcaster said. Paley rapped his knuckles on the desk in delight. "I knew I could count on you. Take Bubs down with you, if you want. We'll give 'em a run for their money." The open disrespect Aylesworth showed CBS months earlier, unwilling to recognize the undeveloped network as legitimate competition, still burned Paley. Now he would have his chance, give the big bully on the block something to think about.

Ted agreed to make the trip under muted protest. There was one small problem—inexperience. What Ted knew about describing a horse race he could fit on a single sheet of toilet paper. "I didn't know anything about racing then," Ted admitted. "I'd only seen a few races in my life and hardly knew a horse from a heifer."[177] The uncertainty of his horse calling skills quickly gave way to excitement. Ted, as always, was up for the challenge, any challenge to prove himself. Obviously the boss had confidence in him. Besides, he was right, why let NBC have all the fun. He, too, had issues with Alyesworth and NBC. Flat out rejecting his demands for a raise in salary two years earlier remainedfresh in his mind.

Ted shook Paley's hand and returned to his office bold and invigorated. There was much to do, researching horses and jockeys at the top of the list. Paley immediately called the press, fueling the PR machine. A *New York Herald Tribune* half page profile on Ted and his picture plastered in the Radio Section of the Sunday *Times* reminded listeners that NBC would not have the only microphone at Churchill Downs.[178] Three days later, in the dark of night, Ted's train departed Pennsylvania Station for Kentucky. He left his wife behind.

The broadcaster packed light, sharing his berth with a young engineer who would assist with setup of microphones and technical troubleshooting, among other duties. Two would have to do for the Columbia network. NBC had other ideas. They brought an armed force, fifteen in total, arriving in Lexington on Thursday morning: engineers, staff, and, of course, announcers, intent on one thing, crushing the competition. Leading the charge would be the man, Graham McNamee, host, master of ceremonies, and unknowing nemesis to Ted Husing. Popular, famous, and easily the most recognized voice on radio in the spring of 1929. He embodied all the things that Ted longed to be but was not. Who was Ted Husing compared to Graham McNamee? "The other broadcaster," an enigma of a man. A simple example to that fact, most newspapers merely referred to him as *Edward B. Husing* in their daily radio program listings. The moniker of "Ted" still not recognizable enough, not strong. Radio insiders widely expected a better show from NBC, more networks, more experience, more history, more resources, more everything.

Calling the race for NBC was 46-year-old, Rochester, New York–native Clem McCarthy. McCarthy might have been new to the network, but he was an old hack at horse racing. His father auctioned off thoroughbreds for a living, barking out sales at stables from Maryland to Santa Anita. By the age of ten, Clem had witnessed his first Kentucky Derby. Pale Irish skin, with ears pealed forward and a round derby upon his head, he resembled an oversized leprechaun. As a beat writer and professional handicapper, his syndicated stories appeared in papers such as the *Daily Racing Forum* and *Morning Telegraph*. Then, as the first announcer to call a horse race over a public address system, his unique staccato and infectious rolling Rs became legendary. "R-r-r-r-racing fans, this is Cl-l-l-lem McCarthy!" his signature call before every race. One contemporary said McCarthy's voice "sounded as though he were grinding rocks together at the same time he was talking."[179] Ted himself called McCarthy "the best racing man on the air."[180]

McCarthy's best skill was the uncanny ability to communicate with the thoroughbreds, mimicking a horse whisperer eager to get inside the animal's mind. He often spoke to the horses on the air during a race. Some found his method bizarre, others entertaining. Everyone, without exception, loved it. "Get your head straight or you'll be caught napping boy," he once told a mount at the starting gate. Another tearing down the first turn, "Easy there, Nellie."[181] Remarks he made to himself or to colleagues during a thousand horse races long before they put a microphone in front of his mouth. The life-long passion for the ponies stirred his soul on or off the air. Said racing veteran and friend Chick Lang, "Clem's big thing with me was his enthusiasm. He loved what he was doing. It wasn't just a job."[182]

Also joining the NBC crew was local media celebrity Credo Fitch Harris. He did it all, newspaperman, book author, radio announcer, and managing director of Louisville station WHAS, by then an NBC affiliate. Harris tirelessly advocated for the commercial development of radio, traveling to Washington D.C., sitting in on Department of Commerce meetings, pulling at the sleeve of then department head and future President of the United States, Herbert Hoover. Harris spoke the first words ever heard over the public airwaves of Kentucky, July 18, 1922 saying, "This is WHAS, the radio-telephone broadcast station of the *Courier-Journal* and *Louisville Times* in Louisville, Kentucky."[183] If that wasn't enough, he also helped design the modern state Kentucky flag that today flies over the capitol dome in Frankfurt.

Setting up the day's pageantry and describing the field from the judge's platform was McNamee. Play-by-play was never Mac's forte. He earned his reputation at ad-libs, freeform. Few could talk longer or stronger, with the lone exception of Ted. Calling the race was McCarthy, naturally, but with a new twist. As the field entered the stretch McCarthy was to gamely throw the mike to Harris at the rail for the finish. On paper, the strategy made perfect sense, a fair trade and large thank you to Harris for coordinating the broadcast details. Then again, horses didn't run on paper. Dirt was their surface and sometimes dirt becomes mud.

The networks were not alone in their coverage. Powerhouse Chicago station WGN pulled into Lexington to air the race again with a train full of staff and announcers, five in all, led by Midwest's version of "Mr. Everything" Quin Ryan. Rounding out the WGN team was betting expert Al Sabath, veteran track reporter French Lane, and Harvey T. Woodruff, plus *Racing Forum* writer and Clem McCarthy friend John "Jack" Dempsey.

Ted immersed himself in the environment the minute his train pulled into Lexington. Quickly, the smell of hay and horse manure gave way to picking the brains of trainers, jockeys, groomers, and the most important people at the track, handicappers. They were racetrack lifers, observant of oddities like bottoms of shoes, a horse's smile, the amount of giddy-up at the morning workout, a mount's bowel movement . . . any tangible sign as to how an animal might perform when it really mattered. In the end, Ted was not a fortuneteller or in the game of predicting winners. The key was not to watch the horses, but watch the jockeys. Each stable designed distinctive shirts, better known as "silks," worn by their jockeys on race day. No two were the same, color patterns and logos unique to owners and trainers. But, as Saturday approached, Ted knew that it would take more than a few-days crash course to pick a winner. Calling the first thoroughbred across the line was not the most important thing. It was the only thing. No handicapper or Clem McCarthy or Credo Harris could help in this regard.

The night before the Derby, there was plenty of action along the streets of Louisville. Ted could have done any number of things, crash a plantation party, flirt with girls, find a speakeasy, shoot some pool, or watch a boxing match. He decided on the latter. A short-lived, pre-Derby tradition was watching defenders and contenders slug it out at the Jefferson Country Armory. If a title fight wasn't enough, the Run for the Roses could stir the blood in less than 24 hours. Three ten-round fights were on the card. No memorable punches thrown. No names placed into immortality. But it was enough to give him a buzz, keep his edge for what lay ahead.

By the time Ted returned to his hotel, clocks pushed close to 2 AM. Ears rang with ghosts of cheering fans and prizefight pandemonium. Who won? Who lost? He did not remember. For a moment, Ted missed his wife, longed to kiss his daughter goodnight. A minute ticked by or maybe thirty. His head fell easily on the pillow, a long, full day past equaled exhaustion. A well-earned slumber fell upon him. However, Ted would not sleep long. A new day, a new event to broadcast only a few hours away.

The morning of May 18th broke with drizzle. A low mist lay over Lexington. Streaks of white headlights bounced off the wet pavement from cars stuck in traffic on their way to the track. It would be a record crowd at Churchill Downs, 75,000 strong.[184] One writer described the onslaught as "a veritable army of voracious human locust which quickly gobbled up most of the food in sight and left empty larders for the late risers."[185] Gray clouds and low visibility added more worry for the young announcer. The headlines of the morning paper caught Ted's eye. "Al Capone Sentenced to Jail in Philadelphia." The acid in his empty stomach burned. He knew if he didn't call the winning colors, every radio critic, not to mention his boss William Paley, might throw him into the clink. Gangsters were nothing compared to failure.

Conditions improved throughout the day. By afternoon, nothing but sunshine and breezy temperatures coated the oval track. Outside of the occasional mud splat, most jockeys who mounted for earlier post times crossed the finish line surprisingly clean. However, these early heats were mere warm-ups for the featured race. As the clock struck four, a gentle moisture fell from the clouds.

Ted and the lone engineer set up shop in one of the towers protruding above the grandstand, One hundred and sixty pounds of electronics, a telegraph machine, and two wooden stools stood between them and the bulging crowd below. Ted came on the air at 4:30 pm EST, a full hour before McNamee said hello to the NBC audience. If listeners heard Ted at all, it was a miracle. Better than a dozen airplanes buzzed endlessly above, showing off, priming for the crowd. He rambled steadily about the track conditions—wet, the horses expected to run for the roses, 21 in all; celebrities in attendance, including ex-presidential hopeful Al Smith and publishing magnate Nelson Doubleday among the more noted; and, of course, weather conditions: cloudy and light rain.

One hour passed. Ted was in his element, talking, seeing, looking, describing, his voice without a hint of uncertainty. From the paddock door stood a man dressed in red, black leather riding boots around his feet, and holding a long brass trumpet. Placing the horn to his lips, out blasted *The Call to the Post*. The door opened and out trotted the contenders for the 55th running of the Kentucky Derby.

One by one they came: Bay Beauty, Ben Machree, Blue Larkspur, Calf Roper, Chicatie, Chip, Clyde Van Dusen, Essare, Folking, Karl Eitel, Lord Breedalbone, Minotaur, Naishapur, Panchie, Paraphrase, Paul Bunyan, Prince Pat, The Nut, Veltear, Windy City, and Upset Lady.[186]Then a marching band rose from the multitude, horns, flutes, clarinets, and cymbals began to play the newly adopted state song *My Old Kentucky Home*.[187] Ted knew of the song, but unaware of its impact. Thousands of spectators began to sing.

> *Weep no more my lady,*
> *Oh, weep no more today!*
> *We will sing one song for the old Kentucky home,*
> *For the old Kentucky home far away.*[188]

The song pulled at the crowd's heartstrings, how an infant's smile brings the most calloused father to a pool of blubbering tears. Originally composed in 1853, Stephen C. Foster wrote it as an emotional homage to plantation slaves. Done just right, the tune drips with melancholy, a lamenting call for freedom, a longing for home, and over time became the ultimate ballad of the Old South. Said jockey Jacinto Vasquez, winner of the Derby aboard Foolish Pleasure in 1975 and the filly Genuine Risk in '80, "When they play that song, your heart feels though it will beat right through your chest." Jim McKay, who anchored ABC's Derby telecasts for nearly three decades believed the song "rises like a hymn in the springtime air."[189] The year 1929 was no exception.

Husing's tone dropped, his voice almost at a whisper. Microphones picked up the music and echoing lyrics across the grandstand. An unassuming listener spinning the dial might think a state funeral was in session. The musicians played the final sad notes. Men and women cried, then, silence. Ted described it all beautifully. He never saw anything like it. He would not soon forget. . . . Almost on cue, a lusty roar went up through the crowd. In a few short minutes, the fifth race of the afternoon—The Kentucky Derby. Listening intently to the broadcast back in New York was Paley. Among illegal beer and sandwiches for a few close friends, two radios blasted the action in stereo. One tuned to Ted on CBS, another to the NBC crew. "He's never seen a race before in his life," Paley reminded his guests. "He's up against an army of experts. I'll bet two to one our broadcast is as good as theirs, if not better."[190] Laughter rumbled around the room and outside through an open window. Doubt crept in, gnawing at his guilty conscience. "What have I done?" Soon, they would all know for sure.

As post time neared, the weather changed. The drizzle and hovering mist of morning could not equal the darkness that swept over Churchill Downs. The skies opened and poured raindrops the size of golf balls. The huge crowd scurried for cover. But, it was too late. The horses neared the starting gates itching to run. Most of the money was placed on the favorite Blue Larkspur. The Kentucky-bred horse might have been favored, but lucky he was not drawing the last post position on the far outside. Few liked Clyde Van Dusen. Clearly, he did not inherit the physique of his famous father Man o' War. But, what he lacked in size he made up in fun. A soggy track for this 3-year-old meant play time, the wetter the better. Namesake and trainer Clyde Van Dusen felt so uninspired about the horse that he waited until entering the paddock to introduce horse and rider. Linus "Pony" McAtee confessed later, "In spite of being forewarned, when I saw the horse, my heart sank."[191] McAtee jumped aboard adjusting to the saddle. The reluctant trainer offered a last minute ray of hope, "But don't be discouraged," Van Dusen suggested. "He can run and he can really run in this slop."[192] The jockey smiled as umbrellas popped open across the grandstand.

Ted looked out over the crowded field of twenty-one thoroughbreds. Rain pelted at his back. His concentration rivaled that of a heart surgeon. The last door on the starting gate shut. More drama beckoned. For ten minutes, the field stood trapped, chomping at the bits. Waiting, then waiting some more. Jockeys gripped the reigns of their ride, anxious but cautious, water ran wildly down their already drenched silks and fogging goggles. The only thing left for Ted was talk. Words still came, a cavalcade of description. "A kaleidoscope of colors among the jockeys here this afternoon, ladies and gentlemen. . . . Raining harder now. These unfortunate riders, though brave they are, in for a mud bath today, I'm afraid." Ted listened intently for the starting bell among his own discourse and the pounding rain. "No movement yet, ladies and gentlemen." Finally, a loud ring! BZINGGGGGGGGGGGGG! Ted shouted, "THEY'RE OFF!"

Eighty-four hooves tore into the ground, smashing, splashing! Naishapur dashed first and took the early lead. Within seconds every ride wore the same brown color, caked in ugly clods of sludge. Binocular glasses in one hand and microphone in the other, Ted kept up with the field. Suddenly, BOOM! Then a flash lit up the sky. His eyes darted upward to see what it was. Thunder clapped and lightning ripped the sky in half. The crowd screamed, a sickening combination of fear and delight. Ted's eyes returned to the duty at hand. If the horses were spooked, no one noticed. Ride and rider had enough anxiety going. The mighty animals bunched, moving in unison. A new face took the lead around the first turn. From the 20th post position came little Clyde Van Dusen. The favorite horse Blue Larkspur lagged behind somewhere in the middle. Down the back stretch Clyde Van Dusen remained first. Under a heavy whip and flying chunks of slush was Garner, breathing heavy, a close second. A virtual moat of water six inches deep filled along the rail.

Finally, life from Blue Larkspur as they passed the three-quarter poll. He pushed away from the pack toward the leaders, smoking for home. The crowd rose with anticipation. Would he have enough? Around the clubhouse turn more movement from Panchie and early leader Naishapur. More rain. More mud. All but zero visibility for the broadcasters.

Ted screamed into the microphone, " . . . They're rounding

into the stretch now. Larkspur seems to be tiring. They're bunched up . . . and a big horse is coming up the outside. Still in a bunch—too far to see . . ."[193] Two hundred and fifty yards from the end, clarity defied the broadcaster. " . . . thundering down at us through the mud. What a finish. Van Husen is out ahead now half a length . . . one length as they pass here . . . Larkspur dropping back . . . it looks sure for Van Dusen . . . they're over and! . . .

Ted, crunched into the dangerous spire and 150 yards off the finish line called Clyde Van Dusen "the winner by three lengths!" The conditions were tough, but he was sure he saw it right. He repeated it to the listening audience with even more passion in his voice. "Yes, Clyde Van Dusen, ladies and gentlemen, wins the Kentucky Derby!" Then again, not everyone was convinced. Down at the judge's stand directly across the finish line, Credo Harris of NBC declared Blue Larkspur the certain winner. Who was right? The benefit of the doubt went with familiarity—NBC. Inside a dry New York office, Paley laughed hearty, hiding his disappointment. "Damn! Kid Husing got it wrong." Again, his guests razzed him, reminding of his bold prediction. "The ribbing was good-natured, but you're wrong if you think it didn't hurt," Paley told a writer years after. "I knew how stubborn Ted could get, and I think what hurt most was that he never corrected himself."[194] Trying to save face, Paley immediately wired Ted at Churchill Downs, a humorous note of condolence. SORRY ABOUT THE FINISH. STOP. YOU DID A SWELL JOB KID UP TO THAT POINT. STOP.

Ted read the cable and crumbled it slowly inside his angry fist. Could his eyes have deceived him? The Lexington heavy rains gradually slowed to a steady drizzle. Ted, his joints stiff, clothes soaked, and ego bruised, hustled down to the winner's circle, microphone in hand, steadfast in his initial call. There before him stood Clyde Van Dusen, the traditional wreath of red roses, presented to the winner, glistening off his large neck. Perched on his back, wearing an ear to ear grind, was his jockey Linus McAtee, who patted the horse lovingly on the face as if to say, "That a boy. That a boy!" Larkspur was nowhere near the winner's circle. His strong finish still left him out of the money, a distant and disappointing fourth place. McAtee bragged openly to reporters about his prized horse after the race. "Why he's nothing but a pony. He's nothing but a mud-running fool."[195] Yes, in more ways than one, an underdog proved victorious. David had defeated Goliath. That day, talent and a little good luck turned out better than experience.

Ted held his ground. He had no choice. Buried in live wires and doused with a driving rain, it was a miracle he didn't die by electrocution. Ted was spared. Credo Harris, however, was not so fortunate. The press scorched him for his on-air blunder. The *New York Sun* wrote, "Radio personages are still trying to figure how Mr. Harris, born and bred one might say on the Derby, is explaining his unfortunate mistake . . ."[196] Congratulations for Husing was unanimous. "Around CBS headquarters, there is justified gloating for Ted Husing, it's lone representative. . . . And Ted did a good job of it, too."[197]

Back in New York, Paley and company laughed again, this time sinister, proud, and relieved.[198] NBC learned their lesson. The next year, the man who knew horses, Clem McCarthy, was at the microphone calling the Kentucky Derby from starting gate to finish line. William Paley learned a more tangible lesson—never doubt Husing.

Congratulations would be short lived. Within a few days, Ted was off again on the next uncharted assignment. Waiting on his desk, tickets for a party train packed with jazz musicians due for California. On the agenda, selling cigarettes, making movies, and meeting new friends. But, as Ted soon learned, the biggest task among 6,000 miles of railroad track—finding a replacement for himself.

CHAPTER THIRTEEN

OLD GOLD, NEW PALS

No motives. No jive, just straight talk. Few in radio demon-strated pure honesty like Ted Husing. He could never be charged with phoniness, compelled to tell the truth, on and off the air. That included whom he called a friend. But, there was guilt by association. Hanging out with the right crowd helped the all-important public image—anything to get his name out among consumers. Then there was fame. No one walked the streets of the 1920s in America more famous than Paul Whiteman. If McNamee set the bar for radio announcers, Whiteman stood tall and wide, in a league by himself.

Raised among the mountains of Colorado, Whiteman was always more showman than musician. Marrying four times and weighing nearly 300 pounds, he was a man of excess. His animated features, round and jolly, three patches of thinning black hair about his head, double chin, and a pencil-thin moustache under a wide nose helped draw an odd stare if nothing else. But, the Whiteman talent did not lay in obesity. A violinist, trained in the classics, White-man heard his love of music as entertainment, not eccentric artistry. Short stints in the Denver and San Francisco Symphonies left him unsatisfied. Passion and excitement came from rhythms he heard along the Bay Area's roughneck Barbary Coast bar scene. Jazz, jazz, and more jazz.[199]

Before Whiteman came along, jazz was still dangerous, untamed, unsophisticated, and perhaps too black for most of America. Progressive thought needed a human bridge to enlightenment. By infusing a structure and discipline into the music's improvisational roots, Whiteman unknowingly gave jazz the legitimacy it so desperately craved.[200]

The bandleader scoured the country in search of the best and brightest. Bix Beiderbecke, Tommy Dorsey, Red Nichols, and Eddie Lang, some of the most respected and revered names in jazz history and who at one time or another played under the stick of Paul Whiteman. Adding a personal, attention-grabbing twist, Whiteman conducted with an irreverent sense of humor. "Looking like a Dutch miller, he flicked a small baton, twitched an elbow, or crooked an eyebrow. Virtually his only consistent movement was to wag his head to the band's rhythms."[201]

By the early '20s they were in high demand, earning up to four digits a night. Still, upper-crust socialites by and large dismissed musicians with pitiful contempt. Whiteman and his pearly standards changed all that with one defiant act. Hired by millionaire Caroline Schermerhorn Astor to entertain at her 5th Avenue mansion, Paul and his players showed up at the front door. Astor's butler tried to gently swish them around to more appropriate doors, the servant's entrance. Whiteman refused to budge. High society gasped. "Either we go through the front door or we don't go in at all,"[202] he insisted. The orchestra played into the early morning hours, happy and significantly richer. "Without realizing it, Whiteman had demolished another barrier of society," said radio critic Ben Gross. "Thereafter the kings of jazz could consort as equals with the kings of automobiles, steel, or smoked hams."[203]

Paul Whiteman and his orchestra epitomized the youthful glitz of the roaring '20s. Coonskin coats, highwire acts, nylon stockings, and the hip flask were underscored by hits like *Whispering, Japanese Sandman, Mississippi Mud, Felix the Cat, Ramona, Three o'clock in the Morning* and the ageless classic written by George Gershwin *Rhapsody in Blue.* He billed himself "The King of Jazz." Extensive travel filled concert halls around the world. Recording contracts with (RCA) Victor Talking Machine Company sold untold stacks of vinyl.

Every man, woman, and pageboy in network radio tried lassoing Whiteman down to a weekly show commitment. William Paley's pitch was certainly not the first. Whiteman heard it all before from countless execs and advertising agents. Fearing over-exposure, he kept his appearances to the medium few and far between. By early 1929, endless touring and burnout put Whiteman in a more receptive mood. Paley tracked him down during an engagement at the Drake Hotel in Chicago. "How I persuaded him I no longer remember," wrote Paley years later. "It was late that night or near dawn of the next day when he said, 'By God, you've sold me. I'll try it.'"[204] Then again, Paley's stamina and charm meant nothing without the promise of money, and lots of it.

Before chasing Whiteman, New York advertising agency Lennon & Mitchell promised Paley to back their formidable trucks of cash to the bandleader's name, but only if he made the deal first.[205] L & M had many clients, none more recognized than cigarette giant Old Gold. Their campaign slogan splashed across billboards and newspaper ads, countless smokers traveling America packed into cars and crowded trains, spoke to healthier benefits of inhaling tar and nicotine—"Not a Cough in a Carload."[206] The company jumped at the chance to sponsor the show, agreeing to pay Whiteman a weekly salary of $5,000.[207]

One additional thing that may have swayed Paul Whiteman to radio—the presence of the show's announcer. For sixty minutes, each Tuesday evening, the band was encouraged to play as many tunes as possible. A familiar voice, in between numbers, cracked jokes with Whiteman and read commercial spots at breakneck speed.

The voice belonged to Ted Husing. The two had met before, hanging in the same social circles and drinking at the same speakeasies like Billy La Hiffs. A sports enthusiast himself, Whiteman had become familiar with Ted's work behind the mike calling football, regattas, and other athletic events. Ted was gaining a reputation as the magician in front of a microphone.

Smooth, elegant, commanding, he already won plenty of experience guiding musicians during a live broadcast. The famous bandleader was also well aware of what Ted had done to boost the career of Duke Ellington. Ted's broadcasts from the Cotton Club in 1928 put Ellington and his music in homes across America, not to mention more money in his pocket and pretty women rapping on his door. Whiteman, like the Duke, enjoyed the pleasures of stardom. So did Ted Husing. Calling Paul Whiteman a friend was something people of the press took notice of.

The Old Gold Hour debuted on February 5 over the entire CBS chain of stations. The show became an instant hit, adding to the Whiteman phenomenon. More records were sold. More club dates were booked. The first few broadcasts, the orchestra played "Nola," by then a Whiteman standard. Ted loved the song for obvious reasons. He thought of Helen, wondering if she was listening to the radio and sharing the same notion.

Ted saw a new burst of energy join Whiteman's radio show in mid-March. Rejoined was more the case. Harry Barris, Al Rinker, and a wild man from Tacoma, Washington, named Bing Crosby trained into New York fresh off a six-month Vaudeville tour. They were known as The Rhythm Boys. The Party Boys might have fit better. On stage, they sang, danced, and mugged. Off stage, they drank, played golf, and fraternized with the opposite sex, all to excess. Gifted performers, indeed, Whiteman felt The Boys were getting lazy and exiled them in August of 1928 to get their groove back.[208]

Husing and Crosby hit it off immediately, a new drinking buddy and nightclub chaperon. Two years older than Bing, Ted took on the role of big brother. Ted recognized the unique singing talent in Crosby instantly. During smoke breaks, down hallway stretches, Ted talked up his new friend, planting the seeds in the ear of Whiteman to expand the kid's horizons. "Bing's got a great set of pipes," Ted assured. "Let him solo this week, Paul. The audience'll love it, especially the flappers itching to buy a few more records. . . . Come on!" Whiteman finally agreed after weeks of badgering. Old Gold, however, nixed the grand idea, reminding the bandleader that they had a signed agreement with Johnny Fulton, another Whiteman vocalist. Whiteman never forgot why he liked Husing so much. "I think what first attracted me to Ted in those early days was that habit he never lost of going to bat for his friends."[209]

Crosby would have to wait for solos. The Rhythm Boys, in the meantime, were becoming a force in their own right. The trio's popular song "Mississippi Mud" often made the Old Gold play list on Tuesday nights. Bing's tomfoolery and distinctive baritone prominently showcased. "Mud's" derisive lyrics changed over time, but in 1929, they were simply heard as a catchy little ditty.

When the sun goes down and the tide goes out,
The Darkies gather 'round and they all begin to shout!
Hey, hey Uncle Dud,
It's a treat to beat your feet on the Mississippi mud![210]

As the Rhythm Boys sang, Paul Whiteman and company played on. Off to the side, hands behind his back and beaming with fatherly pride stood Husing. Greenbacks and notoriety flourishing, "The Old Gold Hour" helped put a permanent grin on everyone's face. "Those were great days," Whiteman said years later. "Ted helped make them great."[211]

By late spring, stock in the Whiteman experience grew even more lucrative. Universal Studios wanted to shoot Paul and the boys in a musical film fittingly titled "The King of Jazz" using the medium's latest know-how—technicolor. Whiteman negotiated a bonanza, $50,000 up front, $8,000 a week plus $4,500 to cover the band, use of bungalows, swimming pools, the works. Together, Universal and Old Gold owners P. Lorillard Tobacco Company decided to milk the band for every roll of processed tobacco they could.[212] America loved to smoke and America loved Paul Whiteman. A private ten-car revelry train was commissioned to carry "The King" and his entourage through the heartland en route to California. The PR machine called it—The Old Gold Special.

Before reaching the West Coast, seventeen stops were scheduled to play concerts and live radio remotes. Every Tuesday at 9 PM, the show would continue as scheduled from a CBS affiliate station along the way. Whiteman had not forgotten Ted's stellar work and efforts to promote the band. The producers offered Ted a sparkling role in the picture—announcer. Ted didn't care about typecasting. Prancing like a peacock, Ted felt a charmed life, a budding radio broadcaster one day, movie star the next. The President of the United States himself didn't get the same hype. The Old Gold Special triumphantly pushed off Pennsylvania Station on May 24, 1929. First stop—Philadelphia.

Chugging across Pennsylvania, they next visited Pittsburgh, zigzagging over to Cleveland, up through Detroit, down to Ft. Wayne, then onto Illinois. Seven cities in five days. On Memorial Day, Whiteman's crew backtracked to play a special concert for 40,000 fans at the Indianapolis 500 Motor Speedway. Summer arrived in Indiana early, as it usually did on race day. The mercury burned into the upper 90s. The Old Gold Special arrived late, fighting to get through the massive crowds. Hustled to the spacious infield, Ted introduced the band for their first set. Gazing up toward the press box, Ted noticed something that made him think he had suffered heat stroke. Dangling over the railing flapped a banner with the letters NBC stenciled on it. From a wooden booth sat none other than Graham McNamee and broadcast partner William Lynch calling the race.[213]

"Son of a bitch!" Ted said loudly. No one heard him. The band drowned out the agitated announcer's vulgar reaction. What did McNamee have on him now? He, not Mac, was Hollywood-bound to co-star in a motion picture. While McNamee sat in a boiling broadcast booth trying to make sense of screeching engines and dust-filled tires, Husing, week after week, shared a stage with America's favorite music maker. Still, before leaving Indianapolis the next morning, Ted made a mental note to put the 500 on his May schedule for next season.

The Special moved beyond Mississippi during the first week of June. Stops, concerts, and radio shows in St. Louis, Kansas City, Denver, and Salt Lake City along the way. On Thursday, June 6, 1929, Whiteman, Ted, and the boys pulled into Santa Fe Railway Station. Los Angeles, finally! Soon, musicians, bandleaders, singers, and radio announcers would become actors. But, as they were to find out, not every Hollywood movie glitters with gold. From the beginning, troubles cursed the picture. No one could write an appropriate screenplay. Whiteman was given creative control, turning down several scripts, unhappy with the way he and the band were portrayed.[214] Studio head Carl Laemmle, Jr., ordered his team back to work. Until then, there was nothing to do but wait. Universal held Whiteman and the boys hostage, with pay of course. Their only commitment: the "Old Gold Hour." The boys hit the golf course and California highways in brand-new automobiles fronted by Whiteman.[215]

As much as Ted enjoyed swinging five irons and shifting gears, he preferred to stay busy. Boredom was not the only reason Ted battled uneasy feelings. Director Paul Fejos had promised the role of the announcer to John Boles, Broadway leading man and rising silent film star. When Ted found out about the change, his mood soured. The studio offered another role, something less significant. Ted balked, still miffed. "If they want to hire some other slug it's fine with me. I came out here to blow some dough and make a picture," he reminded Whiteman. "But, if it's all the same to you, I'd rather get my ass back to New York where I'm wanted."

"Look Paul, I appreciate the ride out here," he said to Whiteman. "I'll find you somebody to fill in for the duration. A real pro, don't you worry about a fucking thing." But remember," he said with a resentful tone, "whomever I find, no matter how ABLE or DEFT he might be, he won't be Ted Husing!"

Husing and Whiteman worked the phones, hot to find a replacement. Columbia affiliates on the coast, Variety ads, even word around the lots helped fill the roster of possible candidates. More than 200 auditioned. Early in the process, Ted liked a round-bodied, slick-haired man named Harry von Zell. Originally from Indianapolis, von Zell migrated out to Los Angeles in search of work as a singer and silent film actor. But, he quickly learned that talking was where the money got made. Local radio station KYW kept him busy with a variety of announcing assignments.

When word leaked that Ted was leaving the "Old Gold Hour," he decided to take a stab at the network. Von Zell found himself waiting patiently in line as a 23-year-old unknown hoping to replace one of the biggest voices in radio on one of the hottest network shows. There was an energy about the young man that Ted liked right away. "The eleventh inexperienced kid I tried out had what it took," remembered Ted. "His name was Harry von Zell."[216] Ted was still angry about getting the shaft from Hollywood and was anxious to get away but, von Zell remembered, "I've never forgotten this—despite his hurry to leave for New York, he stayed over long enough to coach me on how to work with Paul Whiteman, how to keep the people from the advertising agency happy, and a hundred other little tips he didn't have to bother giving a rookie. He was really a prince."[217] Von Zell's virgin broadcast aired without a hitch on June 25, the first "Old Gold Hour" without its original announcer.

Ted already felt like a forgotten man, yet he knew his destiny lay not from hanging around sound stages or introducing musical numbers. It would be calling the brutality of sports. His plans were to be back in New York by late June for the annual Poughkeepsie Regatta race and U.S. Open golf tournament at Long Island's Winged Foot course. Besides, it would be tough to kick the radioman around in his own element, on his own turf. "I'd like to hear John Boles call a football game," he said before leaving California. "Goodbye Hollywood. Give my regards to Broadway."

CHAPTER FOURTEEN

HAPPY FEET, STEELY EYES

No one doubted any longer. Skeptics, the non-believers were wrong. For better or for worse radio was here to stay. Clearly, William Paley was convinced. In the spring of 1929 he moved CBS to new headquarters. Sizeable rectangular windows dotted the intricate twenty-two-story beige structure at 485 Madison Avenue. Nothing particular distinguished the building until one looked skyward from the outside. Above the fourteenth floor, the floors cut away taking the look of steps climbing to the heavens. For CBS, the only place to go was up.

The stars of early radio were everyday ordinary people. No rhyme, no reason. A strange voice in the dark talking and singing about almost anything became an extended member of the family. However, radio had entered its Golden Age. The industry was maturing. The public begged to hear more than just "Good evening, ladies and gentlemen." Content and substance, polish and sophistication was what the people wanted. There, like Moses in a lavender suit with slick back hair through a haze of announcers, walked the man from CBS, offering the new and daring. "He gave an added dimension to a brand new business that had no dimension at all," said Gary Stevens. "All of a sudden there was this beacon and it was Ted

Husing." Though he had proven a jack of all trades, clearly sports broadcasts demonstrated his best gems. Preparation took on a new urgency, writing his own copy and lead-ins to open a game, usually the night before.

He began to study dictionaries and thesauruses, heightening his senses, expanding his vocabulary. Ted studied as if cramming for a midterm final. Once he found a word, Ted worked it around his mouth a few times, writing it out, counting syllables, perfecting accents and pronunciation. The final test was using the word in three different sentences. Once all these tedious steps were mastered, could the new word be used on a broadcast? He practiced first with Helen, then anybody who would play the odd game.

Enter any sports broadcast booth, and the first thing one wants to do is call the maid. Littered about are paper cups, score sheets, press guides, notepads, and reams of useless statistics. Among the mess sit nervous announcers, wiry microphones, and an engineer who juices the show with electrical power. It is a pile of necessary evils, each element having a special role to play. Yet, by far the most important tools in any football broadcasting booth are spotting boards and the spotters who operate them. Spotting boards come in a variety of shapes, sizes, and colors; they're filled with names, numbers, positions, even stats and biographical information. They are designed on personal taste and distinctive style. No two are alike. But, there is one thing they all share in common. An announcer is lost without them.

The real unsung hero in the booth is the spotter. He is the eyes of the play-by-play man in a literal sense. The sole job description: make the announcer look good. Following the movements of twenty-two flying bodies around the grid is tough work. See the action, identify the player or players, and point to them on the chart for the broadcaster—the quicker the better. Getting it right is everything. The job is undistinguished and thankless.

Ted was not the first football announcer to use a spotting

board and spotters. He was the first to use them as a cohesive unit. Ted early on recognized their depth and influence. "The system is everything in doing the game," shared Chris Schenkel. "At least that's what we thought and he did, too. The shortest cut to getting a name to come out is the best system." The evolution of the spotting board goes back to the very first broadcasts. A simple game program or scribbled notes were early versions. Ted later created a large frame made of apartment-house doorbell panels with slots for players' names. Bulky charts of pasted names and positions was another Husing invention. When spotting in 1925–26, Ted admitted that these methods were unsuccessful. "I had tried to help Major White by writing out information on paper or by pointing with my pencil to names on a program. Either way was bad, for the paper came between the broadcaster's eyes and the playing field."[218] Technology of the day restricted movement by a broadcaster. Guess work was the norm and gaffes aplenty. The listeners hardly knew the difference in those early days. Graham McNamee never let his lack of comprehensive sports knowledge take away from his exciting play-by-play.

Mac created his own art form, hell bent on bringing the listener everything from the battle on the field to a fight in the stands. Nothing was ignored. He worked himself up so much that describing a sports event was often a dizzying experience. "Being enthusiastic has one drawback, however, it's physically exhausting," joked McNamee later in his career. "After every big broadcast, I feel as though I were the one who had taken the beating."[219] Many were initially struck by the announcer's obvious anxiety. "My first impression of Graham was that he was of a high nervous temperament," said a friend, "which didn't surprise me after listening to his hysterical, high-speed manner of broadcasting track meets and football games."[220]

He was known to sip the bottle for calming effects before a broadcast. Buoyancy was needed and alcohol seemed to give the NBC man an extra lift. Stage fright, nervous energy, deer caught in the headlights—actors to singers to radiomen called the fear of performing many things. McNamee was not the first radio presenter to use the drug as a crutch. Nor would he be the last. As big a name in broadcasting, the stories of his brittle nerves and manic pacing before going live were just as large.[221]

Ted's entire approach was clearly different. He wanted to concentrate on the game. He wanted to give the listener more than just color and pageantry. He wanted to present fact, not fiction. Privately, the radioman had other motivations for change. Ted should have been the last person ever used as a spotter. He was nearsighted. Without glasses, far away objects were blurred. He knew that once he started broadcasting on his own, things would have to be different. Ted began tinkering with a box of flashing red lights to identify players, four on each side of the ball. Names and positions were posted below. His assistant would identify the player and push the button for that name and position. The box sat perched just below his eyes. A quick glance down told him everything he needed to know. Who made the tackle. What receiver caught the ball. Ted called it the "Annunciator." Nothing like it had ever been seen before or since. Most football people were amazed how it worked. "Knute Rockne was a great admirer of the machine," bragged Husing later.

In the past, Ted used a variety of spotters and assistants. No doubt his demanding traits and acerbic attitude turned a few away from future assignments. Beginning with the 1929 football season, Ted began working with the perfect partner, one who loved the gizmo with equal abandon. His name was Les Quailey. After joining team Husing that summer, Quailey got busy perfecting the unique spotting board. An engineer at CBS named Jack Norton was brought in to add technical advice. The Annunciator was expanded to twenty-two bulbs with glass-enclosed slots, eleven for offense, eleven for defense. A separate keyboard was designed to control the lights. Special carrying cases were made for the batteries and for the box itself. Les had a pair of wide-lens Zeiss binoculars custom made in Germany to expand his field vision. They were attached to a stationary mount with swivel pole in case he had to look away. "I talk straight ahead, relying entirely on the box for the players involved," stated Ted. "In advance, I have fixed the names of all players in my mind, identifying them with their light positions. If a substitution is made, it only takes my memory an instant to make the adjustment."[222]

Raymond Lester Quailey was a tough man of Irish decent, a native Brooklynite, firm and direct with his comments. Quailey was everything Husing, minus the ego. He lacked something else distinctly Husing, a commanding voice. What he lacked in voice quality he more than made up in administrative skills and sports knowledge, especially football. The two first met as schoolmates at Commerce High School. Following graduation, Quailey traveled upstate to continue playing at tiny Alfred University. He was the team's starting quarterback. Earning a Bachelor of Science degree in the spring of 1923, Quailey was offered a chance to coach high school kids in nearby Buffalo. He chose instead to return to New York, his playing days not over yet. Quailey dashed about Central Park, throwing passes for the same semi-pro football team Ted played on, the Prescotts.

In Quailey, Ted met the perfect partner. He shared the knowledge, passion, and nuances of the game. More importantly, he shared Ted's unquenching desire to do things right. They both hated the shoddy, undisciplined airing of football. Ted was the eyes. Les was the brains. Chris Schenkel remembered Quailey as a combination of divine knowledge and devilish insight. "He was this little tiny guy with eagle-like piercing eyes, blue as can be. He didn't miss anything. Whatever it was, if you needed your cigarette lit, he was at it before you could make a draw on the matches." The partnership freed up Ted to concentrate on the play-by-play, go out on a limb, jump out where no broadcaster had dared go before. And if he fell, if he strayed out beyond parameters, Quailey would provide the safety net. Among all the pressures, a broadcast location was always on the verge of combustion. With Quailey, Saturday afternoon became controlled chaos, the way a hot restaurant kitchen sweats on a busy Saturday night.

The system worked like a charm. Mistakes were diminished, guesswork eliminated. More importantly, Ted's new assistant deciphered the action faster than an outlaw to his six-shooter. If Ted hesitated on the air, it was his own fault. A bonding trust grew between the broadcaster and his spotter. Ted understood that with Quailey by his side, no one could be better. "Most announcers broadcast from sight. We broadcast from knowledge."[223] Flubs did happen, as rare as they were. The affects were not pretty. Ted lashed out, scolding Quailey or whatever innocent bystanders happened to be in earshot. He internalized imperfection as failure, sometimes losing his appetite, sulking for hours until sufficiently punished.[224]

When Ted and Quailey worked football, the platoon system was not yet in vogue. Substitutions were rare. The eleven players on offense were usually the same eleven on defense. A good pile-up, however, caused plenty of confusion, especially in the mud. Once while broadcasting the Army versus Notre Dame game of 1930, Ted lost his glasses. The inclement whether of rain and fog added to his already distorted vision. The CBS broadcast team never wavered. Quailey's accurate spots led to a flawless Husing play-by-play. This peculiar panel of flashing lights and coded information was the third eye in the booth.

The Annunciator became a holy grail, a mystery, guarded from curious onlookers, hidden away from copycats eager to know how it really worked. A wise choice or restless paranoia, Ted saw the device as the ultimate operative against the enemy. The machine became legend, taking on a life of its own, adding a new dimension to Ted's own reputation as ruler of all football announcers. In time, the spotting board was protected better than the President of the United States. "He covered it up if you came near him," chuckled Chris Schenkel. "I was doing a Harvard versus Army game once in 1947. Ted worked on top of the colonnade. I go into the booth and he didn't know me from Adam. He took his coat and covered the

spotting boards. Here I am, an announcer, no way threatening him
. . . He didn't want me to see his preparation and method. I would
have done the same thing." Curt Gowdy witnessed similar stories.
"They'd go in the stadium and cover it up like a secret miracle weapon. He wouldn't let anybody see it."

Yes, the Annunciator might have been cloaked from view.
But there was no secrecy behind the machine's true importance.
There was a carrot dangling before Husing, varnished in a network
of colors, orange, red, and blue. Beat NBC. Beat McNamee. The
flames of the radio wars simmered low. Each passing day, a new
event, a fresh opportunity to gain listeners. Exclusives were rare.
Nothing could be taken for granted. A sporting event, political convention, an air-machine landing, it was all worth covering.

Ted's more measured on-air approach did not mean he was
without passion. He possessed the energy of a jackrabbit, a kid at
heart playing in a grown man's world. The popular song of the day
"Happy Feet" could have easily played the sound track to his existence. Ted enjoyed the chase, thriving in the role of underdog. "We
were hot on the mercurial heels of NBC, breathing right down their
necks," he bragged in later years.

The New Year broke new ground. Paley gave Ted permission to devote the first two Saturdays of the year to football. Inside
Palo Alto, California, a hop, skip, and a touchdown pass from San
Francisco's rolling hills, was a giant stadium furnished with 80,000
seats, oval track, and a lush green football field. The campus of
Stanford University benefited greatly, hosting the annual East versus
West All-Star game on January 1. Sitting in the stadium's new broadcast booth was Ted Husing, smoldering cigarette, hot microphone,
and all. The game marked the first time Pacific Coast sports aired
on the Columbia chain. By winter's end, Ted returned to the nation's
capital to broadcast the inauguration of President Hoover. An estimated 63 million listeners tuned in nationwide.[225]

The fast-paced life of radio announcer kept Ted's bags

119

packed, stomach empty, and appearance deceiving. Even at the age of twenty-eight, his hairline was in full retreat, short above the ears with a thin part down the middle and slicked back nicely with a dab of Brylcreem. It gave him a rugged, distinguished look, a look far beyond his years. With his glasses around the face, Ted could appear downright professorial. "He's a tall man but his hard lanky thinness make him look smaller than he really is," a female reporter once described him. "You think that if he could fill out the shoulders of his coat and fill in the hollows of his cheeks he might be good-looking."[226] The scale rarely bounced above 160 pounds. Bare-chested, one could count his ribs. But Ted Husing didn't have time to stuff his face with heavy food. He was a man on the go, blazing his way up the radio ladder of success. Catching Graham McNamee would take more than a knife and fork. It would take a motor mouth, a determined spirit, and a fighting chance. He told himself, "Be prepared and stay ready."

Helen slept in a lonely bed for most of 1929. Her husband caught his Zs in strange hotel rooms and bouncy train berths, presuming he slept at all. If the CBS man thought his schedule was dizzying, by fall he would be ready to faint. The month of October not only brought Ted close to his rival. He could have practically worn his shoes. Ted called his second World Series on the network, this time working solo. McNamee anchored the coverage on NBC, getting help from newcomers George Hicks and Gene Rouse.[227] The series between the Athletics and Cubs bounced back and forth from Chicago to Philadelphia. It took five games before Connie Mack's As were crowned champions on October 14. Five days later, Husing and Quailey introduced the "Annunciator," calling the Penn versus Cal football game from Franklin Field. On the other side of the broadcast booth sat McNamee describing the same game for his audience.[228]

Ted returned to New York that evening thinking that a few days of well-deserved rest were in order before next Saturday's football broadcast. It wasn't to be. An urgent message from CBS news director Herb Glover told him to board a train for Detroit. Everyone knew about it. Lights Golden Jubilee was hardly news. October 21 marked the 50th anniversary of Thomas Edison's invention of the incandescent light bulb. With the flick of a switch, the modern age had arrived. Never again would the world be dark. Edison still lived at his home in New Jersey, slowed but able at age eighty-two. Fellow inventor Henry Ford decided to throw his friend a celebration near his auto plants in Dearborn, Michigan.

Ford pulled out all the stops, using the event to dedicate Greenfield Village, a living assemblage of buildings where Edison refined his works—the VIP dinner for 500 was held in astate of the art museum, with plenty of pomp and circumstance. He gathered the greatest names of American ingenuity to participate, John Rockefeller, Jr.; Harvey Firestone; Orville Wright; Ransom Olds; and Charles Schwab, among the best and brightest. Edison would be flanked by President Hoover himself the entire day. The United States Post Office released a commemorative $.02 stamp to salute Edison.[229] Radio made plans to be there in full force, sharing all the events except one, NBC had exclusive broadcast rights to the main event—Edison's staged reenactment.

Ted knew the drill on arrival. He and the CBS team scrambled to make the best of an unenviable situation. They were used to playing catch up. Brought in to help Ted on the broadcast was Washington affiliate announcer Frederick Wile. A steady rain fell about Dearborn. Gray skies and cold temperatures added more frustration. To make matters worse, CBS had little idea of schedule and time of events. Keeping up with NBC would be daunting. Beating them to the punch, impossible. Ted didn't have to ask who was announcing for NBC. He already knew.

While setting up broadcast lines, Ted stumbled upon some good luck. He found an itemized schedule for the gala, exact times and locations, left behind by an unknowing NBC crewmember. Now they had a chance. Ted and Wile's coverage flanked NBC's, racing about from the train depot in downtown Detroit to various locales about Greenfield Village. As night fell, a true test of broadcast will faced the network.

President Hoover was scheduled to speak at Feneuil Hall during dinner. Missing any presidential remarks in those early days of radio was unforgivable. The fast-talking Norton finagled a microphone into the banquet room, giving them access. Still, a microphone had to be inside Menlo Lab for the grand finale. Ford constructed, to the square foot, the very building Edison made his brilliant discovery and placed it in the center of the village. The inventor would again, from his upstairs, lab touch wires as he did fifty years earlier. Only this time, a blinding grid of lights would beam around Dearborn, and then following: bells ring, horns honk, thousands cheer.

Norton tried his persuasive tongue once more. He came up empty. Officials refused CBS access to the lab. The room belonged to McNamee, no exceptions. Luckily, for Norton, Ted was there. The announcer did not yield, maneuvering best under pressure. He was determined to get on the air. His creative juices energized by the slightest challenge.

The rain had never stopped. The dirt roads of Greenfield Village turned to mud puddles. Ford even rented horse-drawn buggies to chauffer his guest from the wetness.[230] Edison stood inside with Henry Ford and President Hoover, holding on to two wires, waiting for his cue. Darkness blanketed the lab lit ever so slightly by patches of candle light flickering from giant candelabras. On their left stood McNamee.[231] He spoke in quiet, rapid tones, describing the historic scene. "I have attended many celebrations, but I cannot recall even attempting to describe one staged in a more perfect setting."[232] Ted mouthed similar words into his mike, leaning gingerly on the top rung of a ladder outside the lab, peering through a half-opened window.

Raindrops pummeled him like tiny bullets whizzing uncontrollably. Ted pulled his hat over his dripping head to use as shelter.

Norton tried to cover the brave announcer with an umbrella. It was useless, really; they were both soaked from head to toe. There was so much water that their socks squished as they walked. However, Ted held his ground, finding strength in the moisture. "I was becoming as closely associated with water as a duck."[233] Wrapped in electrical wires, like the Kentucky Derby five months earlier, he could have fried to death in mid-sentence. The thought never crossed his mind.

As McNamee talked, Edison became impatient. Unprovoked and ahead of schedule, he touched the wires together, setting off the glorified display. Those inside Menlo Lab heard cheers but could not see the lighting. Ted had the advantage of being outside. He described the scene long before McNamee realized what was happening.[234] Millions of radio listeners plugged into the broadcast, turned off their lights, regressing to a time before electricity, sharing the darkness. As Edison reenacted his invention, they simultaneously turned their lights back on, wiser, amazed, and glad it wasn't 1879.

In many ways, the Golden Lights Jubilee represented the final celebration for many Americans. The tides were changing, more in the way a massive wave capsizes a ship. The happy feet of the 1920s stopped dancing October 24, 1929. The Stock Market crashed. Fortunes crumbled. Bread lines six blocks long formed in cities like Chicago, Detroit, Philadelphia, even Washington D.C. Along the Bowery and Lower East Side, they were twice as long.

The country would rely on the radio during the coming decade more than ever for news, information, entertainment, fantasy, anything to make them feel better, put the smile back on their faces. Living in a world of uncertainty, listeners gravitated toward the voice of confidence and trust, one they could rely on for telling them the truth. Through pouring rains, endless miles of tired train tracks, alone against the deep resources of the opposition, Ted Husing got it right. He had earned not only their ear. He earned their respect.

CHAPTER FIFTEEN

TIME MARCHES ON

The large galleries at Interlochen Country Club near Minneapolis gave the CBS announcer odd stares. More than 13,000 pairs of eyes to be exact.[235] Husing knew why. No one on an American golf course had ever seen a radio announcer before 1930. Even more peculiar was the fact that the radioman wore large headphones and walked the course talking into a microphone. Strapped to his back was thirty-five pounds of transmitter. From its mass, a thick, wiry antenna protruded five feet high.[236] It did not have a name. Most simply referred to the piece as "portable short-wave broadcast equipment"[237] Ted first tested the contraption at the Penn Relays in April. Fans and runners wondered who the space alien was in the middle of the track infield. Yacht workers laughed when he told them he was boarding their vessel to broadcast a regatta race along the Thames River in New London, Connecticut.[238] McNamee relied on the old method, following the action from a rail car.

Ted kept up with the most modern advancements in radio. Sounds of the game were more readily heard with parabolic reflector microphones. The new invention gave everything from marching bands to the crack of a baseball bat more pronounced reverberation. They were strategically placed around stadiums, close to the crowd, closer to the field. Throughout a broadcast Ted and his engineer could make adjustments. Though able to control more aspects of sports announcing, Ted felt restrained. He wanted to walk around and get close to the action. Broadcast locations for baseball and football for the most part served announcers well: a stationary position high above the field where plays unfolded clearly. However, the lay of land was different when doing the more intimate events like golf or track and field.

The boys at Bell Laboratories had Ted in mind when they designed the mobile handheld microphone set. The ability to walk and talk at the same time finally became a reality. Ted was able to move about freely describing the action. Point-to-point coverage around a quarter mile of oval was instantly possible. From the 1,500 meters to the sands of the high jump, no athlete was out of reach. Among the massive acreage of a golf course, Ted was free to travel with the top players.

Between the Annunciator and portable transmitter, Ted was becoming high tech, if not better physically conditioned. What seemed like a technological marvel to the listener was a backbreaking expedition. It was more like an army backpack strapped to the shoulders, loaded with enough food and ammunition for a ten-day hike. Yet, Husing protested little, willing to work his muscles to gain any advantage for himself and the broadcast. Besides, wearing the new mobile, he was more pronounced than anyone around him. If a fan didn't know about "Ted Husing, radio announcer," all they had to do was follow the man togged up in the large box and sweating more than any competitor on the course.

Minnesota was famous for it brutal winters but this was summer and the July heat reached three digits strong. As he walked the course at Interlochen, the weight of the pack grew with each passing hole. He prayed the scheduled two-hour broadcast would go quickly. As hot as Ted felt, Bobby Jones might have felt hotter. Jones, after all, was chasing history. Barely the age of twenty-eight, he was already destined for immortality, one of the four great names of the Gilded Age of sports. Equaled in talent and legend to Bill Tilden of tennis, football's Red Grange, and Babe Ruth, the ambassador to the national pastime. Where the others gravitated to the public eye, Jones shied away, preferring to show his Georgia, southern pedigree.

Jones also worked his magic for free, accepting no prize money. Technically, he was considered nonprofessional, on par financially with the caddy who carried his clubs. But those who watched him knew there was nothing amateurish about his game. He performed things on a golf course never seen before or since. Coming into the U.S. Open at Interlochen, no one had ever won all four major tournaments in the same year. Jones was halfway there, winning the British Amateur and the Open Championship, better known as the British Open. Press coverage swelled, as did rumors of his pending retirement. The sport's prolific writer O.B. Keeler saw the parallel of Jones' booming drives and slick putting skill to baseball and the great Bambino's mammoth home runs. He called it the "Grand Slam."[239]

Jones did not disappoint. Captivating the gallery throughout the afternoon, working out of trouble and keeping the competition at bay. As Jones played, Ted talked, and walked. Mostly, he ran. He solicited plenty of help that day. Quailey set up shop outside the clubhouse near the 18th green, providing information via short wave. Ted also dipped into his pocket for coins often to pay Boy Scouts who relayed action and scoring updates. The best sources were the players themselves. Ted got many to give brief interviews between holes, perhaps mesmerized by the dangling antenna and present microphone. Gene Sarazan, Johnny Farrell, Walter Hagen, and others laughed softly and talked club selection with Ted.[240] Well out of contention, it was the only thing left for them to do.

Jones birdied the final hole, finding the cup with a fifty-foot chip shot from the fringe. The crowd exploded, littering the green with hats and delaying the action. Ted hustled over to Jones hoping for an interview, but the champion was whisked away to the club-house. None of it mattered. Ted wasn't even on the air. The network had broken away to air the running of the Arlington Stakes from Chicago. Ted complained, demanding more time. After Gallant Fox crossed the finish line a winner, New York threw the air back to Interlachen. Ted asked Jones how he felt about the win. "I was just a little lucky that's all," he humbly told the listening audience. [241] A few weeks later at Philadelphia's Merion Country Club, more luck followed. Bobby Jones won the U.S. Amateur by three strokes, com-pleting the Grand Slam, hailed as an American hero.[242]

Paley continued to call upon his #1 broadcast talent often in the early part of the new decade. It seemed every day a new assign-ment, a new broadcasting first, was blazing past his mind. "It's like everything else—forgotten history to me," he told the press. "All I do now is look ahead."[243] No doubt Ted looked forward to the eve-ning of July 21, 1931. A truly original experience, in reality, had little to do with radio. At 10:15 PM, Ted spoke into the CBS microphone with his customary smooth manner. Only this time, he also looked straight ahead into the lens of an unwieldy object called a television camera.

The Columbia Broadcasting Company decided to launch its pilot station W2XAB as an experiment. Few had access to a set. Much of the public was still getting acclimated to having a radio in the house. If no one watched, Paley would have smiled, a feather in the cap for CBS, beating the competition soundly. It would be another year before NBC jumped into TV. Paley tapped Husing as the show's master of ceremonies. "Good evening, ladies and gentle-men," he began. "We know there are many of you who will be hear-ing this program but not seeing the artists, and no doubt there are others who will be seeing us but not hearing us speak. You know, as I think of it, I've been talking to you radio listeners over a period of years now, and you haven't been able to talk back to me. Now your day has come—with television, like this, you can look at me, and I can't possibly see you."[244] Appearing on the simulcast were an array of stars such as composer George Gershwin, New York mayor and Husing drinking buddy Jimmy Walker, funny man Ed Wynn, and a new female singer recently signed by the boss named Kate Smith.

Being the signature voice of the network, every company who sponsored a CBS show wanted Husing attached. He stayed selective, not wanting to lock himself down to a certain time slot or day of the week. One product he did agree to plug was Time, Inc. sponsors of the *March of Time*. The publishing company engaged in the radio business as a way to promote their weekly news periodical by the same name. The concept was simple: dramatically recreate the latest news stories using actors and sound affects. Narrating each episode was the "voice of time," Ted Husing. His baritone was perfectly cast for the serial, authoritative, commanding voice of God. Ted ended each show with an affected sound dripping with drama, "AND . . . TIME MARCHES ON!" The words would be mocked and copied, becoming iconic in the annals of broadcast history.

The early shows were nothing iconic, staggering out of the gate. "The March of Time" introduced itself rather appropriately on March 6, 1931. But, once found by the public, became a sensation, running for fourteen consecutive years, six on CBS.[245] Paul White, who rose from his post as Director of Special Events at CBS to the first ever Director of News, called it "a series which had more imitators than John Barrymore."[246] Agnes Moorhead became a star from her reoccurring portrayal of first lady Eleanor Roosevelt. The show was also a huge time commitment for everyone involved, a literal mountain climbed each week. Before an episode ever hit the air, a thousand hours of labor, casting, research, writing, and rehearsals were lived.[247] If only the listeners knew. Ted Husing did and quickly surmised that he was not long for the show.

September and October loomed. Ted saw conflict with his growing claim to fame, football. The "March of Time" aired on Friday nights. How could Ted be in a New York studio on Friday and back in the stadium radio booth, fresh and upbeat, calling football on Saturday afternoon? It was impossible. No way sports would take a back seat. Ted cut his losses and recommended Harry von Zell for the job. Gary Stevens was hired several times as a voice extra during the shows initial months. "Harry got me on the 'March of Time' as a mumbler," chuckled Stevens. "That was a big thing for me to get a five dollar bill when I was only making fifteen or eighteen dollars a week. Harry was very kind."

It was becoming clear that Ted's skill shone brightest in the arena of athletics. Those days as a young teenage boy absorbing the sports scene as Columbia University's team mascot paid high dividends for CBS. He aired almost every sport imagined. There wasn't a dormant season on the broadcast calendar with baseball, boxing, horse racing, regattas, football, and a host of other seasonal competitions. "Most of us were good at some sports. Ted was great at all of them," swore Chris Schenkel. Bill Mazer, a broadcast contemporary of Schenkel's who called a variety of sports in New York, preferred Husing's work on track and field events. "I thought his knowledge of track and field was beyond any kind of comparison. He knew it and the voice was just superlative." Then again, *Radio Guide* called Ted, "one of the ablest golf reporters working in radio or any other medium."[248]

Hall of Fame tennis aficionado Bud Collins laughed at his attempts to cover tennis on radio late in his illustrious television career. "Tennis on radio, imagine that if you can,"[249] he once exclaimed. Well, long before Collins, there was Husing. And his descriptions of such fringe events continued to fascinate. "Husing had the ability that if you were listening to him on the radio covering tennis, you found your head moving," said longtime caller of Baltimore sports Chuck Thompson. Former Boston Bruins voice Fred Cusick was also struck by Husing's tennis authority. "I can remember I grew up in Boston, Brighten. And in Brookline, they held at the Longwood Cricket Club, the National Doubles, and he used to cover it all alone. A whole Saturday afternoon, I mean he'd be on four hours and handle it with elegance. He was just great." Mazer agreed. "I think football in its broad scope never compacted him like doing tennis. You would have had to hear Husing do a match . . . He was just that great."[250]

Despite how some raved, for most, it was football that carried the Husing brand name. America loved the pigskin. America loved Husing. His voice, rythmn, and commanding presence captured the game like none other. His legion of fans around the nation were growing. Respect for the voice of football magnified only by the respect Ted had for the rugged game himself. He brought a bravado never heard before, unafraid to criticize poor play, call out second-rate officiating, or any other indignity he thought worth mentioning. "The guy was a superb broadcaster," remembered the former Cleveland Browns announcer Ken Coleman. "Husing had one of those rare voices that when he spoke you listened." The Husing influence continued to be heard on the air. He never actually figured to make a strong impact on the field of play. That, sure to say, came with a little assistance from "the brains," Les Quailey.

Ted hated guesswork, dedicating his entire approach to the elimination of it. The Annunciator was only the beginning. For team CBS, the football season did not start in the fall. The winter and summer months was when the real work happened. Ted and Quailey criss-crossed the nation visiting coaches, compiling rosters, dissecting plays. The more knowledge, the better. More of the same came during the season—interviewing players, boldly requesting to look at playbooks and *even* watch practice. No broadcaster had dared to do that before. To his surprise, most coaches complied with the unusual requests. Ted's gallant moves and arduous study paid subtle dividends to his broadcast. "Husing was not only an announcer. He was a fan," said Glickman. Once the referee, dressed in a black bowtie and white cap, blew the opening whistle on game day, there would be few surprises.[251] One aspect of a football game did remain ambiguous. Ironically, it was the men with the whistles that kept Ted in the dark.

His frustration had been mounting for some time. Among the chaos and violence of football existed plenty of delays, mostly to grant timeouts or enforce penalty infractions. Clipping, roughing, and piling on were only a few of the more egregious offenses.[252] It brought the action to a grinding, if not confusing halt. A whistle or horn blew most of the time. Yet, few heard it above the bellowing crowd noise. The only time fans in the seats, or radio announcers for that matter, knew anything was when they observed officials marking off yardage, then re-spotting the ball to resume play. Questions remained. What was the exact penalty? What team called the timeout? Ted had enough and begged for clarity.

In October of 1929, Ted and Quailey traveled to upstate New York to broadcast the Cornell versus Syracuse gridiron war. Prior to kickoff, Quailey asked head referee Elwood Geiges if his crew could devise a strategy for keeping his partner more informed of what was happening on the field. Geiges devised four hand signals indicating offside, holding, illegal shift, and time out.[253] Whenever Geiges called a foul, he marched to midfield, faced Ted's broadcast area and motioned through the sign. Ted so loved the creations he insisted the same be used during subsequent games. The penalty signal was born. Hand signals had been used sparingly before. Elmer Layden, then head coach at Duquesne, asked officials to use a few helpful gestures during a 1928 contest against Thiel College.[254] But the practice was inconsistent, at best haphazard and unconventional. Ted insisted that all officiating crews adopt Geiges penalty signals for the betterment of the game. Not to mention, his broadcasts. Soon, the practice of penalty signals became a binding part of the sport.

There was still much to be desired in the early days of radio wars. In the listener's mind, there was only one king—NBC. Twenty-four of the top twenty-five shows of 1930–31 season originated from either the studios of the Red or Blue Network.[255] Paley still had

Husing and without him they might be out of business. Columbia, if nothing else, had the weekend—sports. Ted continued to push the envelope. And with that came headlines.

Paley never worried. By allowing Ted to fly unbridled, he was already beginning to apply his formula for success. Where the Peacock's more corporate approach centered on radio sales,[256] Paley's gut told him that the real winners lay in the expertise and artistry of the human spirit. Substance not quantity. Talent is what would attract listeners, not product.[257] "He was always proud that he had something that NBC didn't have," noticed Gary Stevens. "He knew Ted was the best. Just like when he had Bing Crosby or Kate Smith." When Paley arrived at CBS, Husing came with the territory. An old sturdy wall looking for a fresh coat of paint. Getting Crosby in tow came merely by chance. But, like everything else around CBS to that point, new talent didn't come to the network without the aid of one Mr. Ted Husing. That included Bing.

It took a European cruise aboard the SS Europa in the summer of 1931 for Paley to be formally introduced to Bing Crosby. He actually never set eyes on the singer. Crosby never left port, 3,000 miles and half an ocean away, in California with new wife Dixie Lee, recording records and sharpening his acting chops in several movie shorts. Crosby was not yet a household name. But, his solo recording career was in full bloom and some began to notice, especially a passenger booked in a stateroom near Paley's on the ship. "Each time I circled the deck I would pass a teenage boy on a deckchair, listening to a phonograph recording of the same song, 'I Surrender Dear.'"[258] Paley became instantly smitten with Crosby and cabled New York to sign him.

Radio looked to be the ideal medium for Crosby. His relaxed, cozy style and playful song strokes was tailor made for the intimacy of radio. The term "crooner" was about to be revolutionized. "When Crosby came of age, most successful male singers were effeminate tenors and recording artists were encouraged to be bland," stated Crosby biographer Gary Giddins. "Bing perfected the use of the microphone, which transfigured concerts, records, radio, movies—even the nature of social intercourse. Bing was the first to render the lyrics of a modern ballad with purpose, the first to suggest an erotic undercurrent."[259]

The Old Gold days of 1929 blurred into the past. If Paley ever did shake Crosby's hand, it was forgotten. Things changed two years later. Negotiations began on the boss's return from Europe. He recently penned an exciting fresh female songster named Kate Smith at a weekly holding salary of $500.[260] Paley figured getting Crosby in at the same amount. How wrong he was. The Crosby price began and ended at $1,500 a week. Paley drove a hard bargain, but the rising singer never budged. The CBS leader was desperate to sign new talent. Crosby sported the look of a winner and Paley knew that if he didn't corral him in, then they would suck him up across the street, that being NBC. The two sides then brainstormed the right vehicle to showcase Bing's talents.

A weekly fifteen-minute show, Monday through Saturday, was formulated. Airtime 11 PM, coast-to-coast on more than seventy stations.[261] The title made perfect sense: "Fifteen Minutes with Bing Crosby." The premier broadcast scheduled for August 31, 1931. Chosen as the show's announcer was none other than Harry von Zell. After the infamous Old Gold excursion, von Zell stayed in New York, quickly rising up the ranks as one of busiest talents at CBS. Bing trusted they would work great together, just as before. However, von Zell was not Crosby's first choice. Big time radio gigs needed big time radio star power. At CBS, that meant only one man—Ted Husing. Crosby asked about his friend's availability, but was told Husing's price could not be met. Unfortunately, for Bing, the show had yet to secure a sponsor with deep pockets. A limited budget remained. No money, no Husing. "If he'd only mentioned this beforehand, I'd have gladly donated my services," Ted admitted years later.[262]

Crosby arrived in New York two weeks before the big premier. From the minute his foot hit the platform at Penn Station, Crosby was on the move non-stop, especially his vocal cords. Meeting with arrangers, rehearsing songs, and reacquainting himself with Manhattan's finest social spots and parties. The grinding schedule, stress, or a melding combination, caught up to the young crooner at the worst time possible—opening night. Widening his mouth on the morning of August 31, Crosby's mellow voice had been replaced by the deafening sounds of horror. He could not talk, much less sing. Panic set in, polar opposite the singer's cool persona.

Paley was not happy. He poured network currency into the Crosby machine. Now this. He ordered hourly reports on the singer's condition from agent Francis "Cork" O'Keefe. Hot tea with lemon, lozenges, a hooker, anything to get Crosby to the studio ready to thrill. Following a late afternoon rehearsal, it was clear Bing's throat was simply too raw to perform. The first broadcast would have to be altered. Paley and his staff agreed. Studio One buzzed with nervous anticipation. CBS house band, lead by Andy Kostelanetz, went through sound checks, unsure if they would play without the show's namesake and star attraction. Engineers tweaked microphones. Like the rest, von Zell waited and wondered.

From his office on the 18th floor, Ted got wind of Bing's bad luck. Venturing up to Studio One, Ted stood by offering moral support to his ailing friend. "Shit Bing, I told you not to bark at those chorus girls so much, they'll wear anybody out." Husing said shaking his head. "Don't worry about it. You'll be great tomorrow night." The singer sheepishly smiled knowing what the announcer tried to do. Crosby paced nervously, staying quiet, distraught by his present condition, feeling helpless, not wanting to disappoint. The build up, the opportunity. Yes, there was always tomorrow, but would audiences tune in? Then, fear hit hard below the belt. The sound of sets clicking off echoed about his worried mind. Was his radio career over before it ever really began?

Among all the talent that hovered around Studio One that afternoon, Crosby knew no one matched the clout of Ted Husing. Radio audiences trusted him. If one of the biggest names in the business could lend his influential voice there might be room for a second chance. He witnessed firsthand how the announcer handled Whiteman during the Old Gold show. Maybe something could be done for a beginner down on his luck. In a soft, raspy voice, trying not to strain, trying not to beg, Crosby asked Ted if he could put in a kind word to the audience. Try to explain. Before he finished, Ted sprang into action. A promising career was on the line. Moreover, a buddy needed help. "Consider it done, my boy," he said charging with confidence. "Get out of here. Nothing left to do. Go get some rest."

As 11 o'clock neared, everything was set. In the hours before the broadcast Ted called in a few chips. Spinning record disks on radio was not a common practice in the year 1931. The American Federation of Musicians and the composer's union ASCAP fought mightily to protect its members. The networks especially were glad to hire live musicians, compete within the rules, and pay everyone accordingly. Ted enjoyed breaking rules. Live dangerous. Live strong. Extraordinary circumstances called for extraordinary measures. He reasoned that if listeners expected Bing Crosby, then Crosby they should have. Live in the flesh or some other means. That other means meant playing a Crosby record, live on the radio. He calculated the effort Paley put into hyping the show for CBS. The boss quickly agreed. But to get around the union gatekeepers, how? If Ted stood willing to put his own reputation on the line, then William Paley decided do the same. All in the effort of topping anything NBC aired during the same time slot.

Paley trumpeted his new catch to the newspapers hoping America wanted much more of Bing than just fifteen minutes. *The New York Times* featured a large photo of Bing in their Sunday Radio Section, drawing attention to Monday's primetime broadcast. The audience would be sizeable, if all went as planned. But, what happened before them now possessed all the ingredients of a disaster. The mike stand stood tall, about five feet, headed by the microphone itself, CBS in large block letters bolted across the top. Among the hustle and bustle, no one noticed a phonograph machine placed on a small nearby table.

Ted gazed into the microphone and began the broadcast precisely at 11 o'clock. What he would say, for the moment, remained a mystery. "Good evening, ladies and gentlemen, this is Ted Husing coming to you from our CBS studios in New York . . . " Von Zell leaned against a wall off to the side, watching, listening, studying the master at work. Kicked to the side, he wouldn't have missed it for anything. The injured star Crosby sat in a chair near the control booth hoping to stay inconspicuous. Kostelanetz, with baton in hand, stood at the ready to lead. The flow of words continued from Ted, explaining about Crosby's unfortunate case of laryngitis, promising they would love him when he did appear.

Then Ted did something never attempted on the Columbia Network. "Ladies and gentlemen, now I'm going to play a record of his and let you be the judge if you want to hear more of this singer—live . . ."[263] Ted angled the microphone toward the megaphone and clipped the needle to the waiting piece of vinyl. Out blared Crosby's version of "Dancing in the Dark." The studio assembly couldn't believe their ears, shocked, looking about for answers, wondering if the Husing humor was at play. Who played records on radio? No laughter could be heard. Bing himself described Ted's stunt as " . . . something that would have floored me if I hadn't already been flat on my back."[264]

The summer of 1931 already had "Dancing in the Dark" as a songbook standard. But Crosby poured his talent all over the tune, making it his own, bubbling and popping—a deep baritone one bar, high soprano the next—pleading to a sweetheart for compassion, understanding, and mercy. Irony never requires innuendo. Ted chose the song for good reason. The lyrics reflected many of the hopes and desires everyone experienced throughout the precarious afternoon, primarily Crosby.

> *Looking for the light of a new love,*
> *To brighten up the night, I have you, love*
> *And we can face the music together*
> *Dancing in the Dark.*[265]

When the record ended, Ted thanked the patient listeners and threw back to bandleader Andre Kostelanetz for the finale. A tight fifteen minutes. The longest fifteen minutes in Bing Crosby's short radio life. The trick, however, worked. Telegrams and phone messages flooded the Columbia offices, the public response overwhelmingly positive. On Wednesday, September 2, two days later, Crosby—rested, healed, and ready—debuted in style. Seven songs without a scratch. Fans continued to chime in, loving his fresh sound. The press hounded him for interviews. America suddenly aglow with everything Crosby. By October, the Crosby show expanded with an official sponsor, Cremo Cigars; a new title; new announcer; and substantial raise in salary, $3000 a week. The immortal triple-threat career of Bing Crosby, movies, records, and radio was underway. But not without a memorable start that almost didn't happen.

Years later, Crosby marveled at the cleverness of a single man that black night of August, 1931, who helped clench a sinking career from the jaws of danger. "Only Ted Husing would have thought of it. And only Ted could have gotten the network's permission."[266] Husing proved, yet again, perhaps his best skill in radio was getting out of trouble. The Harry Houdini of the airwaves. As he soon found out, some assignments brought more than trouble.

CHAPTER SIXTEEN

PUTRID

The first weekend of November came quickly. It was always a bitter-sweet month for Husing. He could celebrate his birthday, but outside of that rare December game, Ted had to inevitably face the sad ending of autumn and football. Few lived life more exciting than Ted. But during the football season blood seemed to pump through his organs with a more determined purpose. He loved the game. Each year was different. Ted lived off the rush of watching wins and loses; heroes and goats come and go.

Going into the 1931 campaign, expectations were high and the need great. Harvard, the original Beast of the East, had not hoisted the championship trophy in twelve long, grueling years. Head Coach Eddie Casey was feeling pressure. The legacy of past success was waking his restful summers. WIN! WIN! WIN! That was the only thing ever expected at Harvard. Under the guiding eye of then head coach Robert Fisher, the Crimson had won or shared seven national titles. The last, capping the 1919 season with a 7–6 defeat of Oregon in the Rose Bowl. A trip to Pasadena was always the goal. It was the first—the ultimate post-season bowl game— "The Grand Daddy of them All." The Rose Bowl meant perfection, usually. Next to beating poisoned rival Yale, it was a feather in the cap for Harvard men. And with the game being broadcast coast to coast on NBC, it was the dream showcase for any program. Coach Casey liked his chances to end the drought. They vowed that nothing would get in their way. As summer faded and practices began, a new fight song could be heard from locker room to dinning hall—Al Jolsen's "California Hear I Come."

W. Barry Wood, Jr., was an amiable, good-looking student athlete. He was about 6'–2", strong frame with a shotgun for an arm. There were few in the land better at throwing a football than the Harvard quarterback. His athletic skills went well beyond the gridiron. His glove-popping fastball and blue line moves on ice earned him letters in both baseball and hockey. But on the Saturday football field, he was a superstar. Harvard along with the service academies and most of its Ivy League constituents were national powers in collegiate athletics, especially football. Long before Red-Shirt Freshman, computer rankings, and The Bowl Championship Series, there was the Gilded Age of college gridiron. Kicked around in a cloud of dust, competition was blood fierce and the game's top talent godlike in legend and stature. Barry Wood possessed all the beguiling of a star.

"He was just a great all-around athlete," said fellow Harvard graduate and one time Boston Marathon race director Will Cloney. "He could have gone in the major leagues I'm sure."[267]

Harvard Stadium, the place that housed the gridiron gladiators, was also special. Originally opened in 1903, the horseshoe-shaped stadium had expanded to spacious lodgings. The seats to watch the Crimson buckheads stretched better than 55,000. When full, the stadium looked more like a gothic coliseum. Atop the building ran a ten-foot-high, closed-in walkway supported by thin concrete columns. Roman! Classic! Bold—Harvard. Above, the walkway on one side was a huge press box. The perch above made for ideal broadcast accommodations. In a day when stadiums offered cramped enclosures or, quite often, no broadcast booth at all, Harvard was a welcomed post. Site lines were straight, true; and the view from above, unobstructed. For this reason alone one would think Ted enjoyed his visits to Cambridge. However, looking around the campus surfaced feelings of anger, resentment, and uncertainty for the broadcaster. "Fuck Harvard, those elitist pricks," he often mumbled under his breath. With no college diploma hanging on his office wall, the glass of success was always half-empty for Ted.

"Not until years later did I gain a better insight into myself and learn that I suffered from a terrible hidden insecurity, especially about my lack of a college background," said Husing in retrospect. "And what was the college with the greatest background? Fair Harvard, of course."[268]

By Saturday, November 7, the Crimson were in the middle of an undefeated season. Barry Wood had played brilliantly, living up to the All-American hype. Early season wins over Virginia and Texas were impressive. But, a hard fought, forceful spanking of the rugged Army Cadets made them think a year of destiny was at hand. The Yale game loomed ahead. Casey warned his team not to look forward. Keep the eye on the prize, one opponent at a time. The challenger on this particular Saturday was hardly a challenge. It was Dartmouth. The Indians were not enjoying one of their better seasons. They came into Cambridge with a losing record. But coming from a tie with the mighty Yale Bulldogs a week before gave them confidence. It would take more than confidence to upset Barry Wood and the Crimson, however.

All across the country, stadiums were packed with hardy fans cheering and booing. When nearly twenty-five percent of the nation stood in line for bread, it seemed the rest stood in line for football tickets. That same weekend, a record crowd of 65,000 filled Yankee Stadium to watch NYU top Georgia 7–6. Boat trips were being advertised in newspapers to "beat the heavy automobile traffic to and from New England football contest."[269] From middle-America, more than 60,000 watched Ohio State roll away Navy at Columbus. Over the mountains near the Pacific, 95,000 faithful crowded the new Los Angeles Coliseum to witness USC's defeat of Stanford. Most of the 57,000 plus who pushed into Soldiers Field expected a cake-walk for Harvard. What they got was a classic.

Was there any doubt college football was supreme? And by the sound of things, Husing was the vocal knight who helped promote its supremacy. As much as Ted wanted to believe that, the public thought different. McNamee was still the name that came to everyone's mind first, habitually gravitating to his spine-tingling descriptions. A writer once asked NBC President Merlin H. Aylesworth, "What does McNamee actually know about football?" Aylesworth responded with, "Damned little, but he certainly puts on a great show."[270] All of that was about to change. On one chilled Saturday afternoon in the year 1931 outside Boston, three weeks shy of his thirtieth birthday, the CBS announcer became the nation's most polarizing figure, a household word.

Originally, Ted scheduled himself to do the Navy versus Ohio State game on the network. But circumstances changed his mind. In two weeks was the big clash between Harvard and Yale. Ted and Les Quailey knew the media would converge on Boston and McNamee and NBC would do the game. Ted didn't like sharing the airwaves with anyone, especially Mac. Knowing he wouldn't see Harvard again for the remainder of the year, Ted wanted one more look, one more eyeful of the great Barry Wood.

"So I thought that in covering the Harvard–Dartmouth set I could predict the Yale–Harvard result and let it go at that," he said.[271]

With the pageantry of autumn in Massachusetts, the afternoon was in full swing. It snowed a kaleidoscope of leaves. Gapping holes of bare tree limbs allowed the sun to shine through with a clarity rarely seen. Just before 2 PM, Ted settled into his press box seat. On the right side was Les Quailey. On the left, a young spotter from Harvard who would quietly help identify players. Behind them sat a nervous gum-chewing engineer named Les Farkas, ready at the controls. The network channel was clearing from Manhattan. Once open, Dartmouth versus Harvard would be heard from coast-to-coast. Ted sipped long on a mug of lukewarm coffee, cleared his throat, and leaned into the microphone.

"Good afternoon, everyone, everywhere. This is Ted Husing coming to you from Soldiers Field on the Campus of Harvard College . . . " For the broadcaster, it was business as usual. And from the opening, it appeared to be the same for Harvard.

Their first offensive series looked familiar—a touchdown march. Left halfback Jack Crickard chewed yards and spit out would-be tacklers. Wood pitched the ball back and simply watched the graceful runner methodically descend into enemy territory. A Crimson score looked imminent. Fans cheered happily. To them it would be the first of many. At the Dartmouth twenty-two-yard line, suddenly the drive stopped. The underdogs, dressed in green jerseys, got stingy.

"Harvard trying to stuff that ball into an impenetrable wall of humanity," barked Ted's call of the action. "Head coach Eddie Casey ought to teach his back how to run."

Fourth down and stuck, Wood dropped back to punt the ball away. It would be the first of ten times the pigskin left his foot that afternoon.

Coach Casey knew there would be other scoring opportunities, lots of opportunities to put points on the board. He was mistaken. The usually sure-handed Wood fumbled three times and shanked two punts for a total of only twenty-one yards. Dartmouth could not convert the turnovers into points. Patience, however, was on their side. On Harvard's next shot at the end zone, their quarterback slipped again. Ted's rapid-fire description sensed the moment.

"Wood back to pass, cocks his arm looking for a receiver downfield. Throws that ball and is stolen out of air. That ball is intercepted by Will Morton of Dartmouth. To the thirty-five, cuts outside to the thirty and is wrestled out of bounds hard at the Harvard twenty-seven-yard line!"

Dartmouth saw the goal line and resolved to score. Flip flopping the action, Morton took the first snap from scrimmage and hit his right halfback Bill McCall for a touchdown. The extra point was blocked. The only sounds heard for the moment were a small section of Dartmouth faithful cheering in the corner of the stadium. The second quarter brought more reasons for Indian fans to applaud. Pinned deep in their own territory, Dartmouth was able to punt themselves out of several jams. Wood's play remained poor as he threw a second interception just before half. As time expired, the two teams ran for the tunnel. Intermission was upon them. Ted sat stunned, groping with words to describe this most unusual two quarters.

"The sunshine covering the field but not on Harvard's all-American today so far. Yes sir, for a commentary on this game, a stellar second half or at least much improved performance for Wood is needed if Harvard is to come from behind. Make no mistake about it."

Dartmouth was a weak football team. Ted never really gave them much consideration. [272] They had played the role of spoiler nicely, but the second half would surely prove their glass slipper a rotting pumpkin. Ted saw the greatness of Wood enough to know how potent his skills were. The third quarter proved him wrong. He tripped and stammered up and down like an ageing cripple, botching punts and grounding passes. As the last quarter began, hope seemed to fade.

After graduation, Barry Wood would become a Rhodes Scholar and doctor of microbiology. Important posts at Washington University Hospital in St. Louis and John Hopkins in Maryland beckoned. His work with penicillin and pyrogen isolation is renown in the field of medicine. Buildings and infirmary wings would be named in his honor. But on this cool, crunched autumn afternoon, he was simply a quarterback. He was not playing well, obviously.

Allison Danzig, who covered the game for the *New York Times* described the Harvard offense as "a team that had been wasting scoring opportunities prodigally all through the game." Jimmy Powers of the *New York Daily News* was just as critical of the all-American's first half play:

"His passing aim was bad and the only aerial he tried went into Morton's arms and was indirectly responsible for Dartmouth's touchdown."[273]

The growing question around the stadium echoed "What's wrong with Barry?" His play was beyond confusing. It was sinful. And if a loss was pending, Barry was to blame. "He lapsed into his old habits, seldom hit his man, seldom left his feet, and frequently turned to watch his runner," said H.R. Hardwick of the *Boston Globe.* "I believe that therein lay the main seat of Harvard's inability to run-up a sizeable score."[274]

Ted watched Casey pace the sidelines in frustration. He thought of strategy. He thought of Coach Rockne and wondered, *If Knute was in charge would the scenario be different?* The radioman talked as the Indians clung to the improbable 6–0 lead.

". . . and Wood is sacked under an avalanche of green jerseys. And what now, ladies and gentlemen? Fourth down and five and Barry Wood set to kick the ball away yet again. Six minutes show on the scoreboard clock. Not much sand remains in the hourglass for Harvard's unblemished record."

Harvard's "D" had to hold. And they did, stopping Dartmouth unmoved in four plays.

Just over four minutes remained. Harvard's anemic offense needed a quick shoot of vitamin "T"—"T" for Touchdown that was. Everything stood in the balance. It was score now or the sugar plum visions of Southern California would end. On the first snap of the series, Wood looked for his left-halfback Jack Crickard. The man was open for a moment, but Dartmouth's pressure blinded Wood. He gripped the ball hard and threw it toward Crickard. The pigskin sailed out of his hand, landing incomplete. On second down, the Harvard quarterback hurried another pass, missing his receiver by three yards. The crowd grew restless with a humming of audible boos and frantic encouragement.

"Barry Wood threw one of the worst forward passes I have ever seen," remembered Ted. "It was incomplete, of course, but on the next play he repeated with one equally as bad."[275]

Ted's mood grew colder with the afternoon. He was out of patience. He was confused. Why was Wood's play just a week ago so much finer, precise—sharp? Inside the booth, the urge, an impulse took over. Something had to be said.

"Barry Wood is playing putrid football today compared to his performance last week," he cried to the listening audience. "That's right, putrid, ladies and gentlemen. And why? Even this announcer cannot answer such confounding, inexplicable questions."

Ted stopped talking. For a brief moment, life in the booth came to a grinding halt. The young student spotter sat dumb-founded. The gum-chewing Farkas at the electronic controls swallowed hard. Even Quailey, who was numb to Ted's acerbic tongue off the air, felt the blow. None were sure they knew the meaning of the word "putrid." With its tough sounding consonants, the expression swam in ugliness and malice. It was a phrase rarely used in everyday conversation. Perhaps they heard wrong. Did he say something else? What was he trying to convey? Among the confusion one thing was clear, the tall, thin man sitting in front of the microphone used the word "putrid" exceedingly well. And it landed with a loud thud.

Ted shot a glance at Quailey. His eyes grew black and large. The moment seemed to linger. Ted saw the fear of his compatriots, but did not understand. Were they not watching the same game he was? Had they not seen the same rotten, decomposed, and foul-smelling play from the Harvard all-American? Husing, the master of words, was sure he had found the proper one to describe Wood's performance. If "putrid" did not convey that, no word in a good college dictionary could.

Sucked back into reality, Ted remained undaunted. If Barry Wood had, indeed, been putrid on the previous play, he acted anything but that on the next. On third down, Wood again dropped back to pass. His eyes fixed on right-end Carl Hageman sprinting down field. Two green-jersey defensive backs pursued in earnest. Hageman pulled ahead by a yard. He was open. Wood stepped up in the pocket and with one foot on the forty-yard line heaved the brown leather pill forward.

"On this one he went way back, winding up like a sandlot pitcher,"[276] described Westbrook Pegler for the *Chicago Daily News*.

The ball spiraled long, tight and true. It touched on the fingers of Hageman at the three and bounced up in the air toward the end zone. The Harvard faithful rose from the hard, cold seats and held their collective breath. Like a soft floating snowflake, gravity pulled the football back to the lunging Hageman and landed safely in his arms—Touchdown!

"Oh boy, a perfect trajectory by Barry Wood to tie this game," the broadcaster shouted. Harvard was on the board and just in the nick of time. "As if to eat my words,"[277] Ted recalled later.

Wood drop-kicked the extra point through the uprights. Harvard Stadium exploded into pandemonium, finally something to cheer for, finally the lead. Dartmouth took the ensuing kick off and scared the living hell out of Harvard one more time. Morton passed the Indians down to the Crimson fifteen-yard line. But, Harvard's defense squashed their last two attempts to score before the clock ran down to zero.

Umpire W.R. Crowley pulled a starter's gun from his pocket and fired it toward the sky. The game was over. A collective sigh of relief could be heard all over Boston. Ted gave some concluding stats and wrapped up the broadcast with the final score, Harvard 7, Dartmouth 6. As they packed their belongings, Les stood wryly amused. He wondered if Ted had any idea of the backlash that possibly waited for him beyond the stadium gates.

"One hell of a game, glad we got a good one," he said to Quailey. "Thanks for the help." Les had one more query, "You sure have balls, Husing. Putrid? Where in Sam Hill did you get that one?"

The exciting events of the day gave much to talk over. However, Ted was a busy man. He had a train to catch—game today, gone tomorrow. Ted was soon reminded, nonetheless, that this particular game was destined to stay. As fans filed out toward the parking lot they talked of the game's inconsistent play and wild finish. Yet, within twenty-four hours, the talk was only about one thing—Husing.

Ted's apparent name-calling of Barry Wood during the broadcast spread faster than soft margarine on a piece of bread. "Putrid" was suddenly the most compelling word in the English language. Such a word, such language was never heard on a broadcast before, much less a football game. But, when Ted spoke on Saturday afternoon, the earth shook. The shakiest fault-line stood under Soldiers Field. Some fans were outraged, mainly those of Harvard. A downpour of letters and telegrams quickly found their way to CBS and Harvard's athletic office asking for an explanation, asking for Husing's head. Leading the lynch mob of reaction was Harvard Athletic Director William J. Bingham. A former track star at the college and the university's first ever Director of Athletics, Bingham was a stiffly conservative thinker who possessed strong views about integrity and fairness.

"He was a very strict, hue-to-the-line sort of administrator," recalled Will Cloney. "If he got an idea in his head he would follow it. He was kind of an Avery Brundage type."

Bingham was just not shocked, he was offended. In his mind, Ted's word description was taken as a personal affront to the scholastic and athletic prowess of Harvard. How dare anyone try to offer a challenge? And if it were to be questioned, it would happen in the ancient halls of academia, on the brutal fields of athletic competition—not by some "radio announcer." Judge, jury, and executioner, he threw the switch and chucked Ted from Harvard's announcing seat—permanently.

"I don't think anyone speaking over the air has a right to refer to anybody of any team as 'putrid.' Let it be emphatically stated as coming from me that he will never again be admitted to the Harvard Stadium for the purposes of broadcasting a football contest."[278]

Observers took sides and offered opinions on the "putrid" uproar. Intellectuals debated its relevance. Newspapers wrote editorials. Some, on the other hand, didn't care. Cloney, who graduated from Harvard in 1933, was a junior at the time. In the past, he helped Ted on broadcasts as a field spotter. On that infamous day, Cloney was in the stands watching. He remembered the reaction of the Cambridge campus to Ted's inflammatory words.

"Harvard doesn't get in an uproar over things like that," he laughed. "A few people were upset about it. I mean the closer you got to football the more upset you got. But, an awful lot of people at Harvard aren't interested in football."

However, Ted's banning brought to the surface volatile issues like first amendment rights and freedom of the press.

"That was a national story that this guy called a quarterback putrid," said long-time Detroit Tiger's announcer Ernie Harwell. "You say that today, no one would no the difference."

The following week at Pittsburgh, Ted was flanked in the booth by two graduate managers from each school, watching his every move, censoring every word.

"Thinking it over, I was glad I hadn't called any of the Army players 'putrid,'" he joked. "The Army carries guns."[279]

While Gandhi was in London talking peace with Hindus and Muslims, William Paley was back in New York discussing peace with Harvard over Husing's words.

"Paley believed in backing his subordinates as long as they performed," wrote Paley biographer Lewis Paper.[280]

The fact that the nation was buzzing about one of his employees was proof that Ted had performed—and then some. The boss supported his man with a firm sense of diplomacy. He made sure that the network's official statement reflected that.

"All our announcers are under rigid instructions to cover each event with scrupulous fairness and we make continual effort to see that they are fair. It would be a pity, however, if the work of one of the country's most distinguished sports announcers is censored and hampered to this extent because of the choice of an unfortunate word in the stress of covering a football game."[281]

While in Buffalo, reporters tracked Paley down and asked if he thought the word "putrid" had crossed the line of decency. "I can't answer that. I personally see no reason, however, why a radio announcer should be legislated against any more than various types of news writers."[282]

The CBS Chairman was not the only one of influence to defend Ted. Westbrook Pegler once said, "I claim authority to speak for the rabble because I am a member of the rabble in good standing."

His syndicated articles backed king rabble-rouser Husing one hundred percent. The eccentric *New York World* contributor Heywood Broun also took umbrage with Bingham's remarks.

From his popular "It Seems to Me" column, Broun wrote, "It was only another aspect of the menace Harvard offers to human liberty."[283] To Broun, the Husing affair became very personal—any reason to get back at Harvard. Once a student at the college, the deans refused to graduate Broun based on failing marks in elementary French.

Ted had opened up the lid to a simmering Pandora's box. All of a sudden it was open season on the network sports announcer. One week after Ted was barred from Harvard, the Yale Athletic Association politely asked Graham McNamee never to return to the Yale Bowl. Evidently, Mac's sketchy details and mispronunciation of names had ruffled too many feathers.

"Something had to be done about Mr. McNamee," said a

university official. "When we got home after these football games we had a terrible time squaring our story of the contest with what our wives and children had heard on the air."[284]

Fellow NBC football voice Bill Munday was getting similar pressure from the University of Notre Dame. Bill's liberal use of the nickname "Fighting Irish," especially when referring to players like Jaskwich, Sheeketski, and Melinkovitch, was upsetting some of the South- Bend boosters.

With a tongue and cheek remark, one Notre Dame coach said, "The first thing you know, people will be getting the idea that only Irish boys are allowed on the team."[285]

Even the brass at West Point expressed displeasure with the overall broadcasting fraternity. "We have tried them all and are satisfied that there isn't a broadcaster who can describe a football game the way it is played."[286]

For the first time ever, more football fanatics were talking about what was happening in the radio announcer's booth than what was taking place on the field. Ted was the focus, the lightening rod for this new flood of attention. Princeton, in the midst of a tragic 1–7 year, believed Ted's use of the word "putrid" was ideal for describing their team and begged him to announce the last two games on the schedule.

"That adjective is not strong enough to describe the playing of the Tiger team this season," said a Princeton supporter. "You ought to hear the words used by some of the fans."[287]

Reluctantly, Ted apologized to those offended, but remained defiant saying, "I certainly had no intention to do so . . . As a sports announcer, I can only say that if I and my fellow announcers are to serve the public, we must not be unduly constrained by deference to either side in the sports we cover." [288]

Ted's complex personality did not allow him to fully enjoy his newfound celebrity. Ted shunned the attention, saying it was only part of the job, but snarled if no one noticed him. The gravity of confidence pulled Ted's feet firmly on the ground. He never mentioned the incident unless someone brought it up first. The broadcaster seemed to be the only one unfazed by all the attention. Yet in reality, his stomach splashed like a pig on a fresh pile of manure.

Ted got the expected razzing and roasting from the boys at the office. "What did you say Husing?" they asked. "Come on tell us. What really happened?"

"Wood played like shit, something had to be said," he told them, arrogance dripping with every word. "Besides, the kid got the last laugh. Harvard won the game, didn't they?"

Publicly, Barry Wood never spoke of the infamous incident. He was an intrinsically modest man who felt the attention he received as a student athlete was embarrassing. Yet, after his playing days, he did write a book called *What Price Football*—a defense of the game he loved so dearly and played so well. Openly critical of the writing press, a more compassionate tone was uttered about radiomen.

"Then comes the temptation to editorialize. Since he has no time to reflect, but can only utter the first thought that comes into his head, he is hardly in a position to pass judgment upon what he has seen. . . . that his account of the game be both clear and colorful, and that he is blamed for all inaccurate statements, we readily agree that the radio announcer's job is not an easy one."[289]

Three weeks later, Yale defeated Barry Wood and Harvard 3–0 killing any chance of a national title. Ted's season of calling football would end shortly as well, a season few would ever forget.

On New Year's Day, 1932, Ted clicked on his radio and listened to Don Wilson and Don Thompson call the Rose Bowl for NBC. Harvard, once again, was not invited. Southern Cal put a bow on a stellar season, beating Tulane 21–12—at last for the Trojans, a National Championship. Ted was a fan that day. Just one of the millions who wished he, too, could view the game inside the huge bowl, surrounded by picturesque sun-drenched mountains. Yet, because of the events that transpired some seven weeks earlier inside a smaller stadium near seaside Boston, Ted Husing was quickly becoming America's most famous sports announcer. For most, including Ted, he already was.

CHAPTER SEVENTEEN

MOVE OF THE CENTURY

What News From New York?
Stocks go up. A baby murdered a gangster.
Nothing more?
Nothing. Radios blare in the street.

Those were some of the things F. Scott Fitzgerald described of New York in his 1932 classic lament, *My Lost City*.[290] New York was no longer a town of emerald-laced streets and endless possibility. The champagne of the roaring '20s stopped flowing and the good times irrevocably changed forever. Radio, however, seemed to benefit. People stopped going out and started staying in. Nightclubs and theater tickets cost money. Radio was free. Fitzgerald's city may have been lost. But for Ted, the good times were just getting started.

The year did not open with a party, or a game, or a family holiday with wife and child. It began with something better, an award. Ted was named top sports announcer of 1931 by the United Press. MacNamee finished a close second. Thrilled and invigorated, Ted embarked upon the traditional zigzag, coast-to-coast traveling show of the Columbia Broadcasting System. The first week of February, he trudged through the upstate snow and broadcast the Winter Olympics from Lake Placid, covering hockey for the first time.

He returned to New York ten days later to take on a new assignment. The folks at Mennen, the makers of men's deodorant, paid him handsomely to host "Sportslant," a weekly montage of scores and commentary sprinkled in with the occasional profile of the famous and not-so-famous figures of sports.[291] "Sportslant's" popularity expanded to the silver screen, the Husing voice narrating the short films in movie houses from California to Cape Cod. The Husing face would soon become as familiar as the Husing sound.

Ted was the most confident man in the business and for good reason. With confidence came speed. It was said that Ted could fire off better than 400 words a minute "without sacrificing accuracy and lucidity," as one writer described.[292] A newspaper once hired stenographers to try and keep pace with the nimble-tongued radioman. They couldn't. Industry insiders referred to him as "Mile-a-Minute Husing."[293] Still, the CBS announcer's obvious prowess unearthed detractors. Not everyone was a fan. Some found his brash style and uncensored comments, especially on football games, repugnant. The word "putrid" never officially went away, working like a double-edge sword, branding him as a criminal while intriguing others to wonder what he might say next. *Radio Guide* reviewer Mike Porter was one who wished to hear less from Ted. "I could and would chuck a dozen of the same orchids to the networks if ever they should train news event announcers or employ trained observers for outside happenings and keep the Husings and McNamees in the studios— where they belong.[294]

Ted liked critics, as long as they wrote something nice about him. If they did not, there was hell to pay. No one took a challenge more seriously than the most serious man in radio. If Ted disagreed with a criticism, which was often, he went out of his way to confront them, picking fights, using wit and sarcasm as his weapon of choice. For the more baneful cases, he used his fist.[295] "On most newspapers the radio critic is simply a bum reporter who couldn't make good on any other job," he wrote in the mid-'30s. "The music critic probably doesn't know he exists. The dramatic critic meets him in the elevator and thinks he's the office boy. Even the movie critic lives in a different world."[296]

His acerbic attitude won him few friends among the press, to no one's surprise. Following a scrap or impromptu war of words, many used their columns for revenge, torching the CBS man worse than before. Oddly, he seemed to feed off the tension, creating enemies just for spite, allowing him to stay aloof. When the threat dissipated, Ted's charm returned, calling a truce, even offering a conciliatory handshake. He was even known to apologize. Jimmy Cannon, before becoming a legendary sports columnist, started as a radio critic for the *New York Post*. He was also a sworn enemy of Ted Husing. Once he left the newspaper, focusing more on features and politics, Ted invited him to his apartment for breakfast. "There is a strange man," Cannon said later. "He insulted me when I could do him some good. He made a friend out of me when my days of boosting and bad notices were over."[297]

Ted was blessed with many obvious talents. Patience, however, was not one of them. He saw the world in simple terms, direct, black and white, and nothing in between. Anyone who challenged that view, namely critics, became *persona non grata*. The only way was the Husing way, in life, love, and radio. Some saw it as arrogance, others insecurity. And as was the custom, that usually meant conflict. "I don't go around acting superior to anybody," he blandly concluded. "I don't like pretense of any kind, consequently I suffer. I'm not conceited. I'm me. That's all the excuse I can make."[298]

Ted's talents as a domestic lacked everything his broadcasts did not—care, knowledge, preparation, and a willingness to speak his mind. Pegge, no longer a baby, growing fast, spent more time listening to the radio than most grade school kids. It was the only chance she got to spend quality time with her father. Friends tried to intercede, suggest, ask questions, and talk sense. Ted promised to change, welcome more the comforts of family life.[299] It never lasted more than twenty-four hours. Then he was back on the road, out on the town. For whatever reason, family was not his priority. "You would never know that Ted was married," said former CBS and Warner Brothers press agent Gary Stevens. "Most married people have someone else to answer to, have a limitation of their times. Not Ted. He seemed to be able to go anywhere or anyplace he wanted."

Loved ones were not the only thing Ted ignored, taking a similar approach to the nagging stomach cramps he felt through late spring. *Indigestion,* Ted thought, *and nothing more.* Quailey suggested he have it looked at, just in case. Instead, Ted boarded a train for Chicago. Next on the CBS broadcast schedule, the Democratic National Convention staring June 27. Herb Glover, Paul White, and two other announcers, old pal Frederick Wile and newspaperman turned broadcaster H.V. Kaltenborn, headed the Columbia team. Par usual, Ted would anchor the coverage. Most of the time, Ted was doubled over in pain, suffering from an acute case of appendicitis. The hotel doctor warned him to cut it soon or pay the consequences later, perhaps at his own funeral. Ted held on, gripping the microphone with one hand and his irritated gut with the other. On July 2, the DNC nominated Franklin D. Roosevelt as their presidential candidate.

Three days later, back in the Big Apple, Ted reluctantly checked himself into New York Hospital for the operation. A nurse slipped an ether cone over his nose. When he awoke, the angry appendix had been removed. Doctors told him to rest. For the next several weeks no work and no play made Ted an unpleasant soul to care for. Trying to get the radio man to shut his mouth and give over to the bedside manners of the nurses, namely Helen and Bertha, was about as difficult as getting him to have the appendectomy in the first place. "You have to lie down and be quite during an operation," he joked later. "But Bubs came to the hospital daily; though I wasn't very good company even for her then."[300]

To alter his mood and sooth his wife's feelings, he decided two weeks in Atlantic City would do the trick. He told Helen and Pegge he would find them a holiday sooner or later to make up for so much time spent apart. It became a family affair. Henry and Bertha also joined Ted at the Traymore Hotel on the Boardwalk for some well-meaning R and R. But good intentions turned to bad medicine. Bertha nagged her son about relaxation. Pegge whined for attention. All the while, Helen begged for affection. Ted wished he were somewhere else. A photograph taken of the Husing family standing in the cool sea air during the infamous vacation said everything: forced eyes, sullen looks, and no smiles.[301] The two-week vacation lasted six days. The only way to get Ted feeling better was to get back on the air.

Through the summer into the fall, Ted continued on the move. Two cross-country trips—calling the Olympic Games from Los Angeles—Chicago back and forth, and come October back to the Windy City again, this time for the World Series. By no means was baseball his best showcase sport for the air. It's leisurely pace and broken action ran counter to Ted's loquacious, commanding build and rapid-fire delivery. Nonetheless, with streams of statistics, unusual information, and vigorous preparation, Ted approached a baseball game like any other broadcast. His work was well respected. In fact for the last two weeks of the regular season, Ted was asked to sit in for the ailing Pat Flanagan as voice of the Cubs on CBS affiliate WBBM. It was especially unusual because the announcer was sent on the road to call the games—live.[302] Prima Brewing Company sponsored the games, pleased to have the great Ted Husing plugging their product.

Ted heard the newspapers rail against his baseball broadcasts. Some of the adjectives used to describe his work were unflattering words like: "rambling," "unbalanced," and just plain "bad." He was anxious to prove his critics wrong and jumped at the chance to do more games, or in the least, improve. Ted was certainly gaining a reputation for taking chances, but going to Chicago to broadcast baseball looked to be nothing short of career suicide. If he wasn't out-flanked by better talent, he was certainly outnumbered.

Second to New York, which housed three major league teams, Chicago was the liveliest baseball town on the map. The White Sox ruled the southside while the Cubs wore blue a bit to the north. Baseball was so popular in Chicago that three different stations all with a different trio of announcers called the games. In an era when most owners were terrified to put live games on the air, Chicago teams welcomed the broadcasts with open arms. Ted knew a well-educated baseball audience would be listening to hear if the "football man" really could talk America's past time.

The most popular of Chicago's hardball announcers included Bob Elson, a fixture of Chicago super station WGN. Across the dial, Hal Totten sat behind the microphone representing station WMAQ. Both, however, broadcast in the shadow of Midwest trailblazer Quin Ryan, who had voiced everything from the World Series to Big Ten Conference football games to the controversial Scopes "Monkey Trial" in Dayton, Tennessee. By the time Ted arrived in Chicago that fall, Ryan was semi-retired, all but gone from the airwaves. Listeners spoke of his greatness, his sound still fresh in their ears. Chasing one living legend was more than enough to keep him busy. McNamee may have set the mold for the New York radioman. In Chicago, everybody wanted the life of Ryan.

Ted's work turned out to be good luck, if nothing else. The Cubs held off the Pirates to win the National League pennant by four games. Ted's baseball senses, not to mention his pipes, were sufficiently polished for his next assignment—the World Series. It looked to be a good one, underscored by the return of former Chicago skipper Joe McCarthy. His walking into Wrigley Field was painful enough for Cub fans. Worse was the fact that he managed the New York Yankees. "Murder's Row" was still in tact, Gehrig, Lazarri, Combs, and, of course, the big guy roaming right field—Babe Ruth.

Flannagan was healed from his mystery illness and joined Ted at the CBS mike along with fellow Series virgin Bob Elson.

The Yankees swept in four straight, winning decisively, outscoring the Cubs 37–19.[303] The American League champs came as billed, carrying loaded bats and a dugout full of drama. Chicago hit three homeruns compared to the eight smacked by the Bombers, none more famous than the monster shot Ruth hit off Charlie Root in Game 3. Over the years, the story would erode into urban legend. The moment debated endlessly. Did Ruth actually call his shot, boldly pointing toward the place he would hit the homer? Or was he toying with the Cub faithful. Did he lift his bat to scratch an itch? Or did the famed Yankee possess magical powers? According to Ted Husing, Ruth did all of those things and then some. The way Husing saw it from the booth, there was no controversy. "By a gesture he told them that was where he was going to park the next one," Ted said in retrospect. "He turned to the Cub's bench and repeated the gesture. I'll say one thing for Charlie Root—he pitched to Ruth."[304]

During the summer of 1933, Ted had ideas of calling an event rarely heard on radio: track and field. Peaking his interest was a meet pitting the world's best milers on the same track. New Zealand star Jack Lovelock versus Princeton challenger Bill Bonthron. Initially the CBS brass balked, but changed their mind only after Ted guaranteed a world record. Bill Bonthron had never run a mile faster than 4:23 compared to the more able Lovelock who sported a personal best of 4:12.[305] Even in perfect conditions, the record of 4:09 looked to be safe. The man who held the mark, Jules Ladoumegue, was at home in Paris, eternally banned from the sport for accepting illegal payments.[306] At the opening gun, Bonthron bolted out to the lead, hard, aggressive, fast, hoping to leave all comers in the dust. The stadium rose in bedlam. Everyone was surprised except Lovelock. He took the bait and stayed on Bonthron's heels, waiting to make his move.

Into the final lap, Bonthron stayed strong, already showing his famous kick. "BONTHRON WITH A SIX YARD LEAD AND ONLY EIGHTY YARDS TO GO!" Husing screamed trying to stay above the deafening crowd. Suddenly, Lovelock pumped his arms harder, accelerating his pace. The two ran neck and neck. Lovelock proved stronger, breaking the tape at 4:07 His time bettered the world mile record by almost two seconds. A spent Bonthron crossed the line at 4:08, setting a new American mile record. Ted topped his own bold prediction, voicing not one record but two, a portable transmitter strapped to his back the entire broadcast.

The race helped usher in a new era for track and field. It was the Husing influence again at work. Newsreels got in on the act showing the sport's top personalities, sprinters, and distance runners on movie screens from coast to coast.[307] Ted's thundering broadcast brought attention to a sport once in the shadow of baseball and football. CBS monopolized track and field on radio throughout the decade, shinning brightest at the biggest indoor event of the season—The Millrose Games—and showcasing the most exciting race, The Wanamaker Mile. The track meet began on the first Friday of February, 1908, as a day of athletic competition for the employees of Wanamaker's department stores. By 1914, an overflow of crowds forced the meet to a much larger venue, Madison Square Garden in New York. Ted made it a spectacle. At exactly 10 o'clock, the house lights dimmed, Ted hit the air, and the world's top middle-distance runners raced for a place in history. "He was the center of everything at the Millrose Games," remembered Joe Kleinerman, who witnessed sixty-eight Millrose Games, several as an assistant coach. "They had a big spotlight on him. Then they had a big spot on all the runners, announcing them as they came up to the line. Oh God, it was a big deal."[308]

As Ted's fortunes rose, those of Graham McNamee turned in a decidedly different direction. His high-strung act was growing tired among many in radio land. Whether it be a football game or some other assignment, listeners were never sure what they were going to get. [309] McNamee was ribbed mercilessly after saying "gasaloon" instead of gasoline on the popular show "The Fire Chief," starring comedian Ed Wynn. "It was a sensational boner," remembered Wynn. "It became a by-word across the country overnight; a national joke."[310] Mac took it in stride, but never healed from the affects. He would never again be heard as a serious announcer, reduced to a stooge bumbling into the mike.

Ted continued to win awards and attention as radio's favorite sports announcer. The newspaper syndicate Scripps–Howard that year ran a nationwide radio announcers poll for the first time. In the sports announcing category, Ted placed first.[311] The United Press named Husing top sports announcer for the second straight year. In both polls, Graham McNamee placed a distant second. Ted's skills as a sports broadcaster had grown to epic proportions. He never did like the term "sports broadcaster." He considered himself an announcer, capable of taking on any assignment, and he had. "It seems to me that any life spent in the promotion of athletics is a life well spent, but what burns me up is that people regard me only as a sports broadcaster."[312] Like any craftsman, Ted was never fully satisfied with the work. He wanted to be everywhere doing a wide variety of events.

However, inside the shrinking world of radio developed "the specialist." The days of "Mr. Everything" were no longer in vogue. Nor did it make much sense. By the early '30s, both CBS and NBC started their own news departments. Gathering news, breaking stories, and reporting the hard, cold facts was a newsman's job. Paley and Paul White entrusted the meat and bones of news broadcasts at CBS more to the likes of Wile, Kaltenborn, and a strong-willed Englishman named Boake Carter. Lowell Thomas did similar mike work for NBC. All, without exception, were veteran newspaper journalists.

When it came to news, Paley would always "favor the good newsmen over the pleasant speaking voice."[313] Ted's assignments in the areas of "special events" began to taper off. By no means was it a demotion. Paley appreciated Ted's tenacity and stamina. But, there wasn't a person in radio who didn't know where the strengths of Ted Husing lay. Paley and White both believed in putting talent in the best position to succeed. Clearly, the Husing mastery was calling sports.

Whether Ted realized it or not, he had founded a movement. Taking what McNamee kick-started and making it the work of a maestro. His descriptions were a mix of impressionistic art, textbook science, and blank verse. His football broadcast got the best of the bunch. The mind's eye of the listener was finally given sight. A retreating pass play behind the line of scrimmage led by a wall of blockers, he called a "screen pass." Position players on the field were given locations, "Half-Backs," "Full-Backs," to "Wide-Outs." The field of play for him became a strategic map of geography. Defensive backs roamed the "secondary." The "Safety," the last one standing between ball carrier and goal line, became a "Tertiary." Runners were either brought down by "a whole host of tacklers" or "snowed under." When Ted was feeling especially raw and amorous, deceptive bootleg runs or reverses were called "naked." Punts angling inside the opponent's ten-yard line were headed for the "coffin-corner."

His adjectives were simple, to the point, and memorable. For Ted, word usage was a mind-altering drug. For the fan listening on radio, the experience was similar. His broadcast had become an explosion of the senses. "He was Caruso, Verdi, and Toscanini all wrapped in one," wrote *L.A. Times* sports writing great Jim Murray. "So far as the fans were concerned, he invented the sport."[314] And like any great artist of the day, Ted was paid handsomely.

In the early '30s Paley named Husing head of the network's sports department. The title was more convenience than prestige. No one doubted who ran the show when it came to sports at CBS. Paley simply got out of the way, relying on Ted's superior judgment and talent. He paid him a combined base salary of better than $20,000 annually, considerable income in those days.[315] With sports, his wages increased a separate, non-negotiable category. Whatever the event, the announcer usually received a slice of the advertising pie, football Saturdays in autumn being the biggest cash cow. He and McNamee took home an additional grand each week.

Once a star, Ted Husing wanted nothing to do with a common existence. In early 1933, he moved his wife and daughter to an art deco building at 25 Central Park West dubbed The Century Apartments. The new plush, state-of-the-art living quarters stood on the site of the old performance space originally referred to as the New York Theater, later to become the Century Opera House. Ted Husing was not the only big name to call The Century home. The list of prominent leaseholders included Broadway stage stars Bert Lahr and Ethel Merman, ex-heavy weight champ Jack Dempsey, George Gershwin — and Graham McNamee.[316] It seemed only fitting that the two most famous announcers in America shared the same address.

The Husing's tenth-floor apartment came equipped with all the perks of luxurious living, modern kitchen appliances, an envious view of Central Park, and spacious closets where Helen could keep her fine jewelry and French lamé brocade dresses. A Harlem woman in her mid-thirties named Eva Lee was hired as housekeeper.[317] Lee became a pseudo member of the family with a separate bedroom, sometimes taking on the role of nanny to Peggemae. Helen would have never hesitated trading it all in for one blissful night alone with her man.

Sprinkled about the apartment were plush leather sofas; thick, mahogany wood dresser draws; and perhaps the most impressive fixture placed in the living room, a baby grand piano. Ted couldn't play a note, but it did not matter. The fact that he could afford one was the ultimate sign of prosperity. The instrument never sat dormant, happily touched by his many friends who could play. "Once I came into the apartment, Ted wasn't there, so I went into the living room and there was this big piano," recalled Stanley Wertheim. "And a guy was playing, so I sat down and listened to him.

After a while he said, 'I'm Bing Crosby,' like I was supposed to know who that was."[318]

The move offered Ted distance from the riffraff members of the press who often hung around the old neighborhood in search of a good story and photo opportunity. He had changed. But, all the while, Henry and Bertha remained simple and unpretentious. Forty plus years American, still immigrant Germans more comfortable wringing out a wet mop than resting on hard-earned laurels. They were a constant source of anxiety for Ted, who worried their lifestyle would reflect poorly on him.[319]

No doubt Ted was a man of his time. In the days of Depression, it was either feast or famine for most Americans. You had it or you didn't. And there was little doubt that Ted Husing had "the it." And Ted's warbrode reflected that fact. His ties were silk in a variety of pastel colors or polka dots. His suits Italian-made, black, beige, brown, or pinstripe, tailor cut to perfectly fit his lean arms and long regal legs. He also had his shirts specially made with low neckline collars, as not to inhibit his precious vocal chords. On his left wrist, always a shiny, Swiss-made watch. His shoes of the softest cow leather and alligator skin all topped with a shaded hat, worn like a crown just above his eyes. "He carried himself like a star," remembered Hall of Fame broadcaster Bob Wolff. "He was a fastidious dresser, immaculate and sharp. He always had cologne on his hands as well as his face. So when you shook hands with him, it stayed with you all day."

Ted's career passed many names, many figures in the game of numerology. Seventh place on a listener poll inflicted an unforgiving combination of joy and disappointment. He was a different man then, unknown, hungry, willing to do anything, go anywhere to be the best. Two outs, round three, first and ten yards to go. Nearly a decade in, the CBS man reached the summit of his profession—#1. New numbers would keep him busy, transfixed on everything but love.

CHAPTER EIGHTEEN

THE BOYS IN THE BACK ROOM

A New York aristocrat with polio had been elected president. His victory represented hope for a broke, sagging nation. An uplifting motto trumpeted the inauguration, "Happy Days Are Here Again." When he started office in March of 1933, Franklin Delano Roosevelt's first order of business, repeal Prohibition. If society couldn't get a job, at least they could get a good stiff drink. Roosevelt favored dry martinis after a long day in the oval office.[320] With the passing of the Twenty-First Amendment, the bottle of drinking and debauchery popped wide open. It seemed on every corner of America, a new bar or gin joint opened for business, this time without the fear of raids. No one place bared witness to the new free-flowing happy days than West 52nd Street in New York City.

Stretching a quarter mile west from 5th Avenue past 6th dotted a plethora of posh eateries and lively dance clubs. Of course, many were well established, skulking in the shadows under false pretense. After the Twenty-Firt Amendment passed through Congress, no one had to hide. Over thirty joints backed up traffic from dusk to dawn, alluring devils tempting even the most stringent souls of a puritan society. Taste one or see them all. For every occasion, for every wallet size, there was something on West 52nd.

Comedians made them laugh at Leon and Eddie's, Club 18, and the like. Exotic dancers made married men forget about their wives at places such as Caliente or Club Rumba. If hunger called, exquisite meals could be created at Chalet Suisse and Chez Lina, to name a few.[321] Music, however, namely jazz, got them to stay. Jazz took center stage as the road's main attraction. Singers, horn blowers, pianists, or percussionists, acts big and small, esteemed talent or soon to be, all made the avenue come alive. The Famous Door, Onyx, Tony's, and the Three Deuces were just a few sizzlers. Before long, no one called it West 52nd Street, they simply called it what it was—"Swing Street." Jazz great Dizzy Gillespie perhaps said it best, "Fifty-second Street was a mother. I say mother—and I don't mean motherfucker, though it was that, too."[322]

If anybody was anyone, they shopped the pleasures of the avenue. If they wanted to be seen, they went to the 21 Club. Few nightspots equaled the charm, allure, and sophistication of 21. Standards second to none, owners unwilling to compromise, prices fixed to accommodate only the wealthiest, an uncommon build, and a legendary reputation within a year of its opening drew everyone to its door. During Prohibition, it was estimated that over 35,000 speakeasies operated in New York City[323]—38 on "Swing Street" alone. None was more reputed than the 21 Club.

Owned by John "Jack" Kriendler and his plump, nearsighted cousin Charlie Berns, the 21 Club opened on New Year's Eve, 1929. It was a far cry from the other joints the two previously ran, including one in Greenwich Village called the Redhead. Working the door as a cashier was Mark Hellinger, then a young, aspiring newspaper writer. Years later, Hellinger jokingly said that it was the happiest period of his life because he sat collecting cover charges and pocketing the profits.[324] However, one thing about Jack and Charlie's places never changed, high standards. A stringent, uncompromising dress code was set. Men wore ties, no exceptions. Ladies were to always be accompanied by a gentleman.

Dining at 21 was a heavenly experience. It was also expensive. Jack and Charlie hired the most respected chefs and dressed the dining room in elegant red and white checkered tablecloths. "We do not charge high prices to rob people, but to keep the heels out of the joint," Kriendler once said.[325] The club's best customers were the barons of business, Hollywood starlets, and political heavies to a self-assured radio star named Ted Husing. Dragged in with the fat bank accounts were bloated egos and battles of wit that rivaled any Cotton Club floorshow. The red and white checkered tablecloths seemed to symbolize an ongoing chess match that the rich and famous subconsciously played amongst each other. "Of all the unlawful establishments on 52nd, none could vie in elegance and snob appeal with Jack and Charlie's 21," said writer Arnold Shaw. "And no one joined the national game of beat the booze hunters with more zest than its owners."[326]

The club was raided often during Prohibition. But Jack and Charlie were never caught, due in large part to their extensive "bailing" system. At the push of a button, walls opened, shelves moved, and bottles dropped through a chute, trashing all evidence.[327] The most coveted secret Jack and Charlie kept away from authorities was the whereabouts of their wine cellar. Located in the basement of 19 West 52nd Street, the cellar was hidden behind a two-ton door opened only with an 18" meat skewer.[328] Inside sat the finest wine collection this side of the French Riviera. Unlike other clubs, "21" was never about music or dancing. It was about good food, stirring conversation and an ambiance of macho zeal that could put hair on anyone's chest.

Ted began frequenting the club when it operated as a speakeasy. The man's face was a mystery at first—hallow cheeks, eye glasses, and fedora hat peeled above his dark eyes—his voice, however, a calling card. Ted was making a name on his own. People recognized him by the mere sound of his accent. "I thought I knew that voice.

Boy, I love your football games. You make it sound so serious." Meeting Ted for the first time, Jack Kriendler had similar things to say. The two became fast friends. He went beyond a regular, spending so much time at the club some might have thought he owned the place.

Ted's more attractive qualities of pretentious self-worth and cocky 10th Avenue flair fit right in with 21's code of ethics. Jack and Charlie knew it well, street survivors, outcasts. Once marginalized, now the toast of the town. Ted was drawn to Jack Kriendler for many reasons. Above any, he related to Kriendler's sense of style and panache. His collection of clothes varied from pinstripe suits and saddle shoes to cowboy boots and bolo tie. Columnist Louis Sobol described Jack as "handsome, dudish, congenial" toward those he liked, "haughty and aloof " to those he didn't.[329] Sobol might have described Ted the same way. He also possessed certain intangible qualities that any good restaurateur appreciates. Husing, the broadcaster, learned well from Hellinger, the newspaper man. He became unflinching with a roll of cash and fiercely loyal to his friends. His paycheck became an expression of his fame, opening the floodgates to an extravagance rarely seen. "Fred Astaire had grace. Husing had style," said Gary Stevens. "Nobody could throw a twenty dollar bill down on a table like Husing."[330]

Ted found his throne inside the club, holding court, showcasing the brass tacks of America's most famous radio personality. "Table 11, first table on the left when you entered the main bar," remembered Charlie Berns' younger brother Jerry, who was brought to the club in the late '30s to help with administrative duties. Situated across a cigar counter and steps away from the door, Table 11 was a magnet for those who wanted to be seen and heard. Berns believed Husing to be ideally placed, his commanding presence on display for all to witness. "He was an outspoken and friendly person. Anybody sitting at that table would have to be because anyone who came in or left, that was the table that stared the exiting people in the face. When they knew he was coming it was left open for him."

Helen, as before, was left at home or left to her own devices. She came to understand that 21 was his, a special place, providing in ways she could not. Yes, Ted was spending less and less time with his wife. But, if nothing else, Helen knew where her husband was most evenings. "He made 21 more of his home than he did where he was supposed to live," wrote Red Barber with a critical tone. "It was 21 that gave Ted status, or he thought it did, and he made it his headquarters."[331]

Jack and Charlie offered all the amenities of the modern cosmopolitan man atop the upper floors, away from the main bar and dining area. Grunts could be heard emanating from a fitness room with steam cabinet, free weights, and a heavy bag that hung from the ceiling. A gifted Swede named Sven Erickson provided an invigorating rub down. John the barber was hired to give haircuts, a shave, even a manicure. Afterwards, a short pour of Ballentine Scotch, a club standard, and a hand or two of bridge. A man named Tony shined shoes so well that dentists considered using them to help clean teeth. Jack and Charlie offered these extras only to their favorite clients, an inner circle of close friends: Louis Sobol, Mark Hellinger, Bill Corum, and Ted Husing, among the chosen few. They became known as "the boys in the back room."[332]

But, what attracted Ted to the club of Jack Kriendler and Charlie Berns most would never be found on the menu, at table 11, or an upstairs private room. In those moments of darkness, self-doubt, or private pain, he could always find refuge. If he ever needed to think, if he ever needed to talk, if he ever needed to ground himself and be reminded of who he was as a strong and capable man, if he ever needed a place to just get away, there was always 21. Always! Influential *Look Magazine* food critic Marilyn Kaytor once wrote, "21 is a very special place, not a bar, not a restaurant, but a great jolly drinking and dining establishment with an aura of self-assurance and an intimate masculine flavor that sets it apart from other gin mills into almost the private club category, yet it doesn't suffer from the parochialism of a private club. It is home to those in need of sensitive shelter."[333] At 21, with all the other lovable losers of domestic life, Ted felt safe—like family.

Ted was known to sneak away from 21 on occasion. His fame was not exclusive. If the spot was hot, he'd show his face and money at other establishments, too. Sherman Billingsly at the Stork Club on East 53rd Street enjoyed seeing Ted. So did Walter Winchell who had a special table in the back. "The Stork, like 21, was fussy about its patronage," wrote famous Broadway columnist Louis Sobol. "And perhaps, because so many were refused entry, it became a must spot for the night imbibers, that is, those for whom the open sesame sign was flashed."[334] The famed King Cole Room at the St. Regis Hotel in midtown found Ted sipping Red Snappers, later known as Bloody Marys, a creation of the Room's head bartender Fernand Petiot.[335] Each night, the famous mixologist carried a leather-bound autograph book, collecting the signatures of his equally famous clientele. The famous announcer gladly scrawled his name boldly among its rippled pages.

Another Husing favorite was the Barbary Room. A quick escape from the office only because it was located directly across from CBS on Madison and 52nd Street. The network's orchestra leader Freddie Rich also used the place as a different kind of escape. The law was after him when his wife Pegge wanted a divorce. Court process servers hounded Rich for weeks trying to get official papers in his hands. Ted helped by hiring page boys to cover the orchestra leader's face so the inevitable divorce documents could not be served.[336] Once through the lobby, the Barbary Room became a safe haven.

Time and time again, Ted would return to Billy LaHiffs. The original sports bar, packed each night with ball players, beat writers, and has-beens. Billy was dead by 1934. His son ran the bar with less passion, less interest in bloodshot eyes from another late night. A new employee of the club, however, had other ideas. A penchant for the nightlife and a passion for taking chances and a dream to one day call the place his own.

Ted first met the man with the funny name around 1931. He was new in town, hired to watch the door and "take the trash out" at Owney Madden's other joint, the 5 o'clock Club. The radioman reacted the same as everyone else, laughter. Who in their right mind calls themselves Toots? But, the man called "Toots" won over Ted the same way he had all the others, an overwhelming, bone-jarring zest to live everyday as if it was his last.

Bernard "Toots" Shor was large, capable, and Jewish. He learned to handle himself growing up in the no-nonsense neighborhood of South Philadelphia, surrounded by Irish and Italian Catholics. Soon people found out Shor just wasn't another New York club bouncer. He liked to talk. He liked to smile more than he liked breaking heads. He gambled to excess and drank with equal profligacy. His most endearing trait, however, was a big heart, loyal, generous, and sensitive as a papercut. One friend said of his emotions, "You can make Toots cry with card tricks."[337]

Soon, club owners gave the 6'–2", 250-pound Shor the title of "greeter." Business perked wherever he went, as did his salary. His list of friends grew as well, Mark Hellinger one of his closest. Stops along the way included, Napoleon Club, Eddie and Leon's, and the infamous LaHiffs Tavern, graduating to manager and minority owner. As Ted had done a few years earlier, Shor watched Hellinger maneuver through New York's social scene, well dressed, well liked, and unafraid to spend money. The three became inseparable in time—rich, successful, and married to former Ziegfeld girls. Hellinger even tried radio, doing his best Ted Husing impression as voice of Columbia football form 1931–33. The effort turned out to be more comedy than play-by-play.[338] The trio did not stay in tact. Hellinger's savvy prose brought him out to Hollywood for good, as a writer and producer.

He did teach his star pupils well. Shor and Husing could stand on their own. The name Toots Shor would soon grace the front of a restaurant and become legend. As for Husing, in the world of radio, his star was only just beginning to ascend. He was the king, king of the nighttime world, and reigning monarch of the sports airwaves.

CHAPTER NINETEEN

A MOUNTAIN CALLED KENESAW

Husing no longer needed to be greeted at the door and given formal introduction. He had arrived—one of the biggest radio stars in the business. There were signs of his new status. Ted graced the cover of top selling magazine *Radio Guide* in April of 1933 in a large charcoal profile sketch by celebrated artist James Montgomery Flagg. The subtitle: "Who Is This Husing?" Ted wrote the article himself—none of it factual. He told all about his upbringing in Deming, New Mexico, and how he worked in the aviation department for New York's finest before entering radio. Being honest on the air was one thing. Stretching the truth in the pages of an image building publication was something altogether different.

There, of course, were more tangible signs of success—additional on-air work. Whether he was hosting a Broadway opening like "Jumbo," celebrating the birthday of Irving Berlin, or welcoming the Queen Mary to the New York harbor, Ted was there to add a distinctive level of class to an event. If Husing was on the mike, it had to be important. The network wanted Ted to help showcase some of their best talent away from the athletic fields. Ted was also front and center as announcer to radio's hottest comedy duo, George Burns and Gracie Allen. Ted flitted back and forth from sports assignments, never wanting to miss the antics of the gifted husband and wife team.

But nothing could have made Ted smile brighter than receiving perhaps the highest complement at the track. On the afternoon of July 26, 1935, at Boston's Suffolk Downs, a horse named *Ted Husing* ran in the third race. Minus fanfare, the thoroughbred finished sixth that day. But, it did not matter. Graham McNamee, Phillips Carlin, or Quin Ryan never had a horse named after them. Husing, the famous radio announcer and racing enthusiast, had come full circle. The United Press voted him again the country's top broadcaster of sports, four years running. With more accolades, however, came more competition.

Bill Slater was a rigid, frugal man. A man so stingy about money, he would on a whim offer to buy a friend dinner, and then walk endless blocks in search of a bargain blue-plate special.[339] Being raised in the black poverty of West Virginia coalmines chiseled his humble, careful disposition. He was accepted at West Point, sprouting to 6'–3" and over 220 pounds. However, in time, a career in the broadcast booth not the battlefield would be his. Critics praised his work after sharing the CBS microphone with Ted during the Army versus Navy contest of 1933, and NBC quickly signed him to a deal, the heir apparent to McNamee.[340]

Wimbledon, Indy, New Orleans, for the Sugar Bowl and a dozen or two of the prettiest college campuses ever seen were only some of the places Bill Slater, NBC's top sports announcer of the mid 1930s, traveled. "I loved to hear him," said Chris Schenkel of Slater. "He was very lyrical. His voice was up and down like a good opera singer." As popular as Slater was, he never topped Ted. Poll after poll, the CBS man continued as king of radio sports. "He lacked the publicity that the other guys had," shared Marty Glickman of Slater's work. "He lacked the charisma. I don't think he was flamboyant in his way, but he was a very good announcer." Bill Slater was a proud man and approached his sportscasting like he did everything in life—serious. Yet, he knew the truth as all others did.[341] There was only one Ted Husing.

October 1, 1934 marked the arrival of a newcomer to the radio conglomeration of networks. "The Lone Ranger," a western adventure serial about a vigilante Texas Ranger and his faithful companion Tonto had piqued the ears of listeners outside its origins of Detroit station WXYZ. Joining WOR New York, WGN Chicago, and the vigorous 500,000 watts of WLW Cincinnati, these four stations introduced America to the Mutual Broadcasting System.[342] Cliffhanger endings made "The Lone Ranger" a smash hit, spawning comic strips, movies, and a slew of copycat sequels. Soon Mutual stretched from coast to coast.

What really made NBC and CBS take notice was when Mutual added sports to their schedule. Baseball first, then the World Series followed quickly by football. Before the close of the 1930s, Mutual held a firm grip on the airing of the annual mid-summer All-Star Game, World Series, and Notre Dame football with former Irish assistant coach Joe Bolan at the mike. Initially, Mutual entered the broadcast booth in the autumn of 1935 not with a bang, not a whimper but a wiry southern twang. The voice was meek, straightforward and crackling with a phraseology heard more around the back porch than on a radio describing sports. He was simply known as "Red."

John Clark made it happen. The boisterous general manager of Cincinnati station WLW pulled strings and negotiated deals. "Get on the train tonight for Detroit. You're on the World Series broadcast tomorrow," Clark told his startled young announcer on the other end of the phone. "I agreed that WLW would take the broadcast from Mutual instead of NBC, provided you were one of the announcers. Report to Quin Ryan and Bob Elson of WGN, Chicago, they'll be at the Statler Hotel. . . . Good luck."[343] Far away from his home state of Florida, year after year, Walter "Red" Barber listened to the Fall Classic on radio. The sounds of Graham Mc-

Namee and Ted Husing instilled a hope in Barber to do the same. "Someday you're going to hear me announcing the World Series," he told friends.[344] Two seasons as voice of the Cinncinnati Reds and a tap on the shoulder by radio's powers that be, the dream became reality. With lavish red hair, clean socks, pressed pants, and a worn duffle bag, the Mississippi native hustled for the Union Terminal in downtown, off to the Motor City. He was about to meet his broadcast heroes, then work along side them. Barber was twenty-six years of age, one year younger than Ted when he called his first World Series seven Octobers earlier.

Red Barber would become a different kind of big event sports announcer, averting attention and playing coy while the rest, Ted included, put a huge stake in press clippings and social status. To Barber, little of that mattered. Attending Sunday church service, putting in a hard day's work, and staying married did. His on-air style was southern to the core. "Walking in tall cotton," "Sitting in the catbird seat," or "High on the hog," came from the mouth of Mr. Barber first, making their way to the lexicon of American language. Sports fans, especially baseball lovers in Brooklyn, cherished him.

Few of those admiring devotees came from his broadcast contemporaries. To Barber, the fraternity of mike men was special, a place void of monkey business, no time for male bonding allowed. He was quick to disapprove, always expecting more. Taskmaster, perfectionist, cold, aloof, even sanctimonious: all adjectives used for Barber by colleagues in a not-so-complimentary fashion. "It was so easy to listen to him," described a befuddled Marty Glickman, who worked with Barber in the early '50s. "He was the warmest guy in broadcasting, I'd know. He'd come off the air and be another person entirely." Bob Edwards who worked with Barber for twelve years at NPR came across a bit more understanding. "He did not suffer fools. He was candid, perhaps to a fault though he didn't see it that way. He expected others to have the same professional approach to the job that he had."[345]

Barber had great respect for Ted. A friend, however, he would never become. He chose to keep his distance, in awe of the Husing talent, in utter contempt of the way he lived his life, sickened by the man's brash behavior and callous approach. "Ted was devious. He schemed. He defied me to like him, with an arrogance he must have thought was the image he had to sustain,"[346] Barber observed. "He claimed the entire United States for himself and CBS. You played ball with Husing or else—he didn't hesitate to draw a bead on you."[347]

Whatever Ted said or did made headlines, a household name, recognition equal to Lindberg, Roosevelt, or Ruth. No other announcer on radio wielded more power. He could say or do almost anything he wished, without repercussions. "He goes his own way in spite of hell or high water," wrote a magazine reporter. "He says he likes to have his own way because it has never failed him."[348] Of course, not everyone enjoyed the Husing way. During the fall of 1935, the "Husing way"would be tested like never before. Ted was about to meet his real arch nemesis, a power even he could not stop. The biggest threat to Ted Husing did not come from another spunky, determined broadcaster. It did not come from a rival network. It came from an unmovable force, a mountain called Kenesaw.

Baseball, the Major Leagues, never had a commissioner before. Team owners were a miserly but honest bunch enjoying the love of a nation as keepers of America's pastime. Chicago owner Charles Comiskey was easily the most tight-fisted, refusing to even pick up the team's laundry expenses. The 1919 White Sox became known as the Black Sox. Uniforms hung with a dirty, soiled look but their play sparkled. Chick Gandil, Buck Weaver, and an outfielder sensation named Shoeless Joe Jackson helped the Sox capture the American League Pennant. Things oddly changed at the World Series. Errors, erratic pitching, and a well oil gambling ring gave the championship to Cincinnati. Eight White Sox players admitted to taking bribes and throwing games. The public outcry left a defining scar. Goodness vanished. The field of dreams, innocence, and fair play tarnished irrevocably. Baseball was in trouble. Something had to be done. Someone needed to take control.

Owners had no idea of the consequences when they selected Kenesaw Mountain Landis Commissioner of Baseball, November 20, 1920. Born in Ohio, Landis was named by his father Abraham, a Union Army physician wounded at Kenesaw Mountain, Georgia during the Civil War. Throughout his life, the name fit perfectly. He obtained a law degree without ever finishing high school or college. In 1905, Landis was appointed an Illinois federal judgeship, ruling on such high profile cases involving Standard Oil antitrust and monopoly of Major League Baseball by the upstart Federal League. "Any blows to the thing called baseball would be regarded by this court as a blow to a national institution," Landis stated.[349] As commissioner, his power was limitless. Some called him czar, others a dictator. With sprouts of wild white hair and a scouring treebark face, he appeared disheveled and crude. His opinions, however, were clean, clear, and transparent as a mountain lake. His job—restore the game back to it's pastoral roots—was humble, pure, and peaceful. The new commish banned the Black Sox Eight for life, suspended the mighty Babe for barnstorming illegally, and threatened to investigate Ty Cobb's business practices. No one dared oppose Landis, that was until Ted Husing came along.

Landis didn't like Ted. He saw the broadcaster's big mouth and blunt on-air editorials as a threat to the innocence of baseball he tried so diligently to restore. King Landis told the networks that he and he alone picked what announcers voiced the World Series. Within that, certain rules of etiquette were to be followed: no questioning umpire calls, no mentioning of celebrities in attendance, and, most important, no editorializing or personal opinions. Convey what you see, not what you feel. "If you see men putting up a gallows in center field," he instructed the rank and file, "and then see them lead me out to it and hang me on it, describe it into the microphone but don't question the justice of the hanging."[350]

The riff with Landis had been brewing for some time. Never once did Ted alter his approach to broadcasting a baseball game, remaining bold and outspoken, purposely ignoring the Landis Rules. He wasn't only ticking off Landis, but some sports writers as well who saw his on-air antics as intrusive and unprofessional. [351] The Commissioner had finally booted Ted from the booth prior to Game 5 of the 1933 Series between the Washington Senators and the New York Giants. Ted told the press that his sick wife and mother needed emergency attention. What ailed them exactly and why he boarded a plane to Rochester, never was explained. [352] In truth, most knew the reason—Landis.

The 1934 Series was to be Graham McNamee's twelfth and Ted's seventh. And it looked to be a dandy. Detroit blasted out of April in quick fashion, winning ten of their first fifteen games. Behind the "G-Men" of Gehringer, Greenberg, and Gosslin, the Tigers kept the Yankees at bay by seven games and cruised to the American League Pennant. The National League flag was won in more nail-biting fashion. The Cards, spurred by the talents of two hillbilly brothers from Arkansas named Paul and Dizzy Dean, lapped the Giants in the last week of the season and ended a three-year dry spell from post-season play.

Ted would be flanked by St. Louis broadcaster France Laux and old Chicago pal Pat Flanagan on CBS. The assignment, strangely, came with a new wrinkle. "Ted, I'd like for you to focus on other areas of the broadcast," Landis strongly suggested to Husing. "Let Flanagan and Laux call the action. That's what I'd like to hear. I'm sure you'll find something to talk about . . . It's funny, you know, I can't imagine a World Series without Ted Husing. Can you?" With a sly grin, Ted let the remark go unchallenged. He appreciated, better than anyone, the Commissioner's backhanded humor. And what did he mean by "other areas of the broadcast?"

Ted looked forward to the '34 World Series assignment. He

knew Flanagan and Laux were solid announcers, more experienced and better qualified. His new role of "not describing play-by-play" he accepted without incident. Still present, still in the booth holding a live microphone, still "the" principal member of the CBS broadcast team. For Fran Laux, the elevated status in the network hot seat was nothing new having worked the games with CBS the previous year. Ted considered him the finest baseball play-by-play man he ever heard.[353] But, if a St. Louis man was to grace the broadcast, then it only made sense a Detroit voice would have to counter.

Everyone was expecting Ty Tyson, Tigers radioman on local station WWJ, to get the nod for NBC. But from his office in Chicago, Landis declared that McNamee would work with his usual suspects Tom Manning and Ford Bond. In the best interest of baseball, he kept the Detroit broadcaster away from the booth thinking he was "too excessively partisan."

Tiger fans didn't care what was good for baseball. They wanted to hear Tyson's voice on the broadcast. "Ty was so vivid, he made games come alive," remembered Tigers fan Maynard Good Stoddard. "Ty talked real slow, but he had an urgency inside him and he transmitted that to us."[354] A few days before Game 1 in Detroit, the Tyson faithful circulated a petition to have the broadcaster's voice heard on the air. Over six hundred thousand angry loyalists signed it. Landis eventually reversed his earlier decision, with one minor alteration. Tyson could work the broadcast, but only on hometown Detroit station WWJ. It was a blemished victory, but a victory nonetheless. Matters of broadcasting, for the moment, were set. An overcast sky covered Navin Field in Detroit as the World Series began Wednesday, October 3, 1934.

The opener resembled more of a comedy of errors than a baseball game. Balls dropped, bases overthrown, and ground balls booted. Seven errors in all were tallied as Dizzy Dean pitched a complete game 8–3 victory for the Cards. Games 2 and 3 were split before St. Louis's play suddenly turned soft. The Cardinals struggled, outplayed and outscored, losing the next two games. Intimidation, perhaps their best weapon, also failed them. Stabbing players in the hands and legs with high spikes made most National League opponents think twice. The boys from the American League proved to be a different bunch, unfazed by such boorish antics. If St. Louis kicked, the Tigers kicked harder, dishing out a dose of their own rough play. "It was a series of gleaming, slashing spikes," wrote the *New York Post*. "The boys were trying to cut one another down at nearly every base."[355] Detroit's best attack came from the pitchers mound. Keeping the Gashouse Gang off the bases kept the sharp spikes, dirty mouths, and soiled uniforms in the dugout, away from harm. The Tigers exited St. Louis the intimidators, in charge three games to two. One more win and Detroit would be crowned champions.

The radio talk, all the while, buzzed along the ebb and flow. Laux and Flanagan voiced their usual strong play-by-play. In between, Ted added color, chuckled through the absurdities he witnessed, an editorial in itself, and strongly critiqued the umpires when he felt needed. Still, something was missing. The overall tone of the show came across bare. Apparently, Landis' warnings had everyone in the booth spooked, including Ted. Radio critic Ben Gross noticed the change of speaking duties in the booth, the lack of Ted's play-by-play, and found an unusually conservative, scaled-down show. "What we have in 1934 is a cold, calm, almost matter of fact description, of the games . . . more accurate perhaps than before . . . but from a dramatic standpoint not quite so exciting."[356]

The Motor City buzzed with anticipation, October 8th. Navin Field never saw a bigger crowd. Better than 44,000 pushed through the turnstiles. All signs pointed toward a Tiger's win—momentum, home field advantage, and their unbeatable ace Lynwood "Schoolboy" Rowe slatted to pitch the sixth game. Schoolboy was at the top of the class during the 1934 season. The long-limbed Texan tossed sixteen consecutive wins in a segment from June through August, but saved his A game for the Fall Classic. His gutsy twelve-inning, complete game gem in Game 2 was nothing short of remarkable. As Game 6 loomed, rested and ready, how could anyone expect anything less from the Schoolboy?

However, Schoolboy was not invincible on this day. The pesky Gashouse Gang refused to leave quietly, scratching out a 4–3 lead through seven innings. As well as Schoolboy pitched, Paul Dean of the Cardinals pitched better, and hit better, knocking in the winning run with a bloop single. He shut down St. Louis the rest of the way for his second series win. On the brink of disaster, a new day dawned. Game 7, the clincher.

Energized again, St. Louis rushed to the finale confident. Now the Tigers worried. For the first time, there would be no tomorrow. One last battle, winner takes all. Radio announcers like ball players, too, had one more chance to "get it right." If Ted felt stifled through out the World Series broadcasts, the final game offered plenty of opportunity to unburden his soul. How far could Ted go? He, the commissioner of baseball, and an audience of millions were about to find out.

The only thing that stood in the Tigers's way from a title was the right arm of thirty-game winner Dizzy Dean. Detroit handed the ball to Elden Auker, trying to accomplish what Schoolboy couldn't a day earlier. But before St. Louis finished batting in the third inning, Schoolboy was back on the mound trying to do what Auker couldn't, get somebody out. A laugher was underway. The Cards scored seven times through the first five innings. All the while, the Tiger attack lay limp and lifeless. Things worsened in the sixth. An additional run for St. Louis scored, then another when the red hot Joe Medwick knocked in Pepper Martin with a triple. A nine-run lead loomed over Navin Field. Dark, insurmountable, impossible. The game and the Series was essentially over. The rough stuff, however, stayed a little while longer.

As Medwick headed for third, the relay throw flew behind, sliding hard, spikes high, taking no chances. Safe! Detroit third-baseman Marvin Owen figured if he couldn't beat St. Louis on the scoreboard then he would just simply beat them down. Owen took his spikes and slashed Medwick's chest, sending him sprawled to the ground. Fighting pain, fighting rage—rage won. Medwick leapt from the ground and kicked Owen full force in the knee. The two rolled around the dirt, trying unsuccessfully to beat the hell out of each other. Benches cleared. Umpire Bill Klem bravely stepped between and separated the brawlers. Order soon restored. Medwick, feeling friendly, extended a hand in reconciliation. Owen looked at Medwick's calloused palm, turned his back, and walked away.

Marvin Owen was not the only one irked. The boo birds echoed their disapproval around the stadium. As Medwick ran to his left field position at the bottom half of the inning, more boos reigned down, louder, this time sinister, evil. Clearly Medwick had become the target of the fans fury. "TAKE HIM OUT! TAKE HIM OUT!" they screamed. What they meant to say, "KILL HIM!" Curse words from the mouths of men and women alike landed on the back of Medwick. Then, whole apples, followed by bananas. Oranges came next. Finally, glass bottles, half empty with soda, milk and beer filled the outfield grass.[357] They were no longer a crowd of sports fans. They were now a mob. The game stopped. Cardinals' players grouped together, away from the flying objects, hoping to avoid bodily harm. Chaos ruled the day. Outnumbered, police stood idly by unable to intervene.

Scheduled to work the sixth inning on the CBS chain was Fran Laux. His quiet, low-key style perfectly suited the uneventful balls and strikes that remained. Once the melee broke, everything changed. Emotions ran askew. How could the Landis rules of no editorials apply? Someone had to say something relevant. A player, a spectator could get hurt, blood shed, or, worse, death. Laux didn't have the stomach for it. This was Husing country. He reintroduced the Master, took a deep breath and listened.

"This probably is the most unusual demonstration a man

has ever witnessed," Ted began. "After the little incident at third base when "Ducky Wucky" Medwick went out toward the left field bleachers, almost unabashed, there arose and very, very dangerously, started tossing pop bottles and these oranges. Then after a while, growing stronger and bolder, they came at a regular torrential flood until they flooded that left corner of the field. . ." [358]

A volatile scene continued to unfold. Camera men engulfed the combat area hoping for a prize-winning shot. Medwick and Dean clowned around, juggling fruit and playing shadow ball, anything to lighten the mood.[359] Instead they incited the wild crowd to a second round of abuse. Ted stayed focused, keeping up with the riot below, passion creeping into his voice. "Of course, the incident was reported to you when Joe "Ducky Wucky" Medwick picked up a full ripe orange and tossed it at the head of a brown-suited photographer, WHO STILL WILL NOT GET OFF THAT DIAMOND and is just tempting a punch in the jaw!"[360]

Would the game be forfeited? Could the army be deployed? No one had answers. But at least one member of the broadcast crew had opinions and was not keeping them to himself. Every rule Landis set shattered on the floor of the broadcast booth. Again the question begged, how far could Ted go? Instinct took over, inspired by revenge. If Ted was going out, he was exiting in perfect Husing style, his way.

"This unusual demonstration is certainly going down as a BLACK NOTE against the fans of Detroit. However, they have good cause, in one respect, for a little roughing that goes on during the game. But, after all, these men are playing for money. They are professional ballplayers They are out to give their best. They are taking no chances. . . . But at this point, we suddenly discover that the fans are entering into the ballgame's spirit because their $1.10 or $3.30 admits them to giving their spirit and feelings up on the afternoon air."[361]

Several minutes passed. Medwick slipped his glove on and

tried again to take the field. The worse abuse yet followed.

"And the bottles start again so help me Hanna," cried Ted. "And the crowd lets up a lusty roar. THEY WILL NOT LET JOE MEDWICK GO OUT INTO LEFT FIELD! And don't kid yourself that it" just one or two pop bottles or two or three oranges. It's a whole torrential Niagara. It's a flood that roars onto the diamond, an echo that will be heard around the world against the Detroit fans."[362] Ted wasn't kidding. And neither were the Tiger faithful in showing their disfavor of Medwick's perceived dirty play. Ted offered a weak disclaimer for his harsh words. "Not that I, in any sense, wish to editorialize regarding this, but, they have demonstrated . . . "[363]

Suddenly, manager Mickey Cochrane jogged from the Tiger dugout toward left field and pleaded for peace. "He's going to swing this entire demonstration," he declared. "He's asking the fans to let Joe Medwick play . . . I think that's the impression that you get, isn't it Fran, because that's certainly the impression I get."[364] Boos changed to cheers. Groundskeepers bagged the debris, making the field playable. But once Medwick took his position, a new layer of hate littered the outfield. The Commissioner, as last resort, intervened. There was only one way to get the game restored, give the people what they wanted. Landis ordered Cardinal skipper Frankie Frisch to remove Medwick from the field, for his own safety. Boos afresh crashed like cannons as Joe Medwick walked to the clubhouse under police guard. Satisfied, the fans allowed the action to resume. Five more pitchers took the mound for the Tigers before the damage ended. St. Louis included two more runs in the seventh, adding insult to injury. Final score, Cardinals 11, Tigers nothing.

The fan's outburst surprised everyone. Even the hometown players, who had fondly welcomed the support, were caught off guard by the mutiny in left field. "I don't know where they were getting all that stuff from," said Detroit second-baseman Charlie Gehringer. "It was like they were backing produce trucks up to the gate and supplying everybody."[365]

Ted had to know repercussions were forthcoming, but if he did, the man was on the fast track, too busy to care. After the game, Ted bolted for the steamy platforms of the Michigan Central Depot. He had a train to catch. He and Quailey were behind on their preparation for Saturday's Ohio State versus Illinois football broadcast.[366]

The Judge obviously had his own opinion of Ted's radio rhetoric. But, Landis did have a certain appreciation for descriptive language. Proof was given when he fined St. Louis catcher Bill Delancey fifty bucks for an outburst of curse words during Game 5. Umpire Bill Klem was leveled the same treatment for nasty remarks thrown at Tiger pitcher Goose Goslin in a hotel lobby. "He (Klem) followed the retreating and embarrassed Goslin in detail the length of the lobby, discussing his antecedents in langue that withered all the potted rubber plants and curled the paint of the room clerk's desk."[367] Landis was done with the 1934 World Series, for the moment, witnessing things he hoped never to see or hear again. But, it would be another year before the matter was officially closed. Left on the docket: how to discipline a certain radio announcer.

News spread throughout the summer of '35, off the record, and the rumor mill whispered that Ted would not return. Landis had enough of him, and McNamee for that matter. A strong suggestion came to CBS early in the season not to submit Husing for any baseball assignments.[368] That suggestion came from Leslie O'Connor, Landis' assistant. On July 27, a full three months before post-season began, *Washington Post* reporter Shirley Povich wrote, "If the Giants get into the World Series, Manager Bill Terry will go to the front for his friend Ted Husing, who is banned as a baseball broadcaster."[369] Yes, Husing, too, heard the stories of his perceptible downfall. But, the famous radioman believed cooler heads, strong allies, celebrity status, and tradition would prevail.

The 1935 baseball season played out with the Tigers and Cubs in the World Series. Once the pennants were clinched, Ted expected his traditional call from the Commissioner's Office. To him, the assignment was never in doubt. It was always a matter of not "if" but "when."

A week before Game 1, the lines of communications from the Commissioner's office were unusually quiet. In the past, Landis called a good two weeks before divvying out assignments and even asking Ted for logistical advice. He was hoping to be teamed up again with his favorite baseball voice Franz Laux from St. Louis. But he knew the chances were slim since the Cardinals didn't get in. It didn't matter who he got to mix it up with. Maybe his old chum Pat Flanagan might get the network nod. The fun of extracurricular activity was discussed with Quailey. "Book us our usual suites at the Plaza," he suggested to his friend. "When we get to Detroit, maybe we can jump across to Canada and see a hockey game."

But two days before the series there was still no word. The two partners, were busy preparing for the broadcast, pouring over old box scores and calling on connections in Detroit and Chicago. Finally, a knock on the door. There stood Paul White, head of the network news and sports division. A telegram dangled in his hand. On the top of the envelope was marked:

K.M. Landis, Office of Commissioner, Major League Baseball.

Ted eye-balled the letter and grabbed it from White. He then smoothly waved it at Quailey. "About time the old heel got his shit together." He unfolded one side and read it, his eyes passing quickly from left to right across the page.

Dear Mr. White:
Please find below my decision of radio broad-cast assignments for this year's World Series. Stop.
CBS—Fran Laux, Jack Graney, Truman Bradley.
MBS—Bob Elson, Hal Totten, Walter Barber.

NBC—Ty Tyson, Hal Totten, Boake Carter.[370]
Please contact your announcers. Rooms booked
at Statler. Meeting scheduled with me morning of
Game 1. Good Luck.
Hon. Kenesaw M. Landis
Commissioner of Organized Major League Baseball

Ted chuckled slightly as a broad, cynical smile moved onto his face. "Guess who got the boot again?" he asked Quailey, pushing the cable toward his friend. Smiles quickly turned to frowns. "Does Paley know about this?" Ted sternly asked Paul White. "Yes. Look Ted he tried," White replied, trying to sound sympathetic. "He really did. You know the way the old man is. He just doesn't want you." Paley tried to reason with Landis, even promising to have Ted self-censor the usual candid approach. Landis refused. "I want baseball men who know baseball on the microphone," he told Paley. "Ted's not a baseball man. He's trouble!" He also reminded Paley of Mc-Namee's scaled-down participation on NBC during the Series the last few years. Mac willingly did what Landis wanted, accepting his demotion with quiet dignity.[371] He slipped into the background, his voice scarcely heard anymore during baseball's crown jewel.

Ted would never stand for such an insult. "Fine, if the old fart doesn't want me at the ballpark, I can spend more time on campus," Ted reasoned. Football was more his style anyway. Yes, it's true that he witnessed some of the greatest moments in baseball history form his broadcast perch. Describing them with an indelible flair and lasting poetry was something else. Ted himself admitted that relating World Series action was a challenge beyond even his talents. "Covering the Series is radio's toughest sports job because you're talking to the world's largest expert audience," he shared with a writer. "They'll call you on every error you make, so you've got to be right and be right the first time."[372] For the first time in seven years, Ted would not call the Series for CBS, relegated to listening on the radio like the rest of America.

Indeed, for Ted the emphasis shone again on football. No more distractions, no more detours from the grid. Yet, anger ate at his soul in the fall of '35. The star had fallen. For Husing, shaking the World Series assignment, or lack of it, proved difficult. He never stopped having to prove himself. It brought him back to the old neighborhood, black eyes, bruised skin, German blood. What Ted needed was an epic gridiron battle, a fight for No. 1 to make him great again. He found it in two very special teams, one very close to his heart and a skirmish to the last second in a place they called The Horseshoe.

CHAPTER TWENTY

WAKE UP THE ECHOES

Cheer, cheer for old Notre Dame,
Wake up the echoes cheering her name,
Send a volley cheer on high,
Shake down the thunder from the sky.
What though the odds be great or small
Old Notre Dame will win over all,
While her loyal sons are marching
Onward to victory.[373]

Ted heard the song countless times, in his head, on the train, at parties, just before kickoff. But how the fight song played loud by a feisty marching band, sung by a group of hearty alum, inspired the boys it was meant for! How they ran! How they tackled! How they won for old Notre Dame! Playing in front of 50,000 South Bend home fans came easy, but what about the road? Could "Wake Up the Echoes" shake down the thunder against a new powerhouse football team from Columbus, Ohio, one who marched to the beat of a different drum?

Though Ohio State University could not brag of a National Championship, the Buckeyes also flaunted a proud football tradition of skilled players, rollicking fight songs, and an imposing 80,000-seat concrete stadium known as "The Horseshoe." But, in the end, disappointment always seemed to conquer them. No doubt the worst offense was falling to conference archrival Michigan for what seemed like every year. But in the season of 1934, bright, cloudless signs of changing fortunes finally came.

The press called it "razzle-dazzle." Long passes, double-, sometimes triple-reverses, and runningbacks lined up from something never seen before called the "I-formation."[374] When Ohio State hired Francis A. Schmidt as their new head coach, they thought they chose a serious, no-nonsense, God-fearing Kansan. But underneath his bow tie and straight-laced manner, lurked a madman, prone to fits of rage, four-letter words, spitting tobacco, and a wild imagination, especially on the offensive side of the football.[375] The Buckeyes literally ran, passed, and kicked their opponents ragged by scoring an astonishing 267 points his first year at the helm. They finished with a 7–1 record and second in the Big Ten, then known as the Western Conference, and topped it all off with a 34–0 shellacking of hated Michigan. "As for Michigan," he told reporters after the game. "Well, shucks, I guess we've learned they put their pants on one leg at time just like everybody else."[376]

Schmidt brought more than razzle-dazzle to Columbus, he brought attention. Ohio State football had arrived, finally. Fans talked of a Big Ten championship. Behind closed doors, they spoke of bigger accomplishments, a national title. But Schmidt remained guarded. He knew that to be the best, one must defeat the best. Beating Michigan was one thing. Taking down the great Notre Dame Fighting Irish was everything. Schmidt worked the phones and scheduled a home series beginning in 1935, with the Horseshoe to host the opener. Ohio State was about to find out if they were ready to be called the best college football team in the land.

The Buckeyes entered the '35 campaign brimming with confidence. They had a talent pool deep in all-Americans like Junior end Mike Wendt, Beefy lineman Charles Hamrick, all Big-ten center Gomer Jones, and the secret weapon, sensational sophomore half-back Joe Williams. On October 5, the season launched against Kentucky. The offense sputtered, but Ohio State managed a 19–6 win. The ensuing week, Schmidt dosed the razzle-dazzle in rocket fuel. The Buckeyes broke the scoreboard in a laugher against Drake, 85–7. Two tough conference games against Northwestern and Indiana followed with easy wins. Ohio State stood undefeated. Sportswriters and football pundits were already calling them #1.

The year Francis Schmidt ushered in a new age of football at OSU, Elmer Layden had taken the reigns at Notre Dame. The former Notre Dame star tailback felt compelled to return to his alma mater, ten years beyond his playing days and hoping to restore the Irish to greatness.[377] The Layden era started with a thud, losing a heartbreaker to Texas 7–6. Two midseason losses put the season in jeopardy. Yet the Irish rallied, finishing strong with impressive wins over Army and Southern Cal. Team supporters sensed good things right around the corner. "Next year, the title will be ours."

South Bend welcomed the 1935 football season with a win over the University of Kansas. Most talked glowingly of the impressive Irish offense, winning by three touchdowns. Wally Fromhart, Wayne Millner, and Vic Wojenhowski became the new fan favorites. Also among the talented squad was Bill Shakespeare, a slim, elusive H-Back not quite as well known, at least not yet. More victories came, topped off by an impressive 14–0 win over traditional foe Navy in Baltimore. Five opponents and five wins, on top, unbeaten, and untied. On a collision coarse came two teams without a blemish. Who was really #1? The answer was forthcoming on Saturday, November 2, at the Horseshoe.

Ted put in the miles, loving every minute. Nine, sometimes ten weeks a year, from late September to early December, he broadcast football on college campuses all over America: New Haven, Connecticut, Annapolis, Maryland, Champaign, Illinois, and Atlanta,

Georgia. Westward locations included Eugene, Oregon, and Palo Alto, California. No doubt, Ted enjoyed one school above the rest. Perhaps influenced by the late Knute Rockne, the big brother he never really had.

By the time Ted became a broadcast fixture on Saturday afternoons in fall, Rockne was already an icon. Notre Dame and national championships were synonymous. "Win one for the Gipper" had become the benchmark for pre-game pep, and the Four Horsemen hauntingly mythical as "The Legend of Sleepy Hallow." Rockne and his boyish thrill put football on the map. He was P.T. Barnum with a whistle and cleats. Ted had great respect for the innovative football mind. In turn, the coach recognized the growing reach of Husing's microphone. The two quickly bonded, and spoke often in season and off about formations, plays, and strategy. "He said to me, 'If I were broadcasting a football game, I'd watch the offensive line and the defensive backs. Then you'll know where the ball is going and whether the play works.' Every football game I ever broadcast was conditioned by that advice."[378]

At Notre Dame existed a visceral temperament, without question, the determined attitude of a small Catholic college in nowhere Indiana, never letting go, striving for excellence, enduring the pain, showing the world how to be goddamn tough season after season after season. One thing was expected when playing at Notre Dame—wins. Ted understood the ND mentality better than anyone. No one remembered who finished second.

Notre Dame and Ohio State were not the only perfect teams entering the first weekend of November, 1935. Army, Princeton, and USC were among the unblemished. Most seemed to forget that defending National Champions Minnesota, without a loss, sat atop the Western Conference standings tied with the Buckeyes. Ted Husing and his traveling microphone could have gone to any one of these settings. He wanted crisis, excitement, and a solid football contest, a backdrop that would milk what he called, "the annual autumnal madness."[379] There was only one place he wanted to be, Columbus, Ohio. However, the door to the Horseshoe's broadcast booth remained, for the moment, locked.

Securing broadcast locations for radio was a bit more involved. The Ohio Oil Company owned exclusive rights to the entire package of OSU home games. Each broadcast emanating across the state had Red Barber at the microphone, the same man who called the World Series a few weeks earlier. His southern sounds had been a kind fixture of Ohio sports the past two years calling football and baseball. But with a game of such magnitude, every network, CBS, NBC, and a new kid on the block, Mutual, wanted a piece of the action. That Monday they asked Ohio Oil to waive their contract. A respectful but definitive reply came back—*No!*

Ted chewed at the ear of his bosses to see if something could be done. "The game of the year and we can't do it!" he grumbled. "My farts don't stink as bad as that fetid deal." NBC joined to fight the power. The unit turned every rock, making calls to New York, Chicago, Columbus, and even the headquarters of the stubborn petroleum company in Findlay, Ohio. By Thursday, sufficient pressure had been applied and Ohio Oil relented. The networks scrambled to dispatch announcers. Mutual looked no further than plugging into Barber's broadcast. Late Friday morning, Ted, Les Quailey, and the Annunciator boarded a plane for Columbus.

The usual week of preparation was obviously altered. Viewing the team's Friday practice would likely be scratched. Fortunately, Ted knew the squads fairly well, and concluded that Buckeye PR man Jim Rennick or a coach would help with spotting boards once they got settled. Delays finally landed the CBS crew as night began to close on Columbus. No one was available from the university to help. The teams were holed up in an undisclosed location and Rennick was too busy. Ted got agitated. They needed to finish their homework. A solid broadcast depended on it. He grabbed the phone and called. "Well, Goddamnit Jim! We come all the way out here to put you guys on the network and can't get a little cooperation. I'd say that's pretty insolent don't you?" Rennick tried to pacify Ted to no avail. " . . . I don't fucking care who it is, Jim. Just send somebody up here, please."

Rennick knew just the guy, Red Barber! He tracked the young announcer down at the Deschler-Wallick Hotel hobnobbing at the pre-game press smoker. He entreated Red to lend a hand for the CBS crew. He was happy to oblige, any excuse to meet the famous Ted Husing. He raced up the elevator and knocked on the door. Quailey greeted him cordially and thanked him for coming. Over near a table sat Ted sipping a drink and pulling nervously at a rubber band. He again showed the teeth of a bad mood. "He was mad that only a kid announcer had showed up," Barber surmised. "He barely grunted when Quailey introduced us. He didn't get out of his chair."[380] As Ted sulked, he studied the stranger. He tried to think of where he knew this Barber fellow.

Like a lightening bolt, it hit him—The World Series. He heard the young man's voice on the Mutual chain just last month calling baseball. Ted's bruised ego found new life. Thoughts of the hated commissioner fueled an existing anger. Landis dumped experienced announcers like himself and for a mere rookie? Ted became nasty and belligerent. As Barber tried to answer Quailey's roster questions, Ted cut in retorting as some immature school student trying to impress the teacher. Red had seen enough. "Husing was not only rude and overbearing, he was also profane . . . dirty profane. I didn't take much of that. I got up and left."[381]

Quailey ran down the hall after him. "Hey, Barber, don't think anything about Ted. That's the way he gets sometimes. I need the dope on the squad. I've got to run the players' charts—not Ted. Be a good guy and let me come to your room, will you?"[382] Barber agreed. A few minutes later, NBC mike man Bill Slater came panting at Barber's door. He, too, was desperate for help with his player charts and spotting boards. The three worked into the night. Ted retreated downstairs to the press smoker in complete trust of Quailey and hoping to pick up a few game tidbits of his own.

The next day, whatever demon was eating at Ted had been expelled. He entered the booth excited and prepared. Ted looked out the window over the swaying multitude scurrying up and down aisles, flags briskly flapping along the top rows, the way heat rolls off a stretch of burning asphalt. The crowded press box found room for two more announcers, Tom Mannning, calling the action on Cleveland station WTAM, and a thin 25-year-old Detroit son named Jim Britt.[383] His voice would be piped into South Bend, Indiana, on local station WSND.[384] Again, Ohio Stadium broke records. Better than 81,000 sat in the big Horseshoe. Counterfeiters pawned off some 2,000 fake tickets. Scalpers sold forty-dollar seats to gain entrance, an insane amount of money in such cash-strapped times.

The Horseshoe transformed into an insane asylum. Bands of students blared trumpets and crashed cymbals. Bookies offered 7–5 odds in favor of Ohio State. Most agreed. They had home field advantage and an unstoppable offense. With a sea of red, and not a friend in sight, Coach Layden consented and played the underdog role well, "We hope to hold the score to 40 points,"[385] he told a reporter before the game.

The gladiators of Notre Dame entered the arena first to a chorus of boos. "GO HOME CATHOLICS!" yapped several OSU fanatics.[386] The clock on the radio booth wall read 1:59 PM. Quailey sat at his usual place, lost in concentration. Annunciator lit, the microphone wide-opened. Sound exploded and an unmistakable voice hit the air. "Good afternoon everyone, this is Ted Husing coming to you from Ohio Stadium in Columbus, Ohio. And if you have been without newspaper or radio this entire week then you are in for what should be the football clash of the year . . ." Ted continued with the opening, as he had countless times before, setting the scene, giving the starting line-ups and key match-ups. From the first snap, it was clear to Ted and anyone else watching, that the Irish left one small arsenal of their game plan behind in the locker room—the will to fight.

The Buckeyes came roaring from the tunnel and never seemed to stop. The defense brought the Horseshoe to its feet first. The battle, three minutes old, Ohio State defensive-back Frankie Antenucci intercepted an errant pass by Elmer Layden's younger brother Mike Layden. Antenucci saw daylight and headed up field gaining ten yards before opposing players closed to make the tackle. Instinct took over and he flipped the ball back to teammate Frank Boucher who bolted down the sidelines sixty-five more yards for a score. "Thundering down the sideline like a crimson red thoroughbred. He's got two men to beat," said Ted keeping up with Boucher's every step. " . . . at the ten, five . . . Touchdown! . . . Wow! We should have known a little deception could happen even on the defensive side for the Buckeyes." Dicky Beltz drop-kicked the ball through for the extra point. Ohio State 7, Notre Dame 0.

The first quarter clock had ticked down when the Buckeye defense struck again. Heavy pressure forced young Bill Shakespeare to throw to the wrong color jersey again. Fired up, Ohio State took over at midfield. Blockers Hamrick, Karcher, and the big boys, Merle Wendt and Gomer Jones, a combined one-ton bulldozer, pushed Notre Dame's front line all over the field. The four blasted holes large enough for a freight truck convoy to drive through. Antenucci and Boucher, doing double duty, carried most of the load. The second quarter started with the Buckeyes at the three-yard line banging on the door. Next play entered the secret weapon, Joe Williams, who shot through the right side into the endzone untouched. The crowd rang out in song, hugging, laughing, jumping. Ohio State led by a healthy 13–0 margin.

Notre Dame accomplished very little. The Buckeye rushed for nine first downs. Their first half-ground attack, in complete control, more than doubled the inept Irish 118 yards to sixty. "Notre Dame simply did not have the physical power to stand up against such Herculean strength," said the *New York Times*.[387] Schmidt and his high-powered offense had yet to crank it up. The rout looked to be on. The referee's gun sounded. Intermission came. The Irish walked off dejected, confused, lifeless. The lead seemed insurmountable. Sounds of glee ricocheted off every building in the city limits. Ted's reporting implied that the football battle, built up with such eagerness and anticipation, was finished by the half. "And ladies and gentleman this game looks all but over for a limp and unresponsive Notre Dame team. Coach Francis Schmidt and the Ohio State faithful are smiling now."

During the first two quarters, Ted tried to provoke Notre Dame into making a game of it. On more than one occasion, he described the Irish play in the first half as that of a "high school team." Like any good sports reporter, Ted wanted one thing, a good game. With a closeknit, back-and-forth contest stewed the boiling ingredients of a better broadcast. No one understood that better than he. If the game turned into a lopsided affair, Ted had no intention of describing the surrounding Columbus skyline or the fall Ohio foliage on campus. Ted wanted to talk football. And he hoped the second half would bring better opportunities for such eloquence.

With nothing to lose, coach Layden decided to mix things up by starting his second line unit. Fresh bodies, he figured; and, if needed, the first stringers could rest. "They won the first half," Layden told his players. "Now it's your turn. Go out and win this half for yourselves."[388]

Senior running back Andy Pilney began the third quarter at quarterback for the Irish, tag teaming with Mike Layden as signal caller. The move added a spark to the sluggish offense. Drives began. First downs mounted. And the Ohio State front line started to bend, tiring as the afternoon wore on. But, the Buckeye "D" proved tough, forcing Notre Dame back into a familiar situation—punt. Bill Shakespeare's deep kicks never gave Schmidt's "razzle-dazzle" much room to maneuver, forcing the Buckeyes to do some punting of their own. It looked to be Ohio State's day when Wojenhowski fumbled deep in Buckeye territory, squandering Notre Dame's best opportunity for points. Things were shifting down on the field of play. The scoreboard, however, stayed the same. Ohio State 13, ND 0.

Third quarter action was about to pass into the fourth and final frame. Four seconds remained. Pilney dropped deep, awaiting another Ohio State punt at midfield. The tight end-over-end kick landed softly in his brawny arms. Cut right, cut left. The crowd rose to their feet, eager, nervous, excited. Pilney zig-zagged through the Buckeye pursuit before being tackled at the nineteen-yard line. It was the biggest gain of the day for Notre Dame. Pilney's legs brought the Irish closer to a much-needed score. His arm did the rest, gunning a seventeen-yard bullet to Francis Gaul then handing off to Steve Miller for a two-yard dive into the end zone. "Touchdown, Notre Dame," Ted declared with a firm voice. "They have broken the Ohio State stranglehold and may make a game of this yet." But Ken Stilley's PAT hit the cross bar and bounced wide. "No good," Ted told the radio millions.

For the next few possessions, defense told the story as Ohio State clung to a 13–6 advantage. Ted's voice pounded back and forth as one big tackle begot another. With five and a half minutes left in the game, Quailey rubbed his eyes and looked over at the clock. This one was about finished. Wait. Notre Dame had the ball and pushed for significant yardage, one first down then another then another. Standing at the one, Pilney pitched the ball to his fullback Miller for what looked like an easy six points. Jim Karcher from behind stripped Miller of the ball and recovered it for a harmless touchback. Another great stop for Ohio State. Another turnover for the Irish. Another opportunity for victory lost. The Horseshoe, drenched in sweat, mopped its collective brow and the party of 81,031 fans continued.

Notre Dame hunkered down, trying anything to get the ball back. They grabbed, lunged, even punched—all for a lost cause. The Buckeyes, tired, would not succumb to the pressure and held on for dear life. Their approach remained predictably conservative. The main strategy, eat the clock. "Cross-buck play, Beltz again smashes into the line and is slapped down hard by the Irish front line. And if Beltz gained a yard on that play, he was lucky. It'll be fourth down and a likely punt on the way . . ." Just under three minutes remained. New life found the men in blue and gold jerseys on their next possession, digging deep into the chilly Ohio Stadium field. Elmer Layden threw caution to the wind, time no longer an ally. It was the ideal occasion to pass.

From the twenty-one-yard line, the Ohio State goal line appeared distant. Mike Layden, back at quarterback, connected perfectly with Wally Fromhart and Andy Pilney on bombs. Bang. Suddenly, from the fifteen-yard line, the Ohio State goal line looked fat and attainable. The Buckeye "D" shuffled about, hearts racing, looking for oxygen. The voice of Husing percolated, in the zone, anticipating the action before it happened. Here, the now, Ted was at his best. What once resembled a blowout turned desperate. The stadium clock ticked down: 2:06, 2:05, 2:04 . . . The next play, Pilney returned to the passing position and found Layden on a corner rout for six more points. "Touchdown!" yelled Ted to the radio listeners. "These resilient players of Notre Dame have reminded everyone that this contest is not over yet. Oh, boy, let me say, ladies and gentlemen, these Ohio State fans have become awfully quiet compared to the ruckus we heard only an hour or so ago." Miracle of miracles! Dead one minute, ND lined up at the two-yard line to tie the game.

Schmidt fumed on the sidelines, chain smoking, screaming four- and thirteen-letter expletives rarely heard, disgusted with his crumbling defense. He yanked several starters and installed new bodies hoping to block the extra point. Wally Fromhart, in relief of Stilley, dropped back to attempt the kick for Notre Dame. The Ohio State defense jawed at full volume and waved their arms, trying anything to draw a penalty. The crowd rose once again. HIKE! The ball snapped high pulling Fromhart from his mark. All eleven Buckeyes stormed the line. Fromhart panicked. His foot slipped trying desperately to get the kick away. THUMP! The ball angled three yards into a wall of red jerseys and caromed away. "NO GOOD!" said Ted, this time his voice breaking with rare emotion.

The city of Columbus exhaled with relief. It was Pilney's second touchdown pass of the half. He had played well, all for naught. Ohio State dodged the bullet. Ted continued regaining his composer. "Dicky Beltz's point after touchdown way back in the first quarter of action is looming ever larger now, the only difference that appears to be the winner for the Bucks." Notre Dame trailed by a single point 13–12 and needed a miracle to win. Only one weapon remained. The two kickoff teams lined up knowing what was coming next, Notre Dame's only chance, an onside kick. The ball squabbled the necessary ten yards falling gingerly in the waiting arms of Charles Gales for OSU. Seventy-five seconds hung on the game clock. One man dressed in soiled blue and gold stayed on the field believing. Andy Pilney wiggled his fingers, barked hellish instructions to his mates and zeroed in on the ball.

Quarterback Stan Pincura handed the pill to Dick Beltz who ran wide for OSU trying to kill the precious seconds left in the match. He looked up field for the first down markers. Pilney darted parallel to the running back, possessed, mad, hungry for contact. The senior cut off the angle and hit Beltz with a bone-crunching tackle. Screams of "FUMBLE" were unleashed on both benches. Ted said the same thing, the word shrieking throughout the broadcast booth. "Fumble! The ball is loose!" The football glanced off the hands of nose-tackle Hank Pojam before rolling out of bounds. Possession was awarded to Notre Dame near mid-field. The Ohio State faithful covered their heads in shame. A loss was not possible. The cries of "GO HOME, CATHOLICS" were replaced by "PLEASE GOD, PLEASE."

Ted's play-by-play kicked up a notch. A shot of adrenaline got the booth buzzing once more. Ted leaned hard into the mike, his lips kissing the electric steel. Quailey punched at the Annunciator trying to keep up with the frantic changes. Fear ruled Ohio State. Could they stop the rising, chocking tide? For the Irish the goal was easy, score in a hurry. Pilney, the one-man wrecking crew soldiered on with lethal force. Back to pass, he looked for an open receiver, every friendly face covered. The quarterback tucked the ball under his arm and ran as hard as he could for pay dirt. Jumping, slipping, juking would-be tacklers, Pilney made it to the Ohio State nineteen before being driven out of bounds. A loud pop echoed off the pile of bodies. The play was over, but the senior could not get up. Ligaments torn, ripped, and dangled, left his knee unmovable. The contest came to a stretching halt. Exhausted fans, depleted players, and unraveled broadcasters took a deep breath. Fifteen minutes passed. A medical crew busily worked Pilney's damaged leg, poking, prodding, setting . . . and did the only human thing possible. They carted him off the field on an army stretcher. Bill Shakespeare, from the bench, listened for the play from his coach, nodded and sprinted back on the field.

When play resumed, a spent Mike Layden was back at QB. Forty ticks remained. With Ohio State still weak in the secondary, big brother Layden continued the passing attack. Little brother Mike cocked his arm and saw Shakespeare open in the end zone. Who he failed to see was Dick Beltz roaming the precious territory for Ohio State. Layden's tired arm gave witness. The ball fell woefully short of Shakespeare and into the waiting hands of Beltz. Amazingly, the football slipped through Beltz's hands, bounded off his thin shoulderpads and fell to the ground incomplete. Ted cried out in utter disdain, giggling half-way through his opinion, trying to make sense of the madness. "Unbelievable! The sun just refuses to shine advantageously in this fourth quarter for the Bucks . . . Aaaaaaa—all the breaks leaning toward the men from South Bend, Indiana!"

Mike Layden was clearly done for the day. Fatigue cast him in the role of decoy. Running out of skill players, coach Layden looked to reserve QB Jim McKenna to pull out a miracle, if any more existed. McKenna was not scheduled to make the road trip, oddly enough. He was left off the traveling squad, nursing an injury sustained in practice. Yet, big games call for bold moves. He snuck onto the train Thursday night and hid in a teammate's berth.[389] Confusion rocked the press box. No one could identify the fresh pair of legs. Quailey tore through his notes trying to find a name. Nothing. Suddenly, Les remembered what Red Barber had told him on Friday night about McKenna. "I knew the Ohio State squad and I knew the Notre Dame squad," recalled Barber. "I was never so ready for a game in my life."[390] Thanks to Barber, the mystery man was identified. Husing introduced him to the audience, setting the frenzied situation. His words boiled with anticipation.

The new quarterback appeared rusty. Timid strides brought him to the Notre Dame huddle. His teammates spanked his buttock, slapped his back, building confidence, wondering if Coach Layden had brought them the right man, the correct winning play. "Expect another pass from the Irish," Ted warned his audience. "Ohio State on their heels, vulnerable to the aerial assault this entire fourth quarter." McKenna took the snap and tripped, moving away from pursuit. Ted stayed with the play, "McKenna back to pass, flushed out of the pocket . . ." Somehow he kept on his feet and pitched the ball to tailback Billy Shakespeare. "He flips the ball to his tailback. It's Shakespeare now with the ball . . ." Ohio State bruiser Chuck Hamrick was closing in for the game-saving tackle. Shakespeare shut his eyes and heaved the ball down field. Streaking across the goal line was Wayne Millner, open for an instant. The ball struck his hands in stride just out of the lunging reach of the unluckiest man on the field, Dick Beltz. Millner slipped across the endzone clenching the ball. Ted's voice exploded, "The ball is CAUGHT by Wayne Millner in the endzone for a TOUCHDOWN! It's a Touchdown, Notre Dame!"

Ted stopped talking. Silence filled the Horseshoe. The stunned Buckeye faithful could not speak. No cheers, no boos, no words could form in their mouths. Thousands gazed up on the stadium scoreboard, trying to convince themselves that what they saw was a mirage. Ted looked over at the scoreboard with them and spoke once again. "The craziest play you will ever see, fans . . . Notre Dame, once thought for dead, has come all the way back, and now leads by five with some thirty-one seconds remaining." The Irish bench rushed toward their heroes, Shakespeare, Millner, and the new guy McKenna pummeling them with congratulations. The real hero Andy Pilney lay on his back near the clubhouse doorway, half conscious, fully aware of Millner's go-ahead touchdown. The rest stood in shocked silence. Again, Notre Dame missed the extra point, but it did not matter. The impossible had happened. The Fighting Irish led for the first time. Only seconds were left on the clock. Could there be time for one more miracle, this time for Ohio State?

The secret weapon, Joe Williams dropped deep hoping for a big return. Notre Dame would have none of it. Instead, the safer squib kick dribbled up near the thirty-five-yard-line. Precious seconds disappeared. Buckeye Lineman Gus Zarnas secured the ball with his wide body, stopping the clock. Time allowed one maybe two plays for a near comatose offense. Ohio State had gained only one first down and zero points during the entire second half compared to nine for the Irish, three unanswered scores and the most important feature—the lead. Schmidt looked to showcase "razzle-dazzle" one last desperate time.

Pincura faded eight, ten, then twelve yards behind the line of scrimmage, pumping the ball hard. His receivers sprinted up field in search of an opening. Five defenders rushed the passer, breaking a feeble wall of resistance. Ted thundered into the final stanza of play-by-play. "Snowed under by a swarm of blue shirts at the thirty-two-yard line. . . Pincura trying to hurry . . . And this– one– is– over! It is over! The final score: Notre Dame 18, Ohio State 13!" Ted stopped momentarily to fill his empty lungs. Quailey continued to work feverishly on final statistics. "Swooh! . . . I must admit, ladies and gentlemen, that I have never been so weak in my life . . . In a most improbable game, a football contest that would make the immortal Charles Dickens proud, this truly was 'a tale of two halves.' The Buckeyes of Ohio State controlling the first two periods, could do no wrong. The last and most important two quarters belonged to the University of Notre Dame Ramblers who came alive due in large part to the sensational play of one Andy Pilney. All-World this afternoon and perhaps All-American by year's end."

Notre Dame ran for the locker room in giddy triumph. The handful of Irish fans in attendance stormed the field. No one tried to stop them. Uprooting the goalpost at the open end of the Horseshoe, the happy mob carried off a souvenir to celebrate into the night. Newspapermen rushed the winners' dressing room to begin writing their stories. "In the annals of gridiron lore are countless tales of famous rallies," began Wilfrid Smith of the *Chicago Tribune*. "But, no Notre Dame team ever has written a more brilliant page in football's history than these boys today."[391] Grantland Rice, the man who witnessed more games, more heroics than anyone present gazed in awe at Andy Pilney and said to the dazed athlete, "Andy, I've been writing and watching football for over forty years now and that is the greatest single performance I've ever seen."[392] The losers had a much different outlook. "It was probably the greatest football show I ever saw," Francis Schmidt told reporters. "And it was just our misfortune to be on the losing end. My heart is broken. The boy who fumbled can't be blamed. Every back fumbles at some time or other and this one just happened at the wrong time."[393]

No one believed what they had seen. Others could not believe what they had heard emanating from their radios. Chicago broadcast luminary Jack Brickhouse remembered the game with fond distinction. "I will never forget the end of the 1935 Ohio State–Notre Dame with Husing doing the play-by-play. Husing's description of the finish is absolute must-listening for any aspiring broadcast student."[394] Legendary sports columnist Jim Murray also harked back listening to Ted's call. "It was a funny thing, but you remembered a game Husing broadcast better than a game you saw in person. He made a Notre Dame–Ohio State game the most famous football match of a generation at once by the quality of his description."[395]

Also listening to Ted's broadcast was a young Curt Gowdy. A then wide-eyed sixteen -year-old, Curt was especially thrilled. He lived in Wyoming, but cheered hard for the Fighting Irish. "The greatest game on radio I ever heard was the Notre Dame versus Ohio State game of 1935. I was at Cheyenne High School and I was handling the chains at the Cheyenne versus Douglas High game. Ohio State was leading 13–0 going into the fourth quarter. I paid a kid a quarter to continue to do my job on the sideline. I went in a car and listened to the last part of that game. It was the greatest, most memorable radio broadcast I ever heard."[396]

Ted did not have time to relish in his accomplishments. He boarded a train. First stop Pittsburgh, then Philadelphia, and finally New York City. He would be home only for a while. A National Championship may have ended for the Buckeyes of Ohio State. But, for America's top football voice, the season was far from over. Ted Husing and the Columbia Broadcasting System would again be on the air from some lucky college grounds, capturing the rollicking sounds of the "the annual autumnal madness." Before then, there was much to do—study dictionaries, secure broadcast rites, and prepare the Annunciator for four more quarters of flashing lights.

CHAPTER TWENTY-ONE

THE PRICE TO PAY

S pace was a constant issue, room to maneuver limited. At times it seemed 485 Madison was simply inadequate. "The urinals stank, the toilets hardly flushed, and there was no air-conditioning," remembered former president Frank Stanton.[397] Worst of all, the only live audience studio, Studio One, was located on the twenty-second floor. The network rented additional studio space throughout the city. Compared to NBC, Columbia was operating on bare bones. There were whispers of a new CBS broadcast center, but plans never materialized during the tough economy. The little network that could pushed forward, always under the shadow of NBC and its brand new state of the art facilities at Rockefeller Center offices and studios topped off by Radio City Music Hall, a palace representing the grandeur of live radio. "You had to be pretty stupid not to be impressed with the seventy stories of the RCA Building," laughed Stanton. "But, what counted as far as we were concerned was what came over the air not where it came from."[398]

During radio's golden age, the real money came from advertisers. Ted's first ten years in the business, he played it safe, choosing to keep his options open. Several announcers grabbed the big payday instead of honing their skills. Ted stuck to his guns, waiting patiently, digging trenches as the company man while building an impeccable reputation doing everything. "I had seasoning and experience that no other announcer could compete with and I'd finally built up a name that was worth something."[399] By 1934, all bets were off. To the highest bidder came a new commercial spokesman. White Owl Cigars offered him a bucket of cash and plenty of smokes to introduce Guy Lombardo and his friends to the listening audience. Camel cigarettes kept the habit stocked sponsoring "Ted Husing's Sports Caravan."

The network gave eccentric singer Ruth Etting her own show starting in February of 1934. Oldsmobile flitted the bill and paid Ted to be the show's spokesman. It all went back to his days with Whiteman, talking up the sponsor while playfully engaging the show's star, seamless, commanding, and smooth. In between, Paramount Pictures hired him to narrate their show biz movie shorts, chronicling the latest on Broadway and in Hollywood. The schedule was tough, but Ted did not object. More fame, media hype, and practically doubling his take-home pay. "I never dicker or bargain," he admitted to a reporter. "I state my price and get it, or else."[400]

Negotiating took a special skill, one Ted did not readily have, tip toeing around with small talk while holding the hard line. Ted needed help. Once again, he followed his instincts and relied on someone from the old neighborhood. Someone he could trust. Before the likes of smooth chatting "super agents" like Michael Ovitz there was the cantankerous yet bewitching Mark Hanna. Ernest Lehman, Oscar winning screen writer and author of *The Sweet Smell of Success*, once described him as, "A saturnine, silver-haired, elegantly dressed man who was so much more colorful than any of the make-believe figures I was trying to turn into a writing career that I wonder why I never attempted even once to 'use' him as a character in a short story."[401] A one-time sales representative living in exotic Shanghai, China, his clients included writers Ring Lardner and John O'Hara, actors Douglas Fairbanks Sr., and Helen Hayes, plus musician Benny Goodman.

Hanna helped Ted ink lucrative endorsement deals with Seagram's, Goodrich Tires, and Chrysler. During the late 1930s, Ted pushed the automobile makers' luxury gem, the Desoto, into prominence with countless magazine and billboard ads. Pictures were nice, words, however, were immortal. "I never signed a document without Mark's approval," said Husing. "He was my guardian angel."[402] To help protect his earnings, Ted also began his relationship with long-time attorney Harry H. Oshrin. To top it off, the broadcaster hired his own chauffer, a man called Fereschi. Strong build and wrinkled face, Fereschi became his jack of all trades, running errands, making pick-ups and drop offs, and playing the role of muscle, in case Ted got into trouble.

As always, Ted went for the best in everything. The best clothes, the best representatives, and the best schools for his daughter. Ted and Helen decided to send Pegge away for schooling at Friends Academy on Long Island. The Quaker institution provided all the amenities a wealthy radio announcer could want for his child, discipline, room and board, plus a top-shelf education. Above anything, it provided an isolated environment, away from marital problems and intrusive members of the press. Ted knew of the private school through friend and star bandleader Tommy Dorsey, who's daughter Patricia attended Friends.[403] Both girls were born only days apart. The classmates bonded quickly, sharing the trials and tribulations of an atypical existence.

In 1935, Hanna parlayed his client into the book world. Publishing brothers Stanley and Fredrick Rinehart with partner John Farrar wanted to cash in on Ted's insatiable popularity. Issued in November of that year was the broadcaster's autobiography *Ten Years Before the Mike*. The book moved well on the day's best-seller list. The author was no F. Scott Fitzgerald, and never claimed to be. But, Ted had always been a fan of the lucid and respected writers. He was proud to place himself in such literary company, even if it was his own cheesy story. *Ten Years Before the Mike* was loaded with what both reader and listener came to expect from Ted, candid opinion and scratchy humor. The inside sleeve read, "Ted Husing tells very nearly all." He saw the book as another tool to place his soul on the treasured consciousness of history. "I didn't know whether I could write a book successfully or not," he divulged. "But, I figured I could talk and I ought to be able to get talk on paper. It turned out to be a cinch."[404]

Most critics and literary insiders took the author's assessment of himself in typical Husing stride. His pompous, acerbic yet riveting on-air style translated perfectly to the page. The *New York Times* endorsed Ted's written prose as a must read. "Mr. Husing is known especially as a sports announcer, and he gives a good deal of space to the beginnings and developments of this factor of broadcasting . . . But, he has done many other kinds of work also and his book overflows with stories of them, inside stories that are cynical, amusing, slangy, replete with all that happens in the world behind the mike."[405] The broadcaster did have his detractors nonetheless. Other reviews weren't so glowing. "There is altogether too much of dames and janes and hubbies and socks-in-pusses. Altogether too much Husing,"[406] wrote the *Boston Transcript*. Ted's former bosses at the newspaper perhaps knew the real Ted Husing all too well. However, in the end, they wrote that the $2.50 investment to buy his book was worth it. "Ted Husing is obviously fond of himself as well as being, in his own words, 'one of the most garrulous guys in America.' Yet, it is worth overlooking these irritating flaws for the sake of some of these recollections."[407]

On air, Ted was being mimicked endlessly. If it worked for him it had to work for others. "A lot of people who came along later imitated Husing," said Ernie Harwell. "Very smooth, very sophisticated voice."[408] In the world of sports announcing, everyone wanted to sound like Ted Husing. Dozens tried, most failed. One fall afternoon of 1934, Ted heard a voice from Texas on the radio vaguely familiar. The play-by-play was coarse and inconsistent. However, something about the young man's sound and temperament made him listen still. The announcer's resonating voice, talkative yet demonstrative style reminded the network star of another caller of football—Ted Husing. The voice belonged to Byrum Saam. Ted blushed with delight. He knew his power and grace were setting new standards in the industry. Finally, from the far-off Lone Star state came physical proof.

Ted tracked Saam down and called him at his Forth Worth home with praise. "Had the nearest thing in voice quality and technique to Ted Husing I ever heard,"[409] flattered Chris Schenkel about his friend Saam. Ted and Quailey soon persuaded contacts on Saam's behalf. It would kick-start an illustrious thirty-three-year career as voice of Philadelphia sports from 1937–70, Phillies and Athletics baseball, two World Series on radio, college football galore, and Wilt Chamberlain's 100-point game in Hershey, just to name some of his more noted highlights. Saam's younger brother Robert recalled what Husing's guidance meant. "My brother was really very influenced by his call and the connection and the interest. I just remembered because my mother was so impressed. He was very moved by that whole thing."

For some in the field of sports announcing, the Husing influence was not immediately felt. Four decades after Husing burst onto the dial, the name Howard Cosell stirred the emotions and raised the blood pressure of anyone who owned a television set from the height of Vietnam to the dawn of Reagan-omics. His presence at sporting events oftentimes was the event. The legend and influence of Cosell as a sports broadcaster only underscores the greatness of Husing. Anything that Howard accomplished, Husing did first. "The sound of their voices was very different and Husing would have sneered at Cosell's bombast," wrote *Sports Illustrated* critic William Taaffe. "In other respects, however, Cosell seemed to be his alter ego."[410]

Both men were loud, magnetic, pompous, controversial,

and used a mike-side verbiage that confused the most intelligent viewer. Yet in a world years apart, big enough to share these two giant personalities, there was only one Ted Husing. "Doing sports games he had used three-syllable words when everyone said "spit" he'd say "expectorate" or something like that," remembered Goff Lebhar, son of New York sports announcer Bert Lee. "He was way before Cosell in using the English language." ABC Sports legend Keith Jackson worked on the same network with Cosell. He grew up listening to the yarns spun by the Master. "Husing was wonderful at creating phrases," shared Jackson. "He was—how should I say this and be gracious about it—he was a calmer Cosell. He loved the English language, as Howard obviously did, and he used it very artfully."[411] Cosell himself called Ted "incomparable."[412] But perhaps Curt Gowdy put the whole assessment of the two in perspective when he quipped. "Yeah, there are similarities between them. But, Ted wasn't always investigating you like Howard."[413]

His influence in the industry was clear, obvious and multidimensional. Ted adored radio work. It was never a spitefull job, painfully watching the clock until quitting time. It was fun, creative, and the ultimate platform to prove himself.[414] To his wife and daughter, perhaps his two biggest fans, the "Husing influence" never seemed to have the same effect. His love affair with a live microphone, with things other than them, hurt. Pegge was now ten years old. Where had the years gone? Ted could not explain. The father wished to be around to see his daughter grow, share an intimate dinner with his wife. But, there was always something—work. And then work again. Sand trickled through the hourglass. He had turned it over several times, but never seemed to sit long enough to watch the grains drop peacefully to the other side. He always told himself there would be plenty of time. Time to prepare for the next broadcast. Time to catch the next train. Time to visit 21 or the Stork. Time to catch Graham McNamee. Time for everything, except her.

CHAPTER TWENTY-TWO

THE MICKEY MOUSE MUSICIAN

The minute Ted walked through the door Helen noticed something different about him.

"Where is your hat?" she asked.

The question caught him by surprise. A trapping sense of guilt slurped at his veins, a kid caught with his hand in the cookie jar. He couldn't speak a word. Instead, a nervous smile and breathless chuckle answered his wife's query. His sullen brown eyes darted from side to side. Perhaps the fedora was at the club or maybe in the cab he just paid. He could always get another hat. But, could he ever find another woman like Helen? Among hundreds, a lone question bounced around his conflicting head. Is this what he wanted, to leave the woman he loved? His left arm, his right leg, his life meant nothing without her.

The words spilled from his mouth, stinging like citrus to the eye.

"I'm no good, baby. You deserve better than a half-minded husband like me," he said. "I want a divorce!" He corrected himself. "I mean, I want to give you a divorce."

Ted felt uncomfortable, a stranger in his own home. He reached for his cigarettes trying to make himself feel better and realized they weren't there. They, too, like the fedora hat, lost in the confusion. Helen sat stunned. She felt relieved. She felt hurt. She was content—finally. She tried to remind herself that this was not one of his broadcasts, but their marriage that he was talking about. She wondered why he didn't fight to stay. But, she knew better.

"We stood facing each other and examining each other as if this were the first time we had ever met," Husing said later. "As if all those wondrous nights had never happened when we clung to each other rapturously in a warm bed of love, or watched snow fall past the window and laughed away the hours until dawn."[415]

Whatever was left, they agreed to settle later, alimony, bank accounts, and child support. Divorce—the word seemed foreign. It sounded so final, so wrong. Ted went in to gaze upon his young daughter sleeping the night away. He kissed her goodbye. Pegge did not stir; sound asleep in a world of innocence. Ted Husing, however, was heavy with feelings of remorse, fully aware of why his marriage had crumbled. [416]

Ted closed the apartment door and retreated downstairs. Outside the Century, standing on the street, a revolution tore at his mind: the memory of a ten-year marriage, the fights, the make-ups, cuddling his daughter, making love, the countless pep-talks by a Cherokee-blooded dove who told him if radio is what he wanted than show them the best.

"Oh, God! What have I done?" Ted whispered. "Help me, please."

Praying was not something he was used to. But, Ted was desperate. The inner monologue of contradictions continued. He tried to gain control.

"You've made the right decision. It's over," he told himself. "Now be a man and move on!"

But it was all too much. A tidal wave of emotions tackled him. He buried his face in his hands and cried for the first time since the birth of Pegge. His tearful sobs echoed off the building and against the trees of Central Park. Rage filled him simultaneously, kicking the side of the building with his shoe, cursing. "God Dammit! God Fucking Dammit!"

Suddenly, seemingly from everywhere and yet nowhere, a kind voice spoke slowly from the madness,

"Looks like another storm doesn't it?"

It was a sound vaguely familiar, one with equal parts of compassion and firmness. Ted was startled.

"What did you say?" Ted asked without facing the sound.

"I said it looks like another storm." Ted remained frozen with his head bowed down. "Mr. Husing. Mr. Husing, everything all right there?"

Ted reached for some courage and cautiously turned around. Standing in front of him was the Century doorman, a tall man in full regalia, overcoat, and hat. Finding his masculine composure, Ted straightened his spine and answered with a direct face,

"Just something in my eye that's all. I'll be all right. Find me a cab, will ya?"

The doorman threw up his hand and blew a small whistle dangling from his neck. Like magic a yellow car appeared. He opened the back door and waited for the injured radioman to enter. From under his large coat he presented a dark lavender fedora.

"I believe this belongs to you, Mr. Husing. A cabbie said you left it in his car. Good thing he came back. Looks like it's going to be a rough night."

For a moment Ted watched as if he was somewhere else, in some other time. The skill of this perceptive doorman was surely remarkable. Ted dug into his pocket and offered a few singles as compensation.

"No sir, not tonight, Mr. Husing," he said. "This one's on me. Good night, sir."

Taking the hat, Ted looked at him and sat gingerly on the cool leather seat. As the door shut beside him, Ted wondered if he was dreaming.

By the spring of 1934, it was clear that Helen and Ted's marriage was over. Husing had ascended to the top. Things were moving too fast for Ted to sit idly in an Upper West Side apartment tending to domestic life. Quiet evenings with his wife and young daughter didn't crack the lips on his face like carousing with his buddies—male and female. Ted was a celebrity and he was not going to cultivate the glowing lights of fame from his living room.

"He was the perennial gadfly at 21 and the perennial bachelor though married," described his friend Gary Stevens. "If you met him anytime when he was around the bar, nobody, if they didn't know him, would have thought he was married. He was always looking at some young thing who was coming in and making a comment."[417]

Ted Husing was no different than most red-blooded men of celebrity. Big money and beautiful women were the premier signs of success. He was enjoying the fruits of his hard labor like a kid in a candy store surrounded by a smorgasbord of soft ice cream and shapely assorted chocolates. All the while, the truth was being ignored. He was no longer a youngster, but an adult man with grown-up obligations—a child, a wife. Helen wasn't naïve. She knew the lifestyle, once the showgirl herself in swifter days—the glazed look in his eye, a smell of strange perfume seeping through his clothes. The magic touch of femininity could make a man do almost anything. Ted, however, remained faithful to Helen as long as her wedding ring circled his finger.

"I may have possessed a thousand faults, but infidelity to Bubs was not one of them," he admitted.[418] The husband may have been true, but the wife was not convinced.

While Ted was everywhere and anywhere but home, Helen lay in a bed filled with loneliness and unfulfilled desires. The patchy circles of several unsuccessful sleeps wore on her face. Every time Helen looked into the mirror, she saw the darkness of fatigue staring back. But she noticed something else. She was, surprisingly, still an attractive woman. Helen Husing may have felt over the hill but, she was only twenty-eight years old. Her yellow hair and pure, regal looks were still in tact. Anyone with a clear eye could see she was still a catch. She, like Ted, had needs and vices. Helen, like Ted, enjoyed the creatures of the night. A soothing belt of the sauce and bubbly music was the perfect remedy to mend a broken heart. On one occasion, she met a young bandleader by the name of Lennie Hayton.

Leonard George Hayton was born a New York City kid, February 13, 1908. By the age of six he was waxing his fingers on piano keys. Lennie had a gentle, subtle pitched voice that matched his pint-sized body. At seventeen he dropped out of school to pursue work as a musician. In 1926, Hayton landed his first pay gigs with Spencer Clark and The Little Ramblers. One year later, he was kicking it around with his neighborhood friend Cass Hagan and his orchestra at one of 7ᵗʰ Avenue's more upscale stops, a place called the Hotel Manger. One night, Paul Whiteman walked into the Manger looking for new talent. He walked out begging Lennie to join his band. Initially, Hayton balked at Whiteman's offer, wanting to stay loyal to Cass Hagan. But, logic got the better of him. For more than two years, Lennie was Whiteman's keyboard extraordinaire and fill-in conductor.[419] He was part of the infamous Old Gold Train of 1929, whistle-stopping across America. He often shared his berth with a radio announcer named Husing.

Crunched into a two-person seat, Hayton looked like an old duffle bag uncaringly tossed aside. He was playing a solo game of backgammon. When Ted approached, Hayton saw a new partner for his favorite pastime.

"Husing, how about a few rolls of the dice?" he asked. "We just pulled out of Penn Station and you guys got a game of craps going already?" Ted joked.

Unfolding his posture, Hayton revealed a crisp dark lavender outfit with a white silk handkerchief neatly tucked in the breast pocket. On his feet was a flickering pair of soft leather saddle shoes.

They shook hands and exchanged pleasantries.

"Sorry, I'm not much of a sportsman Ted," admitted Hayton shyly. "I don't give a shit about that," coached Ted. "Where'd you get the suit?"

Ted sat down, offered a smoke and studied his new acquaintance. Lennie's skin was the color of pale Spanish olives. Protruding large ears waved beyond his hair, black as the other side of the moon. But, a thin moustache gave him a swashbuckling, cavalier look. Hayton was known as "The Mickey Mouse Musician." In other circles he was called "The Wolf."[420]

Ted and Lennie shared a passion for music. The two could talk for what seemed like hours about bluesy riffs and up-beat quarter notes. Where Ted was more impulsive and extroverted, Lennie was more laid back, often playing the mystery man, a devilish, knowing smile on his face. But, they certainly had other things in common, a roving eye for beautiful women and late nights.

"Lennie likes a Bohemian existence," wrote Martin Lewis of *Radio Guide*. "He goes to bed never earlier than 4 AM, though more often it is nearer six or seven. Then he arises at noon, in time to just about make the afternoon rehearsals."[421]

The only thing that separated these two dashing New Yorkers seemed to be the fact that Ted was married and Lennie was not. In fact, Lennie so enjoyed being single and free, he denounced any intentions of ever being married.

"Go ahead," laughed Hayton to a writer once, "get yourself a ball and chain, but the day I get myself hitched, I'll hand you a hundred dollars of fine United States currency!"[422]

Before too long, Hayton became a maestro leading his own orchestra. Ted knew talent and insisted that his friend have a spot on the network. With a word from Ted, The Chesterfield Quarter-Hour had Lennie leading an orchestra in 1932 on the CBS schedule.[423]

In January of 1933, Bing Crosby hired Lennie to play tunes on his radio show also sponsored by Chesterfield. Both men were aware of how Ted had helped their careers. Working together in the beehive of CBS provided Ted and the Mickey Mouse Musician with ample time to develop their friendship. The Old Gold days were always fodder for storytelling. Chatting in the hallways became a natural springboard to the buzzing merry-make on the city streets, visiting each other's tailor, buying cigarettes and, of course, flirting with the ladies. They were determined to experience together the glittering allure of New York nightlife, one club, one corner booth at a time.

"In more care-free days, Husing and Hayton roamed Broadway arm in arm after their perspective stints in the Columbia Broadcast System programs. They were radio land's Damon and Pythias."[424]

Ted and Lennie shared many things. But, never in Ted's wildest smoke-laced, scotch-drenched dreams did he ever think they would share the same wife.

Their initial meetings were easily forgotten. To Helen, Lennie was cute, fun, and talented. His best quality she believed was that he was simply a good friend to her husband. Yet, Helen knew there was an attraction between them. She noticed a selflessness about Lennie, a certain sensitivity that was simply communicated best through his music. Ironically, Ted, the professional announcer and champion of words, could never find the right ones to say.

"I could reach millions just by sending my voice over the air waves, but I had built an invisible barrier between myself and my own wife," said Ted in retrospect. "I don't know if she realized that I still loved her. I could no longer tell her."[425]

Lennie began spending less time with Ted Husing and spending more time with Ted Husing's wife. At first, he played the role of confidante. Helen had plenty of obvious questions about her absentee husband. Where was he frittering his nights away? Was there another woman? Before long his compassionate hugs took on a more intimate caress. Lennie rekindled Helen's forgotten sexual passions, provided the attention she craved, and restored confidence.

Above anything, he made her smile again.

In him, Helen had found the opposite of Ted. Lennie was supportive and patient. Ted could be volatile and cross. While Ted ignored her, Hayton listened. "Lennie knew what he was, who he was, what he could do and was very secure in that," said concert singer and friend Donald Shirley. "That's rare! And when you're that secure as a human being, then everything else in life becomes very quiet and very smooth. That's exactly what Lennie was."[426]

By the middle of 1933, Helen's relationship with Lennie was no longer platonic. They were seen kissing in the corner after gigs. Long walks and afternoon lunches lasted all day. Among their mutual friends and social contacts, it did not take long for Ted to find out. News of the affair traveled quickly among CBS office secretaries who pined for the sultry details.[427] Ted was rarely surprised about anything. But, clearly the tables had been turned. Ted's pride became a festering wound.

"There was a period there where Ted was very disturbed," remembered Gary Stevens. "In September of 1932, I started college at the University of Chicago. When I returned to CBS the following summer, there was a change in Ted and it was obvious. He just wasn't in control of himself. He seemed to be nervous. He seemed to be edgy and mumbled something about his personal life that he was having a lot of trouble. He mentioned Lennie a few times."[428]

Stoned by the sharp rocks of jealousy, Ted wasn't going to let go of Helen easily. They had built a life together, he convinced himself. But, holding on to her was spiteful, angry, and possessive. He wasn't like that. If being with Lennie Hayton or some other man made her happy so be it. She had earned that much at least. She had stroked, probed, built, cuddled, and caressed Ted's fragile sense of self from the beginning. If it wasn't for her, his early days may have been his only days.

The matter was not just a split between a famous husband and his discouraged wife. It was a separation between a mother and father and an innocent child, the break up of a family. Pegge knew nothing of unrequited love, late nights, or burning desires of a healthy grown-up body. All she knew was that her parents were not happy. Why were they fighting? Why were they not together? No hasty decisions were made. Ted and Helen talked about working things out, spending more quality time together. The announcer even considered cutting back on work and losing his key to the front door of the 21 Club. If time healed deep wounds, then reconciliation was possible. Helen was conflicted, in love with two men. She cooled her affair with Lennie, only to rekindle the flames again. Weeks went by. Hope prevailed and slipped into months. Still, Ted did not mend easily.

Friends like Mark Hellinger encouraged him and tried to keep him on the straight and narrow. But, the damage had been done. His broadcast schedule remained heavy, the pull of celebrity too much. Visions of his wife making love to someone he thought was his friend turned his stomach. Not making love to her made him sicker. Given a vacation for the first time in years, Ted spent New Year's Day of 1934 in Los Angeles and watched the next day's Rose Bowl game between Stanford and Columbia, assisting in the NBC broadcast booth as a spotter.[429] Helen spent the holidays in New York without him. Five months later, the white flags of surrender were hoisted. Helen packed her bags and boarded a train for the desert town of Reno where only six weeks of residence was needed to obtain a divorce. In the seat next to her sat little Peggemae, learning the ways of love, growing up faster than her parents ever expected.

Ted and Helen agreed to an amicable, quiet procedure. However, they both knew walls and water coolers had ears. Helen was supposed to be just another woman in town getting divorced. But, when the man you're divorcing is a famous radio announcer, the outside world becomes interested. Besides her attorney Felice Cohn, Helen had few friends in Reno. Ted provided finances, wiring money from New York and coaching her on how to spot unsavory media types. Lennie, too, called, even keeled, reminding Helen that he loved her.

Helen used an alias at the hotel and restaurants as to deflect attention. The plan worked at first, but the situation quickly changed after a diligent reporter discovered Pegge had registered at a local horse-riding stable under her real name. When news hit the papers, Ted tried to play dumb telling the press, "I don't know anything about it. I don't know where she is."[430]

But, even that wasn't very convincing. Everyone knew. Few were surprised. Helen was left holding the bag, trying to elude the press and protect Pegge. She tossed them a bone saying it was the pressures of radio that broke up a once happy home. In the end, skirting the press was easy compared to occupying their time. The "biggest little city in the world" prided itself on adult entertainment for obvious reasons, exotic shopping sprees, burlesque shows, and enough alcohol to bring back Prohibition.[431] Not exactly ideal activates for a nine-year-old. Horses, movies, and a gallon of ice cream sundaes helped pass the days best for the Husing girls. Alone and lonely, plunged into a strange land, under unwanted circumstances, mother and daughter held on tight for support. "I think my mom and Helen really bonded those two months in Reno," said Peggemae's youngest daughter Kate. "They became closer than ever before."

After Judge Thomas Moran granted an official divorce on July 18, 1934, Helen took the traditional walk from the Washoe County Courthouse to the Virginia Avenue Bridge and tossed the wedding ring Ted gave her into the cool, still water below. The next day, Helen returned to New York a single woman.

Helen moved into Essex House, a few short blocks from the Century, overlooking Central Park South. The art deco residency hotel was the perfect environment to start anew. Opening in 1931, it offered all the high standards of living of which she had become accustomed: plush carpeting, high ceilings, doorman, maid service, and a dining hall. Also keeping a room at the Essex was the "Mickey

Mouse Musician."

The two lovers picked up where they left off. For all intents and purposes, they were living together. Talk of marriage came up often. The fact that Hayton even considered it marked maturation in the man. If Helen was to try again, she wanted to be sure—safe. A long train ride to Reno was something she did not want to endure again.

With his own orchestra, Lennie landed the "Lucky Strike Hit Parade" on NBC. The Ha Ha Club, one of the city's swankiest jazz joints, remained his favorite hangout, gigging several nights a week. Lennie's dream of owning his own club became a reality when the band pooled their resources together and bought the Famous Door in March of 1935. Swing Street had a new hot spot. With acts like Louie Prima, a regular part of the floor show, business was good. But, the fun was gone. Something was missing. Lennie had to convince Helen he was serious about making her his wife. First, he quit the "Hit Parade." In May, he sold his share of the Famous Door.[432] A once confirmed bachelor, Lennie Hayton had changed.

"Sooner or later, we all settle down," he came to realize. "Chasing around doesn't do anything for people except waste their time."[433]

In a simple afternoon civil ceremony in Metuchan, New Jersey, flanked by maid of honor Dorothy Link and best man Jack Colt, Helen and Lennie were married. The date was June 16, 1935.[434]

Something about being domesticated immediately appealed to Hayton. "I didn't even begin to find out what life was all about and why I was living, until I was married," Lenny said. "I had the idea it was just a three-ring circus."[435]

Helen had no intention of becoming a prude. However, she had no intention of losing her second husband to the night stalkers that had devoured her first. She enjoyed being a traditional house-wife, a romantic at heart. Helen suggested that the couple entertain at their apartment. The more snug gatherings became simply known as "Lennie Hayton's Home Parties."

"They were just as gay, just as much fun as night club evenings—but somehow, it always happened that not later than one o'clock in the morning nobody except Lennie and Helen were left in the Hayton's establishment."[436]

Helen's newfound happiness highlighted Ted's unpredictable mood shifts. Subordinates received the worst, a tongue lashing for things otherwise overlooked. "I must confess that the news of her marriage put me into a foul humor," admitted Ted years later. "It made me mad at myself for not filling the bill as husband."[437]

The shadows of insecurity rolled back like a blinding lakeside fog. Paranoia and suspicion registered as truth. Now that she was gone, he wanted her more than ever. And the more he thought of Helen, the more he hated the man he once called freind.[438]

"I asked Lennie about it many, many years later," remembered Gary Stevens. "Oh God! Lennie refused to discuss it with me. 'I have nothing to say. Don't ask me,' he said. And I knew Lennie very well."

Ted, at the same time, was hell bent on proving that life was better off without the former Mrs. Husing. Once the word of Ted's divorce hit the street, it seemed every woman citywide wanted a piece of Ted, including the listeners. One admirer exemplified the Husing effect on many females. In a July 1934, letter to the editor of *Radio Guide* magazine, Jeanette Herman of the Bronx, begged the magazine to put more men on the cover. Ted, however, got the juices flowing a few more degrees than most.

"Personally for your first male cover, may I nominate Ted Husing," she wrote. "I know from my personal contacts that most women go for his suave and sophisticated style and he is certainly deserving of a lot more publicity than he gets. I just live from Thanksgiving to Thanksgiving to hear him do those thrilling Penn–Cornell games. So I urge you again, give us an occasional man on the cover, but Husing first."[439] In case Ted was interested, Ms. Herman enclosed a photograph with the correspondence.

Unchained by the oneness of marriage, Ted was able to stretch his legs and play the field. His reputation was always free and easy with the opposite sex, a quip, a quiver, a look, or stare. Always soliciting a reaction. Gary Stevens remembered one such evening that epitomized Ted's flirtatious character.

"Ted took me to the Cotton Club one night. And there was a line of showgirls dancing with all kinds of gyrations and hip swinging. At the end of the show Cab Calloway, who was a friend of Ted's, came over to the table. He had that great sense of humor and he laughed and he said, 'Well, the prescription was really right tonight,' referring to the chorus girls. 'Shake well before Husing!'"[440]

Up in Harlem or the middle of Broadway, he was spotted all over town with several young ingénues. Blond bombshell Jean Harlow was rumored to have the hots for Ted and was seen arm and arm whenever she was in town. Word on the street had Ted having affairs with everyone from silent film star Estelle Taylor, vaudevillian Pegge Joyce Hopkins, and singing star Kate Smith. As laughable as the gossip was it proved something, Ted soaked up the role of lover with gusto. One girl, however, seemed to attract special attention from him.

Dancer Ann St. George helped grind the Husing nuptial rumor mill more than any other. Her stellar reviews of the 1935 revival "Scandals" and limbering kicks in the Vincent Minnelli-directed musical "At Home Abroad" put her in fashion.[441] Seen cuddling up with the recently divorced radio icon put St. George on the fast track— the fast track to wife of Ted Husing. When she first moved to New York as a teenager in search of stardom, St. George waved short, snow-white hair on top of a plump, round body. By her twenty-third birthday, the baby fat gave way to an athletic, leg lengthy shape. She even won a diving competition, splashing with chorus girls in Hollywood in 1935. The newspapers reported that she had "more than a casual interest in Ted Husing."[442] Between the constant prying eye of the press and clinking of glasses, it sounded like marriage to everyone except Ann St. George. Whenever Ted broached the question, which was often, she became evasive, coy, unsure.

"I've wanted to marry her for over two years and I'm still trying but she won't say yes," Ted told a reporter in the spring of 1936. "I don't think St. George is ready to marry yet, she thinks she wants a career first, partly, and for the rest of the reason, I don't know."[443]

Ted had used every trick in the book to win the heart of his woman. He escorted her home every night from the Winter Garden stage door after performances, cut back on poker pleasure with the backroom boys at 21, and even wooed her with an engagement ring costing more than six grand. Ted was frustrated by his lack of persuasion—he had a need, a burning desire to fill a void left by someone else. He was looking for another chance, another opportunity to be a good husband. If that was, indeed, what he hoped to discover, it was obvious that Ted was looking for Mrs. Husing II—in all the wrong places.

CHAPTER TWENTY-THREE

LEMME SLEEP, WILLYA?

April 27, 1936, was a popping spring day. The workweek had just begun. Central Park was alive with green. Flowers bloomed and birds sang their songs. The streets roared with car horns, scurrying feet, and high-pitched paperboys hocked their trade. It was the kind of spring day that could put a smile on anyone's face. But Ted Husing still burned with envy. Helen lying in the same bed with Hayton! The thought was unthinkable. Nothing else mattered. Divorce was what he had wanted, he assured himself. But, why did he feel so lousy? What did his old friend Lennie have that he didn't? Ted could have any woman he wanted. The one he wanted, he already had, and let go but wanted again. He couldn't go back, could he?

The last two years chasing Ann St. George seemed like a waste. Would she ever bend to his romantic desires? But, Ted was hopelessly in love, one in the past and one in the present. Sandwiched between the new Mrs. Hayton and a young Ms. St. George, the walls were caving in. All day, Ted was a caged lion. He paced in his office. He snapped at Quailey. Les was used to that. But, even he was a bit perplexed at Ted's mood. The two had been discussing the upcoming Berlin Summer Games. The usual stuff: names, dates, schedule, and statistics. Paley had OK'd the voyage for Ted and Company to cover the event for the network. A chance to visit the birthplace of his mother and father was energizing for obvious reason and for those less apparent. The radioman was equally curious about the new German chancellor, the one they called the Der Fuhrer.

He had seen photographs of Adolph Hitler, the small patch of moustache above his lip, short-cropped hair, and charismatic presence. This man knew how to captivate an audience. The newsreels didn't lie. From one communicator to another, Ted admired that about him. Like many others, Ted had heard the rumors. Like many others, he refused to believe them. However, like many others, questions lingered. "The boss, Bill Paley, was a Jew. Close friends, Jack Kriendler and Charlie Berns, Mark Hellinger—they were Jews. Mother was Jewish—once. If she had stayed in Bielefeld, would she be an outcast? Or worse, would she be . . . ? Could he, Ted Husing, be . . . seen as a Jew?"

Ted and Quailey also exchanged a word or two about the baseball commissioner's newest proclamation from Chicago.

"Pending further notice, all major and minor league clubs will refrain from making any additional commitments, arrangements, or authorizations for radio broadcast of ball games."[444]

Ted knew the owners were worried about gate receipts. Dwindling attendance at baseball games had nothing to do with a depressed economy. Paranoid fantasies of fans staying home and listening to live broadcast were to blame. Or so they thought. As a broadcaster, Ted smiled. The power of the mike and the voice that spoke into it could be godly. No one wanted to believe that more than Ted. Yet, he knew the premise was uncivilized as the commissioner's hair. Athletes and the sports they played existed long before radio announcers. But, to Ted, Kenesaw Mountain Landis was unsavory and just the thought of the man irritated him.

"Let's call it a day Ted," Quailey suggested. "We'll walk over to 21. I'll buy you a drink." Ted shrugged his shoulders no. "How about La Hiff's? It'll give Toots a thrill!" Quailey tried again. "Shit, you don't want to be with me tonight. Lester, my man," Ted said with a churlish tongue, "I'll see ya tomorrow."

There was a hum of melancholy in his voice. Les knew his friend and didn't bother changing Ted's mind. With a slap on the back, he reached for the door and went to the place Ted should have gone—home.

Only moments after Quailey had left, another familiar face entered. Ted's eighteenth-floor office often rotated with a sweep of activity, in and out, to and fro. A change of pace was welcomed. Ted remembered an interview scheduled with freelance writer Alice Pegg. He enjoyed talking with the female reporter and saw it as an opportunity to lift his spirits and unburden himself. Pegg was well aware of Ted's potent mind and couldn't wait to get her fingers on a typewriter after one of their meetings.

"He talks freely on even the more personal subjects, he never stalls or generalizes," she said. "He's probably the most colorful copy of anybody in radio."[445]

The subject and his interviewer talked a wide range of juicy topics, especially past and present lovers. Helen was handled with an insightful combination of shadowy regret and polite pleasantries. Ted knew that some affairs were meant to stay in the dark. He was not about to divulge secret love triangles and broken promises with anyone, especially a newspaper pen.

"Our marriage was the most beautiful relationship I have ever known," he told the female reporter. "It had to end and it did and I'm sorry. Bubs is a wonderful woman."[446]

However, when the subject turned to Ann St. George, the broadcaster seemed to gush a fresh sense of purpose found his tongue.

"Ted grinned when I mentioned Ann's name and promptly launched into a raving session about her that lasted the remainder of my visit," Pegg wrote. "He was beaming like a schoolboy and there was an undeniable ring of proud possessiveness in his voice."[447]

Ted may have convinced Alice Pegg of his romantic intentions but there was no fooling himself. Ted Husing was a man of truth, honesty eating at the core of his soul, worms to the rotting apple. The guilt ate at his throat the more he sat with the reporter. Ted never had a problem pushing bravado to promote his greatness as a radioman. In the booth, in front of microphone he was the best, a true winner, all others paled in comparison. In the ways of love, he could not show the same arrogance. In the ways of love, Ted would be the one chasing the greatness of those more successful. Would he ever marry again? Could he ever find a woman to accept his proposal? Was he a man capable of finding true domestic tranquility? He had to know. He had to know now.

With the clock slipping past 5 PM, Ted decided to say no more. A relaxed, straightforward chat about volatile subjects had suddenly become all too real. He mustered every ounce of cordial civility and charm he could and said good night to the female columnist. The evening was young. Ted had something to prove. The Stork Club was right around the corner on Eeast 53rd Street. That was as good a place as any. Perhaps he'd visit the Kriendler's later. He wanted a woman. But, Ted had no perimeters—as long as she was soft and female, willing and able. He would even marry her tonight if he had to.

Ted powered through the door with purpose. He was wearing silver-rimmed spectacles and a silk purple tie. The owner of the club, Sherman Billingsly, darted over and shook Ted's hand. "Jack Kriendler finally had enough of you, hah?" he teased. Born and raised in Oklahoma, Billingsly was more homestead maître d' than farmhouse wrangler. His initial pile of money was made in a chain of grocery stores and pharmacies. But, when he moved to New York in 1923 he brought with him $5,000 and an ambition of opening a restaurant he called "a nice place where people can come for a good time and where I can bring my family without their seeing anything I wouldn't want them to see."[448] In reality, there was plenty to hide. Like most speakeasies, Billingsly earned his reputation as a champion bootlegger. After prohibition, he was equally notorious for his public spats with celebrity guests. Yet, the unadorned talking Sooner was a businessman first. He coddled to people like star columnist Walter Winchell. The gossip king's free plugs on radio and newspaper were money in the bank and a waiting list of reservations for the Stork Club.[449] Likewise, Ted was good for business wherever he went.

"Great to see you, Ted. Enjoy yourself," reminded Sherm. "And let me know if you need anything."

Such hospitality was never more meaningful. As much as Ted preferred the 21 Club, Jack and Charlie's place didn't really sport what Ted was looking for—women. The first one Ted saw that night was the cigarette girl. She was young and slender and appeared to be overpowered by the black bulky serving cart strapped around her neck. She couldn't have been more than twenty years old, if that. Buying a pack, he gave the girl a wink and a dollar and thought about asking for her hand. But, he retreated to the bar to smooth the craving and see if the urge would pass.

Monday at the Stork was lottery night. Ted was a gambling man. So he dug into his pocket, shelled out fifty cents, and purchased a ticket. The winning prize was $100. Ted didn't need the money. Outside of a porter or bus boy, no one at the Stork Club needed the money. What they lived for was the adrenaline rush, the thrill of the chase. He fit in well with the crowd around him. Ted understood the odds. As in life, some times you win and some times you don't. And he knew the only way to find out was to be a player. The house band strummed soft, upbeat interludes. After an hour or so of chat and cocktails, Husing was ready. He spun in his barstool, clapped his hands, and made a bold proclamation.

"Watch the door," he ordered his friends. "Because I'm going to marry the next girl who walks through that door."[450]

"She was a blonde with a tight, short skirt. Her hair was upswept. I don't remember the dress, but I'm sure she must have been wearing one," Ted later remembered. "In fact, I don't remember anything except approaching her and leading her to a table."[451]

They weren't exactly strangers, having met once or twice before. Among mutual friends they exchanged a pleasant hello, a handshake, a glancing look. By that evening's end, their relationship was much more than just casual. Born near Savannah, Georgia, Francis Sizer was in the youthful style of the day, bright and perky with a thin waist and button nose. Moving to New York, the first thing she did was change her name to Celia Ryland, one of a thousand young beauties searching for stardust as an actress.[452] Her diligent speech lessons had erased any trace of an accent.

But, the more Celia drank that night, the sloppier her mouth moved. Traces of her southern roots would drawl out on occasion. Ted didn't care. Like the booze, she consumed him. There was something exciting about Ryland—sexy. Ted was in love, for the moment. The couple moved on the dance floor to continue their impromptu seduction. She pressed herself against him. He wantonly took her in. Ray Nobel's haunting lullaby "The Very Thought of You" underscored each step. Ted towered over her standing on the parquet floor. But, somehow Celia pulled Ted closer. She put her lips to his ear and sang the lyrics softly.

I see your face in every flower,
Your eyes in stars above.
It's just the thought of you, the very thought of you, my love.[453]

The actress seemed to know her role instinctively. Celia played every line Ted fed her. He promised her a mink coat. Size, cost, or the hour, none of that mattered to Ted. He was caught up in the rush, aching to sooth the pain. Besides, luck was in the air that night for the budding couple. When the band broke and the announcement was made to claim the lotto's 100 bucks, Ryland's number was called. Ted's new girl held the winning ticket. As if rubbing the genie from an ancient lantern, Ted next coaxed more luck from the beautiful performer.

"Now that you're rich, you wouldn't want to marry me, would you?' he wise-cracked soberly to his companion. 'Here's your answer,' she said simply and handed him the $100."

Like that he was engaged. The answer that had eluded him for two years with Ann St. George had been handed to him by Ms. Ryland in just two hours. With a burning desire and the clock ticking, the couple had no intention of wasting time.

Who would perform the ceremony? Where? He was reminded that it was Monday night and a long week lay ahead. But, to Husing it felt like New Year's Eve. Ted took the club owner up on his early suggestion and asked him to help.

"Hell, if ya want to get married Ted, why not the Blessed Event Room," cracked Billingsly. "I'd say the Cub Room, maybe. But, if Winchell gets wind of it, things will be on the front page before you can say 'I do.'"

Ted was not laughing. He was serious. Billingsly knew a judge in Westchester. But, the hour was getting late for the suburbs. It was nearly 10 o'clock and rain began to fall. With an address in hand, the two drunken lovers staggered out the door into Ted's automobile. Behind the wheel sat Fereschi, waiting for instructions. Ted melted into the backseat while Celia clung to her man's shoulder. They were giddy with laughter, determined. Ted looked over at his companion and caught the smiling face of Helen, the alluring face of Ann. A flash of lightning and a misty nighttime drive could play tricks with the mind. Who was this woman? What were they doing? It did not matter. No one else was around to care.

The two saw a sign for Harrison, New York, and knew they were close. Through the darkness and side streets, they found a house. On the mailbox near the driveway was a name: Hon. Leo

Mintzer. He answered the door and welcomed the bustling travelers inside. Ted shook his hand and thanked him. Celia stood quietly with glassy eyes and an ear-to-ear grin. It was past 11 o'clock. Mintzer knew the look. He had seen it all before, one time, many times, or just enough times to know that these two people should not be getting married. They were much more committed to the gin and cigarettes of which they reeked than to each other. But, those were his morals not theirs. If they wanted to be married, then so be it. He'd take their money. From an old cigar box, the judge kept cheap costume jewelry. His clients could choose temporary bands for such occasions—free of charge.

The ceremony was brief. In a flash, it was over. Ted and Celia were married. The newlyweds looked at each other. What now? Ted slipped the judge a wrinkled one-hundred dollar bill from his pocket and thanked him again. It was the luckiest $100 that Celia Ryland and Ted Husing would ever spend. They leaped for the car and raced back to Manhattan. In due course, Ted Husing and his new wife stumbled back to the Century to consummate their relationship. Sleep would have to come and it did. *What would everything look like in the morning,* Ted wondered? They had barely been married seven hours. Already, it seemed too long.

Then . . . he was awake. One eye popped open, then the other. Wherever Ted had been, he was no longer. The surroundings of his tenth-floor apartment were familiar again. According to the clock on his dresser, noon was approaching. Ted was still boiling, moisture formed on his scalp. The heat from the radiator was blasting out with might. The pipes clanged with excitement. "Don't those fuckers know it's the middle of spring," Ted cursed to himself. He was beginning to feel the effects of a king-sized hangover.

From the pain hitting him square between the eyes, it felt as if the pointed top of the Chrysler Building dug into his head. He was not dreaming anymore. Or maybe the dream had changed. From inside the sheets, Ted felt a smooth leg rubbing against his.

He woke up to see a sweet naked woman lying next to him. Ted was confused—in a fog. What had happened? He looked down at his left hand and noticed a gold band on the ring finger.

His house phone was ringing. The doorman informed him that reporters had gathered downstairs hoping to get a word and photo with the happy couple. *What happy couple*, Ted thought? *Jesus Christ!* He pulled on a pair of brown trousers, grabbed his Camels, and staggered down to chat with the press boys. Perhaps they knew more of what had happened than he did.

"I'm very sleepy . . . I won't talk . . . I won't pose for pictures . . . All I want to do is sleep."[454]

Ted tried to smile. He tried to be accommodating. The questions were coming too fast. He couldn't keep up. Besides, he didn't want to. Ted yawned and swallowed what tasted like a large bud of cotton. His cool demeanor was quickly spent. He was sobering with impatience.

"This marriage is neither gag nor wise-crack," he explained with confidence. "We're both very happy and sure that it will last."[455]

He took a long drag on his cigarette and threw it into the street. "We've known each other for quite a while, but unfortunately we've not been engaged a long time . . . Yeah, it happened at 11 o'clock . . . Seems years ago now. Mrs. Husing is asleep and I'm sleepy, too . . . Very sleepy . . . Lemme sleep, will ya?"[456]

The warm spring sun crashed into his tired eyes. He wanted to get out. He couldn't. Ted was trapped. He was married now. Mumbling, he went back inside and disappeared into the elevator. A formal introduction to his wife was in order. If only he could remember her name.

Boyhood Husing, circa 1910

Helen "Bubs" Gelderman

Radio pioneer and first president of CBS Major J. Andrew White at ringside before a broadcast.

Graham McNamee calls the 1924 World Series.

Husing announces for "Old Gold Hour" with jazz great
Paul Whiteman, 1929.

Ted calls football game while loyal assistant Les Quailey works the
spotting board, circa 1930.

Husing showcases his portable broadcast pack at
Penn Relays, early 1930's.

COLUMBIA

Husing calls the 1932 Winter Olympics from Lake Placid for CBS.

Publicity photo for "March of Time," on CBS, 1931.

Jack Kriendler (right) and Charlie Berns (glasses)
in front of the "21 Club" around 1932.

Mark Hellinger with actress Linda Darnell,
his wife Gladys Glad and writer Louis Sobol.

Publicity photo of Lennie Hayton sitting at piano with "America's Sweetheart of Song" Ruth Etting for The Chesterfield Quarter-Hour on CBS. Hatyon was the show's musical director 1932-33.

Husing interviews track star Glenn Cunningham of Kansas.

From left to right - restaurateur Joe Moss with Ted, Ethel Merman, Bob Hope and writer Louis Sobol at L.A. charity event.

Ann St. George

Ted shares a cigarette and drinks with second wife Celia Ryland.

Ted and his second trusted assistant Jimmy Dolan worry over pre-game preparations for a football broadcast.

Ted interviews boxing great Joe Louis following his win over
Jack Sharkey August 17, 1936.

Husing and Jimmy Dolan joke around with football squads
during a light Friday practice session.

Husing interviews witnesses of Hindenburg disaster at Lakehurst, NJ. May 6, 1937. Husing and CBS broadcast until 3AM the next morning.

Ted broadcasts 1938 PGA Tourney at Shawnee-on-Delaware from back of lawn tractor.

Ted poses with then girlfriend Betty Lawford.

Two American legends, Ted Husing and Babe Ruth.

Husing takes part in a charity rodeo event with Bing Crosby (foreground left) and actress Dorothy Lamour (far right).

Ted flirts with models on the beach in Miami during Orange Bowl Week, circa 1938.

NBC publicity photo of Bill Stern around mid 1940's.

Ted dines with his third wife Iris Lemerise, circa late 1940's.

[David Husing]

Ted laughs it up with some members of the Skeeters Club.
Among the group, Toots Shor, third from right,
and Walter Kennedy, second from left.)

[David Husing]

Ted, on WHN, spins records for the "Ted Husing Bandstand."

[David Husing]

Ted sits for photo session during "This Is Your Life"
appearance May 8, 1957. With Ted is host Ralph Edwards,
mother Bertha and daughter Pegge.

[Ralph Edwards Productions]

Jesse Owens (middle) talks with Ted as Ralph Edwards (left)
looks on during "This Is Your Life," May 8, 1957.

[Thomas Pryor]

Fr. Benedict Dudley, Ted's friend and confessor, poses with young parishioner Thomas Pryor while pastor of St. Stephen's on E. 82nd Street.

[Stanley Wertheim.]

Stanley Wertheim, who Husing helped escape Nazi Germany, pictured in Central Park circa 1940. Wertheim went on to become a professor of English at William Patterson University in New Jersey.

Young David Husing pictured with Bertha and Iris
at his Confirmation late 50's.

Ted chats with Tom Harmon at Del Mar Racetrack, 1957. Pictured
on the left is Harmon's wife Elyse Knox Harmon.

Ted catches up with two old friends, Hollywood actor
Pat O'Brien (left) and a Cuban musician turned American
TV icon named Desi Arnaz (white hat).

Husing works with physical therapist during rehab session.

CHAPTER TWENTY-FOUR

KEEP YOUR FRIENDS CLOSE AND ENEMIES CLOSER

Ted's second honeymoon did not last long. A few days after the whirlwind marriage to Celia Ryland, he was on a train bound for Lexington to anchor the network's coverage of the Kentucky Derby.

A long shot horse named Bold Venture captured the run for the roses that year. A two-dollar mutual bet paid winners forty-three dollars. Similar odds could have been placed on Husing's recent nuptials. It, too, was a long shot. Betting the house or even two dollars would have paid handsomely had Ted and Celia crossed the finish line together. The point was moot. No one dared wager. Everyone knew it was not meant to last, even the happy couple. Ann St. George seemed unfazed and quickly moved on to other fish. Millionaire playboy Alexis Thompson, heir to the Inland Steel Company fortune, took the bait. Within four months, they were engaged. In less than four months, Ted was divorced, again.

As much as things changed they seemed to stay the same. Ted had exhausted himself in search of a new wife. But, as everyone eventually found out, he never relinquished the old. Ted and Helen were officially split, but hardly behaved like typical divorcees. She kept her key to the Century apartment and was spotted there enough that some doormen still referred to her as "Mrs. Husing." Ted affectionately called her "My Helen," as if they were still together. Some found it sweet, others twisted.[457] Whispered telephone conversations were frequent, many letters were written, even anniversary cards sent. A need to stay close compelled them forward, but an unspoken sadness remained. Writer Jimmy Cannon, a friend of the couple, referred to it as "a secret sorrow."

"One thing I really remember my mother telling me was that after their divorce they talked on the phone every day for years," revealed Ted's granddaughter Kate Lacey. "There was a friendship that totally endured. They were always connected. I wouldn't be surprised if he just felt the whole thing was a big mistake."[458]

The summer of 1936 could not have arrived sooner. Ted was salivating to get away from his troubles. He was thirty-five years old. With the Olympics scheduled to begin on August 1, in Berlin, Ted set sail for Europe on the USS Normandie on the first day of July. Also sailing on the Normandie was St. George and her new fiancé. Thompson boarded the ship as an athlete, a member of the U.S. Olympic men's field hockey team. Ted might have liked the Yale man in other circumstances. Thompson later became a world-class bobsledder and owned two NFL football teams, the Steelers and Eagles.[459] On a cruise-liner filled with happy party sailors, Ted was determined to be one of those contented spirits. "Let the kid have her fun," he thought. "She had her chance. Now I guess it's over."

Ted was excited to be in Berlin. For the first time in his life he was proud of the German blood that flowed through his body. Better yet, he was proud to be American, especially after the showing of a black bullet sprinter from Ohio named Jesse Owens. The man's performance was spectacular. With fists pumping and feet flying, Owens' four gold medals turned the Hitler Olympics into Jesse's Games. Four years earlier at the NCAA Track Invitational in Chicago, Owens stunned the crowd when he set a new world record in the hundred. He was a senior in high school. Everyone knew they witnessed something special. He was still black, however. Newspapermen and radio pundits begrudgingly stayed away—all except for Husing. The CBS man did not care about skin color. He was there to do a job. He found the young sprinter and placed the microphone gently in front of his mouth. The audience deserved a word or two from the world's fastest man. Owens never forgot the bold gesture.

In Berlin, Hitler refused to shake the sprinter's hand, but the German citizenry applauded wildly. They crowded around him in public outside the stadium, grasping to touch the American's glistening exotic features. Yet, the biggest fan of German decent was none other than another American, Ted Husing.

"He gave me a tremendous thrill that week in Berlin," said Husing. "And another one a few weeks later."

Following the Games, Owens and his teammates barnstormed track events in France and England until September. When he finally returned to New York, thousands, including newspapermen and radio announcers lined the streets hoping to see their new hero.

"You can picture the kick I got when Jesse worked his way through the mob and came looking for me," Ted recalled. Owens also remembered seeking out Ted during his triumphant return to New York. He personally thanked the CBS announcer some two decades after the fact by saying, "You put me on the radio the first time when I was in high school. Nobody else wanted me on the radio then and you were nice to me, so I thought maybe I could return the favor."[460] Returning favors was one motivation for Owens, fear being the other. "I was scared stiff when the huge reception was at the pier. And you took charge . . . you gave me the confidence that was needed for the press and the radio."[461]

Ted's descriptions of Berlin were superior, as always, calling the events with precision, weaving words, setting the scene with detail of everything from a runner's shoes to weather reports. He shared the duties with Los Angeles announcer and Olympic historian Bill Henry. As a technical adviser to the International Olympic

Committee and main organizer of the 1932 Games in California, few added more insight to worldwide sport than Mr. Henry.[462] However, radio critics weren't writing about Bill Henry. They again were drawn to Ted.

"A gripping word picture of the 1,500-meter classic was described by (guess who?) Ted Husing," wrote the *New York Daily News*. "Ted let himself go with his entire two-fisted vocabulary in praise of the sensational New Zealander Jack Lovelock, who ran our own Glenn Cunningham into the ground. 'Specs' Towns upheld American prestige by winning the 400-meter hurdles, thus coming in for his share of the Husing encomiums."[463]

Secretly, Ted's real work in the German capitol during the Games of the XI Olympiad had little to do with cinder tracks, javelins, swimming pools, or gold medals. The stakes were much higher, a matter of life and death.

The festive atmosphere surrounding the Berlin Games brilliantly hid from the world a systematic evil of epic proportions. The flame burning above the Olympic Stadium represented peace and unity, a brotherhood of man. For Adolph Hitler, the fire symbolized an extermination of a particular people, a purging already underway. An ordinance known as The Nuremberg Laws passed quietly a year before the Games, stripping Jews of citizenship and marital status. Fines, prison sentences, and general harassment soon followed. It was only the beginning, as time would tell for German–Jewish families. One of those families in trouble was Bertha Husing's nephew Max Wertheim, his wife, and their 6-year-old son Stanley. A former decorated army officer, Wertheim hardly believed his Jewish ethnicity could be a target for organized, governmental malice. He dragged his feet, unmoved to action. Wertheim was finally persuaded to leave the country by friends and co-workers, many of them Nazis sympathetic to their plight.[464] "My parents were people, for some reason, who had a great sense of entitlement," believed Stanley Wertheim. "They felt people owed them something. I really have no idea where it came from. It's hard to explain because it isn't rational."[465]

The logical place of exile for any unwanted strays remained, as it always had, the United States. No better place than New York City, home of lady liberty, the beacon of freedom. Better yet, the displaced Wertheim's knew people in the thriving metropolis, not just people but flesh and blood—Henry and Bertha Husing. A letter asking for help soon arrived. In order to gain entrance, a sponsor was needed, a promise to Uncle Sam that foreign refugees would not be a financial liability. That promise, however, did not come so readily from Henry and his wife. Bitterness still lingered. Wertheim, Hecht—the same side of the family who some four decades before refused to embrace the marriage of a certain Jew to an unwanted Gentile.

From their reluctance, up rose Ted. He accepted the Wertheim burden, if one was to come.[466] He did not harbor the same feelings as his parents. Wishing to shun unwanted publicity, Ted convinced Henry to be the front man, steering his father to connections at the State Department, extraditing paper work, and securing an otherwise complicated process. He made plans to meet Wertheim in person during the Olympics. His two weeks in Berlin would be busier, if not riskier, than anyone imagined. Throughout the day, Ted battled the sun, chased athletes, and, of course, called the action from his stadium perch. At night, he and his newfound cousin discussed escape routes, contact information, and political realities.

Somehow Wertheim did not recognize the same bomb ticking that those around him did. He remained in the dark, unconvinced that danger lurked about. Ted reminded him again and again to stay clear of Gestapo agents and other untrustworthy types. "Ted would always say my father had a great sense of unreality," Stanley Wertheim remembered. "Of course, he was right. I think Ted was afraid. It was imminently dangerous for both my father and Ted."[467]

By February of 1937, flight ultimately came for the Wertheim's from Germany to New York. At Pier 72 on the West Side of Manhattan, Ted's personal driver Mr. Fareschi sat inside a long, black car with bright chrome bumpers and spotless cream wall tires waiting to pick them up. The refugees moved into the Wilsonian Apartment Building on West 69th Street, next-door neighbors to Henry and Bertha Husing. They were free from the Third Reich but new inquiring eyes followed. Hitler's war machine made anyone of German citizenry living in the States an enemy, especially in the years leading up to World War II. Little distinction was made between immigrants. All were viewed with suspicion. The Wertheim's being no exception, under constant surveillance within a year of their arrival. Husing's connections had no relevance in matters of national security. Government operatives checked radios for shortwave capabilities and asked an endless array of questions. "The FBI man was so consistent that I used to call him Mr. Monday," laughed Stanley Wertheim. "I thought that was his name."

No doubt, the most plentiful piles of resentment toward the new German fugitives living on New York's Westside came off the shovel of Henry Husing. He would never let them forget. "His favorite thing he always said to me was 'The *Goy* saved your life,' a Yiddish term meaning *Christian*," explained Stanley Wertheim. "German Jews didn't speak much Yiddish but he picked it up someplace."[468] Ridicule aside, Stanley Wertheim embraced gratitude, understanding the sacrifice made on his behalf by the Husings. The famous radio announcer and his parents were more than family. "If it wasn't for them, we never would have gotten here. We owe Ted everything in that sense. He saved our lives."[469]

The sea air and visit to the Fatherland was just what the doctor ordered. Ted felt surprisingly refreshed even amongst the pressure-filled broadcasts and covert spy games. September was just around the bend. Ted was ready to chew the miles once again. From college town to big city metropolis, it was time for cooler temperatures and Americas favorite attraction—football. Unfortunately, his trusted assistant and friend would not be joining him. In the six years that Les Quailey and Ted Husing worked together, a lifetime had passed between them. They were no longer two skinny kids desperate to make their mark in a world of radio professionals. Ted was a star. Quailey the dutiful subordinate. "In a very closeted way, he idolized Ted," believed Gary Stevens. "He was Ted's alter ego."[470]

His contribution to molding the modern sports announcer was just as important as Ted's. Quailey never had the driving desire to be an on-air personality. His talents were in "running the show." He was proud of his work with Ted. And like Ted was convinced that the way they broadcasted sports was the only way. During their travels, he knew of many a young sports announcer who didn't want to be compared to the great Ted Husing. The ground was fertile. It was a bustling field of specialties in dire need of a guiding hand and the time was right to mass market the technique, make it universal. Recruit, teach, and mold.

By the mid '30s, Philadelphia advertising agency NW Ayer was beginning to see the power of broadcasting sports and the selling of their client's product. The lofty goals of early radio as a tool for information and education were long gone. Radio was about commercial sponsors and making money. One of the agency's biggest clients was the Atlantic Refinery Oil Company. From traveling salesman to weekend road warrior, America was forever linked to the automobile. America was forever linked to rabid sports fans as well. From northern New England, across the Ohio Valley to the Carolinas, Atlantic tied their message to every baseball and football contest they could get. One problem remained. New talent was needed to broadcast the games that Atlantic had agreed to sponsor. Quailey was hired by the agency to enlist and train the best and the brightest of sports announcers on how to broadcast a game correctly, but sell the sponsor as well.[471] Some of the biggest names in the history of sports announcing were initially showcased and trained by Les Quailey. Names like Curt Gowdy, Chris Schenkel, Ken Coleman, By Saam, Rosey Rosewell, Bob Prince, Richie Ashburn, Bill Campbell, Arch McDonald, and Chuck Thompson all felt the guidance of

Ted's former assistant.

"Les Quailey from Ted Husing brought that book about the do's and don'ts of play-by-play broadcasting," said Chuck Thompson. "And what I found was probably the right way to do it. Football, basically, every play—down, yardage, team possession, and then set it up. Basketball, its possession and direction—every play. In baseball, it's the same thing. A ball is never hit to a person. It's always hit to a position."[472]

No one was surprised when Atlantic inked Ted as one of their first national spokesmen. They sponsored Ted's sports recap show three times a week on the network. Like Husing, Quailey became a father figure to many young voices.

"He was a tremendous influence on my brother. He was the one who got my brother to come to Philadelphia," said Byrum Saam's younger brother Robert. "From then on, Les Quailey was sort of a family member for a long time."[473]

The real hero behind the success of Ted Husing was no doubt Quailey. He was the man who took the brilliance of Husing and shaped it into seamless organization.

"Les is the eyes and pretty much the brains of the combination; I am the voice," admitted Ted.

Above anything else, Quailey over the years had familiarized himself with Ted's shifting temperament better than any wife or girlfriend ever could. He knew just the right buttons to push with the man. And he often found the right words as well.

"I think he was maybe Ted's best PR man," said Chris Schenkel. "He let everybody know how good Ted was if they didn't know already. He was there to tell Ted."[474]

Finding a replacement for Quailey would be a daunting task. It had to be someone of boundless energy, loyal, bright, dedicated, a man–child who could eat up sports facts and spit them back at the most belligerent of 21 bar-sitters. Ted knew of just the man. James Michael Dolan was raised a Catholic on Manhattan's West Side. His parents were fresh from the shores of the Old Country. While his father worked for the Post Office, mother steered her son in the more traditional activities of life—church.[475] St. Paul the Apostle parish on West 59th Street became home away from home for young Jimmy. He served dutifully as an altar boy and was forever moved by the solemn rituals he took part in.[476]

If Jimmy wasn't busy with the prayerful activities at St. Paul's, he was playing sports. One of the neighborhood mutts he befriended in Hell's Kitchen was none other than Ted Husing, attending Commerce together and later suiting up alongside Ted and Quailey as a lineman on the infamous Prescotts football squad. All three survived the weekend ass wipings and learned to laugh them off. Not one of the three were very good athletes—boys among the men. Tearing the eyes out of one's opponent was measured by a less physical yardstick.

Following the Prescotts, Dolan struggled to find his true calling. A few uninspired semesters at Columbia University pushed him to drop out. He worked at the Paulist Athletic Club as an officer and even considered the priesthood. What truly stirred the man was a life of sports and when Ted called about a job at CBS, Jimmy jumped at the chance. Dolan was everything Ted wanted in a man: honest, passionate, and smart. His stubby legs, bulging ears, and short arms gave him the look of a Leprechaun. The quirky features underestimated a quick brain power that most recognized as genius.

"He was a Johnny Irishman," laughed Chris Schenkel of his friend. "His mind worked faster than he could talk."[477]

Dolan wore his emotions on his sleeve. He was hospitable and warm yet equally shy and sensitive. Jimmy learned to express himself best through writing. Pen and paper were never far from reach. If Ted unburdened his innermost thoughts to a live microphone, Jimmy buried his with words on the page.

"He had a little brown book he was always writing in," remembered Gary Stevens. "When he had lunch with me at Sardis many times he was always creating some poem or something."[478]

Dolan also picked up the role of protector from Les Quailey. Jimmy was willing to defend the methods of Ted Husing with anyone who dared to challenge him.

"Dolan was, what shall I say, like a father to his child," said Bill Mazer. "Though there was nothing infantile about Husing. He was very guarded about Ted. I made the mistake of saying to Dolan one day that the only time I heard Husing miss a beat was during a two-mile race at the Penn Relays . . . When I mentioned it, Christ I thought he was going to whack me."[479]

Ted had every trust in Dolan. Seeing his wide eyes and fresh energy everyday at the office made the transition from Quailey seamless. 1936 had been a strange year. Much of what he knew to be absolute and unquestioned became distorted. It was comforting for Ted to know who was looking out for his best interest. Ted had learned a painful lesson about friendship. Sometimes friends who watch your back may end up stabbing you there. If Ted ever saw Lennie Hayton again it would be too soon. Unfortunately, too soon became too often. He couldn't get away from bumping into Hayton either on the airwaves or the hallways, playing tunes for several CBS shows including a new version of the "Ed Wynn Show," minus "the voice with a smile."

Graham McNamee was by now, less and less of a threat. The NBC announcer's waning talents were beginning to dip like a glorious sunset just above the stark horizon. His schedule remained heavy as announcer for the popular "Major Bowes Radio Hour," newsreels for Universal Pictures and a few odd sporting events, including football. Gone, however, were the glamour events of yesteryear, including the Rose Bowl. Mac had shot himself in the foot one too often. The growing legends of sports fans could no longer take his blunders for granted.

But, his effect on Ted wasn't without one last power pack punch. In the spring of 1936, Wynn switched the show back to

NBC and a glorious, though short lived, reunion with Mac. Lennie Hayton stayed on as bandleader. McNamee and Hayton! The irony was heavy enough to break the back of Hercules. Ted's most spirited rival of the microphone and his soul-pierced rival in love were now paired together. *Together to do what?* A shot of paranoia passed through his mind, and then quickly disappeared. Mere coincidence, or a warning sign? Ted's ears must have burned wondering if either thought of him as much as he did them. Keep your friends close and your enemies closer. If it worked for gangsters and gunman, it also worked for Ted Husing.

CHAPTER TWENTY-FIVE

COLOR ME ORANGE

No one was better. Husing and football were the perfect fit, a match made in broadcasting heaven. His knowledge was scholastic. His voice pounded with authority. His style and word usage captured a rhythmic essence of the game itself—hits, slaps, hand-offs, and tackles!

From his royal castle above the gridiron fray, nothing negative could touch him. Hateful critics, two failed marriages, and nagging insecurity vanished. Behind the mike, Husing was Teflon. He had finally outlived the "putrid" fiasco. William Bingham, the Harvard AD, came to understand that Husing in the broadcast booth was much better than no Husing at all. By 1934, the entire episode was forgiven and Harvard home games were back on the CBS football schedule. Tough talk was expected on air, even welcomed by then. Hearing Ted Husing's voice on Saturday afternoon was like hearing one of President Roosevelt's "Fire-side Chats." It had become part of the game itself, sewn into the fabric, required listening for all those who loved football.[480]

The only time greatness eluded him was the same day it did every year, the first day of January. Ted felt emptiness. He craved to do the Rose Bowl. The New Year's Day game was not only the pinnacle contest of the season, it was arguably the broadcast event of the year. Millions tuned in, rabid fans clinging around the radio, hanging on every word. It seemed unfair that football's top announcer sat home gagged, forced into silence. Every fall new hope rose, but the chances unlikely, as long as he remained at CBS. The Rose Bowl was one of the few exclusives in broadcasting at the time. The game belonged to NBC. The event brought in big numbers of listeners and big bucks from advertisers. Ted was starved for the action, salivating, almost praying for a miracle. Every year, hope dissolved into reality. The answer remained the same, "NO!"

Ted did the next best thing, broadcast the annual Tournament of Roses Parade the same morning for CBS. [481] Ted sounded excited, describing the pageantry and sharing the stage with the new Ms. Rose Bowl Queen. But it never seemed to take thunder away from the competition. Chatting with the beautiful college coeds was no substitute for a live microphone inside the cathedral of college football. More than anything, Ted wanted the spotlight turned to him. No one respected the legacy of Graham McNamee more. But, he understood that the man was yesterday's news. Ted was in his prime, ready to take his rightful place in the annals of broadcasting.

Ted Husing never realized the answer stood above him on the parade route every New Year's morning. Just beyond the Rose Bowl's large, empty parking lot was Colorado Boulevard. The main drag cut scenically through the heart of Pasadena with homes, stores, and palm trees reaching for the mountains due east. Hundreds of eager spectators lined the street as early as 6 AM hoping for a prime view. Shortly after 9 AM, the parade marched wide with colorful floats and bass drum bands. Ted could see everything from his broadcast perch, except the street signs. Before it turned on Colorado, the parade began on another road, one filled with irony, a path significant of the future—Orange Grove Boulevard. Whomever named the street seemed to know life's destiny better than the man himself.

Like any urban community during the Great Depression, Miami, Florida was looking for ways to boost its sleeping economy. The land lifting days of the area's real-estate boom during the '20s was over. When the economy tanked, many investors lost their property and were forced to relocate. Others simply left in search of employment. One of those individuals was a young Connecticut native named Claude Morgan and his wife Regina.

"Before I was born, my parents lived in Miami," said their daughter Ann Lewis. "They had a car and good money. When the market crashed, they lost everything. My father went up to New York and found work as an electrician with the local union. Once he had that, he sent for my mother."[482] The Morgan's story was true of many in the early '30s.

Rich or poor, playboy or panhandler, the weather of South Florida was one thing that never went belly-up. Balmy temperatures and slicing rays of sunshine were always in season. Miami appealed to affluent Northeasterners whose teeth chattered for white beaches and warm-lit cabanas. The annual migration didn't happen until mid-January centering on world-class thoroughbred racing at Hialeah Park and the Flamingo Stakes.

The city desperately needed money. Local politicians searched for ways to stretch the season and add to the kitty. The popularity of football appealed to some Miamians as a way for the horse enthusiasts to come a month early, enjoy a game, and work on their tan, if so desired. Talk of a holiday gridiron contest began to circulate. Tropical Park Race Track in nearby Coral Gables accommodated by moving the post times up to late December. "Have a Green Christmas in Miami" became the motto. The entire state of Florida stood to benefit from the plan. "Tourists arriving in Miami would make other stops on the way down and on their return."[483] It seemed like the perfect proposal. South Florida offered the same attractive accoutrements as Southern California. And the success of the annual Rose Bowl was the model for a waiting financial windfall.

The game was initially referred to as the Palm Festival, debuting on New Year's Day, 1933. From the beginning it was clear that the game's organizers had an uphill battle to fight. The football contest played inside tiny Moore Park at the outskirts of town. Bought on credit, temporary wooden bleachers created a horseshoe that could accommodate only 5,000 fans.[484] The Rose Bowl, when packed, exceeded 90,000 strong. If the city was promoting green, there was little to show on the field of Moore Park. After a vicious tackle, brown dirt, sharp rocks, and hot sand typically broke a player's fall. The Rose Bowl was a virtual Garden of Eden, lavish, deep-rooted grass almost too pretty to run on.

The host school, the University of Miami, invited any college willing to make the trek south, expenses not included. Miami was far from a worthy opponent, the school three-years removed from bankruptcy. Supplying the team with black cleats, leather helmets, and clean uniforms, the standard tools of the trade, challenged budgeters and coaching staff alike. Looking to leave the snow and cold winds of the northeast behind was Manhattan College. The team was one of the best in the land. They ripped through 1932 with only two losses. Big crowds watched their games in famous stadiums like Ebbits Field and the Polo Grounds. The school's administration saw the Palm Festival as a way of rewarding the boys and enjoying some warm tropical skies. An easy win was a forgone conclusion. The team promised to keep the margin within three touchdowns.

The minute the powerhouse team arrived, though, trouble followed. The two-day boat trip left many of the players queasy. More ill feelings surfaced when it was discovered the game's organizers were cash-strapped. Manhattan's head coach Chick Meehan refused to step on the field until the full $3,000 appearance fee was paid in full. Local bookies with bulging pockets stepped in to cover the cost.[485] In front of 3,500 sleepy fans, Miami upset the heavily favored squad from New York 7–0. Few seemed to care. Many of the tickets unsold by game time were given away to passers-by and stragglers looking to see the game free. After Duquesne University came down from Pittsburgh a year later for the sun and fun, crushing the Hurricanes 33–7, the Palm Festival seemed doomed for a short life. Then came help.

Earnie Seiler was a football man all the way. Originally from Oklahoma, he played college ball in the dust of Stillwater at Oklahoma A&M. After his playing days, he drifted to South Florida with an architectural degree and became head coach at Miami High School. Two years later he was named Athletic Director of the Miami Recreation Department.[486] Seiler had a solid frame, wore glasses around his balding head, and smoked nervously on thick ten-cent cigars. It soon became apparent that Seiler was more than just a sports jock. He was an idea man. They called him the "Mad Genius."[487] Seiler was asked by Palm Festival head W. Keith Phillips to be the point-man for change. Maybe it was the architect inside or a daydreamer's imagination, but Seiler knew that if this "little game that could" were ever going to get anywhere, he would have to build the event into a spectacular show. One that people noticed.

His first suggestion was to find a new title for the game. Phillips and Miami Herald sports editor Dinty Dennis came up with the name "Orange Bowl." The new tag was an immediate improvement. Rose Bowl! Orange Bowl! Already, they felt closer to Pasadena. A pre-game parade and beauty queen pageant came next. For the 1935 contest, Bucknell trained down from Pennsylvania and steamrolled Miami 26–0. The game was a dull, one-sided affair. Even Seiler's glitzy new half-time show barely woke the crowd from their apathy. The big wigs and their money stayed north. The purpose of creating the game first and foremost was to generate cash, bring life. Hotels remained half-booked. Florida talked about the new Orange Bowl, but the other forty-eight states did not care. Obviously, Seiler, Phillips and the Committee had more work ahead.

The host team was turning out to be easy prey for the more elite eastern powers. The University of Miami's shocking win over

Manhattan three years earlier was clearly a fluke. The school's football program stepped on the field losers before most games ever started, bone thin, under-sized, and unequipped. Phillips and Seiler wanted to up the ante.

Red tape and last-minute refusals gave everyone pause in 1936. Many top-ranked colleges stayed unsold on the Orange Bowl. They heard the stories of unsavory conditions and empty bank accounts. Vanderbilt, Villanova, Ohio, Duke, North Carolina, Texas Christian, and NYU all politely turned down invitations.[488] Adding insult, the University of Miami even rejected a last-minute request. Finally, on December 9, Ole Miss agreed to play Catholic University. *The Miami Herald* reported that committee members "departed for their respective homes late yesterday afternoon, red-eyed, exhausted but happy."[489] The PR machine was way behind. By now, the Orange Bowl was only one of several holiday bowl games. Along with the Rose Bowl, gridiron brawls in Dallas, New Orleans, the Bacardi Bowl in Havana, and East versus West All-Stars in San Francisco were hyped.[490] Seiler needed a boost. The Orange Bowl was less than three weeks away. The Committee had to act quickly. Pacing his office with the radio on, the "Mad Genius" pondered the next move. From the talking box came inspiration. A booming voice shook the man deep in thought. "Good evening everyone, everywhere, this is Ted Husing in New York . . ."

Everyone knew that NBC was airing the Rose Bowl and added the spanking new Sugar Bowl to its New Year's broadcast schedule. What about CBS? Seiler could not blow the horn of publicity alone. Strong lungs and a set a pipes that turned heads was needed. A lone voice possessed the power to take the tiny Orange Bowl game out of Miami and feed it to the hungry football masses of America. That singular voice was the undisputed sound of football—Ted Husing.

The fading calendar did not work in Seiler's favor. With such little time to promote the game through the affiliates, Ted turned down the assignment. He, too, understood the art of show business. A grand event took time to cultivate and a great event required a grand entrance. It had to be right. He knew little about Miami. He knew even less about Earnie Seiler and the Orange Bowl Committee. Like any celebrity, however, Ted liked being stroked. But the idea of having his own Bowl game to call on New Year's Day was more than vanity could control.

"Husing desperately wanted a New Year's Day game for himself and for CBS," recalled Red Barber. "Ted was fit to be tied."[491]

The seeds were planted. He decided to wait until next year. He wondered if this was his golden ticket, the final dagger to hush the legacy of the "voice with a smile."

In the absence of Husing, not all was lost on the upcoming '36 contest. The network found the game attractive enough to offer the Committee access to some of their southern regional stations. With the affiliates lined up, the question of who would broadcast remained. They needed a name, someone with excitement, someone with weight. The man they got was the original voice of the south, Bill Munday.

William Shenault Munday burst onto the radio scene like a comet during the Rose Bowl broadcast of January 1, 1929. Munday's wild rodeo description of the game and spicy southern colloquialisms charmed the radio audience right out of their chairs. By the time Roy Reigals of Cal ran back an arrant Georgia Tech fumble the wrong way, listeners had forgotten about McNamee. "Bill Munday was a left-handed baseball pitcher and was also a left-handed sports announcer," chuckled longtime friend Dan Magill.[492] Fellow friend and Georgian Ernie Harwell agreed. "Bill Munday made Red Barber sound like a Connecticut Yankee. He was a beauty."[493] A player just wasn't tackled, but brought down to "terra firma." When the offense huddled they went into a "crap-shooters formation" and a touchdown scored brought the runner into "the land of milk and honey" instead of the end zone.

As colorful as Munday talked, he drank booze with equal abandon. Though his rowdy, untamed descriptions continued throughout the early '30s, crude, offensive comments began leaking into his broadcasts. Bill's work suffered and whispers of drunken escapades had NBC executives worried. The final straw came at a regular season contest between Georgia Tech and Alabama where Munday opened up his broadcast in bold fashion, "This is Bill Munday from Legion Field in Birmingham, a town of hard drinkers and fast women."[494] He was suspended and soon fired. Bill Munday did not know that a stumbling life of feeble employment awaited him. Even worse, begging for money on the corners of Atlanta to feed his addiction lasted nearly a decade.[495] When Seiler came calling he had not yet hit rock bottom. Munday continued to freelance his way around the old confederacy calling football and announcing public addresses. Earnie heard the gossip about the former network star, but was willing to give the man the benefit of the doubt. "What southern gentleman doesn't enjoy a good belt of rye every once in awhile," Seiler convinced himself. "Bill just likes his before, during, and after the game, that's all."

Seiler shelled out $500 to pay the line cost and for the first time, the Orange Bowl was on the air.[496] Watching the game from the stands while gazing up at the broadcast booth, Seiler anxiously chomped at his cigar. Catholic U beat out Ole Miss on a missed extra point 20–19. Munday's call of the game went without a hitch. By 1937 the Committee had learned from four years of baby steps, stumbling, tumbling, that the Orange Bowl child still looked feeble compared to the giant bouquet of roses in Pasadena. It was time to grow up. The Committee promised that the January 1, 1937, contest would be the beginning of something spectacular.

"Get Husing" became the cry! It didn't take long to see movement. Part-time planning turned into a twelve-month crusade for perfection. By the early summer of '36, Ted was hearing stories from Seiler about the "hugeness and grandness of the Orange

Bowl." Seiler abandoned the meek facilities at Moore Park and decided to move the game to grounds called Miami Stadium. Cynics defied anyone to tell the difference, however. Temporary bleachers, patches of grass, and a wobbly press box made up the latest place to play the Orange Bowl. Yet, Sieler pushed on.

He bragged to the CBS announcer how delicious the stadium and modern the broadcast facilities looked. Seiler made the location sound like a palace fit for royals. He was not about to let the truth get in the way of a good sales pitch. What he sold was pure fantasy. If Ted needed any more coaxing, he heard enough. He agreed to do the game and began sharing his plans for New Year's Eve with friends. The idea of catching McNamee swirled his imagination. Ted Husing had never been to Miami. For a man who prided himself on preparation, Ted was willing to let the little fine points be worked out later. The only thing Ted cared about was the football game. Ted Husing had his sights set, but remained deaf, dumb, and blind on the realities of the Orange Bowl.

While Ted dreamed, Seiler worked feverishly. Ted had taken the bait. Feeding a worm to the big fish did not guarantee anything.

Seiler traveled to Washington during the late summer and convinced Congress to pay for a new stadium through the Public Works Administration. He used every trick in the book. Seiler discovered that Charlie Grimm, a fraternity brother from Okalahoma A&M, was a member of the WPA board. He talked up the virtues of Miami and the need for employment. When Seiler discovered that Post Master General James Farley was a graduate of Catholic University, he invited the team to play in the next Orange Bowl game.[497] Seiler never failed to share with the governing body if Mr. Ted Husing was going to be part of the festivities. For how long, no one knew.

Extra money to finance the facility would be raised by selling bonds to local businessmen.[498] Purchase of a bond meant pick of the litter for fifty-yard-line seats at the new site. Seiler hoped to stretch the money from goal line to goal line.

The "Mad Genius" had done a stellar job of convincing Washington that South Florida needed a new football playground. The big hurdle, convincing the good people of Miami. In October of 1936, city property owners passed a seven to one resolution in favor of breaking ground. The Committee danced in celebration. Then, the music stopped. Those who opposed the stadium cried foul. Many qualified voters were allegedly denied ballots based on misinformation, paperwork errors, or, worse, fraud. The courts agreed and overturned the decision.[499]

The setback was only temporary. Seiler raised enough stink to have a fresh count scheduled for early December. With Miami mayor A.D.H. Fossey helping promote the resolution, the Committee this time made sure all their "Is" were dotted and Ts crossed. They even went so far as to list over 6,000 names of eligible voters and their districts in local newspapers. This time, in a landslide decision, the stadium finally passed.

The new stadium loomed, in plan only. For the time being, the old one remained. So did its appalling reputation, crumbling structure, and minor league press box facilities. Somehow, Ted seemed to be the only one in the dark. A negative word never reached his ears. Blind ignorance or wishful thinking, the radioman actually looked forward to his trip to Miami. A hero's welcome was expected, a coronation for Ted Husing, the new king of New Year's Day. Then again, he had yet to lay eyes on Miami Field's broadcast booth.

All throughout the 1936 campaign, Ted fervently plugged the Orange Bowl. Seiler himself wrote the promotional copy expounding upon the virtues of Miami Beach and the city's rich football tradition, wiring them each week for Ted to read over the air. By Christmas, fans from Syracuse to Seattle heard the sounds of warm Atlantic surf and shoulderpads crashing in their ears. The final piece of the puzzle, find the teams.

Making their second trip to Gator Country in three years

was Duquesne University. Florida was a long way from Pittsburgh, but beginning to feel like home. Led by all-American linebacker Mike Basrak, the Dukes were hoping to reprise their previous visit, hot sand and a big win. This time, the opponent would not be the University of Miami. Unfortunately, for Duquesne, Mississippi State was chosen to represent the south in the game. This group of quick-hitting farm boys brought a different brand of football with them to Miami. They would prove to be much stiffer competition.

The new stadium meant a step in the right direction. However, Seiler and Company knew that it was worthless without fans to fill the seats. The future looked dim, everything riding on Husing. Seiler and Company feared Ted might throw a fit once he saw the hen house called broadcast booth and jump the first train back to New York.[500] Everything the committee worked so hard to garner— lost forever. If the new Orange Bowl was to rival what happened every New Year's in Pasadena, it needed a big-time broadcaster. America trusted his voice. If Ted was at the game, it had to be great. Everyone knew Ted was coming to Miami, but would he stay?

The Committee wondered how to handle the temperamental broadcaster. His sullen reputation arriving long before he ever did. They found out that Ted liked to have fun. Perhaps that was an area they could exploit, work to their advantage. Ted loved to gamble on fast horses and flashy women. Miami had plenty of both. The plan was to keep the star broadcaster occupied until game time. And for God's sake, don't let him see the booth!

The Committee booked Ted into the high-flying Roney Plaza on the strip. The place was a spiderweb of delight, a 400-seat, five-star restaurant, spacious beach front rooms, well-stocked bars with sun umbrellas stretched along the sand, and a giant kidney-shaped swimming pool surrounded by beautiful girls in bathing suits. The hotel billed itself as "play headquarters for the world's most respected minds."[501] There was little doubt that Ted saw himself as one and he expected to be treated accordingly.

Ted and his assistant Jimmy Dolan arrived in Miami on December 28, four days before the big game. There were others in the Husing entourage. Also making the trip south was his guiding light of the high-life Mark Hellinger and Max Kriendler, younger brother of 21 Club co-owner Jack Kriendler. Newspaper columnist Heywood Broun, who defended him during the "putrid" calamity, also hopped onboard.[502] They looked forward to visiting former heavyweight champion Jack Dempsey and his new Miami restaurant, among others.[503] If the Orange Bowl assignment turned out to be a bust, Ted assured himself he would not drink alone, 21 Miami style.

Football and work however came first. In typical Husing fashion, his first instinct was to visit the stadium and check out the unfamiliar radio works. Seiler understood that Ted's sensitive eyes and broad ego were not ready for the shock quite yet. Whenever Ted mentioned work, Seiler steered him in a new direction. Racetracks, Jai Alai matches, and the city's hottest club spots purposely filled Ted's agenda, day and night.

"We knew Ted was a swinger, and the Roney was a big-league hotel," recalled Seiler years later. "When Ted got in a cabana, got a glass in his hand, saw the pretty girls around the place, he forgot about going to the football field. We took him around to the nightclubs and kept his glass filled, and every time he said something about going to the stadium, we said just as soon as we had another drink."[504]

Seiler toyed with the idea of driving Ted over to the new stadium sight, simply a huge pile of dirt and a bulldozer on the corner of 3rd Street and 16th Avenue. He thought it too risky considering it was a stone's throw away from the very place he did not want the announcer to see. Instead, Seiler talked about the glory of the future and the modern accoutrements of advanced architecture, like a working elevator to the press box.[505] Ted didn't care about the future. He was much more concerned about the now. The broadcaster had a football game to call and was feeling ill prepared.

"What about the stadium, Earnie? I'd really like to have a gander," insisted Ted. "Sure, sure we'll go see," assured Seiler. "I want to run by the hotel first. There's a girl I want you to meet."

For the time being the diversions worked. As the clock struck twelve on the morning of January 1, 1937, Ted toasted in the New Year. He shook his friend's hands, kissed a few of the females, and retired to bed—alone. He had a long day ahead of him and sleep was important. As much as Ted liked the nightlife, he was a man who knew control.

"Surprisingly, he never drank much," remembered Jimmy Dolan. "I mentioned that when he was with the guys he would have a scotch and soda. He never finished one. When the drink was half gone, he would ask the waiter for a fresh one, so if the rest of the crowd had six drinks, he had only three."[506]

After an early breakfast, Ted and Jimmy went over some last-minute preparations, rewriting the opening, checking rosters of the two squads, and making sure the blessed Annunciator was up to snuff. Ted rapped his spoon rhythmically against a coffee cup. He was getting nervous, as time ticked away. The game kicked off in less than four hours. Finally, he tracked down Seiler and demanded to see the broadcast site. The "Mad Genius" tried to buy more time. He suggested they watch the brand new Orange Bowl Parade float down Flagler Street.

"Later," the broadcaster insisted. "Just show me the god-damn booth!"

Dolan grabbed the spotting board and sat next to Ted in the car. Seiler swallowed hard and jumped into the passenger seat. No one knew what to expect. How would Ted react to the deplorable conditions once he saw it? Would he laugh or storm away insulted, looking for the next train back to Manhattan?

The twenty-block ride from Roney Plaza to the field did not take long. The broadcaster jumped out of the car and jogged up toward the front gate. Ted had always been drawn to stadiums, the lush green grass, painted white lines, and rows of seats cutting into the earth's bending horizon. He could also count on the smell of boiled franks and freshly roasted peanuts buried in salt and oil tickling his nostrils. What he saw, however, was the sports ground in its worst possible condition, depleted, lifeless, and empty. The only movements came from a few tired hands pushing lawn mowers and hammering nails. Evidently, some details remained unfinished. Seiler and his crew stayed cautiously behind. "The boys really worked overtime trying to get the place ready," Seiler chimed in. "Once this spot gets full of people it'll make Yankee Stadium sound like a funeral parlor."

Ted nodded his head up and down in apathetic agreement and finally asked, "Where's the booth?"

Seiler ushered Ted and Dolan further inside the stadium while keeping the mood light.

"Duquesne Dukes! I hate when the school nickname sounds just like the school itself. Confuses the hell out of everybody don't it?" he said. "Hell, I don't care what they call themselves as long as they play a good game."

Ted grew impatient. With a raised voice, he asked again about the booth. Seiler dreaded this moment and pointed up toward the chicken coop press box sitting on top of the grandstands. Ted turned around and studied the small work place. He noticed a green box made of wood with four open-air windows. Covering two of the windows was what looked like to be chicken wire. The structure reminded Ted of a tree-fort he often played on during his boyhood in Gloversville. Underneath hung a yellow banner with the words TED HUSING, COLUMBIA BROADCASTING SYSTEM stenciled in black letters.[507] A thin thirty-foot ladder stretched up the side walls. It was the only way to enter the press box. Dolan shook his head back and forth, eyes looking out toward the late morning sun. The little Irishman knew the boss was not happy. He, too, was disappointed. Extra work would have to be put in to save the broadcast.

With his left hand, Ted simulated a climbing motion toward

Seiler, as if asking about the seriousness of the situation. He tried to speak, but Ted cut him off.

"Christ's sake, Earnie, I didn't expect air-conditioning, but this fucking thing is more suited to broadcast a cock fight than a football game."

Seiler tried to keep Ted from losing his cool.

"I'm sorry Ted, I know you're upset but this is the best we could do with the old dump. If I told you the truth you would've never come down. Once the new stadium's finished for next year, I promise you that booth will have shiny glass and a gold microphone to boot. Can't tell me the Rose Bowl will have that."

Ted knew that the Rose Bowl would possess no such things. He also knew that Earnie was shoveling the bull deep and heavy by now. But, Ted was impressed with the man's fortitude and passion. Seiler was the kind of guy that could make things happen, even if a few white lies were told along the way. If Earnie believed in making the Orange Bowl special then Ted could help make it the radio sports event of the year. What else did he come down to Miami to do? Ted was still a bit perturbed. His large ego and stellar reputation told him he deserved better conditions. Yet up till now, Ted had to admit he was enjoying everything Miami. Thanks in large part to Seiler and his hospitable staff giving a whirlwind tour of sights, sounds, and smells. If they were willing to go the extra mile in making him feel welcomed, then Ted reasoned he could be a little uncomfortable for three hours in the hot seat. After all, Ted practically invented the "shit-hole" broadcast condition.

"So far, I've never broadcast from a barbed-wire fence or a trapeze," Ted once told a writer. "But, I think I've covered all the other thorny sites."[508]

The press box at Miami Field was about to be added to his resume. It was settled—Ted would stay. As the sweat formed on Earnie Seiler's fast-talking lips, Ted knew there was only one thing left to do.

"What time's the first race tomorrow at Hialeah?" Ted barked at Seiler.

Earnie stood dumbfounded.

"Hialeah? They're not up for a couple more weeks," Ted corrected himself, "I meant Tropical Park."

Earnie tried to stay up with the questioning announcer.

"One forty-five, I think," he answered.[509]

"Well, depending on how much champagne I drink tonight, I expect to have a good tip and a winning ticket by then," Ted gruffly stated. "If not, lunch with a sophisticated lady will do, none of those ditzy broads you've been feeding me the last couple nights."

Earnie answered with relief and a smile.

"I think that can be arranged, Ted, my boy. I most definitely think we can."

Ted waved to Dolan and they both ascended the steps toward the chicken coop.

Under partly sunny skies, a seventy-two-degree day glossed over the New Year. Exactly 9,210 fans squeezed into the temporary bleachers at Miami Stadium.[510] Though the action was fierce on the field, many gazed up at the three-story broadcast booth. A celebrity was in their midst and curiosity roused the senses. Below, Duquesne and Mississippi State were digging in. An old-fashioned football game was being played the way Husing and the Committee hoped for—close.

Minutes after Ted opened the broadcast, it looked to be Mississippi State's day. The Maroons crossed the goal line first on an Ike Pickle plunge from ten yards out. Both teams played hard, but in the end, quarterback Boyd Brumbaugh engineered a stunning 13–12 come-from-behind win for the Dukes. Brumbaugh hit right end Ernie Hifferle late in the fourth quarter for a dixty-seven-yard touchdown strike, completing the Duquesne comeback. Drums pounded. Dust kicked and Ted Husing fell in love with football one more time.

Following the game, everyone wore smiles, including the

broadcaster. By late afternoon, the sun pushed toward the west. Ted looked around and saw his many newspaper friends and cohorts filing out of the booth.[511] Pencil marks, darkened cigarette burns, and white crumbled paper covered the cramped wooden quarters. He thought of next year and hoped this place would be nothing but a heap of ashes and memory, chicken wire and all. He unplugged the Annunciator and placed it safely inside its case. Dolan tucked the machine under his arm and stepped gingerly toward the ladder outside. The two partners shook hands, another job well done. This one was special. They both felt it. "Same time next year, my friend?" Ted joked. Dolan wisely answered back. "For our sake let's hope they get the new stadium built. Air-conditioning would be nice." Descending the steps, Ted thought of McNamee and hoped he, too, was aware of the Orange Bowl like the rest of America.

The real evidence, however, was at the bank. Ted brought money. Phones rang. Hotels filled. And turn-styles at the gate swung open with plenty of hungry sports fans. The following year attendance doubled as 18,000 plus opened the new Orange Bowl sight, then known as Burdine Stadium. By 1939, nearly 40,000 crunched into the expanding facilities to watch Tennessee upset top-ranked Oklahoma 17–0.[512] The sensational growth of the Orange Bowl sprouted like a giant backyard weed in the wet Florida marsh. Husing had radio-land talking about the fresh, sleek events in Miami. There was a new party on New Year's Day and it was not in Southern California or on NBC. It was brought to the listeners by Ted Husing and the Columbia Broadcasting Company.

"If it wasn't for him, it might have been after the late '40s or early '50s before the Orange Bowl took off, said Seiler's son Peter. "Having someone with that kind of personality and the name he had really made a big difference."[513]

Seiler's gamble worked. He hooked broadcasting's big fish, and would be eternally grateful to the instant credibility the Husing name brought. For the next ten years, Ted became a fixture in Miami during New Year's.

"From then on he helped make it a truly great event," Earnie Seiler emphatically stated. "He helped us get good teams. For years he rode in the parade the night before the game and broadcast to the folks on the stret with a public-address system."[514]

"Ted Husing was a very big man in the growth of the Orange Bowl," wrote Red Barber decades later. "I have dwelt upon it at this length because it is THE example of *one*, the power of radio and, *two*, the power of Husing."[515]

Snow fell hard on New York City. Wind and air several degrees below freezing sliced pain at the face and ears. The warm Atlantic breeze blowing about the Orange Bowl agreed with him. He would stay a few extra days. Before the game, most feared his stay in Miami to be brief. Throughout the winter, Ted's schedule was open, his assignments up North limited. Why rush back, he figured? The area's professional golf and tennis tournaments grabbed his attention. Baseball spring training camps hummed with activity. The CBS man soaked up the track and hotel hospitality through February.[516]

Clearly, Ted was captivated by the charm of Miami. Preliminary ideas were discussed with Earnie Seiler and the Committee about next year's festivities.[517] The broadcaster wanted to be better prepared. His next Orange Bowl assignment was less than ten months away.

CHAPTER TWENTY-SIX

SOCIAL SECURITY

I t was a thick piece of gray paper about half the size of a bank check. Typed in bold font on the front was his name and nine curious numbers below. A few days before traveling to Miami, Ted received his first social security card in the mail.[518] President Roosevelt seemed like a nice enough fellow, and Ted was all for helping people in need. But retirement and old age were far away. The day would never come, if Ted had his druthers. Being without money and the ability to make obscene amounts of it was unthinkable. Enjoying South Florida as one of the richest, most famous voices in radio, such matters never crossed his mind. By spring, duty called and he returned to the thriving metropolis with a dark rich tan and a shit-eating grin.

Ted did complain. But, much of his professional discontent was done for show. The year of 1937 was not five months old and he was on his way to yet another #1 showing in the annual United Press Poll as radio's Top Sports Announcer. He loved it, feeding off the opulence the way a sponge grows large in water. None of the success surprised anyone, especially Ted. Now he wore all the trapping of success, the chauffer, the money, the attitude. "Ted doesn't wait for the world to tell him he's good. He admits it," wrote *Radio*

Guide. "Whenever he turns up at any event of importance, his favorite greeting is: 'Okay, you can start the parade. Husing is here!'"[519]

Ted's dominance often kept people at bay. The stories of his large ego and volatile personality were now legendary. Over-zealous fans hoping for an autograph often received a grunt, cold shoulder, or, the worst slight of all, a nasty quip of the Husing's acerbic tongue. An excited father once mistakenly approached the radioman with photographs of his newborn baby. Ted took a dismissive glance at the pictures, called the child "ugly" and walked away.[520] Colleagues mostly approached him with kid gloves, not knowing which side of his temperament would appear. Jimmy Dolan described his friend's force of personality this way. "People said he was temperamental. Most people with great talent are. Egotistical? Yes! But, what do you do with a man who tells you he is the best in his profession and then goes out and proves it."[521]

Ted's vanity was mainly surface, a shield to protect an otherwise gentle, sensitive heart. Once the harsh exterior was dropped, lasting friendships formed. West Coast announcer Don Wilson joined NBC in the early '30s to do sports. Everyone at the network warned him to beware Husing, saying "he's high and mighty and sits in a little white castle all his own."[522] After meeting the CBS man on a frozen Solider Field in Chicago, Wilson came away pleasantly surprised. "Ted was instantly the exact antithesis of what he'd been described to me. He was the most generous man that you've ever known about in your life and he was the most knowledgeable."[523]

Trying to figure Ted out was ordinarily a lost cause. Winning him over was futile. He pegged some as enemies, a threat to his domain, while others were simply accepted on face value, not a question asked. Everyone agreed, being on the good side of Husing was the preferred choice. He used his influence to lift underdogs, or further causes he believed in. When the local New York musician union considered a strike in 1935 over broadcast remote residuals, Ted sat in on meetings, coaching his pals on how to deal with network executives.[524] The union never did strike.

On May 6, 1937, Ted got the chance to show his range as a newsman once more. The days of the Graf Zeppelin were well behind him. German airship landings at Lakehurst, New Jersey, had become so commonplace that radio rarely put them on the broadcast schedule anymore. Numerous flights a year made a spotting in the skies over New York run of the mill. Except when the unthinkable happened. Germany's latest helium wonder, the Hindenburg, exploded just above its mooring and burned within minutes. Thirty-five passengers including one person on the ground died in the fiery blaze. Flames shot 400–500 feet in the air and could be seen from miles around. When the news reached CBS headquarters, Ted raced over to the horrific sight. Unbeknownst to most, NBC already had a man at the location, Chicago announcer Herb Morrison.

His station WLS, an NBC affiliate, assigned him to cover the landing of the airship. Though Morrison spoke into a microphone, his words were not going over the air live. The network was merely testing new wire recording equipment for a possible future broadcast. Morrison never expected a late afternoon of mortality for some and immortality for himself. His hysterical, mournful cries of "It's crashing. It's burning . . . Oooh, one of the worst catastrophes in the world" were replayed over and over. Morrison's raw emotions made the back-bone of a nation tingle with horror.[525] Death and smoke were alive in the air once Ted arrived. He grabbed his mike and interviewed several eyewitnesses.[526] His reporting, as always, was quick, calm, and factual. Because NBC's account was not to broadcast, or rebroadcast, until later that night, Husing and Columbia were actually first on the air with spot coverage. But, Morrison and his crackling voice would rightfully take its place in history. Trumped by the competition, Ted would merely be a footnote to one of the worst aviation disasters ever.

He continued seeing more and more of Helen in spite of his ever-increasing calendar. No one quite understood Ted and

Helen's relationship after divorce, especially Hayton. He understood there was a child involved, a shared concern. For that reason alone, a certain level of civility was expected. But, the bandleader noticed what everyone else did, the latenight telephone calls, shared meals, even the occasional gift. Ted suddenly found time to spend with his wife, except for the fact that she now was his ex-wife? Hayton saw the vulnerability in Helen. He dealt with jealousy in a much different way than Ted. Instead of a fight, Hayton took flight. He accepted an offer to become Bing Crosby's musical director in films, and relocated with Helen to Hollywood. [527] This time for good.

Pegge also made the move, spending her summers in California. Each year, the same routine unfolded. After three months of horseback riding and visiting movie lots, she returned east in the fall for another semester at Friends. A solid, loving relationship developed between stepdaughter and stepfather. "I know my mother absolutely adored him," said Kate Lacey. "They were very close. She felt that Lennie was just the salt of the earth."[528] Ted did his best to stay close to his daughter.[529] On her thirteenth birthday, he pulled out all the stops, an unforgettable lunch at 21. Pegge and several of her friends were given the royal treatment, a full tour of the club, including wine cellar, run of the menu topped off with cake and ice cream. The giddy teenagers left with autograph books filled with signatures of Ted's famous friends. "When he paid attention to her it was terrific," said Pegge's daughter Kim.[530] For the most part, moments of closeness and affection remained rare.

Following the '38 Orange Bowl, Ted again set up shop in Miami for a few weeks. Instead of soaking up the sun like he did the previous year, he decided to eat up the night. His remotes from Miami's hottest music clubs were a fixture on the network. And he again showed his eye for discovering new talent. A young Cuban performer named Desi Arnaz became the latest find. Since his early teens, Arnaz was a transplanted refugee to Miami. His father was a wealthy landowner and member of the Cuban senate. The family enjoyed the benefits of power in his hometown of Santiago. Yet, after a political uprising, the father was jailed and the rest of the family fled to the States penniless.[531] Desi turned to singing and music to make a living. In the spring of '37, he was hired for an eight-month backup stint with rumba star Xavier Cugat in New York. An impatient Arnaz, however, burned to make it on his own.

Receiving Cugat's blessing, he quit, returning to Florida to take a shot as leader with his own band. Arnaz put his life on the line, a make or break situation. "I had my mind made up—if I was a flop, I'd go back to Cuba and stay there."[532] He landed a gig at a brand new room called La Conga Club. From the start, the gig went poorly. On opening night, empty tables and an unresponsive audience seemed to finish the Latin bandleader before he left the stage. After a brief set of songs, the owner Bob Kelly heard enough. He promised to fire them on the spot. Sitting at Kelly's table that night was Husing. The broadcaster had other ideas, offering Kelly a deal he couldn't refuse.

"Luckily for me, Ted Husing was there when we were fired," remembered Desi years later. "And Ted told the owner, 'The band isn't much, but the young lead singer has something. If you'll keep him, I'll broadcast his music every night free on my radio program.'"[533] That's exactly what Ted did. Desi Arnaz was on his way. Sprouting from the airwaves of Miami, the conga craze shook America from coast-to-coast. Within four months, Desi was in New York headlining. Fame beckoned, Hollywood called, and an inspiring romance with a fiery redheaded actress named Lucy soon followed.

"All the wonderful things that have since happened to me would have been impossible without Ted Husing," Desi admitted.[534] To Desi Arnaz, that night at the La Conga changed his life forever. In contrast, Ted never mentioned it to anyone, most notably Desi Arnaz. It was years later that Arnaz was told what Ted had done to save his career. Ted never gave it another thought. He was just one more kid with talent who needed a helping hand. As with so many before and many after, Ted was willing to back his reputation on their promise.

On West 69th Street in the old neighborhod, Ted's father's complaints of pain reached a fever pitch. Bertha had grown accustomed to her husband's shallow breathing due to asthma, exacerbated by decades of heavy smoking. Now he complained of sharp jabs near his groin and stomach. The family admitted him to New York Hospital on August 2, 1938. Doctors discovered a hernia and operated immediately.[535] His damaged, 70-year-old body did not respond well. Eleven days later, Henry Husing, saloonkeeper, maître d', landlord, man of the people, died.

All the accolades, all the fame showered on the radioman for his talent to communicate germinated from the soul of his father. Gone was the man who taught the true power and dexterity of words. Henry, in his food service days, knew how to work a crowd. He continued the practice in the old Hell's Kitchen neighborhood, holding court while respectfully boasting about his famous son. Even Jimmy Walker envied Henry's political savvy, calling him "the mayor of 69th Street."[536] His occasional visits to the Husing home were the talk of the quarter. But, Walker's skills of shaking hands and working a crowd became second to the grace and charisma of dear ole dad. The scars on Henry's face couldn't hide the smile he wore being the father of a radio debutant. Surprisingly, Pegge felt the loss of Henry above any. "She loved him dearly," said Pegge's future husband David Lacey. "He was more of a father to her than her father was because Ted was out being big time and busy so much. He used to take her to Yankee baseball games, Coney Island. Her grandfather and grandmother, both of them, they were like her parents almost particularly after the divorce."[537]

On August 16, the family gathered to bury him at Kenisco Cemetery in White Plains. On the cusp of a scenic hilltop surrounded by names like Schultze, Rudolph, Bleichroeder, and Hindsburg, Henry Husing would call his final resting place. "All my friends from

Germany are buried here," he would often tell his wife. "When I join them I'll have no trouble rounding up a card game."[538] His wish was to have no tombstone. Ted felt his father deserved more than an un-marked grave, but gave way to his father's request. Bertha purchased the lot next to her husband. When her time came, the two could lie together. To soothe his grief, Ted jumped at the usual forms of dis-traction, work—the 21, and continuing his jumbled quest for love.

Around 1939, a new girl floated into Ted's life. Betty Law-ford was different from his other romantic interests. The first thing that attracted him was her accent. Born in England, Lawford arrived in New York more mature, more regal than most for a life in show business. Her father Ernest Lawford dazzled audiences on the West End and on Broadway in critically acclaimed runs of "The Ivory Door" and "Major Barbara."[539] His daughter, however, did more than dazzle on stage. The Broadway hit comedy "The Women" made her many a man's fantasy, including Ted Husing. She sat drip-ping naked in a bubble bath most of the play.[540] Her younger cousin Peter lived in Los Angeles pursuing an acting career in movies.[541] Betty also worked in film, appearing in over forty pictures.[542] The title of one of one her early movies "Love Before Breakfast" may have said everything about her relationship with Ted.

Both were on the rebound. Lawford's marriage to producer Monta Bell recently hit the skids, Ted's marital misfortunes already well documented. The two became an item, seen around town. When "The Women" went on the road, Lawford traveled with the cast, reviving her famous role as Crystal Allen, "the girl in the bath-tub."[543] Ted followed her around the country, trying to match his game assignments near whatever town she happened to be playing. Ted adored her. She was young, insatiably feminine, but at the same time, an independent woman, displaying a dry, British sense of hu-mor equal to that of her lover. "I saw him a lot with Betty Lawford," shared Gary Stevens. "He put his arm around me one day. I don't know how her name came up. He just gave me a little shot in the arm and said what a lady she is."

Lawford met Ted's marriage proposals with a laugh, thinking it was a joke. The actress saw their romance as something other than love, two warm bodies filling a void, companions enjoying each other's company, a roll in the hay. Some couples make better lovers than roommates. Why ruin a perfectly good friendship by getting married? For Husing, there was nothing funny about replacing Helen. Every woman he ever fell for never had a clue, never had a fighting chance. In the end, Ted blamed himself, preserving Lawford's unblemished guise, "I put her on a high pedestal and never once, in my personal estimation, did she fall from her exalted position."[544]

The night before the 1940 Orange Bowl it rained. Ted retired early to bed as usual before a big broadcast. Still he had trouble sleeping. He arrived at the stadium the next day, groggy, restless, out of sorts. His mood lifted as the game approached, a shot of excitement bringing him to airtime. As he closed his eyes to gather himself, he saw a vision of an infant child lying in a crib. It was little Peggemae. She had woken in the dark from a deep, happy slumber and saw the eyes of her father watching her sleep. Even at such a tender, innocent age, Pegge recognized the face. Ted saw her face light up in a wide, toothless smile. Circular shape of her hue green-colored pupils, the diving angle of her lips, the gray shadows of her hallowed cheeks, just like his, engrained in his mind's eye forever. Something, he thought, was tragic, sad, regretful. He saw but understood little. She lifted a hand and waved hello. Or was it goodbye? Or maybe it was come back soon, daddy, I miss you. He missed Pegge. He missed his former wife. He wanted to see her. The announcer opened his eyes and saw the field and action before him. Ted grabbed the mike and welcomed the listening audience. As a fresh decade dawned, life for Ted Husing looked bright and smelled even sweeter. Looks were often deceiving. There was a devil to pay.

CHAPTER TWENTY-SEVEN

THE LAST OF OUR CLAN

R aised voices were scarce. Blood never spilled. Challenging the other side was always accepted in good fun. One thing Ted never tired of was the daily battle of airwave supremacy with NBC. Once during the 1933 World Marble Championships from Atlantic City on CBS, famous Detroit bandleader Vincent Lopez was a guest of Ted's during the broadcast. After innocently plugging his Sunday primetime show for the NBC Blue Network, the Master sprung into action with a quick ad lib. "Of course, we all know what NBC stands for: Never Beats Columbia!"[545] Over the years much of the intense snipping subsided with maturity and age. Ted had proved himself superior, rich, respected, and the undisputed king of the sports airwaves. When everything else faded, however, the shadowy figure of Graham McNamee remained. Graham McNamee represented more than the opposition for Ted. He embodied history, status, and immortality. Those things were more important than a large audience and strong ratings. Numbers changed. A name stayed forever.

With Ted's commanding lead on the competition, NBC brought up a new voice to rival CBS. Bill Stern was more than another sports announcer. He personified the depths opponents would go to draw attention away from Husing. Stern from start to finish was all about the hype. Born and raised in Western New York, he came to the big city as a stage manager working for well-known show producer Sam "Roxy" Rothafel. When Roxy opened Radio City in 1932, Stern came along for the ride.[546] Yet, deep down, he yearned to do radio. NBC gave Stern a shot assisting Graham McNamee on football broadcasts during the 1934 season. Critics loved the newcomer's tense, fast-talking style and begged to hear more.

Network vice president John Royal obliged, ordering McNamee to let the kid call the first quarter of the Army versus Illinois game from Champaign the following week. An overeager Stern asked his friends to flood NBC with telegrams praising his work. The plan backfired when the messages arrived hours before kick-off. Royal wasn't amused and fired Stern on the spot.[547]

The following year, Stern took a job in Shreveport, Louisiana, as football voice of Centenary College. It was not the networks. But, Stern worried little. He was on the air and free to blast his showy descriptions to whomever cared to listen. On a hot October morning that growing world of optimism crashed. While driving back from a broadcast in Austin, Texas, Stern's car skidded off the road and flipped over.[548] Pinned under its massive weight, his left leg was severely damage, amputated within a month, sawed clean from the bone just above the knee. In the car with him was his assistant Jack Gelzer, who miraculously survived without a scratch. Stern lay on the road in excruciating pain, waiting nearly an hour before help arrived. "Gelzer told me he never whimpered. He never made a sound," remembered Bill Mazer. "He never said a word."[549]

Depressed and dashed, Stern recuperated in a New York hospital, convinced his career in radio was finished. His old boss John Royal from NBC stopped by to offer well wishes. In an effort to lift the ailing announcer's spirits, he promised Stern a job when his condition improved. Royal figured he'd never see Bill Stern again. He was wrong. Stern willed himself back to health. Fitted with a prosthesis and aid of a cane, like a spider he crawled into Royal's office ten months later ready to work.

The meteoric climb of Stern as sports announcing star took shape that fall. He returned to assist on football broadcasts, and then pushed his way up as number-two man on the network after Bill Slater quit NBC in 1937 over money issues. With the aging Graham McNamee assigned less and less sports, the stage was set for Stern to usurp power. He was looking for a slick vehicle to showcase his talents as dramatic story-teller and pumping sports enthusiast. In October of 1939, Stern hit the jackpot. His two loves of sports and theater became one with the "Colgate Friday Night Sports Reel."

The fifteen-minute show was suppose to be about sports. It was more "Ripley's Believe It or Not" than anything. The stories he told were pure fiction. Traditional sports fans rolled their eyes. Stern, however, wasn't really concerned about them.[550] It seemed everyone else, from impressionable teenage boys to penned-up housewives couldn't get enough. The show received huge ratings. And Colgate paid him handsomely for his efforts, The year 1940 heard him call a litany of events like track and field, championship fights, and the Rose Bowl. For the first time in nearly a decade, Ted Husing was not voted America's favorite sports announcer by *Radio Daily*.[551] It was Bill Stern. Also joining the rollcall of sports voices was another newcomer, Harry Wismer. The Michigan native was more self-promoter than announcer, too busy name-dropping and shaking hands than following the action. However, his gumption in bargaining with advertisers helped Ted and Stern raise their asking price considerably.[552] Gone completely from the list was "the voice with a smile."

The life, the pressure, the responsibility had taken its toll. He was a forgotten man, relegated to the garbage heap. By the early 1940s, McNamee had plenty of time on his hands to reminisce. He was dropped completely by the network when it came to calling sports, nary a football game, regatta race, or soapbox derby. Universal Pictures also let him go, ending his longtime lucrative duties as newsreel narrator.[553] The only gigs offered McNamee were commercial shows and the rare special events announcer. In 1941, he was brought back to MC, the network's fifteenth anniversary show at the Waldorf Astoria. It was a taste of past glories. He looked thinner, less hair with a shade of gray, the voice not quite as crisp.

McNamee continued wearing a grin, happy to still be in the public eye. Privately, he sulked, dulling his disappointment in alcohol.[554] Radio critic Ben Gross remembered visiting the aging announcer during those waning dark days, a bitter, angry man. "He sat in a room crowded with trophies, countless scrolls, loving cups, and medals bestowed on him by athletic, civic, and patriotic organizations. He spoke with affection of some of his famous broadcasts . . . Suddenly he banged a fist into a palm and frowned, 'They don't want me anymore.'"[555] For someone as famous as McNamee, there was never a good time to step down. The crowds stopped cheering, the mail stopped coming, the perks and keys to almost every city in America no longer worked.

In late February of 1942, the veteran broadcaster developed a persistent fever. Doctors confined him to bed rest.[556] McNamee refused, continuing to keep his schedule as announcer for the "Elsa Maxwell Party Line Show." [557] On April 24, he closed the program in usual fashion. "This is Graham McNamee. Good night all—and goodbye." It would be his final broadcast. The next day, he suffered a heart attack, rushed to St. Luke's Hospital. His condition worsened over an eight-day stay, culminated by a massive stroke that killed him on the evening of May 8. He was fifty-three years of age, a long way from Pasadena, miles beyond the World Series . . . "Over a span of nineteen years, Graham McNamee's voice was heard by more people than any other man alive," wrote sports broadcasting historian Ted Patterson. "His dream was to retire to California so that he could witness that glorious sunset he described at the Rose Bowl. He never got that chance."[558]

Three days later Ted joined over 300 mourners, a who's who

in radio entertainment, at the Campbell Funeral Home on Madison Avenue for a memorial service.[559] Many more stood outside waiting to say goodbye. Nothing could keep him from this place. He wondered . . . *when his time came, would they come in masses? What would they say about him?* The radio wars between McNamee and Husing, the chase, was over. Still the question lingered in his mind. *Who had won?* Stern continued battling, doing his best to keep things hot between them, mirroring football assignments, even trying to cut Ted's wires while precariously hanging out of the broadcast booth with a pair of pliers. [560] But, it just wasn't the same.

With Mac's death, Ted began to feel mortal. "The day of the Ted Husings and Graham McNamees in football broadcasting is near an end," he told a reporter. "We're the last of our clan. For network broadcasting of football games is rapidly on the wane"[561] As in baseball, local announcers and sponsors were doing more of their own live football remotes. But, it was obvious that Ted was in one of his blue moods. Could anyone blame him considering what McNamee had meant? The man dangling the carrot, the voice who had invented the "big broadcast" was no longer around. At age forty, Ted was now the elder statesman.

Peggemae's time at Friend's Academy was drawing to a close. Her interests varied—participating in sports, student council member, and class vice-president. Like father like daughter, she enjoyed listening to Dixieland jazz and eating raw hamburgers. Yet, above everything else, most of Ms. Husing's interest lied in the wonderful world of theater, performing or directing a half dozen school productions.[562] She even acted professionally in 1939, earning her stripes as a Massachusetts summer stock theater member.[563] Her schoolmates appropriately dubbed her "Skip." The Husing name, however, became a hindrance, leery of people's interest only because she was the daughter of the famous radioman.

By May of 1942, Pegge was a budding young woman, with adult dreams and aspirations of her own. Uncertain of the future, she was sure of one thing. As much as young Husing enjoyed acting, a life in show business was never seriously considered. She not only knew the pit falls. She lived them. Broken marriages. Lonely nights. Pegge was not petite and dainty like her mother. She was an imposing figure, tall like her father, wearing awkward spectacles around her eyes. Helen instilled in her the importance of keeping a feminine outward appearance, party dress, flowery shoes, and Sunday best. But, as she matured, Pegge believed that true beauty was found in one's heart. She had seen what pursuing pleasure of the outside world had done to damage her parents. Peggemae saw the ugliness of celebrity and wanted nothing to do with it.

After graduation, she packed her bags, kissed her father goodbye, and headed west, determined to forge a different course. Pomona College in Claremont, California, offered a solid liberal arts education, including studies in theater, in case she had a change of heart. If that wasn't enough, the scenic campus was only thirty miles from mother and Lennie. She brought with her a new hope and unwavering faith. The many years she spent at the safe, close-knit haven of Friends Academy in Locust Valley would stay with her for the rest of her life. The Quaker way, the Quaker religion in many ways saved her. The church's core principles rooted in peace, a fervent passion for humility and grace spoke to her. Within a year, though, Pegge's newly developed faith would be severely tested.

It was happening again. Pegge found her mother's second marriage suddenly on the rocks. Some time in 1943, Lennie began an affair with a beautiful, mocha-skinned singer named Lena Horne.[564] The two met on the MGM lot while Horne was turning heads as an up-and-coming movie star. News of the affair plunged Helen into darkness. Gone were the smiles, replaced by bouts of depression. She was distraught, unglued. When Helen spoke of suicide, many wondered if she might actually do it.

She leaned on friends and daughter for support, trying to sort out the confusion. When she confided in Ted, he reacted with predictable chivalry, threatening to rearrange Hayton's face. He hated the bandleader even more. But in a way, he was glad for her misery. *Could I be getting my Bubbles back, finally?*

The voice cracked and whimpered. Ted did not panic. He was silent, patient. With the receiver end of the phone pressed to his ear, he waited. He knew whom the crying sobs on the other end belonged to. It was Pegge. "What's wrong honey?" Ted inquired. "Tell me what's wrong." Like any good father, he felt confident that whatever teenage angst was troubling her he could fix. He wished he had never asked the question. He wished he had never been born. "She's dead! She's dead. Mother is dead."

Through the tears, Pegge relayed the details the best she could. "She collapsed . . . then they took her to the hospital . . . St. John's . . . in Santa Monica, I think . . . Last night, I mean this morning . . . I don't know! . . . They tried dad. They really tried. Too late. Nothing could be done." Her voice cracked, her sobs heavy. He heard his daughter, but Ted was not listening. Like his child a moment ago, Ted could not speak. Infinite, scattered thoughts of forty-two life years engulfed his mind. He thought of Albert and Elsie, the brother and sister he never knew. He thought of his own father. He thought of McNamee. He thought of a chilly February night in the Bronx nineteen winters ago. A dance contest, a song that started a romance he wished never began. Never ended.

When she's near
The winter turns to spring
Bells begin to ring
There's a magic charm about her

She's divine
And she's mine, all mine
I'm in love
So in love with Nola[565]

The poems, the dreams, the fights, the passions, her touch, her kiss. Death has a funny way of bringing things to life. Was it a quick ending? Did she suffer much or was she happy? Happiness? The last time Ted felt incontestably happy was with Helen. *My Helen!* He wondered why he ever left her. On October 6, 1943, a stroke took her life. Bubs was gone.

"I love you, Dad," Pegge murmured quietly. The words slapped him out of his shock. They wanted to console each other like a father and daughter was supposed to in times of shared sorrow. If the miles of distant wires prevented it, a stoic, German pride made it almost impossible. Peggemae knew she would attend the funeral in California. But, would her father? When it came to the only woman he really loved, Ted wanted to stay forever tormented in the past. "I refused to talk to anyone about Bub's death," he later said. "I didn't even know what claimed her life. To me inquiries into the circumstances of her demise were pointless. Death is final. Bubs would only be perpetuated in my memories."[566]

That unhappy week, Ted felt compelled to say something on the air. He dedicated Saturday's football broadcasting to his dead ex-wife, telling the audience, "She will always have a seat next to me on the fifty-yard line." "I thought it was so touching when he said that," remembered his traveling secretary Kay Sedgwick. "The expression stayed with me all these years."[567]

Ted again decided to use the more traditional route of drowning sorrows, alcohol. Whether at the Stork Club, the Barbary, or 21, Ted stayed later and later. Drinking heavily, feeling more and more maudlin, reminiscing about the past, playing the "what if" game with anyone at the bar who cared to listen. Mr. Fereschi became chaperone, helping Ted find the car door, guiding his wobbly steps toward the elevator at the Century.[568] Sitting around his spacious, lonely apartment, thumbing through old photographs only pushed him further down. In the end, the radioman relied on the job to get him through tough times.

Six months passed since Helen's death. Another harsh New York winter melted into spring and he was beginning to feel alive again. He called Fereschi telling him to bring the car around. It wasn't even noon yet, being a bit early for both. The drive from the Century to the CBS building was usually a short jaunt, even in crosstown traffic. That day, it took a lifetime. With the windows rolled down, Ted tried to quiet his impatient mind. He was eager to see Dolan, dissect the upcoming Derby, look at yesterday's box scores, and laugh at Bill Stern. The building on 52nd and Madison looked somehow different. Clean windows, a paint job, he wondered? He would figure it out later. "Good afternoon, Mr. Husing, and how are you today?" asked a pleasant female voice. He acknowledged the receptionist's greeting with a nod. She had auburn-colored hair and large piercing eyes the size of marbles. Ted never noticed her before. He did now. Turning back, Ted reached for a cigarette, smiled and asked her name.

CHAPTER TWENTY-EIGHT

RED HAIR, GREENER PASTURES

alking into 485 Madison Avenue during the year 1944, the first person one set eyes upon was Mike Donavan. No one could escape him, not Paley, not Ted, not the freckle-face kids working the mailroom. He was literally the eyes and ears of the company.[569] He had neither a desk nor a microphone. He was more than a doorman; he was an institution, a steady fixture from the very beginning. Donavan might have been seen initially, but the first person most people noticed was a talkative receptionist named Iris Louise Lemerise. Her shiny red hair and buxom figure greeted CBS employees and visitors alike during the morning rush. "She was attractive, I'll tell you that," recalled Chris Schenkel. "A substantial female, if you know what I mean."[570]

Iris was born in Burlington, Vermont, the eldest of nine children on March 29, 1912. Her father Joseph, an auto mechanic, struggled to keep his large family above the poverty line. Often-times he didn't. Patchwork shoes, hand-me-down clothes, and cold nights were the norm growing up in the Lemerise household. Raised Catholic, the lessons of servility and abstinence had an adverse af-fect. Iris, at an early age, vowed that when she reached adulthood, a much better financial situation would be hers.[571] A life of tall trees and warm maple syrup was not her idea of excitement. Iris distanced herself from the other siblings, wanting to experience glitter and so-phistication. "We were not close," admitted younger sister Yvonne. "She was completely different than I was. I played with the boys but she was sharp, fashion conscious. She was, how do I say, busy!"[572]

In the early '30s, her father found work with the New York City Transit Authority, moving the family to the outside suburbs of Baldwin, Long Island. The Lemerise fortunes improved little. Iris, however, continued to think big, surrounded by bankers, advertis-ing executives, and radio announcers. Instead, she met a budding musician named Datz, married him and looked forward to a thrill-ing life of nightclubs, travel, and money. The young couple had two sons. From the onset, her dreams of the high-life met resistance. As Iris dove into motherhood, her husband's music career floundered, working day jobs, facing rejection, and feeling the wrath of Iris. It did not take long before she realized the yearnings of abundance would not materialize as a Datz. Frustrated with her lot, Iris packed her bags and walked out the door, leaving a bewildered husband and small boys to fend for themselves.[573]

She had a brief career as a model, loaning out her seductive figure to commercial art photographers.[574] A fresh start and new job at CBS allowed her to dream again of the life she always craved. She remained determined to break the Lemerise mold, never again want-ing, discard the hand-me-downs, and hook a big fish. Once Ted took her in, it did not take long for him to fall. Ted and his new girlfriend started having drinks together at the 21 Club. Next door, Leon and Eddie's started receiving dinner reservations for two under the name of Husing. For Ted, dating became fun again.

By late summer, the rumor mill swayed with the sound of wedding bells. People wondered, waiting for the other shoe to drop. An announcement never came. Ted's close friends and advisors asked questions. Who was this woman? What was she all about? Was this one for real? Could the wild antics of Ted Husing be tamed by a lowly, unknown receptionist?" However, things were already cooking for the two hot lovers. Ted's annual trip to Miami and the Orange Bowl served as the perfect backdrop to shock the world one more time.

The New Year's Day football game was the highlight of the broadcaster's yearly migration south. Parades, Florida girls, young and single, parties, and an entourage of familiar revelers like Hellinger and Kriendler. But when Ted stepped from the train on December 29, everyone understood that this year was to be starkly different. Draped around his arm wearing a long thick coat and a cigarette in hand was Iris. Her heavy wardrobe clashed gamely with the high temperatures and hot Miami sun. She had the look of an overdue Christmas gift in need of unwrapping. The smiling couple was greeted on the platform by a small group of enthusiastic fans, curious reporters, and flashing cameras. Ted wasted no time and announced to the crowd that he was married, again. And this time, he was stone-cold sober.

On the eve of the big game, word splashed across every newspaper in America: "Secret Bride of Husing—Broadcaster Marries." Ted told the press that he and Iris had, in fact, married that spring in a private ceremony while in Louisville covering the Kentucky Derby.[575] He went on to say that the couple felt it was high time to share the happy news. After a few more questions, Ted and Iris thanked the crowd, waved goodbye, and ducked into a car headed for the safety of Roney Plaza. Husing, a man filled with surprises, wasn't done yet. The one thing he conveniently omitted, his new wife was pregnant.

Everyone was caught off guard, including his daughter Pegge. Friends at Pomona razzed her at a social gathering when they read the afternoon papers. "Hey Pegge, your dad gets married and you don't even tell your friends?"[576] She played along knowing nothing of what they spoke. Explanations never came. Friends and family didn't press for details. If they did, especially Iris's sister and seven brothers, she simply stuck to the party line—Louisville. It was a convenient story for a man trying to cover his tracks. By December of 1944, Iris was seven months pregnant and beginning to show. Her protruding abdomen and swollen face said everything. It was important to establish their relationship with the public, get their story straight. "She never confided in me," said Yvonne Britt about her sister. "I never asked any questions."[577] It no longer was about saving the reputation of Ted and Iris. Protecting the future of the life growing inside of her took center stage.

On February 24, 1945, Iris went into labor and gave birth to yet another son. The boy's hair was red. Ted smiled and thought of his redheaded father. The happy couple gave him a strong name, David Edward Britt Husing. They nicknamed him "Duke" in honor of Ted's movie star friend John Wayne. The apartment at the Century was no longer barren, now full with a new wife and active young child. Ted had not been there much for Pegge. He had not been there for Helen. A second chance, a new opportunity awaited. And this time he was determined to be there for both.

Throughout 1945, Paley continued to downsize his responsibilities at CBS. The title of president no longer fit his mold. Chairman of the Board was more the Paley style, concentrating on talent and the expanding horizons of television.[578] The day-to-day operations of the network were handed over to the new president of the network Frank Stanton early the following year.[579] Paley, like Ted, had poured all his energy into catching rival NBC. The owner put his personal stamp on everything on and off the air. Above anything, however, William Paley was a businessman. He intuitively understood the transitions of the modern business world. The Columbia Broadcasting System was no longer the mom-and-pop shop it had started out as some twenty years earlier. It mushroomed into a quagmire of department heads, subsidiary offices, and cold, distant boardrooms.

Ted Husing was none of those things. He was a famous radio announcer. Book-keeping, memos, and the bottom line held no interest. What he only knew of business was money. And he liked to spend it, as much as possible. Lost in the shuffle was the personal touch, one for all and all for one approach to business that the announcer became accustomed. That, too, changed. Gone were the days of contracts sealed with a handshake, a short drink among contemporaries. Ted ignored the new department heads, refusing to return phone calls, demanding only to talk with Paley about business matters, especially his upcoming contract renewal. "Husing was a law unto himself," said Frank Stanton. "He was very popular. He knew it and wanted you to respect him."[580] His belligerence prompted Doug Coulter, new head of programming, to replace him as Sports Department Director, a position created for him by Paley some fifteen years earlier. [581]

Ted felt more and more uncomfortable with the present surroundings, around the office and at The Century. The perceived lack of respect from the new CBS hierarchy rekindled old feelings of insecurity. A gnawing toothache and overdue dental appointment added to his anxiety. He saw Iris and thought of Helen. Gazing down on his new son, Ted thought of Pegge and his promise to be there for both. But, even Ted knew that life as a domestic could be obtained only one way—being home. For the first time, he considered life away from radio. If the network no longer wanted him, then perhaps it was time to give them exactly what they wanted.

Ted's contract was scheduled to expire on August 8, 1946. He remained stubborn, as the summer progressed, holding firm to an eleventh hour meeting with Paley. The boss' call never came; resigned to leave all network decisions in the hands of the new syndicate. That included negotiating with Ted. "If he tripped over me in the lobby, he wouldn't have known who I was," admitted Stanton years later. "I don't say that bitterly. It was an indication of how business was run. I never shook his hand. Not because I didn't want to. It's just because the world in which we lived didn't call for that kind of relationship. He obviously had plans to leave. And when you have plans to leave, you don't stop and start making new acquaintances. There was nothing that I could give him that he didn't already have."[582]

Ted wanted to deal with Paley. And if Paley wasn't around, Ted didn't want to deal at all. "I long ago came to the conclusion that all life is 6 to 5 against," Damon Runyon once said.[583] If ever anyone was Runyon-esc it was Husing. He no doubt turned to the famous author's novels of slick, fast-talking hoodlums and hustlers as inspiration. Ted was a gambling man. His life had been about being bold, taking a chance. In the world of Runyon there was always a fine line between pleasure and pain. Ted knew the odds, willing to play the hand dealt to him. Taking one last look around, he tossed an empty pack of cigarettes in a trashcan and walked out of CBS for good on Thursday, July 11, 1946. By the time Dolan arrived at the office that day, Ted already cleared out his belongings from their eighteenth-floor office. No goodbyes. No farewell party. For the first time in over eighteen years, Ted Husing was unemployed, gone from the network he helped build. He was a free agent and scared to death.

He tried to stay hopeful, adjusting to his newfound freedom. He took walks with Iris and "Duke" through Central Park, pushing the pram, heads turning all the while of those around them who recognized his unmistakable voice. He thought of his friend Bing Crosby singing with the Andrew Sisters their hit song stressing the upside of a positive attitude.

> You've got to accentuate the positive,
> Eliminate the negative,
> Latch on to the affirmative,
> Don't mess with Mr. In-between.
> You've got to spread joy up to the maximum,
> Bring gloom down to the minimum,
> Have faith, or pandemonium
> Liable to walk upon the scene.[584]

Ted talked a big game. His plans were grand. They included starting a new radio network devoted solely to broadcasting sports.[585] If anyone could make such things happen it was Ted. The truth, however, was something different. "There are also disadvantages in having a front-page name," he admitted later. "One is that when you're out of work, you can't answer a want ad. You have to wait for the phone to ring, especially if you have as much false pride as I did in 1946."[586] During the interim, Ted decided to focus on having fun, creating the Skeeters Club with good friend Toots Shor. Together, along with a group of assorted friends, they traveled south to New Jersey's Garden State Park, usually by train, battling the giant mosquitos, betting on the horses, and enjoying an otherwise rousing afternoon of male bonding. [587]

Work offers eventually came and in abundance. The Mutual Broadcasting System immediately called, offering their Saturday college gridiron airings. He quickly accepted. Football without Husing could be akin to Christmas without presents. However, things would not get going until the season commenced in late September. What to do in between? Philadelphia station WCAU offered him a new Sunday morning show called "Sports Scenes." He was given free reign to do what he wished, commenting on the day's sports stories with the usual Husing candor, good or bad. Owners Ike and Leon Levy joined the revelry with Ted and the Skeeters at Garden State. Though they enjoyed seeing Ted, what they saw first were dollar signs. The two brothers hired the announcer to call the daily-featured race at the track live on the air.[588] To listeners, all seemed normal. The station was the city's CBS affiliate.

In the end, it was still football, Saturday or Sunday. Ted watched the pro game with great interest, hanging around the press box, feeding off the energy of the crowd. He even helped out on his off day, if called upon. The close of World War II had many servicemen returning to the booth, including a young officer named Al Helfer. The Western Pennsylvania native, a giant of a man, went on to a solid network career calling World Series, Rose Bowls, and Army versus Navy clashes. Back in civilian clothes, his early assignments included NFL and rival league, the All-American Football Conference. Helfer remembered the shock he received prior to the broadcast of the Brooklyn Dodgers versus Green Bay Packers game at Ebbits Field in 1946. "We were having problems locating a spotter. About an hour before the game, I was preparing when Ted Husing came down the ladder. I thought he was kidding when he said he was my spotter. 'No I'm not Al,' said Ted. 'You've been gone five years and the game has changed. This is your first broadcast back and you're not going to make a mistake.' He wouldn't let me reveal he was in the booth."[589]

Helfer was one of thousands returning to civilian life. And a new generation in music was underway with a new crowd of popular singers and bandleaders to welcome them home. It became known as the "Interlude Era." Names like Frank Sinatra, Perry Como, and Les Brown filled not only nightclubs but also the radio airwaves. Spinning records was rapidly replacing studio orchestras and live music remotes. The brave men who played the music, the "disc jockies," were becoming the new stars of the industry.

Bert Lee was manager at New York station WHN. Born Bert Lebhar, Lee knew radio, the ups and downs, ins and outs. He also knew how to talk. With his special gift of gab, Lee could have sold light bulbs to a blind man. "He was the world's greatest salesman," remembered former advertising executive Adam Young. "He was a real pro in the radio business."[590] While auditioning announcers for New York Ranger hockey games, Lee coached the announcers on how to work the game's sponsor, Pabst Blue Ribbon, into the broadcast. He did it so well that Pabst hired him as the play-by-play man. In between, Lee also figured to get his station into the lucrative record-spinning trade. He didn't know anything about music, but he did know a certain unemployed announcer who might fit the bill.

Ted had done his share of on-air selling. He was not a screamer, a neon voice squawking a catchy little phrase in the night.

Ted Husing was about dignity, class, and commonsense smarts that put any weary shopper at ease. If Husing pushed a product it had to be good. Bert Lee knew the charm and influence the man possessed. That combined with his personal friendship with some of the countries top recording artists, Lee was convinced that the former CBS announcer would be perfect for the show. The only thing he had to do was convince Ted. Initially, he balked at the idea. Most people in the entertainment industry saw DJs as loudmouths with marginal talent. Ted himself referred to them as "a form of animal life."[591] But, once Lee laid out the plan in whole, he quickly reconsidered.

With Lee schmoozing clients and Ted pushing their product, he reasoned they'd both make a fortune. Nedicks fast-food restaurants and Buddy Lee clothing store were only a few of the advertisers happy to jump on board. Lee's son Goff Lebhar remembers watching the duo work their magic. "In those days in our house in New Rochelle, we had a bar downstairs. It was almost like a night club. Husing would come up and they would do a lot of selling. My dad would invite clients over. With a guy like Ted Husing, respected and idolized, boom! There goes his money on the Husing show!"[592] The big bucks and flashy perks no doubt aided Lee in winning over Ted. The fact that the new music show would broadcast from New York clinched the deal in granite. It was a bit of a home coming for the new disc jockey, having broadcast Columbia football games on WHN nearly two decades before. The name Ted Husing was not easily recognized back then. Now, he was a household word.

On Wednesday, October 24, 1946, a packed semblance of peaceful delegates from around the globe gathered in San Francisco. The United Nations celebrated its first birthday reflecting a world tired of war and chaos eager to embrace a softer, more prosperous ideology. If Husing had been present at the historic General Assembly, he may have echoed President Truman's words. However, Ted was in New York preparing for his new career as a disc jockey. Perched in a broadcast booth surrounded by frenzied sports fans was one thing. Sitting in dark studio, alone, surrounded by spinning turntables was all together something else.

He tried to convince himself that leaving CBS was the right move. "I'm not losing any dignity as a disc jockey," he told reporters. "At forty-four, I'm tired of glamour and glory. At CBS I was the highest-paid sports announcer in the business and I got only $27,500. Here, there's no reason why I shouldn't make a quarter of million a year."[593]The station quickly got the PR machine rolling. Ted's smiling face splashed across subway ads and every New York daily newspapers banging the drum. [594] Bert Lee wisecracked with the press saying, "We finally have a guy who can play the records."[595] A dubious public, meanwhile, wondered if the whole thing was a joke.

"Hello Kiddies! This is Ted Husing speaking."[596] The old voice had a new hook. And at 10 o'clock in the morning on Monday, October 28, "The Ted Husing Bandstand" streaked across the city for the first time. A catchy theme song welcomed listeners.

Hi there, Mr. Husing
What's the hottest thing on records, when it starts you to enthusing?
Mix it all, Mr. Husing
Keep that all recorded smile
At 1050 on the dial
Evenings at five, every morning at ten
Keep those turntables spinning at WHN[597]

Many were shocked to hear the most revered sports announcer talking music. Surprise faded into loyal fans and a hit show, embracing him as a natural of the profession. "I remember it was quite a switch in those days for a guy to go from being a very famous sportscaster to being a disc jockey," said veteran New York radio personality Danny Stiles. "I remember as a kid I was an avid follower of records and record spinners and he came out of nowhere." He adapted effortlessly to the new role, occasionally inviting well-known guests to the studio for a little chit chat. By and large, Ted stuck to the script, playing music and augmenting commercial copy. Ted's style as a DJ was much the same as it was when he did a sporting event, slick, informative, but not obtrusive or over the top. "He injected his personality a little bit and he was not obnoxious," added Stiles. "He was pleasant enough to go from record to record."[598]

If Graham McNamee or Bill Stern fueled the man's competitive juices when it came to broadcasting sports, there were a host of names to turn his screws as king record-spinner. Ed Randall in Cleveland. From Chicago came Howard Miller. It seemed more than a dozen large cities nationwide had their famous disc jockeys. Each distinctive. Each strong. In New York, Martin Block posed the biggest threat to Ted and the success of "The Bandstand." The native Californian made a name for himself playing records on station WNEW during the infamous trial of Bruno Richard Hauptmann, the man accused of kidnapping Charles Lindberg's baby. Block called his show the "Make Believe Ballroom."[599] However, there was nothing phony about the show's impact and popularity or the large amounts of money he earned. "Make Believe Ballroom" quickly became an institution and never budged from the top spot during its twenty years on the air. Though no one was openly aware of any simmering rivalry between Block and Husing, others at WNEW were keenly aware of the competition. "Everything's confusing with Husing," became a common wisecrack around the station.[600]

Working for Block at that time was a young disc jockey want-to-be named Joe Franklin. He helped Block pick the records, having his ear closer to what the man on the street wanted to hear. Ted was aware of Franklin's talents and called the young New York native about doing similar duties on "The Bandstand."

"Ted called me about coming to work for him," remembered Franklin. "Boy, what a thrill that was. I wanted to say yes, but I felt loyal to Block and had to turn him down." Franklin would become a New York broadcasting institution himself with various radio and television talkshows over a five-decade career. Known as the "King of Nostalgia," Franklin was surprised at how little both Block and Ted actually knew about music. "You'd figure guys like that really knew their stuff. But, man, both made some bizarre choices, I remember."[601]

Ted certainly did play a genre of music that Block ignored by and large. In between the standard crooners and big band acts, he always featured a quarter-hour block of Dixieland Jazz. He loved the sound, having added to his own private record collection over the years. Ted's personal tastes in music weren't everyone's cup of tea. But, it did seem to have a profound monetary impact. Several Dixieland record labels announced a dramatic surge in sales due to his plugs.[602] Fans of the show were also moved. One such affected was renowned jazz clarinetist Kenny Davern. As a teenager growing up on Long Island, Davern heard his career vocation blaring through the radio. "In those days, I was listening to 'Ted Husing's Bandstand,' and for fifteen minutes of each day he'd play Dixieland Jazz. One particular day, I heard this thing and whack! It was like a baseball bat between the eyes. I stood transfixed. I said, 'I want to spend the rest of my life doing that.'"[603]

Ted was not a pioneer like Block, but his influence soon became obvious. In 1948, Motion Picture giant MGM purchased station WHN, changed the call letters to WMGM, kicking off a hot property to showcase their movie talent and singing stars. They not only increased Ted's salary, but also gave him a slick new million-dollar Manhattan studio to broadcast from. The show continued its large popularity, no more evident during the baseball season. The station owned broadcast rites to Brooklyn Dodgers baseball games. Most games started at 2:30 in the afternoon. "The Bandstand" aired at 5 PM. As popular as the Dodgers were, Husing took precedent, booting Red Barber and his play-by-play off the air, no matter what inning or the situation.[604]

His annual take-home ballooned well over $250,000. Ted's

monetary success elevated the profession to soaring heights. "He was the first big announcer to become a disc jockey, and the switch boosted the strange tribe as nothing else had ever done," wrote the *New York World-Telegram.*[605] It seemed everyone, including a few old friends, entered into the disc jockey fray. Paul Whiteman, Rudy Valee, Dinah Shore, Jimmy Dorsey, Duke Ellington, among others, were given similar radio shows in New York and L.A.[606] Husing wasn't the only sports announcer who sat behind the turntable. Yankee voice Mel Allen was given his own show on station WINS, same format, same direction. Big Band sound, some jazz, and healthy plugs of the show's very expensive sponsors. Mel, too, was paid handsomely for his talents, no thanks to Ted Husing. Not everyone, however, was pleased with Ted's new role. One ruffled columnist wrote, "If stations are so badly in need of record-turners, this department recommends they convert such "sportscasters" as Harry Wismer and Bill Stern and leave experts like Husing to us sports lovers."[607]

Ted also started taking advantage of the latest technology, a 401—magnetic recording machine. He could pre-record his afternoon show and spend more time with family. Old buddy Bing Crosby was a huge proponent of the machine, more eager to be on the golf course than hanging around a recording studio all day. He not only used it. The singer owned Ampex, the company that manufactured them.[608] Before long, both Husing and Block made full use of the device.

Ted sipped a scotch and dragged on his cigarettes satisfied. He rarely thought of CBS. He was sorry he ever said anything derogatory about the disc jockey profession.[609] Ted was enjoying his new digs, richer than he'd ever been in his life. But, more than anything, he was home for dinner and in bed by eleven on weekdays for the first time since puberty. It was all working out for the announcer. Responsible parenting could not have been more pleasant. Being a good husband, however, was becoming less and less desirable.

CHAPTER TWENTY-NINE

IRIS MANAGEMENT CORPORATION

T ed Husing—disc jockey! Never could he ever imagine his career in radio reduced to three inanimate objects, a soft leather
chair, vinyl, and a hot microphone. Almost a quarter century in the business, Ted had seen it all, created half of it, and been
surprised by nothing. Somehow, it made perfect sense. "The Bandstand" was a hit. The money was great and life grand. But, Bert Lee's
well-oiled business socials in New Rochelle soon spawned lucrative
ideas in more traditional areas, namely football. A season of games
with MBS took Husing to the usual places, Ann Arbor, Chicago,
Philly, South Bend. Yet, Lee often heard the famous football announcer turned DJ complain of road burnout, wishing to stay closer
to home. Less than forty-five miles north lay perhaps the most fertile
ground in the college game—West Point.

Army represented the crème de la crème in fighting men.
Their victories, their sacrifice in Europe and Asia, were still fresh in
everyone's mind. The young football cadets reflected the same on
the gridiron during the last two years of World War II. Mr. Inside
and Mr. Outside, Doc Blanchard and Glenn Davis, won back-to-
back Heisman Trophies and national championships. As the 1947
season approached, they were still a national power. As Lee saw

things, all the best football programs in America needed was the best football broadcaster in radio to call their games. Ted loved the idea. He always enjoyed doing the Army versus Navy games during his CBS days. Lee did the rest, using the same formula that made "The Bandstand" a financial juggernaut. The Black Knights and Ted Husing were on the air starting in 1947.[610]

Washington D.C. announcer Bill Brundige worked the Annunciator with Ted on Mutual's "College Game of the Week" the previous fall. He added color to the broadcasts, learning the "Husing method," later molding it to his own play-by-play technique in later years. Brundige's son Tim recalls his father speaking often of Ted. "My father was a big believer in preparation and clarity of facts, let me tell you. He never forgot a thing. It's safe to say he learned that working with Ted Husing."[611] With the new gig, however, came a new assistant. Ted remembered a dark-haired sports enthusiast named Walter Kennedy. A 1934 graduate of Notre Dame, Kennedy returned to his alma mater a few years later as Sports Information Director. The two got to know each other during Husing's many visits to South Bend. Following the war, Kennedy became publicity director of a virgin professional basketball league called the National Basketball Association.[612] When Ted asked him to join the team, Kennedy jumped at the chance.

Working with a living legend was inviting enough. But, the fledgling hoops game needed publicity not to mention on-air exposure. Maybe Ted would be interested in calling a few games. Kennedy kept his Monday through Friday job with the NBA. Saturdays were about football. Like Brundige, Kennedy handled color. But, Ted quickly tapped into Kennedy's sports knowledge and energetic personality. While Ted focused his remarks on the offense, his assistant expounded defensive strategies. Stealing the famous monikers of Doc Blanchard and Glenn Davis as "Mr. Inside" and "Mr. Outside," Husing and Kennedy became "Mr. Offense" and "Mr. Defense." A deep friendship formed, sharing family photos, a love of football, and marital advice.

Bright shiny shoes, crisp tailored suit, discipline, and loyalty—everything about the Army life reflected those innate Husing qualities. Yes, he was a long way from guarding docks on the Hudson as an underage solider. No doubt, Ted felt a binding tie to the sentiment of West Point; bold leaders, winners, excellence at its core. "Duty, Honor, Country, Football."[613] Running the program was head coach Earl "Red" Blaik. When it came to preparation, the broadcaster met his match. To Blaik, football was more than a game. It was an obsession, twenty-four hours a day, eight days a week. His firm style of communication was the spitting image of Husing's on the radio. "Blaik was all understatement—reserved, aloof, outwardly cool," wrote Pulitzer Prize winning author David Maraniss. "He stood alone at football practice, tall and straight in his Army baseball cap, sweatshirt, football trousers cut off below the knee, and woolen socks, barking out crisp commands, rarely needing to modulate his tone of voice, just a nod and a look that said he could not be fooled."[614]

Ted stayed consistent for his adoring public. Arrogance pored from every pore. Home games at the Academy were equal to a coronation. Everyone had their roles. Fereshci made the hour drive with Ted sprawled in the backseat. Once they arrived at Michie Stadium, the car slowly dipped up a ramp behind the press box. Excited fans crushed against the car hoping for a glimpse of the star broadcaster. A then young broadcaster, Hall of Fame sports voice Lindsey Nelson watched and reveled in Ted's pomposity. "As his feet touched the ground, his eyes were straight ahead and he wore a black French beret at a jaunty angle. He had a cigarette in a long holder, and he strode toward the booth, dismissing all cries for autographs, every fiber of his being seemed to shout, 'Get the damned peasants out of the way and make way for the king.' There is something to be said for being true to yourself."[615]

After the game, the role-playing parlayed over to Bear

Mountain Lodge for a feast. It was 21 cut out of the Adirondacks. Ted mingled among politicians, four-star generals and their wives, sipping drinks and eating caviar. All the while, the children played touch football outside, laughing and regurgitating lunch. His gruff attitude at the station remained unchanged as well. When a new employee named Guy LeBow joined WHN as an announcer, Ted immediately put him in his place. "Who the hell are you? Don't talk to me unless I speak to you first!" he barked. LeBow regarded his one-time hero the way many at the station did "as imperious and a pain in the ass."[616]

Professionally, Ted had little to complain about, eight shifts a week with "The Bandstand," half of them taped to be broadcast later. He could be sitting at 21 sipping a scotch and soda while listening to himself on the radio. Army football games on Saturday during the fall seemed to fuel him more than playing music. Often during a "Bandstand" broadcast, Ted gave away tickets for upcoming Army games.[617] He did it more for himself than sports fans or music lovers. The gesture played to his ego, reminding him that it was still sports, not music that got people excited about Mr. Husing. "The bottom line with Ted Husing to me is that he was the only guy who could jump from news to music to sports," said Walter Kennedy's son David. "He was Walter Cronkite, Allan Freid, and Curt Gowdy combined."[618] As for Mrs. Husing, "the life" was a dream come true.

From the onset, Iris enjoyed all the luxuries of being the wife of a celebrity. Everything from shopping sprees, travel to domestic help was taken advantage of. Eva Lee stayed on as housekeeper, her skills more useful to the Husings than ever. Bertha had moved into a residential hotel called the Duaphin Apartments near the old neighborhood.[619] Ted and Iris continued to call upon her for duties tried and true—babysitting. If she wasn't available, Iris often called on her side of the family for help, especially brother Joe, Jr., a New York City cop, and his wife Dee Dee, who raised their family in nearby Queens.

317

Her figure bounced back nicely from childbirth. So did her fresh smile. Ted enjoyed showing off his beautiful wife at Bear Mountain, the Stork Club, and on trips to Philadelphia for lobster at Bookbinders off Walnut Street. She was often seen in shoulderless dresses, bright color belts wrapped snuggly around her thin waist, and thick white pearls dangling from a sultry neckline. In between Iris's new socialite responsibilities, she continued to enjoy her hobbies, knitting among the favorites. She put her skills to work making not only little trinkets for "Duke" but gifts for others' children.[620] Every season Iris purchased the latest fashions, whatever her rich husband could afford—Christian Dior designs, mink coats, hats, shoes, and gloves. The old clothes were carefully wrapped in boxes and given to family and friends, many of the articles hardly worn.

However, an attractive complexion hid a darker side. Iris stayed unapologetic about her childhood convictions. Everything "Husing" now belonged to her. She became protective, isolating her husband and his possessions from those she didn't trust, which turned out to be just about everyone. Stanley Wertheim had been a steady visitor at the Century since moving from Germany. He loved talking with his famous uncle, picking his brain, wondering what celebrity types might he meet on any given stop over. After Iris moved in, the visits stopped. "She used to make me wait outside in the lobby if he wasn't there. Used to talk to me through the door," said Wertheim. "No way she could get away with that if he was around. She really put me off."[621]

Wertheim wasn't the only one. Friends, colleagues, Pegge, even Bertha experienced altercations with Ted's strange new wife. Her cold exterior and disapproving stares generated little warmth. A hot temper and fits of rage came to the surface with ease. They were impartial to no one.[622] Before long, most saw her as an opportunist, a gold digger. "In some ways she was a paradox," believed Dee Dee Lemerise. "She could get very ugly about something and other times could be very sweet."[623] Barely three years old, Ted's third marriage was already vulnerable.

The radioman, however, remained optimistic. He promised a new lease on life with Iris, for better or worse. Quitting CBS, leaving Dolan, leaving Paley, a new disk jockey career would not be in vain. "This time it's going to work," he told himself. "I'd profit by experience. I'm going to succeed."[624] The time to escape the past was upon him, in all ways. On August 13, 1947, Jack Kriendlier, complaining of chest pains, retreated to his upstairs apartment at the 21 Club. An hour later his little brother Peter found him dead on the floor, a heart attack victim. At forty-seven, he was in the prime of his life. Entering 21 would never be the same. On Christmas Eve, Ted helped bury Mark Hellinger, who also met his end by heart attack. He was forty-four years old. Everything Husing knew about the good life came from the newspaperman turned Hollywood guru. How could two men so young, so full of gusto be dead?

The old world appeared faded. Ted saw the passing of his two devoted friends as a wake-up call. Slow down. Take a deep breath and take stock before . . . Before what? The thought was foreign. Ted was a nomad, constantly on the run. The demands of the past gained with every year, every step. The apartment at the Century served him well. But, Ted had more hairs on his balding head than hours he spent truly enjoying it. Helen and her memory still lived at the Century. Divorce. A few one-night stands, the scent of Tina Lawford, Ann St. George, and Celia Ryland lingered there. Another divorce. What Husing needed, committed husband and devoted father, was just not a place to hang his hat. He was ready for a clean break. He was ready for a new home.

Nine years deep into the twentieth century, an architect named Frederick Sterner designed a stretch of upscale New York City apartments from 3rd Avenue west to Irving Place. Two hundred and fifty yards of sprightly, spacious five-floor fashions, all with a view of money and a key to the tree-lined Gramercy Park that dipped around the corner. He called it "The Block Beautiful."[625] Ted

Husing was eight years old at the time. Dreams of living in such luxury were not yet formulated or in the least affordable. By August of 1948, such dreams became a full-blown reality. Thanks to "The Bandstand," anything was possible. Ted bought a spacious nine-room apartment house at 141 East19[th] Street.

He spared no expense, reconstructing to the most modern proportions. The first floor dining room had a huge red brick fireplace, framed by green leather sofas, large benches, and a long table prepared to seat a royal wedding. The low ceilings were stretched by the sun-friendly golden oak wood paneling. If that wasn't cozy enough, Iris could open her brass-handled glass doors leading out to the back garden, which included a pond filled with gold fish. The second-floor living room or "tavern room" was dressed in tall, sturdy bookshelves. Above that was a sewing room for Iris, multiple bathrooms and bedrooms enough for a sorority sleep over.[626]

Ted's pride and joy, however, lay above in the top floors. Peeking down through a roofed skylight was a two-story spiral staircase. The descending steps led directly into Ted's custom-made broadcast booth juiced with the latest broadcasting technology. He called it the "crow's nest."[627] From the street outside, the front door was protected by a six-foot high, black iron gate. Mounted from the white face facade were two horse jockey statues, each with one arm extended as if to say hello. Each spring he had Iris's brother Charlie paint the jockeys the silk colors of the Jersey Stakes winner. Ted once flippantly cracked during a radio interview, "In Gramercy Park, all the people stop and see the disc jockeys."[628] The resemblance to 21 was uncanny. If he couldn't be at the club, he'd bring a piece of the club home to him. The radioman was still king and this was his castle.

Dinners together continued, at home or in one of a dozen selected restaurants, Peter Luger's in Brooklyn, Gallagher's on the Eastside among them. Football catch, bike rides, and a special game called "Twenty Trains" kept father and son close. "As a kid, I used to love trains," remembered David Husing. "We'd go up to the

125th Street station, watch twenty trains go by and then go home. I couldn't get enough."[629] Teaching young "Duke" the valuable lessons of life also became a priority. Thanksgiving was not only spent at Luchows getting stuffed. He made sure the day was spent in the company of orphans, welcomed guests at their table, and at least for a few hours, members of the extended Husing family.[630] Eva Lee made the move from the Century to Gramercy Park, living in the apartment five days a week. Ted paid her well. She seemed to be the only one with the Midas touch, unaffected by Iris's incorrigible demands. Butlers were contracted for special occasions like cocktail receptions or dinner parties. During the Holidays, Ted would hang a speaker outside his office window and play Christmas carols for all of East 19th Street.

The broadcaster finally had his dream home. In reality, the house belonged to Iris. Shrewd, calculating. Right from the start, Iris saw the future. She wanted Ted to plan for retirement, suggesting he invest in real estate and land properties.[631] On the contrary, Ted never believed in savings. There would always be another paycheck to spend. Another show to broadcast. Another game to call. When the idea of purchasing a place in Gramercy Park emerged, Iris convinced him to put the building in her name. She had papers drawn, incorporating her new property, even using the legal services of Ted's long-time attorney Harry Oshrin. She called it "Iris Management Corporation." The name could not have been more fitting. Ted willingly signed over the deed, never hesitating, never thinking twice that he couldn't buy half a dozen Gramercy Park houses if he wished. "I guess she realized my father made money and spent money," believed David Husing. "She wanted a nest egg. Her nest egg was to take everything my father had."[632]

The pressures of home centered mainly on how he handled Iris. The nagging intensified. If her changing mood swings got too much for Ted, he simply piled more work into his already busy schedule. Just before moving into Gramercy Park, he traveled to London, broadcasting the Summer Olympics for Voice of America Radio and the BBC. His side-kick was the irascible former Olympian and ex-Stanford track coach Robert "Dink" Templeton.[633] On New Year's Day, 1949, Ted returned with Kennedy to Florida, this time calling the Gator Bowl in Jacksonville.[634] Listeners were no doubt confused. The game aired on NBC. That fall, he spent his weekends in Baltimore calling Colts football games on radio. The following year, he partnered with Marty Glickman, voicing the New York Giants on WMGM. After two years of the NFL, Ted quit, preferring the passion of the college game. "I never knew anyone to cry when a pro team lost," Husing said, "unless he had a very large wager on it."[635]

Arguments flared, becoming volatile at times. Iris's volcanic reactions were on display for all to see. "One time we're in the station wagon and she hit him while Ted was driving the car," laughed Joe Lemerise, Jr. "I have to guess there was at least five of us in the vehicle. She was not playing. I think she hit him in the gonads quite frankly. Oh Boy! He yelled back at her but I never saw Ted lose his temper."[636] During another memorable fight, Iris let her aggressions out on his Dixieland records, smashing the priceless collection with a hammer.[637] If Iris really wanted to irritate her husband she'd call him a "kike."[638] The happy couple was no more. It didn't take long for them to be living in the same house, but sleeping in separate beds. Iris kept the second-floor master bedroom, while Ted moved into his study just below the crow's nest.[639]

Invariably, Ted retreated to the old hangouts to ground himself. What would Jack Kriendler say if he were alive? How about Hellinger? He missed them both. The broadcaster leaned more and more on Toots for advice, still married to his showgirl "Baby." Ted was twice removed from his. The Husing gruff arrogance intimidated many people. His wife, however, was a different story. She seemed to feed off of it. "I'm sure he was a son of a bitch to live with," said Chris Schenkel, trying to be the devil's advocate. "All those guys with big ego are. Aren't they?"[640]

Ted tried to lose himself in the music he played at work, anything to put a smile on his face. During one particular show, he called upon another old friend, Jimmy Dorsey's version of "The Call of the Canyon." Belting out the lyrics was a young crooner from New Jersey named Frank Sinatra. By the late '40s the song was a standard. Glenn Miller among others covered a version. As the record played on the turntable, he thought again of Bubs.

Standing there alone by the ashes
Of the fire we said would never die
Will I ever find an ember
Burning from the days gone by...?

Then I hear a lonely whisper
As a little spark I see
It's the call of the canyon
Bringing back your answer to me![641]

Iris was becoming a headache, literally. Ted routinely found himself reaching for an aspirin bottle, removing his eyeglasses to massage the pain just above the sinuses. Or was it stress behind his neck? A migraine pushing on his temples? Moments of light-headedness began to happen, breaking out in a cold sweat. Ted was beginning to do the unthinkable, forget words. He brushed it off. Too many late nights. "Life with Iris might make anybody lose their mind," Ted thought to himself. But, Ted's sharp intellect and diamond bright focus was legendary, especially in the broadcast booth. The radioman was often eccentric, but never erratic. Others noticed that something was different. Lindsey Nelson remembered one such incident at Michie Stadium. Nelson was scheduled to call the Army game for the Liberty Broadcast System, a chain of some 500 stations based out of Dallas. Husing and Kennedy were, of course, on the Army web emanating from their flagship station WMGM.

For some reason, that afternoon there was confusion. "Once we were into working position, my booth next to Husing's, he seemed puzzled," recalled Nelson. "I noticed that there was some hurried whispering. And Husing was pointing toward me. Then he came in and was cordial enough as he said, 'Lindsey, I'm Ted Husing.' I refrained from saying that I knew who he was, that I had known who he was since I'd listened to the radio during the years of my extreme youth. He then said, 'I thought I was doing the network broadcast.' I said, 'No, I think I'm doing the network broadcast and you are doing WMGM local.' He said, 'Oh.' And that was all. We went to work."[642] Ted immediately dismissed the error. A rare mistake, an oversight in the chaos of a hectic broadcast booth before a big game. Or . . . was it something else?

CHAPTER THIRTY

A FLICKERING CANDLE IN THE WIND

The general loved football. Army had fans stationed world-wide, none more fervent than Douglass Macarthur. His desires to excel in battle equaled his want of everything Army football. It seemed anyone associated with the program became a "Macarthur Man," Ted included. The decorated veteran was a living legend of history, two world wars, countless tours of duty and the Supreme Commander of the Allied Forces during the Korean conflict. Millions worshiped him. The only one who didn't apparently was the president of the United States, Harry S. Truman, who in 1951 replaced him following a conflict of policy. The broadcaster found himself defending the General following the notorious dismissal. To Ted's surprise, the most quarrelsome debate was with his own daughter. Pegge, by now a grown adult and committed Quaker, found Macarthur to be callous and overly militaristic. "The only argument she really ever had with him was about General Macarthur," laughed Kate Lacey concerning her mother and grandfather. "My mother didn't approve of Macarthur and Ted admired him very much."[643]

Macarthur wasn't the only West Pointer in trouble during the year 1951. A wide-spread cheating scandal nearly rubbed the

Army helmets clean of their gold-colored tarnish. Words like honor, duty, and trust were never taken lightly at the Academy. At summer's end, ninety cadets were expelled, half were from the football team, including Red Blaik's son Bob, a promising young quarterback. The Army program was devastated. Ted and Walter Kennedy were left holding the bag. They tried to punch things up on the air through two losing seasons of 1951–52. A once mighty football power was reduced to just another pile of jockstraps and shoulderpads. The Honor Code Scandal marked a new day for the integrity of college sports. The basketball programs at Bradley and City College were similarly rocked with charges of fixing games. Gangsters and money had wormed its way into the beauty of amateur sports. Purity was in the past. And so was radio. The TV set was quickly becoming a fixture in living rooms and bars across America. Husing, as most other announcers, had every intention of getting in on it, convinced he could glide right into the world of television sports.

Ted's first TV gigs were covering boxing matches. Not everyone, however, thought that his rapid-fire style transferred to the virgin world of television. As conventional wisdom met the camera's eye, there seemed little difference to veteran radio guys like Husing. Talking was talking. Prepare, know your stuff, and describe the action. What most early television sports announcers forgot was that the audience was no longer just listening but watching as well. "Mr. Husing is comparatively new to television and last night he showed it," said a scathing *New York* critic. "He talked and talked and talked, more often than not at just the wrong time."[644] But, it just wasn't newspaper reviewers who attacked him. Many of his colleagues did the same. "In TV he failed miserably," laughed a forgiving Chris Schenkel. "We don't talk about that. Shifting gears after all those years must have been difficult. It was a sad thing. Everything is so indoctrinated deep."[645] Guy LeBow also noticed Ted's deteriorating skills. "Ted Husing's sophisticated, slightly Tony delivery worked over the radio. But, it didn't match what the camera revealed."[646]

Ted wasn't done yet. He would get the chance to answer his critics. On Valentine's Day, 1951, the boxing world awaited anxiously the rematch between middleweights Jake LaMotta and Sugar Ray Robinson. This would be no ordinary fight. The two had danced in the ring together three previous times, all of them classics. Robinson's quick jabs and fancy footwork were in perfect contrast to LaMotta, a bruising street fighter, as tough as they come. They called him "The Bull" for good reason. All 15,000 seats at Chicago Stadium sold in a matter of hours. Hoping to get in on the big payday, CBS placed the fight on the Wednesday night show.

Red Barber, the man who replaced Ted as CBS Sports president, took full advantage, deciding to simulcast. On radio he paired the reliable Russ Hodges with an up and coming announcer from the Midwest named Jack Drees. For the television broadcast, Barber understood that the fight needed to be captioned by a voice as big as the event. He hired Ted Husing. Newspaper ads from coast to coast promoted the broadcasts. Bars and living rooms filled to capacity. One fan called the upcoming bout "fistic history."[647] The previous week's telecast, the announcer plugged the fight in typical Husing fashion. "Any of you planning on getting married next Wednesday night? Better postpone it. You'll miss the Robinson fight."[648]

From the opening bell, he was different. It was no more "Mile a Minute Husing." The fight would be known as "The St. Valentine's Day Massacre." Fists recoiled. Faces caved. Necks jerked from side to side. And blood flowed in buckets. Robinson slammed punches on LaMotta's mouth and body like rough surf against beach rocks. The Chicago Stadium crowd erupted throughout. Ted stayed quiet, measuring his blow-by-blow, willing to let the television pictures tell the story. The broadcaster had learned his lesson. The new medium would not swallow the Master. He swallowed it.

He reminded everyone why they called him the best. Great sports moments often bring out great words in sports announcers. Ted's description was flawless. Corner men barked instructions. Reporters slapped away on their typewriters. Only would Ted interject with information or comments about something the viewer couldn't see. In the fifth round a flurry of punches by Lamota landed squarely on Robinson's nose. Robinson turned his back to the camera, dancing and bobbing to safety. Ted countered with, "That brings blood to Robinson's nostril."[649] Simple. To the point. Some of the most ferocious punching of the Eleventh round had Ted silent. The crowd spoke instead, screaming for the two fighters to kill each other.

Don Dunphy, the industry's quintessential boxing announcer, raved about Husing's work that night. "Ted Husing's vivid description of the bout caught my attention as I watched on television . . . I recall Ted's description of the last round."[650] During the thirteenth round, Robinson leveled more abuse on his opponent. Husing the artist, the wordsmith, emerged, painting the graphic scene in a way only he could. "Round #13, the hard luck number!" he somberly stated. "Robinson is hurting LaMotta now! . . . LaMotta is on queer street, holding on. This is some of the most damaging evidence of punishment I have seen! How he can survive, no one knows! . . . No man can take this pummeling!"[651]

Finally, referee Frankie Sikorfa waved his arms and mercifully stopped the fight. LaMotta was a glutton for punishment. He wobbled but never fell, savoring each smashing Robinson punch. LaMotta proudly said later, "If the referee had let the fight go on for another thirty seconds, Robinson would have collapsed from exhaustion."[652] The ring exploded into chaos. Ted seized the moment. He weaved through the ropes grabbing a corner of the ring. With microphone in hand, Ted stood tall facing the hungry lens of a viewing nation. The television cameras picked up the bright reflection off of his round, bald head. Next to him stood the champ, drained and happy, waiting to be interviewed.

The CBS announcer was cool, confident, almost dwarfing the fighter. For a moment it looked as if Robinson should have been asking Ted the questions. How did you do it? How did you feel? Was this by far your toughest test? It was quintessential Husing, a colossal Neptune in a sea of little fishes. Robinson incoherently talked about a $25,000 check to be presented for the Damon Runyon Cancer Research Fund. Ted kept him on track asking about the fight and his tough opponent before bidding the television audience a good night. Viewers noticed the change, praising his work. "Ted, who made pretty much of a mess of his description of the Louis–Charles battle last summer with his fancy verbiage, has evidently learned something about television since then," wrote his old critic friend Ben Gross. "He confined his comments to a terse minimum and didn't indulge in high-flown language."[653]

Ted again stood tall. Another big broadcast, more national recognition. Wednesdays from St. Nicholas remained prominent on his schedule. But, a new option in television boxing soon came his way. Long before Fox, Dumont was known as the fourth major television network. Its founder was Dr. Alan B. Dumont. During the1920s and '30s, Dumont was a pioneer in the development of television electronics and transmission. With TV programming in its infancy, Dumont decided to mount telecast beginning in 1946. He set up offices at 515 Madison Avenue and went to work. Right away, Alan Dumont struck gold. He managed to showcase his young network with the two biggest names in entertainment, the large comedic antics of Jackie Gleason and the glistening pinstripes of the New York Yankees.[654]

Much of Dumont's success was due in large part to Tom McMahon, the network's head of sports. Producing live sporting events came easy for the small man with glasses. He learned the craft from one of the best, Les Quailey, during his days at N.W. Airey Advertising. McMahon took chances. Seeing the future, he put the growing National Football League on television before anyone.[655] In May of 1952, McMahon had plans to produce a new live sports show called "Boxing From Eastern Parkway." Only, he needed an announcer. He set his sites on the best—Husing. It did not take long before a working agreement was reached and the Master was calling more fights, this time on Monday nights.

Criticism continued against his television work, slipping back into the old ramped word description. Charged with loving the sound of his own voice. Old habits were hard to break. After all, it was radio and CBS that made Husing synonymous in the minds of listeners. For those listening to their local Columbia affiliated on Saturday, August 29, 1952, they heard a familiar quality. Flung to the past, Ted found himself in Williamsport calling the last two innings of the Little League World Series.[656]

CBS booked an hour of coverage and asked Ted to do the honors, traveling by airplane with a contingency of sports writers. For a day, Ted was back among the familiar, idol to all and king of his castle. The gig seemed to make his mood more amorous and upbeat than usual. "He'd get on the plane, he started making fun with all the stewardesses," remembered longtime *Scholastic Coach and Athletic Director* editor Herman Masin, who covered the game for his magazine. "He was a total extrovert. He made everyone laugh and everyone was enjoying it. He was absolutely wild."[657] The United States Rubber Company was the sponsor. Ted's old baseball friend Connie Mack took the tour of Williamsport and threw out the first pitch. Ted and Masin saw the team from Norwalk, Connecticut, take the title.

After that, the Little League World Series became a staple on the late summer network schedule. As usual, the influential broadcaster started something. The Husing magic worked again. Instant respect, class, and recognition were heaped upon Little League like the Orange Bowl nearly two decades before. The following year, two future network sports stars called the title game. CBS expanded the game to television. Jim McKay, a former police reporter for the Baltimore Sun, and his trusting, excitable voice anchored the coverage. In the next booth over was a young lawyer turned broadcaster named Howard Cosell filling the description over ABC radio.[658]

Ted carried on with his hectic schedule, trying to keep pace with the ever-changing modern world. The "Bandstand" radio show, Army games, Monday night TV duties at Eastern Parkway. Iris continued to accompany him to Bear Mountain on weekends, the occasional dinner out, trying to keep some assemblage of their marriage in tact. Another game of "Twenty Trains" with "Duke." Ted was not only a father, but now he was a father-in-law.

Pegge had fallen in love with an advertising writer named David Lacey. The two first met in 1944 while Lacey spent a brief shore leave in New York. Following the war, their relationship bloomed, completing graduate studies at Pomona College. By the early '50s, they were married and settled in California.[659] Iris alienated the couple, to no one's surprise, distributing snide remarks and a dismissive attitude. Ted did his best to be charming with his new son-in-law. But, his paternal instincts often took over. "Of course, I knew who he was when I first met him. I used to listen to all those football games like everyone else," remembered David Lacey. "I never really got to know him very well. It was at a very basic level of conversation. Very guarded, informal. It was your typical in-laws relationship."[660] Father, husband, in-law, acquaintance, or friend, Ted Husing remained complex to the core, rarely dropping his careful approach to people. "He was always a bit mysterious," shared Chris Schenkel. "Ted never really let anyone get close to him—arms length."

On Dumont, Ted worked with his usual proficiency, sitting ringside, controlling the broadcast. But, the camera revealed things out of his control. Ted was over fifty and beginning to show his age. Smoky gray circles shadowed his eyes. A wider mid-section stretched his pants, his head increasingly bare. Though he rebutted his critics, beat the odds, there remained a perception that his best days were behind him. Ted's choice of projects outside sports didn't help in the fickle opinions of the public. As narrator for odd one-timers like "Neptune's Girls," girls attending an underwater school, or "Showman Shooter," a film documenting the exploits of skilled hunter

Herb Parsons, some viewers were left scratching their heads.[661] Was Husing wearing out his welcome? Yes, you can't teach an old dog new tricks. But, Ted wasn't old. He was sick.

It was subtle, slight, almost unnoticed. Ted began to drag his left foot. Each step, scraping back and pushing through ever so slightly. Few of his friends said anything, chalking the hitch up to the everyday wear and tear of being a New Yorker. Foot caught in a cab door. Tripped on a step. Twisted an ankle stepping off the curb. Yet, it was another signal that something was different, something was wrong. Afternoon naps, something he never did, became a regular part of the day. Sagging eyes, slumping posture, and low energy followed. No one dared comment, but it did seem the man at times looked like an ugly monster.

Pegge noticed odd behavior going back to his brief days in Philadelphia. During a summer visit, she saw her father nearly fall to his death from the broadcast perch at Garden State Race Track high atop the roof. He admitted to dizzy spells and promised to see a doctor.[662] He never did. Instead, he had frequent vitamin shots administered to boost his stamina. Fatigue continued. Ted became more belligerent, more than usual, as impossible as that was to measure. Squabbles with Iris increased in number and volume. Drinking binges were more frequent. His trademark discipline approach to work slipped, breaking the cardinal rule of no alcohol before a broadcast. Stanley Wertheim recalled seeing his famous cousin drunk on several occasions. "Once he passed out at the studio before going on the air. Everyone wondered if he would get it together in time. Suddenly, he woke up, grabbed the mike and said, "Hello, Kiddies." He did the whole show as if nothing was wrong."[663]

The broadcaster was hurting, but stayed busy. He charmed Arlene Francis, comedian Steve Allen, and others as a guest panelist on the popular CBS game show "What's My Line." Trying to stump the panel during that September 6, 1953, telecast was Brooklyn Dodger star Roy Campanella.[664] Later that month, another season of

Army football kicked off. Red Blaik's team still struggled to regain the days of championships and front-page headlines. The scares of scandal continued to rear its ugly head. But, on the afternoon of October 17, 1953, both Army and Husing gave fans an opportunity to relive past glories one more time.

On the schedule was Duke University. It was a game, like so many lately, they were supposed to lose. The Blue Devils were enjoying a solid year, 4–0 and ranked in the top ten. The game was originally scheduled for Michie Stadium. But a vicious cry for tickets and media credentials moved the game to the more spacious Polo Grounds in New York. The fact that it was a home game for Army seemed to be the only advantage they had coming into the contest. Duke rumbled onto the field with a run-happy offensive lead by all-American candidate Worth "A Million" Lutz, and a burly group of linemen that created holes the size of moon craters. The crowd gazed down in awe. What the boys from North Carolina expected was an easy victory. What they got instead was an unexpected flood of emotion from the Army defense, fans, and radio broadcasters.

It was a perfect day for football, warm temperatures and sunny skies. Perhaps expecting the worst, less than 22,000 fans showed at the Polo Grounds.[665] Army played the role of underdog to the tilt, wearing their road white uniforms. Duke supposedly had the strong running game. But, it was Army that struck first, scoring on the seven-yard first-quarter touchdown by junior tailback Tommy Bell. Duke woke up in the second quarter on a TD run by Lutz knotting the score at 7–7. Yet, before half-time Army regained the lead 14–7 when Patrick Uebel caught a five-yard option pass from teammate Pete Vann. Lutz of Duke continued to live up to his nickname, finding the end zone one more time during a bruising third quarter. The extra point kick would tie the score again. His attempt sailed left. Miraculously, Army still led.

The crowd, led by the corps of cadets, cheered the Army squad forward. GO! GO! GO! As the final quarter advanced, the

Polo Grounds began to wonder. "Could an upset be in the making?" The question was soon answered—No! Deep in their own territory, Duke runningback Red Smith broke through the line on a double reverse and raced for the Army end zone. Cadet's defender Bob Mischak galloped after Smith a few steps behind, hoping to tackle. Urban legend had Red Blaik screaming from the sidelines as the chase ensued, "Not Yet! Not Yet!"[666] Finally, Mischak lunged, bringing Smith down at the Army seven-yard line. What happened in the next four plays was anything but urban legend. It was stone-cold reality.

The Army defense dug in and held. Duke pushed to the five to the one, then to the one-inch line. On fourth down, the Duke bench tossed the kicking tee onto the field thinking Lutz would boot a chip shot for the win. He threw it back, remembering the missed extra point. Another running play seemed the safer bet. No way the Army line could hold afresh. The quarterback took the ball and dove for the goal line. A wall of white jerseys smashed him back. Ted was right with them as sweat ran down his temples. "Battered at the line! A second effort! . . . NO! NO! He did not get in! The Army refuses to allow Duke a score!"

Not wanting to risk a turn over, Blaik immediately punted the ball back to Duke, trusting his stingy defense to preserve the win. Less than thirty ticks remained on the scoreboard. Enough for Duke to perform a miracle of their own. The crowd remained standing. No one dared sit. The only two people at the Polo Grounds still nailed to their chairs were Walter Kennedy and Ted Husing. Three missed completions by Lutz had the Blue Devils down to one last play. The noise led Lutz to say later, "The savage cheering of GO! GO! GO! from the West Point stands placed our team in a nervous fright of tension and jitters."[667] The chaos not only affected the Duke players, but Ted as well. He set the scene for the listeners, his voice cracking on every syllable. "Duke moving left to right across your radio dial. Fourth down at the Army forty-two-yard line. Army leads by a single point."

Among the Polo Grounds press box sat two former Husing disciples, Curt Gowdy and Joe Hasel, calling the game on NBC radio.[668] They never had a chance that day. The listening audience was mesmerized by another captivating Husing football show. Some also noticed an unlikely vulnerability in his voice. "I do remember him being very emotional, you know, overly excited during the broadcast," said Army football fan Bill Giunco, who tuned in to hear the game on radio. "But, I also remember Kennedy had to hold him up, so to speak. He still called a thrilling game. He was the best."[669]

Ted looked out the window of the cramped broadcast quarters, struggling to focus on the players below. All of Duke's receivers sprinted for the end zone. Lutz dropped back and the crowd swelled. He planted his feet, cocked his arm, and heaved. As the ball floated through the air not a sound was heard. Wide out Jerry Barger was opened in the corner. A second passed, then another. Army defensive-back Pete Vann closed quickly and jumped to the sky batting the ball away. "INCOMPLETE!" the WMGM broadcaster shouted out. The Stadium noise nearly shook Harlem to rubble. No one knew such a small crowd could sound so loud. "The Army have held their ground and it looks like they will accomplish what no one expected them to do here this afternoon! OH BOY! OH WOW! . . . Can you believe this?" Then he said something that no one ever heard him say. "These boys have gotten me so excited, I can't even finish the broadcast. Take over, Walter."[670] Ted pulled away from the microphone and leaned forward in his chair. More sweat moistened his forehead. His eyes, filling with tears, rolled back in his head. The booth began to spin. He tried to regain focus, his breathing heavy and hard. Something was horribly wrong.

Kennedy could hardly believe what he heard. "Take over, Walter." Take over? Take over what? He knew his friend possessed a biting sense of humor. Relinquishing the microphone during the football game of the year was not funny. Two seconds remained.

Army broke their huddle. The confused color commentator saw no change in Husing's demeanor. Kennedy sat moved, concerned for his injured friend. Suddenly, the hysterical crowd brought him back. The more deafening sound of dead air shot fear through his body. Kennedy stood up, turned to the action on the field and grabbed the mike, finishing the broadcast as ordered. Army ran one play to complete the improbable victory.

More than 2,400 cadets stormed the field hoisting their heroes on brawny shoulders.[671] Ted turned to look at his partner. The tears were pouring down his checks. His eyes burned pink with sorrow, hands uncontrollably shaking. Oddly, in the middle of his face, he wore a white ear-to-ear smile. Kennedy barely recognized the person in front of him, a mad man, old and tired. He buried his head into his hands and cried still. The rest of his body quietly sobbing, heaving with emotion. Always the professional, Ted tried not to be heard, biting at his right hand. Kenney kept talking, shouting with a very different brand of emotion. "Army Wins It! Army Wins It! The Army Cadets hold on to take Duke here this afternoon by the score of 14–13. Truly . . . I don't know what to say. What a game!"

After the elation died down and stadium emptied, Ted brushed off the incident, never discussing it, a knowing look passed between them. Kennedy remained troubled but respected his friend well enough not to ask questions. Mr. Offense and Mr. Defense had five more games remaining on the schedule, if Ted could pull himself together. The Army was back in business, sporting a winning record. And above anything, feared again as an eastern football power. Outside of a scoreless tie with Tulane, the rest of the season went without a hitch, on the field and in the booth.

Ted suffered yet another worrisome episode two weeks after the Army versus Navy game. While watching a basketball double header at Madison Square Garden, he passed out on a bathroom floor. Friends, once more, begged him to see a doctor. In the past, he refused to seek help, paranoid they might actually find something.

He equated poor health with instant unemployment, final damnation, and the end of a brilliant career. "I was becoming increasingly jittery over what might happen next. My premonitions were strong," he later confessed.[672] This time, he agreed to an examination at Georgetown Hospital in Washington, using an alias, concealing his voice, away from the roving eyes of the New York press. A battery of tests, X-rays, and spinal tap surprisingly found nothing. A small series of mild strokes was the final diagnosis. They prescribed plenty of rest and cutting down on his heavy schedule. He had already dropped the Dumont boxing show a few months earlier, replaced by a young Chris Schenkel. The only gig left was the "Bandstand." There never was any passion in spinning vinyl records for Ted. It was a job, one that paid handsomely. And if he ever quit that, his friends might insist he visit a doctor of a different kind.

Rest did not help. Food lost its taste, sitting inside his cramping stomach like wet cement. During a large dinner party at Luchow's, he again wobbled uncontrollably before falling to the ground. A grease spot? Wet floor? Helping him to his feet, the party laughed it off. In the paper the next day it was reported that Ted was drunk.[673] The story couldn't have been further form the truth. Christmas came and went with little enjoyment, wondering if it would be his last. His nights were restless, immersed in depression, constantly living in a world of doubt and fear. "Just what the hell is wrong?" He tried to think of a word or words to express the way he felt. He could not. The king of phraseology, the man who studied dictionaries, picked apart thesauruses in his free time was stumped. What came to mind were clichés. To get to heaven you must go through hell. Was this heaven or hell? He was about to find out.

CHAPTER THIRTY-ONE

AM I DEAD OR ALIVE?

Finally, the limp was revealed. The evidence was in the shoes. After recording the next day's broadcast, Ted returned to Grammercy Park. He entered the apartment and climbed the stairs up to his bedroom. He felt tired and drained, stopping a few feet from the top to catch his breath. He chalked it up to old habits, long work hours and longer hours spent out with friends. He knew better. Lunch at 21 could not be called risky living. Stepping into his bedroom, he reached for the corner of the bed and nearly fainted. A cool breeze of thin air filled his lungs, fogged his brain. He sat down on the firm mattress and found his bearings. He took a deep breath and made a mental note to cancel any appointments for that evening. He couldn't remember if he made any or not. It did not matter. Getting comfortable was the only thing that did.

Ted untied his brown suede shoes and tossed them on the floor hoping to find relief in a pair of soft house slippers. Looking down he noticed something. The heel on his left shoe was severely worn down at a sharp angle. The heel on his right shoe, outside of the usual wear and tear, was unchanged. What made the discovery even more peculiar was that the shoes were only a few weeks old. Ted grabbed another pair from the closet and then another and finally one more. The left heel on all of them sported the same worn angle. Some trick he thought. Iris was known for having a volatile temper, but taking a knife to his shoes seemed outside the realm, though not impossible.

Still, Ted played the tough guy well, procrastinating, denying, and ignoring his condition. But, then there's the innocence of a child to motivate the action of a loving father. The one lone positive in his recent "forced retirement" was "Duke." He took full advantage of the extra time with his son. Visits to the WMGM studios, wrestling at the Garden, and, of course, more fun with trains. Come the spring of 1954, the ailing broadcaster and boy played a new sport, one with near tragic consequences.

The sun shone bright, the sky dotted sparingly with white, puffy clouds. The day opened with mild air, staying pleasant by noon. Ted slept late feeling a bit sluggish the night before, a scenario with more and more frequency. But as Ted rose to a late breakfast, he was quickly made aware that not everyone in the house felt the same. David Husing behaved as a typical boy of seven, full of energy and an abundant gusto for excitement. Sunday was his day with dad, no records to spin, no meetings to attend, no quick goodbyes. "Twenty Trains, Pop. You promised," he reminded him more than once. Ted sipped on black coffee and ate hard-boiled eggs, anything to match the boy's enthusiasm. He tried to ignore him, burying his eyes in the morning newspaper. The tepid strategy failed. "Come on dad— Twenty Trains, Twenty Trains! Pleeeeease!" Ted finally relented. "Alright!" he said. "Go tell your mother we're headed out." There was no need for Fereschi, not in quality time between father and son. He grabbed the keys to the car and reached for his hat. "One hundred and twenty-fifth street here we come." The Husing men headed for the door. Again, as things had been at the Husing house of late, family time did not always include the whole family.

Driving in a pink Buick station wagon, they headed uptown. The two shared a bag of M&Ms® purchased at a Lexington Avenue "five and dime" store. They savored the small dark chocolate pills the way a baby drinks a bottle of warm powered milk. Twenty trains soon became twenty-five, then thirty trains. Who was really counting? The simple child's game of counting trains always brought joy. The ride home down 2nd Avenue, however, took on a less jovial mood. Ted's pink four-door cruised along the street purposely, a new type of game being played. "We were traveling at twenty-eight miles per hour because you could cascade the lights in those days," remembered David Husing. "You could go up and down the street and travel with the lights."[674] One after another, 65th Street, 64th, 63rd, a stream of green and red.

Then, in an instant, the fun stopped. Near the corner of 56th Street, a large freight truck pulled out onto 2nd Avenue. A collision with the Buick seemed imminent. Reflex took over. Ted went for the brake again and again. His right leg froze. Ted's mind raced but his right leg stayed unmoved. "I can't lift my leg," he said to his son. He repeated the words, this time in a more anxious tone. "I can't lift my leg!" Unable to brake, Ted turned the wheel, missing the front end of the truck by inches.

Looking ahead, he noticed the traffic signal at 55th Street. It was green, another collision averted. Panic gripped more. The radioman tried the brake once more. His leg remained oddly frozen. "I can't lift my leg!" he uttered again, quieter this time as not to alarm the boy. "Duke" smiled over at his father, wondering if this, too, was part of the cascading lights or a new version of Twenty Trains. Ted dug deep and tried to lift his stagnant leg. This time the limb responded and found the rubber brake pad. Checking the rear view mirror, he pulled the car over safely to the side of the avenue.

By now sweat dripped from his forehead, veins pulsated on his hands that shook like the American flag in a brisk Yankee Stadium wind. The pain of a throbbing headache pushed between his eyes. Ted jerked the keys from the ignition pulling the boy with him to the sidewalk. With new force he lifted his arm, puckered his lips, and whistled for a cab. He ordered the driver to their Gramercy Park address.[675] Thrusting the car keys inside his pocket, Ted thanked a large cluster of lucky stars that tragedy had been avoided. The pink car sat abandoned. Cursed. Possessed by a spirit Ted did not know. What had just transpired and why, he did not have a clue. But, one thing was certain. His driving days were over.

Iris was not home. Ted figured she was out and about doing something important, no doubt. Wherever she was, Ted was glad she was not home alone waiting for him to arrive. If she found out about the shoes, the condition, she might get mad, and in the least she might actually worry. As much as her and Ted fought, Iris still had feelings for the man. She nagged him endlessly about the earlier fainting spells, begging him to see a doctor. Ted staved her off telling her everything was fine. Now he wondered if his wife was right. Fear closed in around him as he sat on the bed. Something was physically wrong, but what? Again, Ted told himself to just slow down. Take a day off, smell the roses. Nothing that a good night sleep wouldn't cure. Focus in on the boy. It was decided, tomorrow, a play date with "Duke." After that, anything was possible.

The twice-a-day "Bandstand" schedule often dwindled down to one, especially during summer months. Dodger games remained a popular fixture on WMGM, also heard on the new fangled FM band as well. Husing's show no longer bumped them from the air. He didn't mind. Mark Hanna renegotiated the contract, making sure his client still got paid.[676] By the end of 1954, the writing was on the wall. The celebrity DJ craze he helped create had peaked. Paul Whiteman, Duke Ellington, Tommy Dorsey, all went back to playing music live on stage instead of a turntable. Even Martin Block said goodbye to his long time employer WNEW, spinning his records on WABC.[677] The songs they played seemed dated. Listeners, younger now, were into a new sound, a rhythm more unencumbered. Disc jockeys remained hot, but Rock-n-Roll was even hotter. As winter rolled in, Ted exited the station and the "Bandstand," aware that there was nothing left to do. Lee sensed a change in his friend, asking religiously about his health. Ted assured him everything was fine. They both knew better. In 1955, WMGM brought in a wild DJ from Kansas City named Peter Tripp. Fans called him "The Curly-Headed Kid in the Front Row." He gave radio's new generation what they wanted, top forty hits, electric guitars, and Elvis Presley. Ted knew nothing about Rock-n-Roll or curly hair. He was off the radio airwaves, lost, wondering if his career was over?

He thought fresh job opportunities might come. They didn't. The phone did not ring. No one wanted to take the chance. Hiring a sick man came with too many liabilities. Real help, real honesty was still forthcoming. No one wanted to confront the stubborn man, too proud to admit deficiency. Ted became more isolated, easily moved to tears, nothing but time on his hands. Iris's frustrations mounted. She was genuine in her concern about his health. But, the fact that he wasn't earning a paycheck concerned her more. His appearance on NBC television, June 19, 1955, a show called "Remembering . . . 1938," caught many by surprise.[678] Surprised how depleted he looked, how slow he moved.

A steady gloom permeated the house on East 19th Street. The endless stream of visitors stopped. Travels for lobster at Bookbinders ended. Even the always-reliable Mr. Fereschi was let go, no longer needed. In September, Iris shipped David upstate to boarding school.[679] Lake Placid was far away from the inevitable trouble that loomed around the corner. Ted missed the boy, calling him often, promising visits that never came.

If anyone was to detect Ted's deepening joylessness, it was his former assistant Jimmy Dolan.[680] The two friends saw less and less of each other, no longer a team, traveling in different circles. When they did see one another, talk of the old days, the old neighborhood dominated their conversation.[681] Dolan could see the glow fading from the Husing fire. His eyes wandered off, gazing into a world already lived. "I don't think Ted was happy when he accepted the big contract to become a disc jockey. He loved music, but I think he missed getting around to the various colleges and other events he covered for years."[682]

Others, too, saw Ted in an ever-melancholy state, raw, sentimental. Joe Lemerise, Jr., remembered one such time. "I remember, we were at home in Bayside and some kid got hit by a car right outside our house. Thank God it wasn't serious. The kid just got bumped. But my uncle (Ted) got all upset. He filled up and got all emotional. I'll never forget it. He was very soft that way. As big as he was he was a pussy cat."[683] Ted's dizzy spells never stopped, more intense, more frightening. Park Avenue South, near Grammercy Park, nearly became a death scene during a spring morning rush hour.[684] Crossing the busy traffic, Ted's vision blurred. Knees buckled. Buildings melted away. The black pavement broke his fall, cutting a deep gash above his eyes. Cars swerved nearly jumping the curb. A few minutes later, he woke trying to figure out why a circle of worried, unfamiliar faces surrounded him. The hand of Providence had averted tragedy, but for how long?

His world was literally spinning out of control. Ted searched everywhere to find security, a sure foot on a slippery slope. The old haunts, the old streets on the walk of fame added more confusion. West 52nd Street, by the middle of the decade, was almost unrecognizable. Gone were many of the classy restaurants and sassy jazz clubs that made the avenue swing. In its place, strip joints and parking lots doted the changing scene. Brownstones were demolished. Music was replaced with the sound of jackhammers. The stench of rubble and lime dust filled the air. The claws of modern society were evident with the rise of giant office buildings. And the trip on evil heroine pushed to outlast the buzz of a stiff vodka martini. The red-hot hay days of intimate charm and fashion were disappearing. Swing Street was now a joke. The long, blue block became known as "Stripty-Second Street."[685]

Three days passed before he visited the club again, the first of April, 1956. Jimmy Collins, the long-standing doorman at 21 helped him from the cab. The two had become quite familiar with each other over the past three decades. Ted walked in wearing a bandage on his head, a small reminder of the incident on Park Avenue South. Charlie Berns met him with a gentle handshake. "What happened here?" he asked pointing to the white bandage. "I got into a fight with the sidewalk," Ted joked, trying to change the subject. Berns did not laugh. He nodded his head, trying not to look serious, but he was. Ted segued into the reason for taking his good pal up on a dinner invitation. "Who's this friend you want me to meet? Some art collector looking to buy Jack's old crap on the cheap?" The 21 owner wished to lighten the atmosphere, speaking in his usual quiet tone. "Remember you said you haven't been yourself lately? I mean a little under the weather. Well, there's a doctor friend I want you to meet. . . No obligation. . . Just talk to him. Maybe he can suggest something that might help."

"Some April Fool's joke," Ted thought. He did not leave. Berns and the rest of the intimate party took it as a positive sign. Walking over to the table, Ted extended his hand and said hello to Dr. Charles Mayo. His Minnesota clinic was already legendary, progressive, state of the art, and in some cases, able to perform medical miracles. The more the doctor talked, the more Ted fell into his confidence. Whenever the radioman needed answers to life's perplexing questions, they were often found at "Jack and Charlie's." Jack was gone, but his spirit very much lived. Within a week, Ted boarded a plane for Rochester.

The tumor was unmistakable. Sizeable, full and benign. Finally, Ted knew. He was almost relieved. It explained much. But, questions remained. Was the cancer a new condition? How did the X-rays at Georgetown Hospital, only eighteen months earlier, miss this? The latter was answered with the simple fact that there was far superior technology, better facilities at the Mayo Clinic. The doctor himself made no bones about it. Surgery was imminent, the sooner the better. Medical jargon was liberally tossed about, prolactinoma, optic-cyasim, meninges, pituitary glands . . . Ted sat motionless in a chair trying to absorb everything they were saying. He nervously reached for a cigarette inside his sports coat but did not find any. An old habit he would have to eliminate. First he called Pegge and shared the bitter-sweet news, then mother. He waited until he arrived back in New York to talk with Iris.

Instead of Rochester, Ted opted for surgery closer to home, New York Hospital. It was the site of Cornell University's Medical facilities. In typical Husing fashion, he would experience nothing but the best. And once again, it took an Ivy League school to make the Master confront his demons. The arrangements were made, the operation scheduled for the 14th day of April. He was admitted feeling confident, joking with the staff, charming the nurses. Ted had it all planned out, a temporary bump in the road, time off to make things right again, then BAM!—back to the top of the broadcasting hierarchy. However, the ailing broadcaster kept his whereabouts quiet. "Where's Ted?" his concerned friends asked. No one knew. He remained obstinate, still unwilling to admit defeat on any level.

It was a cloudy day in New York City. The sky was dark. Showers threatened.Precipitation was not unusual during the early weeks of spring. It was an annual rite of passage. Wet grass, slick streets, and rainouts during baseball season's first month were always expected. As the patient prepared himself for the knife, the operating team diligently primed for the work ahead. Surgeons, anesthesiologists, nurses, interns stirred about. Ted waited in his room, bathed and head fully shaven.

As they all waited, a nurse standing by the window noticed the gloomy weather before her. Ted noticed the woman in white and asked of the day's prospects. "What's it look like out there?" he asked. Jaded by the long hours and hospital environment she answered with a throbbing groan, "Rain, rain, rain! That's all it does these days, you know. Sometimes I wonder what that God's doing up there." Suddenly the nurse caught herself. Someone in the healing profession should be a bit more sensitive, perhaps, especially for a man who was about to have major surgery. She decided to lighten the moment with a rhythm.

April Showers Bring May Flowers!

The worse was over, Ted believed. Yes, indeed, it rained a bounty during the month of April. What he did not recall was that the rains of sorrow also on occasion pour down in May and June and July and . . .

The surgery did not go as planned. The large tumor was found, and then removed by the fine tools and delicate hands. Lifting the brain, however, was not on the original agenda. The doctors figured they could get all the unwanted growth. They were wrong. Complications occurred. Eleven hours later, the patient woke. The drapes in his room on the thirteenth floor were open. Warm rays of sun screamed through. But, Ted could not see the bright light, the blue skies, the pea green drapes. He was blind. "Am I dead or alive?" he asked. He heard sounds, voices, but no one answered. "AM I DEAD OR ALIVE?" he shouted. In reality, the man made not a sound or wimper. He could not, his mouth unable to move, his muscles defective.

Heat radiated through Ted's fingers. Everything he touched seemed to burn. His sense of smell was pungent and alive. "They didn't have MRIs, CAT scans, or ultra-sound, all three means of radio-graphic imaging just wasn't available back then," explained Dr. Laurence Demers, Director of Clinical Pathology Research at Penn State Hershey Medical Center in Hershey, Pennsylvania. "They would take X-rays and get an idea. But, it was almost like garbage clean-up. They'd go in and scrape the area and didn't really know what they were damaging in there. It was guess work."[686]

For the next five weeks, little changed. Remedial counting

games meant to build up his vocal chords were the highlight of his day. A child of five was better skilled. A dark world filled his eyes. Stitches tore at his head still wrapped in thick gauze. The simple pleasure of reading the *Daily Racing Forum* was impossible. "Do you want to listen to the radio, Mr. Husing?" a nurse asked. He dipped his head, mumbled "no," turning his head away. Crushed by his prospects, he stopped eating, moving, caring, losing an astonishing fifty pounds.[687] Desperate to lift his waning spirits, Pegge called a friend.

The large voice bellowed, storming into the small hospital room. "HEY YOU, CRUMB BUMB!" The man's smile usually entered first. Ted, as sick as he felt, instantly recognized the voice peppered with a slight Philadelphia accent. It belonged to one man— Toots. The personal medicine took effect immediately. If Toots Shor couldn't put a grin on Ted's face, nobody could. The saloonkeeper visited often, sneaking in baked potatoes and steak wrapped in tinfoil, hoping to fatten up his skinny friend. Ted stayed pessimistic, begging Shor not to tell anyone where he was.

Ted trusted no one in his present state. On the bad days his head throbbed. Most of the time it just hurt. His heart ached. His soul burned. There was nothing more New York Hospital could do. Scalpels, sutures, and surgeons, taking away his sight, his will to live, was what they had done best. In early June, they transferred him downtown to the Rusk Institute for a change of scenery and intensified treatments. Dr. Howard Rusk brought in a fresh approach to rehabilitation medicine and took a special interest in the famous patient. Rusk's pioneering philosophy of rehab emphasized treating an individual's emotional, psychological, and social needs.[688] Clearly, Ted fit the mold. From the onset, the star patient put up resistance, unmotivated, depressed. Sit, stare, and disappear like lint from a closet. Ted cared little of what they asked of him. There was only one thing he asked of his superiors. NO VISITORS ALLOWED.

By the early summer of 1956, three greats of radio sports were recuperating in various hospitals from serious illness. Ted would have to share his misery. Phantom pain in Bill Stern's amputated leg had turned him into a morphine addict. Overdosing the night before the Sugar Bowl that year, he staggered into the ABC television booth only minutes before going on the air. As Stern stammered incoherently during the opening segment, producers cut his microphone. His assistant Ray Scott was forced to take over the broadcast. Stern checked himself into a rehabilitation center trying to kick the habit once and for all.

Bill Slater suffered uncontrollable shakes due to Parkinson's Disease. His wife's strict religious beliefs did not permit medical interference in times of illness.[689] Finally, friends intervened and admitted him to a New York facility. Lindsey Nelson remembered the impact it had on him as a young broadcaster. "I had observed that, generally speaking, network sports announcers did not tend to live to a ripe old age."[690] June slipped into July. Ted's sight improved slightly, seeing shadows, dim objects at best. Day after day, week after week, no one from the outside looked in to say hello. The general public began to wonder, "What ever happened to Ted Husing?" Rumors were rampant: stroke, alcoholism, schizophrenia, even death. One thing was certain. The broadcaster was not around and few knew where to find him.

On September 15, Ted received a new visitor. A man he hardly knew walked in alone, practically a stranger. Together they walked out bonded friends. Sander Simon was a local New York businessman. Adhesives were his trade. With a busy plant in Long Island City, Simon had amassed a small fortune. His friends called him Sandy. Like Ted, Simon found the buzz of Broadway and lure of its many hangouts enticing. The 21 Club was among his favorites. Both men were giants in their respective fields. A mutual respect seemed natural. Extending a hand seemed fair. Not to Ted. Oftentimes, Ted saw his professional, social, and economic contemporaries as rivals or threats. "The strange part of it was that Sander Simon was anything but a close friend of mine," Ted recalled later.

"Many times I had been impolite to him. I'd been guilty of doing this to rafts of people. Those snubbed by Ted Husing could have formed a picket line long enough to surround the CBS building."[691]

When Simon entered Ted's room, he was treated unreceptively and rude, par for the course for Ted. Simon was not turned off by the broadcaster's gruff exterior. Instead he was challenged to unearth Ted's indistinguishable humanity. "I'd been searching for Ted for months," said Simon. "I finally located him through his daughter."[692] Simon came to Rusk with a single objective, surround Ted with the old digs—sports. He strapped the patient into his car and the two traveled to Harlem and the Polo Grounds. A baseball game was in order. The hometown Giants were hosting Stan Musual and the St. Louis Cardinals. The National League squad was two seasons removed from a World Series championship. Willie Mays and "The Catch" had been the talk of baseball. 1956 was a different story. Wins were rare and forgetting was more the order. That afternoon, they found the winning touch. The Giants shut out the Cardinals 3–0. The victory over St. Louis made everyone feel good, including Ted. Fresh air and the autumn outdoors did him good.

A true friendship now existed, strangers no more. Simon had thrown a line when Ted was sinking. Others were less appreciative of the man. Some saw ulterior motives. Herman Masin saw the man as an egocentric piranha solely interested in stroking Husing because of his fame. He wrote a story backing up such unflattering claims. "The most dreadful hero-worshipper we ever met was a small-time millionaire whom we once had the misfortune to sit next to at a sport luncheon. Some time during the lunch, he leaned over and said, 'would you like to talk to Ted Husing?' We were startled. 'You actually see him and talk to him?' we asked. 'Yeah! I visit him every day. I'm the only person who does.' He smiled radiantly. It was a huge moment in his life. A superstar loved him. 'Would you like to visit with me tomorrow?' We could only stare at him. He wasn't stupid. He wasn't a bad guy. And he was rich. Why did he have to be so appalling?"[693]

Joe Lemerise, Jr., didn't see the adhesive man as an oppor-tunist. He worked briefly as a summer shipping clerk at Simon's fac-tory in Long Island City. "I didn't know him that well. But, my sense was that he was a paternal person," said Lemerise. "He was the boss and everyone treated him with respect. I think he was well-liked. With the people there at the factory, I never heard a negative thing about him."[694] Herman Masin remained skeptical but gave the man his just due. "He doesn't deserve any great plaudits except to play devil's advocate," said Masin. "He did it. Ted needed him and he was there for Ted and that puts him with the angels, really."[695]

Once again, the power of persuasion came by means of a warm body. Good friends brought a better attitude. Ted surprised Rusk, participating in exercises with a fresh purpose. Promises of more sporting events by his new friend, a visit to West Point during football season, kept him focused. Smiles and jokes also returned, a new twist on self-deprecating humor. However, fragility persisted. Fragility often won the battle of wills. Ted remained defiant about no visitors. In reality, he wanted more, enough to fill Madison Square Garden. Every time Simon came, his face lit up. Another visitor came, and returned again. This time, he did not smile. Evil, dark-ness filled his thoughts. Her red hair was gone, replaced by jet-black strands among streaks of gray. It was Iris.

CHAPTER THIRTY-TWO

DELIVER ME FROM THY HELL

Every time she left, Ted wondered why she ever came at all. As much as he hated Rusk, Iris complained more. He asked about "Duke." Instead, she had a fit. "What the hell are these doctors doing anyway?" she whined. "No one gives me any straight answers. 'I don't know, Mrs. Husing. We just have to see how things progress, Mrs. Husing." The patient just sat quiet, bothered by her presence, hoping desperately to shut her mouth. "You know reporters are calling the house asking questions. . . . What am I– suppose– to - tell them?"

"NOTHING!" he shot back.

"Oh, that's your answer?" Iris said pushing a finger into his chest. "Nothing? . . . Just like you're doing now. Every time I come, all you do is sit here and do nothing! . . . What are we going to do, Ted? WHAT AM I GOING TO DO?" He grabbed her arm and pushed her away. It would not be the last such outburst. Several more visits had them exchanging words like gun fire. Ted fought back with his weapon of choice, a cane. One swing nearly missed her head.

Iris not only seemed to have power over his mental state. She also had power of attorney, as long as her husband remained incapacitated. Everything Husing was now hers. Payments on the apartment, "Duke's" tuition, the new spring line of clothes at Bergdorf Goodman. Those were her needs. Rotting in a hospital was his. Ted's huge medical expenses mounted with each passing week and month. Before long, there was nothing left. "My mother was not good with money. Good at spending it, but nothing else," said David Husing about Iris. It did not take long before word leaked that Ted was broke. The alarm had been sounded. The hat was passed on almost a weekly basis at 21 to help the ailing announcer. The Kriendler's made sure Bertha got the money.

The same was done at Toots Shor's. The large man remained in Ted's corner, forever touched by the kindness Husing showed him when he was in trouble with bookies. [696] Growing up, he knew a life of depravity, never thinking he'd be rich one day. "I don't want to be a millionaire. I just want to live like one," he always said. Shor was a simple man who didn't worry about tomorrow. After he lost $100,000 dollar bet on the Joe Louis versus Billy Conn fight, he slept like a baby. "There are savers and there are spenders. I don't hang around with savers," he once said.[697] Ted, too, had been a spender, never safeguarding a single dollar. Now, he wished he had. "I always tried to pay for everyone's fun," Ted said in retrospect. "The motivation was simple: it gave me pleasure."[698]

For Husing the invalid, the days of fun were long gone. Simon continued to come. Surprisingly, on most occasions, he was turned away. "I'm sorry, sir. He wishes to see no one. . . No one!" Apathy returned, sitting in a vegetative state. Baths were discontinued. Food got picked at pushing his fork around the plate in a circular motion. He snarled at nurses, throwing cups, cursing as if speaking in tongues, ordering them to leave his room. Most of the time they did as he wished. On one occasion he overheard staff members discussing some of the more hopeless cases at Rusk being transferred to a "special ward." [699] Everyone understood the code—rubber rooms, numbing medication, even electro shock.

Was Ted's recent behavior that of a mad man? Iris thought so, co-signing the commitment papers. On the line below, Ted himself signed. It was one way to get rid of her. She would never come to visit insanity. "He was probably getting depressed over the fact that he wasn't normal anymore," explained Dr. Larry Demers. "He probably had severe headaches along with the visual field disturbances. They were medicating him and that starts to play tricks with the mind and then they probably thought he was starting to go nuts."[700] There was no turning back. For the next sixty days, he was stuck, contracted to a room of lunatics. Come October, Ted had a new address, Bloomingdale Psyche Hospital in Westchester.

The room was dark. The only light seen was a tiny ray of sun struggling to find life around the drawn thick beige curtains. Random screams came and went. The sound of broken glass was common. It smelled of unclean human flesh and rotting teeth. Ted's apathy was beginning to reveal itself through his personal hygiene habits or lack thereof. Peering into the gloom, Edgar Allan Poe himself would have appreciated the lifeless atmosphere. Nothing could get to Husing except misery. He seemed to love the role of crazy man. Instigating fights and being difficult became a daily routine. Thoughts of suicide oddly gave him peace. The man was blind. In the darkness, suddenly he could see an array of vibrant, clear colors. He saw his father's burned and distorted face. Henry, too, once sat alone, depressed wanting desperately to hide his mangled features from friends and loved ones. How horrible! How wrong! How unfair, he thought. A pool of self-pity seemed more inviting for them both. Like father, like son.

"Not one of my favorite stories," admitted David Lacey. "I don't want to talk about it," snapped Chris Schenkel. "That was between them." Family members and friends were shocked to find out he had been committed. Dee Lemerise remembers her husband confronting Iris after one such visit. "Joe came back after seeing Ted and, oh God, he sailed into Iris. 'What the hell is he doing up there?

353

He shouldn't be there!' She said, 'You don't understand. He got violent with me.'"[701] After Jimmy Dolan found out, he gathered the troops, headed for Westchester and demanded his friend's release.[702] Dolan brought with him fire power, a man who could persuade people. He brought a priest.

Leo Francis Dudley was born October 6, 1904, in Philadelphia. Like so many in his blue-collar neighborhood, he grew into a fervent sports fan. If he wasn't playing ball, he was watching it. Places like Franklin Field and Shibe Park were second homes. He grew to a husky 6–3 frame. His dark features and curly black hair gave him a unique look among the other white kids in the neighborhood. His friends called him "nigger."[703] Running the same South Philly streets was another boy with a large frame, Toots Shor. The two became fast friends, Dudley the Catholic, Shor the Jew. While Shor pursued a life as a saloon-keeper, Dudley became a man of God. He was ordained in 1930 as a Franciscan, taking the name Fr. Benedict Joseph Dudley. From that day forward, his closer associates respectfully referred to him as "Ben Joe."

When the two migrated to New York, their bond continued. Dudley was a frequent guest at his friend's famous restaurant. "When Duds would go to Toots Shor's, he'd just sign the tab," remembered Dudley's colleague Fr. Ed Sullivan. "He never had to pay for anything." One day Shor introduced the tall priest to a radio announcer named Husing. He told the famous announcer that Fr. Dudley was head of the charitable Franciscan Mission Band. Without a beat and in typical fashion, Ted asked the priest, "What instrument do you play, Father?"[704] From that day forward, a bonding friendship developed.

Dudley served in a variety of missionary work throughout the five boroughs. But, in the fall after Sunday services, he headed to Yankee Stadium as Chaplin for the New York Giants pro football squad. He walked the Giant's sideline for more that forty years, beginning in 1934.[705] Oftentimes, he followed the team on the road as well. His large presence seemed to naturally fit among the players. They enjoyed being around the tall man wearing a white collar, comfortable, sharing a drink in public or privately confessing their sins.[706] "Although a reverent man, Fr. Dudley is also a very worldly man," wrote former Giant great Kyle Rote. "Nothing seems to shock him, at least outwardly."[707] Not everyone approved of his toeing the line between the secular and spiritual worlds. Owners of rival teams, seeing his presence as perhaps an unfair advantage, tried to have him banished from the field during games.[708] "I guess some people might have thought he was too much of a publicity hound," said Fr. Sullivan. "That was the nature of the beast. He liked people, especially sportsmen."

In the fall of 1956, one particular man of sports was in need of his help more than any. Ted's languishing appearance was a reflection of his growing apathy. Tiny gray hairs protruding from his nose and ears made him look far beyond his present age of 54. He felt trapped in more ways than one, convinced an asylum was the proper place for him to be. Changing the mind of this stubborn man would be challenging, if not impossible. The man was literally wilting away. When Dolan and the priest first set eyes on what was left of Husing, they hardly recognized him. Betty Farrell remembered how her father Jimmy Dolan reacted to viewing Ted in such a feeble state. "My father went up to see him and saw this old man sitting there with a blanket wrapped around him and said 'Oh My God, its Ted!'"[709]

Things weren't what they appeared to be. The fast-talking Dolan made a strong case for his friend, explaining to administrators the adversarial relationship between Ted and Iris. Dudley, in his usual strong but quiet demeanor, convinced them to reevaluate the patient. The same patient who was once the most recognized voice on radio. Sixty days in a nut house might kill him. Bloomingdale for many was the end of the line. What Ted needed was a fresh start. After several days of deliberation, the facility finally consented under strict conditions. The former radioman was still broken and needed specialized care. They made a recommendation, a convalescent home. Next stop for Ted on the road to recovery, a spacious collection of neo-classic brick buildings called Burke Rehibilitation Center.

When the sixty-acre facility first opened in White Plains, it was designed to treat war-injured soldiers. By the 1950s, Burke was gaining a reputation for assisting "specific needs" patients beyond physical rehabilitation.[710] Bill Stern spent time at Burke correcting his morphine addiction, as did other celebrities for various illnesses.

Toots Shor and Sandy Simon along with the same few familiar faces all came to see him. How Ted greeted them depended upon factors such as appetite, time of day, and his desire for an audience. Sometimes he was a meek kitten, while others a fire-breathing dragon. When Fr. Dudley and Bertha came, they came with a new tact—prayer. It was met with resistence, wishing to rely on self-pity instead. Even Red Barber, an ordained Episcopalian minister, visited once or twice, offering counsel. He faired little better. Ted's acerbic, cynical tongue overshadowed any hope.[711] Walter Kennedy made the trip to White Plains several times and was surprised by the power of a man who looked so weak. "Fuck it! I'm just a mess." Ted would say grabbing his arm. Kennedy tried to lighten the mood, reassure him. "Come on Ted. If you can't be with the Skeeters, we'll bring the club to you." Ted barked back with explicated instructions. "Goddamnit! Keep 'em away, Walt. I can't bare to have them see me like this!" Then the patient got quiet and whispered, the sadness returning. Kennedy knew the look from before. "Please . . . Don't tell the fellas where I am . . . They'll only be disappointed. . . . Please?"

Kennedy vowed not to tell any of Ted's friends where he was. Those outside the inner circle, however, were all ears. "That was a tough promise to make, because it was one I didn't want to make," explained Kennedy later. "Finally, driving home one night, the solution came to me. I had promised Ted I wouldn't tell any of our mutual friends. That left me free to get the news to somebody he didn't know."[712]

John Ferris, a staff writer for the *New York World-Telegram & Sun* had never met the great sports announcer. As close as he got was the same way most did, listening to his many broadcasts. But, for someone who never met Ted Husing, he was able to get closer than anyone else had in recent months. Walter Kennedy made sure of it. The PR man and former Husing broadcast partner had plenty of friends in the press. He could have plopped Ted on the desk of at least a dozen established newspapermen. Ferris was young, hungry, and looking for a good story to sink his journalistic teeth into. No one, especially Ted, could argue with tenacity. On the day 300 mournful friends and family members said goodbye to bandleader Tommy Dorsey in New York City, the world again said hello to Ted Husing. In the November 29 edition of the *World Telegram & Sun*, his veiled secret and hidden world of misery was revealed. A bold, black headline slapped across the front page: "Ted Husing Losing Brain Tumor Fight." In the story below, Ferris described Ted as a man in grave condition. "His health ever and again brings him to deeply morbid states. Depression seizes him. He misses his friends."[713] Many wondered what had become of the once stellar sports announcer turned DJ. Now they knew.

Would Ted be angry now that trusts were broken? His friends shuddered at the thought. Anyone who knew him, knew the wrath of Husing could be harsh and swift. Maybe he wouldn't find out. In one sense, they thanked the creator for Ted's lack of sight. At least he couldn't read the story. The crippled broadcaster didn't have time to be angry. He was too busy opening mail. Cards and letters came pouring in. The switchboard was jammed for days, fans wishing to leave messages.[714] Kennedy's plan worked. The outpouring of the public's affection softened the uncompromising man.

Ted slowly resurfaced with the coming new year. A renewed determination in rehab exercises had staff members applauding. As Christmas rolled in so did more answers to his now daily devotions. Jack Martin, his friend and proprietor of Bear Mountain Lodge, invited Ted to share the holiday with his family near West Point. Drinking cocktails with the Army brass was not on the schedule. Moved, the broadcaster graciously accepted.

Ted's improved attitude had him listening to the radio again, eavesdropping on sports and enjoying music. The morning of January 31, 1957, greeted Ted with eagerness. A special visitor was coming. When he was coming, where they were going, and why, he had not a clue. There was always a mystery about his friend. It made the broadcaster like him even more. On the day when baseball great Ted Williams was set to marry North Carolina model Nelva Mare, Ted Husing could not have been further away from a life of beauty and the glamour of sports.[715] How quickly they forgot. How soon they would remember. By the next day, Ted, once again, was the story.

CHAPTER THIRTY-THREE

PASADENA

He was an angel—beautiful, cooperative, even chatty. There was a new glow about the man. It was a miracle of near biblical proportions. The spirited late January night at the Roosevelt spurned a chain reaction of events. First and foremost, Ted's health began to improve, and dramatically. Within two weeks, his sight returned to near eighty percent. Before were gray shadows, a flash of light. Now, full figures and recognizable faces greeting him with a smile and a "Good goin' Ted, I knew you'd be back." His speech cleared. Gone were the slurs and garbled confusion. Clear, slow but articulate, words flowed from his lips with little effort. The swagger returned. His confidence rising from the rubble of self-pity and pain. Could a broadcast booth and football game be far off?

But the demons soon returned. Did they ever go away? Depression took over and Ted found himself stuck in a chair, alone in a dark room, crying, mumbling. His mood swings, everything from dirty jokes to a tray being thrown across the room, topped the list of grievances at staff meetings. He was clearly a high-maintenance patient. The nurses rolled their eyes as Ted's daily requests started up again, rage-filled and unreasonable like before. The once great Ted Husing had few fans at Burke Rehabilitation Hospital. They wanted him to leave.

Could he have been faking the whole thing? Mind over matter. Or perhaps it was the wishful thinking of others that saw a change that never existed. It was clear, however, that Ted was a better man surrounded by friends and family. Doctors noticed the calming effect that visits from the likes of Toots Shor or Fr. Dudley gave him. But the daily visits became less frequent. Work, life, and Ted's sour disposition kept them away. The flow of get-well cards slowed to a trickle. Of course, Iris stopped coming long ago. She cut off all communications. Any hope of reconciliation well behind them.

Anger and resentment fueled her. She refused young David to see him. She kept Ted's where-abouts a mystery only saying that, "your father is sick." "It breaks my heart not to be able to see my boy now," he told a reporter.[716] Bertha was still at the Dauphin Apartments. People were shocked when she told them her age, eighty-three. Her cheery outlook and youthful energy remained the envy of the old neighborhood. But the visits to White Plains started affecting her as well. She returned to Manhattan appalled at the conditions. "Hospitals are no place for sick people," she would say. "He should be at home."

Pegge noticed them on her visits from California. They were everywhere it seemed. Unfamiliar female admirers with auburn lipstick and rosy cheeks standing at her father's bedside. Nurses, wearing knee-length skirts flirting with the famous patient. To her they were piranha, bloodsuckers, liars. She knew they did not have his best interest in mind. What they saw was an aging celebrity and better yet, dollar signs. None of them were the wiser. Ted's money was long gone. Iris made sure of that. Nevertheless, Ted still had his vices beyond the sixth race at Jersey Park. Even a blind man could smell a pretty woman a mile a way. And Pegge did what she could from protecting the little dignity her father had left. In her mind, a fourth Mrs. Ted Husing was completely out of the question.

She monitored her father's condition as best she could. The

five-hour flights from L.A. began to take its toll. She was starting a new chapter in her own life, motherhood, pregnant for the first time. If only he were closer, in every way. When she told him of the news, Ted sighed with joy on the phone saying, "I wish your mother could be here to see the baby. She would be so proud." Peggemae heard the desperation in his voice. It wasn't in anything he said. More in what he did not. The lingering memories, heartache, disappointment pulled him further into the abyss. She advocated for change. A clean break, a new outlook on life. What her father needed, above all, the surroundings of people he could trust, those who had his best interest in mind. What he needed more than anything was family. And family lived three thousand miles away.

A move to the West Coast made perfect sense. He was more than familiar with Southern California. Work sent him to L.A. many times over the years. Poolside, the Olympics, Hollywood, football games, the Brown Derby, movie stars, and, of course, the Tournament of Roses Parade. No matter what he was doing, Ted always found time to visit the great oval stadium in Pasadena. The Rose Bowl! He had seen it dozens of times, yearning always to work the hallowed booth just once. Many of the cronies from the old days were out there making the sun and warm weather home: Bing Crosby, Paul Douglass, his former #2 man at CBS turned movie star, and other actor friends. Lennie Hayton lived close, too close. Helen's body rested in a grave somewhere in the hills of Glendale. Ted did not want to think about Lennie and Helen for a minute. Instead, he thought about them constantly.

Pegge and her husband David lived in Altadena, an L.A. suburb. With a child soon to come, they would need help. Ted was in no condition to lend a hand. A man closer to death, a man unfamiliar with good parenting, much more experienced at playing caretaker than caregiver. In reality, he required as much attention if not more. Real help required an ability to multi-task, unafraid to get on hands and knees and scrub a floor as well as change a diaper. One very special person fit that profile—Grandma Bertha. Welcoming her completed the picture. Never once did Bertha hesitate on moving. Duty called. No one would stand in the way of taking care of her grandchild or her son. It was settled. Ted and Bertha would live together.

With forty years in the real-estate business, Bertha knew a good piece of property when she saw one. She chose a quaint, single level, three-bedroom house on Cottage Street in Pasadena. Once she was settled, they made arrangment for Ted to move in with her. "It had a porch across the front," remembered Kim Lacey, Ted's oldest granddaugher, who visited often as a small child. "Inside you could go across the house in a circle. I would play games with Bertha. I made up all these marvelous travels and adventures and I would go through the house hollering to her from room to room and come back. Meanwhile she just sat their the whole time. Very clever woman."[717]

Bertha's maternal instincts seemed the perfect remedy. With Ted's weight dipping below 140 pounds, feeding him was a major concern. Ted became like a child again, speaking German with his mother around the dinner table. He was no longer a great man but a boy reduced to one goal, the only goal that any child aspirers, trying to win the affections of a parent. "The touch of my mother's hand rolled back the years," wrote Ted of their time in California. "The German I had not spoken for years came to my tongue, and Mother and I prattled away in the language of my boyhood."[718] By late March, the transplanted New Yorkers were feeling more at ease. New furniture placed. Boxes unpacked. And freshly delivered letters stuffed in a mailbox hanging near the front door. All the while, the shadow of the nearby Rose Bowl stayed.

Many of his old friends, especially back east, helped make the transition smooth. A black telephone rang often those first few weeks, offering hospitality and wishing him well. Louis Sobol recommended a top medical man he knew practicing in Beverly Hills. Dr. Raymond Spritzler was a small, bald, unassuming man, who wore thick glasses, and spoke with a humble demeanor. Spritzler made

Ted an instant priority, seeing him regularly and setting up weekly re-hab sessions at the renowned Cedars of Labanon Hospital in Holly-wood, headed by none other than John Aldes, former University of Minnesota football star. Spritzler just wasn't another doctor, he was also Louis Sobol's son in law.[719] The best ophthalmologists, dentists, and psychiatrists in Los Angeles put Ted on their busy schedules. The famous radio star in his heyday earned more money than any physician in America. Now, he came to them desperate, penniless. All, without exception, offered their exorbitant services for free.[720]

The press found the Husing's new address before long, ask-ing questions, searching for a feel-good story. Instead, they found doom and gloom. "The worst thing is the depression," Ted told Jack Geyer of the *L.A. Times*. "I get terribly depressed."[721] He shared similar feelings with other writers. "I try to be cheerful about my condition," speaking to Mac Davis of the *New York Enquirer*. "I hope I'm progressing as my doctors say I am. But, I don't feel that way inside. Sometimes it feels so hopeless. But, I haven't grown bitter. I try to remember the life I had before my world grew dark."[722] Ted might not have felt bitter reminiscing about the good life he once had. But, Iris, legally still his wife, vented enough bitterness for both of them. She told Davis a much different story. "Ted's countless friends and his busy life often left him little time to be a husband and a father. When Ted was with his rich cronies, he lived as if he were to the manor born."[723]

California was now home and the best thing about the city was that mother was near. She provided love and support. But what Ted craved above anything was opportunity. It came in the way of another dear friend, still with a dimpled chin, now sporting silver hair and a flair for play-by-play. At the University of Michigan, Tom Harmon made football fans forget about the triumphs of Red Grange with incredible feats of his own. Some said he was better. But, as much as the man loved playing football, he never wanted to be another "Galloping Ghost." What he really wanted to be on Saturday afternoons was another Ted Husing.

The famous broadcaster first met the star halfback in the fall of 1938. But, one game in particular during the 1940 season left an indelible imprint, a head to head match-up with Univeristy of Pennsylvania all-American Francis Reagan. Ted, Jimmy Dolan, and the trusty Annunciator stuffed themselves into the radio booth at Michigan Stadium. What they witnessed was complete domination. Harmon collected over 250 yards of total offense, scoring one touchdown while throwing for another. On defense, he patrolled the secondary tackling runners, chasing receivers and deflecting passes.

Down on the sidelines that day, arms filled with chinstraps and shoulderpads, scuttled Fred Knox, Penn student and team equipment manager. Listening to Ted's description on the radio back in California was Knox's younger sister and Harmon's future wife, Elyse. "I remember thinking, Wasn't there anyone other than Tom Harmon? That's the only name I heard. He did everything."[724] In December, the Touchdown Club presented Harmon with the Heisman Trophy as the country's best college football player.

Three years later, Old # 98 went from football stud to war hero, earning accommodations for bravery as an Army Air Corp pilot during World War II. Harmon returned to civilian life, playing two years of pro football with the Los Angeles Rams before joining retired Cleveland Indians outfielder Jack Graney and Marty Glickman, former sprinter and member of the 1936 Olympic team, as the first star athletes to enter the broadcast booth. Harmon called upon Ted for career advice. The CBS man went one better, helping him land early radio gigs at Detroit station WJZ in 1948. Ted even presented him with his first stopwatch, a gold Bolivar, a vital if not symbolic tool to anyone in the broadcasting industry.[725] By 1957, the rising sports announcer ascended to Sports Director of the CBS Pacific Network. Glib and professional, Harmon worked hard at his chosen profession but, he knew he'd never equal his mentor. "Anyone who saw me play football knows I'm no shrinking violet and I think I hold my own behind a microphone. But, if I stick around Ted long enough, learning this business from him and learn to be a 110, I'll never rate top billing over the Master."[726]

Harmon hired himself to host a weekly sports talk show entitled "Sports Final." Programming consisted of scores, recaps, commentary, and interviews with L.A.'s top sports celebrates. The night of March 15, Harmon needed a guest. He knew just the guy. The radio host understood he had a few mountains to climb first. Even if Harmon could persuade the special guest to sit for an interview, could the person actually speak clear enough to be heard? Harmon had less than seventy-two hours to find out. He jumped into his car, turned the engine over, placed it in "Drive" and headed for Pasadena.

"MAKE SURE YOU WEAR A TIE"

He walked into the house on Cottage Street carrying a tan box, nine by seven inches in size. He stood tall, a determined look on his face, the apparatus strapped guardedly around his right shoulder. The mystery box resembled a typewriter case, or a sewing kit perhaps. But, it was none of those things. What would a tough guy like Tom Harmon be doing with a sewing kit? What a man in the radio business might carry was a portable recording machine. Inside rested two reels of dark brown audio tape. On the outside, a series of buttons reading PLAY, STOP, and REWIND. Dangling along the edge peaked a handheld microphone with a large bulbous head.[727] He understood that Ted had a second chance at life. He saw the potential. He wished Ted felt the same.

There before him sat Ted in an easy chair, pleased to see his friend but unable to shake the melancholy that had returned. Depressed. Shoulders sagged. His eyes fixated on the army green carpet below his feet. He barely looked up at Harmon, oblivious to the tan recorder resting by his side. A voice of a man on the radio reading the news filled the background.

When he finally spoke, Ted rattled on about how he missed New York, the old days, the past glory gone and anything else he wished to pile on his sad state of mind. A vicious pattern of emotional highs and lows colored Ted's mood since the operations. Harmon confronted his mentor trying anything to cheer him up. "Coach you can't sit around and let all that talent go to waste. Tape a guest shot for my show."[728] Ted countered with more negativity. The lofty standards Ted set throughout his career could never be reached by a half blind, incoherent "has been" unable to tie his shoes without assistance. Husing was his own worse critic, the curse of every great artist. Cancer changed the man, no doubt. But no one ever saw his condition quite as hopeless as he did. "I think he felt more disabled than he really was," said Husing's son-in-law David Lacey. "He was very sensitive about it."

Ted was down. He required a little more prodding. Harmon stayed focused. He needed a guest for his radio show and wasn't leaving without one. "Fine, you want to talk about the past, let's talk about the past," said Harmon revealing the recorder. "All those great games and thrilling broadcasts. People want to hear about them. The fans. Your fans!" Ted began to soften, looking up from the carpet for the first time. His friend sensed an opening and pushed on. Harmon placed the microphone near Ted's mouth and cued him to speak. "We can do it right here. If you're voice gets tired, we'll stop. Just you and me, pal, just a couple of buddies talking about sports." The microphone became a miracle drug. The sorrow that ravaged Ted's body only a few minutes earlier vanished.

"I was jittery, but before I could protest, Tom put the mike in my hand," he wrote. "It was like shaking hands with an old friend again."[729] The two grown men, sitting in a living room, laughed and joked, recalling great games, great names, and even greater times. Harmon needed more than material for a radio show. He needed to do something for a man who did so much for him. The gift of life, the gift of friendship overwhelmed Ted. He began to cry. The recorder remained on, documenting everything.

March 15, 1957, Harmon's show "Sports Final" aired on

the thunderous 50,000-watt CBS affiliate station KNX. Ted's voice sounded weak, slow.[730] Yet, sprinkled about the fifteen-minute interview, moments of brilliance, rambling quickness, and large vocabulary that belonged to only one man. For the true Husing fan, the day marked the first time Ted's voice was heard on the air, radio, or television in over sixteen months. Thousands heard the show surprised, shocked that Ted Husing was not only alive and well but called California home. Listening that night at his house in West Hollywood was a middle-aged network television personality. He, too, had a show. And like Harmon, he, too, was looking for a very special guest.

"This is Your Life" was one of the most popular television shows of the 1950s. Ralph Edwards, its host and creator, introduced the show to America through network radio starting in 1948. Once it found a home on NBC television, the true impact of the show sprang forth. Beginning in October of 1952, Wednesday nights became electric. The premise was simple, rehash the life story of a person, usually famous, in front of a live studio audience.[731] Stories were told, celebrity guests appeared, gifts lavished, jokes cracked, and tears shed. The show's success was worthless without the element of surprise. The only person not in the "know how" was the principle subject. The sound of a voice heard behind a curtain or closed door and unscripted reaction were the cornerstones of the series' most memorable moments.

Those on the inside held their cards tight to the vest. Plans unfolded. The unknowing subject went about life, all the while a scurry of activity buzzed making sure the ambush remained covert. Half-truths told by friends and loved ones got them to the studio where Edwards sprang upon them a microphone, cameras, and his famous line, "This Is Your Life!" Seeing the reactions, the power of raw emotion made it must-see TV. Of course, almost every television program in those early days came with the same perverse "must see" quality. Once the novelty wore off, the show went with it. But,

Edwards had something special. "This Is Your Life" stayed on. Viewers couldn't get enough, waiting to see who got spoofed next. And better yet, how they would respond.[732]

When Ralph Edwards heard Harmon's interview of Ted on "Sports Final," pleasant memories played again inside his mind. As an impressionable lad, captivated by the radio in his Southern California home, to Edwards, Husing was a god. "I knew two things about radio," Edwards would say, "Marconi invented it. Ted Husing gave it life."[733] Childhood dreams faded. But, desires to follow in the footsteps of his hero never left him. "I remember well the time I first found myself in Ted's physical presence. I had stepped into the elevator in the CBS building in New York. I turned around and there was Ted Husing! To me, it was a privilege to be within arm's length of a man of his eminence. I forgot to call out my floor. It was unimportant. I really didn't want to get off, for I was riding up . . . up . . . up . . . with the foremost master of the spoken word."[734] Edwards was a fan of Tom Harmon and even bigger fan of Ted Husing. What better way to honor him than his own spot on "This Is Your Life." Harmon agreed. The date set for surprise and celebration, May 8, a Wednesday, 1957. Live on NBC Television.

The Husing campaign began in earnest, Harmon, the point man. Phone calls, schedule, travel arrangements, favors, everyone on the same page. Plans would have to be flawless. Ted Husing, half blind, slow to talk, slow to walk, brain tissue soft from surgery, remained sharp, his streetwise instincts still intact. Any whiff of impropriety, the injured radio star might buckle and the show would be off.

To set the wheels in motion, Harmon invited Ted to a small dinner party at one of the finer downtown restaurants. "Where are we going?" he asked his friend. "Don't worry about it, Ted," Harmon promised. "It's some place nice. Just make sure you wear a tie."

The alibis were set. First Bertha and Pegge slipped away in the late afternoon to have an intimate dinner of their own. The story made sense. Since Ted would be out with friends, why not mom? As they departed, up pulled a pallid four-door Oldsmobile station wagon driven by Harmon's young assistant Bob Speck. Speck would become one of L.A.'s most gifted television sports producers. But, on this evening, he was a chauffeur. Harmon and wife Elyse sat in the back.[735]

The minute they saw Ted, however, they knew an adjustment would have to be made. Apparently, Harmon's suggestion of a tie was ignored. Ted looked more dressed for a company picnic, wearing a plain white shirt and dark blue trousers. Without hesitation, the tandem sprang into action. In the trunk of the car, next to his golf clubs, Harmon kept a sky blue tweed sports coat and a few neck ties, with the initials TH stenciled on the front, just in case. Perfect. Tom Harmon or Ted Husing, no one would know the difference.

Timing meant everything. Final destination, Burbank. Traveling L.A.'s freeway system of the late '50s, as it is today, often came with traffic, over-heated engines, three-car pile-ups, and more traffic. Luckily, Pasadena was a short drive away. Speck navigated well, west on Colorado Boulevard, through Glendale into Burbank.

"Ted, do you mind if we make a quick stop at NBC Studios," Harmon coolly asked. "I have to see someone. A little business. Shouldn't take very long." The football star turned sports announcer exited the car and disappeared into the lobby. Ted sat oblivious, content, thinking that a pleasant evening of dinner, good friends, and perhaps a few old faces awaited him. He wasn't completely wrong. A few minutes passed. Then, surprise! Curbside, between a well-tarred parking lot and white lines, stood Ralph Edwards. He pulled elegantly at a microphone and thirty feet of cord. A man carrying a camera perched on his shoulder maneuvered in front. Harmon smoothly guided his friend from the car while Elyse Knox, lavishly dressed in a white pillbox hat and black satin gloves looked on. "Hi ya, Ralph!" Ted excitedly called out. "The last time I saw you was at 21." Clutching the symbolic thick, maroon scrapbook he held each week, Edwards said his famous words, "Ted Husing, the man who the athletes themselves called the greatest sports announcer of all time, this– is– your– life!"[736]

Here was the moment of truth. What would Ted do? How would he reply? Profanity-laced tirade, too proud to be exposed, duck back in the passenger seat of the car and hide? Serenity? Rage? Excitement? Hope? Embarrassment? It echoed the same question so many asked during his rugged, challenged life: Bertha, who in 1917 stunned him with the news of dad's burned, mangled features; an enlistment officer who accused him of being too young for Uncle Sam's army; Harvard College, who banned him from their broadcast facilities for uttering the "P" word; Ann St. George who turned down his marriage proposal for the final time; radio critics who knocked the Husing method; Ernie Seiler, who coaxed him down to Miami in 1937 with a lie; Pegge, who leveled the sting of death that mother was gone. Doctors who showed him ex-rays of a tumor inside of a brain, his brain, a Catholic priest who four months earlier shared that the Graham McNamee Award would be his.

Uncomfortable smiles turned to belly laughs in an instant outside the NBC television studio. Ted's eyes grew the size of golf balls realizing the night would be his. "Oh Boy! You got me!" he repeated.[737] On cue, Harmon took control, adding a touch of class. "Ralph, it couldn't happen to a nicer guy. Anybody in the sportscaster industry knows that Ted's the greatest." Safety abound, the temperamental announcer looked pleased. "I kept a pretty good secret, didn't I?" asked the blond Elyse Knox. Edwards flashing a set of straight white teeth answered, "Yes, not bad for a woman." Ted quipped back matching the host's large, angular smile, "Wait a minute. You can't say that about Elyse."[738] He accepted his fate with no regrets. He was just glad they wanted him, thankful they still cared. Announcer Bob Warren introduced the first commercial break and off they went to face Ted's glorious, sometimes blemished past.

A pronounced limp, an obvious gate in his once steady walk dragged him across the stage. A cane made of ivory offered assurance in case Ted lost balance. There was much happening, much to absorb, enough to make any head spin. Edwards lead the way, aware of time and anxious to get started. A joyful audience applauded. The next half-hour, Ted's body turned with raw emotion. One by one, they came.

First Pegge and Bertha met Ted on stage accompanied by Dr. Spritzler. "I'm so proud of my boy, that they honor you so," she declared to the national TV audience. Ted grabbed his mother with voice cracking. "Thank You, Mommy!"[739] Even in a depleted condition, Ted towered a foot and a half over her tiny body. Peg quickly embraced her father while the good doctor touched on the importance of "friends" as good strong medicine. Ted appeared strong, poised. Actors say that the camera adds weight, height, dimension to the body. The camera never lies. Clearly, Spritzler's medicine was already working. Edwards mentioned the Skeeters and son "Duke," who were watching back east. Ted quickly cupped his left hand and slapped it over his mouth.

Things were just starting. The host began, as he always did, by reading from the thick book tucked firmly under his shoulder. He shared some of Ted's less glorious details, operation to remove a malignant tumor, born in the Bronx, kicked out of Commerce High School . . . Ted finally interjected with some much-needed humor, "Unfortunately, I'm afraid you must have questioned what I did back east."[740] The first guests to say hello were Les Quailey and Jimmy Dolan, teammates and loyalists in every way. As the two entered through a closed door, Ted nearly jumped from his chair. They told stories of a motormouth football center named Husing who stood up to linemen twice his size. "He was such a gabby guy, we knew his voice would be an asset to him one day later,"[741] Quailey joked. Both thanked him for the opportunity he gave them professionally and told him they continued to use the skills he taught them. "Laugh it up, Ted," ordered Dolan, gently stroking Ted's shoulder.[742]

His balding scalp with a few thinning strands of hair gleamed into the television camera. Suddenly, from the sound system came a dull, but familiar male voice. "And as my assistant, Ted showed great promise as a sportscaster . . ." Ted pumped his fist, hoping he recognized the mystery voice correctly. He was right. The round body and white hair of Andrew White appeared, twenty-eight years removed from the presidency of CBS, slower, humble, no longer flashing expensive knickers and driving high-end cars. Before Husing stood a wise old man. "Andy, how are you," Ted yelled slowly. "This is wonderful!"[743] More surprises followed throughout the next half-hour.

Hall of Fame catcher Mickey Cochrane talked with Ted about the stunning comeback by the Philadelphia Athletics against the Cubs in Game 4 of the '29 World Series. A minute later, the well-known cords of the song "Auld Lang Syne" introduced bandleader Guy Lombardo via film clip. Performing in Pittsburgh and unable to attend in person, Lombardo wanted to thank Ted one more time for his incredible generosity. "Ted, do you remember in 1929, you were out in Chicago covering a Big Ten football game," explained Lombardo. "We were just starting our band and playing at the Granada Café. The night before the game, you came out to hear us. You were so enthused that you wired your boss in New York to leave a half hour of network time after the game. That led to our first big radio show and lots of success since then. Ted, the boys and I are eternally grateful. Good luck and God bless!"[744]

Former Michigan football coach Harry Kipke came out to shake hands. Gold medal swimmer Eleanor Holm expressed her undying gratitude toward Ted for suggesting she pin orchids to her bathing suit during the 1932 Olympic trials at Jones Beach. Her stunning photos lead to a Hollywood movie deal. Appearing next was Jessie Owens. He tenderly told of Ted's humane spirit, how he guided the Olympic hero on his triumphant return to New York through a sea of humanity, exploding flashbulbs, and hot radio microphones. "I was scared stiff with the huge reception at the pier," Owens softly said. "Ted, you took control and saved my life."[745] Trying not to ruin the touching moment, Ted added a quick response, "I just wanted to say that in 1935, this guy broke everything except all the hearts of the women in Iowa."[746] The audience erupted in laugher. Former tennis champ Alice Marble and U.S. Open golf winner Ralph Guldahl affectionately shared additional anecdotes. "Ted, you were the greatest and I got lipstick on you," Marble said wiping his face." Not missing a beat, Ted chimed, "I'll take that for being the greatest."[747] "Mr. Inside" and "Mr. Outside," Glenn Davis and Felix "Doc," too, graced the stage, joining the happy reunion.

Following a message from Ivory Soap, a barrage of gifts and mementoes descended on Husing and family—a gold charm bracelet for mother, an eight-millimeter camera and projector, a $1,000 record collection, and cufflinks with matching tie bar from Marshall Jewelers for Ted. "I used to go by the store window," insisted Ted holding out his hand.[748] Off stage, a nervous production assistant firmly held out two fingers toward the host, signaling that the show was winding down. Edwards mentioned the honors recently bestowed by the Sports Broadcasters Association back in New York, the Graham McNamee Award. The mention of the man's name tore through to his heart. Ted's face bent. Tears poured down his face. Edwards finally announced that Crest and Prell Shampoo, longtime sponsors of the show, would kick in $3,000 for the Kreindler Foundation. "Oh, My God!" Ted yelled grabbing his quivering mouth for the last time. Only seconds remained. Edwards rattled on with his own eloquent tribute.

"The voice that was briefly muted.
The personality that was but temporarily dimmed.
Both are regaining their power as they have done in the past,
Will again bring joy and entertainment to America."

The show closed, audience clapping, with Edwards declaring,

"Ted Husing, This Is Your Life.
Good-night and God Bless, You!"

It was over. The Husing charm prevailed throughout. Cracking jokes, a rye one-liner, softened by a broad smile, a genuine hug from the men and supple kisses on the lips of the ladies. Compassion, guilt, shame, exoneration, anguish, fear, courage, pride, self-hatred, forgiveness, loathing! What he felt, above the jumbled mix of colliding emotions, was love. Mother, daughter, friends. How they adored him. How he loved them back.

A room full of revelry awaited Ted and his guests at the Beverly Hilton Hotel. There was good reason to celebrate: supportive friends, bang-up times, and good fortune. Ted seemed to have more lives than a black cat on Halloween, that much was certain. The man, for the moment, felt he might live a few more. Ted decided to ignore his doctor's order and sipped from a flute filled with sweet champagne. An appetite had built inside of him, one that could only be filled on the air.

HOME AGAIN

The coast-to-coast television appearance woke the public from a deep sleep. Ted Husing was not dead and buried as once rumored. He was walking, talking, weakened but still very much alive, and available to work. Screen Gems called and booked Ted for a guest shot on their popular TV sitcom "Father Knows Best,"[749] a spin-off of the radio show by the same name. The show aired that fall with Ted playing himself.

Surprisingly, more work in front of the camera came. Tom Harmon insisted Ted co-host his popular Saturday afternoon racing show from Hollywood Park called the "Winners Circle."[750] Who knew more about horses than Ted? Harmon's idea soon turned ugly. Ted stumbled through the first few telecast, awkward and out of place. Critics praised Harmon while panning his friend. But, performance gradually improved through the summer. "Ted was breezing through words that would have stumped a winner on the $64,000 Question," bragged Harmon. "And covering up for me when I flubbed."[751] The tables, indeed, had turned. Could anyone have guessed Ted Husing would become a TV star?

Other offers came, mainly additional guest appearances on radio and television. "When you're ready, Ted, let us know." However, deep down there was really only one offer Ted hoped would come, that from the Columbia Broadcasting System.

On the night of June 8, William Paley, too, watched Husing's appearance on "This Is Your Life." What he saw pleased him, happy that his longtime employee appeared on the rebound. Paley knew what Ted had meant to the early success of his network. Anywhere, anytime, any place. The broadcaster was always willing to go the extra mile, asking few questions until the gig ended. Ted burned his marriage license along the way. Paley had done the same. They both had their reasons for putting work before family. But, the dog days were over. Mature, wiser, and a penny for your thoughts, one thing separated employer from employee—money.

Paley gladly chipped into the Husing fund at 21 several times. However, most weren't aware that he also floated the ailing announcer an extra $5,000 loan, interest-free, with an open date to repay.[752] No amount was too grand. He also made it clear to Ted that the network had a position for him when he got back on his feet. "I wanted to work, not be given a charitable pension," Husing said. "So I'd always told Bill that when I was ready, I'd call him."[753] In late July, he picked up the phone and dialed long distance, New York City. Husing, the consummate professional, decided to go through channels. He called Mark Hanna and asked him to handle all the details.

Already in Ted's corner stood Jimmy Dolan. He witnessed live the old Husing charm and magic during the "This Is Your Life" telecast. Dolan, as head of CBS Radio Sports division, wanted to sign Ted immediately, though first things first. Convincing Paley took some doing. The CBS chairman focused more and more on the growing television end of his empire. The day-to-day decisions left long ago to men like Frank Stanton. But, this just wasn't another subordinate. The matters of Ted Husing became a priority. "I want to make Goddamn sure he's ready," the boss strongly suggested. "I don't want this backfiring on us." Paley remained guarded, hesitant about finding a place for a "has been." Dolan assured him that their man was fully recovered and strong enough to write his own ticket. Paley was a man of his word and welcomed the broadcaster back to the fold. Ted Husing for the first time in almost three years joined the ranks of the employed. "Belief was held by the web that Husing may eventually return to doing play-by-play," *Variety* reported. "His first assignment has not been picked." [754] Columbia Broadcasting System, the network he had helped make great, offered him a retainer of $150 a week. Ted gladly agreed to the contract on August 6, hoping for the best. [755]

His friends kept at him, especially Dolan and Harmon. Above anyone, they hoped the Master might resurrect to greatness again, rise and reach the pinnacle of the profession, teach this new crop of sports announcers a thing or two. They planned. They plotted, thinking big. Football was right around the corner. Yes, traveling to the booths at Miche Stadium, or the famed "Brick House," home of the University of Minnesota Gophers were out of the question. Then again, the Coliseum, home to USC, UCLA, and the new Los Angeles Dodgers was near. The campuses of Stanford and Cal were a short plane ride up the coast. With steady improvement in his speech, maybe he could do some play-by-play.

But, within a few weeks, Ted retreated. The darkness returned. His condition worsened. The upswing in mood quickly washed away into a melancholy sadness. His vision again blurred. His bones gnawing, chills up and down his spine. Headaches, like before, grew more frequent. The only thing he did throughout the day was sit draped in the afghan and stare at the phone, waiting for it to ring. It would inevitably become a routine part of his day. Recapturing the form that made him a mighty man on the radio proved to be a bigger challenge than even Ted admitted. Back in New York, CBS waited for better news from Harmon and others on positive progress about their newest employee. Would it ever come, some wondered? Active or inactive, payroll cut a weekly check, made to the order of Mr. Ted Husing, and mailed it to the small house on

Cottage Place in Pasadena.

His swings in mood and health confused everyone. Doctors couldn't quite make out his prognosis. One day strong and talkative, the next, slow and muted. Most chalked it up to recurring depression and general aging affects. What they didn't know was that the cancer had returned. "They probably didn't get it all," explained Dr. Laurence Demers. "Because, once again, back then they didn't have CAT scans, only X-rays. And you couldn't tell unless you went back in and tried to re-operate. They weren't going to do that. So the tumor was growing again."[756]

Good people, great friends, trying desperately to save a man who never had a chance to begin with. "He probably got the best care available at that time given his stature in life," believed Demers. "But, he presented too late to do anything constructive. He probably had symptoms he ignored and tried to work through and if he had seen somebody, even with the crude techniques they had, they could have at least removed a much smaller tumor a lot easier. It was down hill from the day he walked in and that large tumor was discovered."[757]

Ted, on the other hand, created his own crude methods of therapy, anything to make himself feel better. Long-distance phone calls became his passion. New York phones rang the most. Toots Shor, Sandy Simon, Louis Sobol, even Les Quailey living in Philadelphia, he telephoned almost on a weekly basis. Ted played favorites, dialing sister-in-law Dee Dee Lemerise every Sunday without fail. He even called Lowell Thomas once, on assignment in India, simply to say hello. "If I weighed the cost against the temporary lift hearing his voice gave me the scale would tilt in favor of the latter," Ted admitted.[758] The phone calls to back east worked, at least for a while. No one could deny the effects. Mother, daughter, and doctor witnessing first hand. Pegge stood the most frustrated and fed up. She tried everything to help her father. Clearly, the best intentions of care fell on deaf ears and altered minds.

The impetus for relocating him to California in the first place came from her belief that New York, the haunting memories, destroyed his will to live. As things turned out, the thought of New York was the only thing that seemed to keep his heart beating. If it was New York Ted wanted, than New York he shall have. Everyone agreed. Ted would fly home for a brief vacation with Spritzler accompanying him on the trip. In the plans was a visit to New York's Mount Sinai, eager to check on the star patient. "Now I'm going home," he excitedly told the press. "I miss the tempo of the city. I want to see Broadway and hear those cab doors slam again."[759]

A mid-October cool welcomed him. The tracks of the elevated "L" along 9th Avenue rattled and clanked. Times Square buzzed with its usual congestion morning, noon, and night. Ted was back in the Big Apple. On command, the doors of taxi cabs slammed, music to his yearning ears. He gathered with his friends, giving the guest of honor little time to reminisce. Everyone chipped in and put him and Dr. Spritzler in a suite at the Roosevelt Hotel, the place of his most recent triumph. Fourteen days of new memories filled his schedule. Familiar company knew how to celebrate, dinner at Toots Shor's, lunch at 21. The most festive party thrown by the Skeeters Club. There was no paddock strong enough to hold these thoroughbreds of beguilement down. The boys from the Skeeters loaded Ted into the car and off they went to relive their old glories—a day at Garden State.

Not all aspects of the trip were fun filled. Looming about was Iris, causing trouble, controlling the Husing fortune or what was left of it. "They didn't talk," remembered David Husing. "I don't think they ever saw each other." Reluctantly, Iris did allow Ted a brief visit with their son. David had not seen his father in nearly ten months. Much had changed in that time. "The old Ted Husing wasn't there," he remembered. "Physically he looked drained. I guess it didn't matter. I was just glad to see him."[760]

Before he knew it, the two-week trip was over. He did not

want to leave. From Pasadena, Bertha and Pegge awaited his return, anxious to hear the details. More interested in seeing the effects the visit had on his health, if any. Seatbelts fastened. The cabin door shut. A 450-yard stretch of runway traveled before take-off. Ted held firmly to the arm of Spritzler as the plane rumble down the tarmac. The long flight back to California began. Ted wondered if he felt the warm lights of Broadway, heard a cab door slam for the very last time. A delicious taste of New York put him fast asleep, happy, satisfied. Yet, like the old days, there was no rest for the weary. Plans were soon underway for another return east. More work beckoned. A fresh weapon appeared assisting the radioman in his battle to reclaim old glory. This time, the pen would be mightier than the sword.

CHAPTER THIRTY-SIX

A LIFE WORTH READING

Remedies never seemed to be far away. Anything was worth trying at least once. Late November was always a special time in the Husing home for obvious reasons. But, this year, 1957, had been particularly memorable. Ted's birthday fell on Wednesday the 27th, followed by Thanksgiving Day, exactly as it had in 1901. The family had much to be grateful for. On Friday, Ted's phone rang loud and often. Most called to wish him a belated Happy Birthday. But, when Mark Hanna called, it usually meant something other than small talk. "I hope you haven't unpacked your suitcase, Ted," the agent calmly asked. "Jerry Lewis wants to do a magazine story." "Jerry Lewis? Ted shot back. "What's he need, a new straight man?" Hanna chuckled mightily, happy his client sounded in good spirits. "No not the comic, smart ass, the writer. And he wants you back in New York."

Hanging about Manhattan's high-end watering holes was a freelance writer named Jerry D. Lewis who had made a name for himself writing full-length, in-depth articles about the underworld, card sharks and showbiz types.[761] Writing about sports figures was something he had little interest in. That all changed when John Ferris' piece in the *World Telegram* about an ailing sports announcer broke. Tim Cohane was sports editor for the bi-weekly magazine *Look*. Similar in style and content to rival *Life* magazine, *Look* billed itself as "the exciting story of people."[762] Cohane got to know Ted during the early 1950s through his friend Vince Lombardi, then a hardworking offensive line coach at West Point. They were two of the many who worshiped the broadcaster from afar, listening religiously to his football work growing up in New York. Both Cohane and Lewis thought that a series of articles on the rise and fall and rise again of Ted Husing was timely.

They agreed on a December sitdown and photo spread. Lewis wanted not only the input of Ted, but loyal friends and steadfast family members who could take readers on a trip down memory lane. Ted cooperated in any way possible, grateful for the attention and blissfully excited about returning to New York. This time, he visited many of the old work haunts, including his former office on Madison Avenue and the site of many early football broadcasts, Baker Field. Accompying Ted on the trip was film producer Emerson Yorke, giving credence to new rumors circulating around a Husing movie.

Lewis had all the key players participating on both coasts. From California, he first interviewed Bertha and Pegge. No one knew the day to day of Ted's life better than they. Next, they visited a typical day at Cedars of Lebanon, Ted working the parallel bars, determined to walk on his own again, joking with staff members. Cameras clicked the whole time, documenting the experience. Paul Whiteman, The King of Jazz, talked about the Old Gold days, Harmon again backed his mentor, while the most famous entertainer in America, Bing Crosby, thanked Ted again and again. In New York, it seemed everyone had a Husing story from William Paley to Sandy Simon to Les Quailey. All were on record, stoking the Husing image the right way.

The magazines flew off newsstands, January 7, 1958. If radio fans still wondered whatever happened to America's most famous sports announcer, they were about to read the thick, wordy details for themselves. *Look* gave Ted official writing credit, adding credibility to the three-part series. Unofficially, Ted talked, Lewis ghosted. In no condition to write, Ted could barely see the zeros on a paycheck much less a typewriter keyboard. The first part entitled "The Ted Husing Story," detailed his shocking news of brain cancer while transgressing to the announcer's early successes in radio. Two weeks later, "My Vanity Was My Undoing," chronicled his fame and self-regard as America's most recognized voice. The February 4 issue of *Look* had Hollywood beauty Ingrid Goude on the outside cover. Inside, Lewis' final segment on Husing could be found. "My Friends Wouldn't Let Me Die" brought the current state of Husing into focus—a humbled man, fighting to regain health. And hopefully, a new phase in his illustrious broadcast career. The piece ended on the cheerful re-signing with CBS. "It's nice to be home. And it sure is."

Ted may have sounded strong, but he looked weak, his cheeks gaunt and thin. His eyes drooped. Reoccurring nightmares, especially one of a dancing, illusive microphone, made sleep sporadic and at best, restless. [763] The few short months from his *Winner's Circle* appearances had not improved his looks. Any prospects of working in television seemed far-fetched. The Husing name, the Husing voice alone, no longer good enough. He still possessed the will. The desire to win them over. As always, his brain refused to cooperate. Walking down three small steps on his front porch, impossible without holding on to mother's hand. A simple phone call, unthinkable without an operator's assistance. No one sat more frustrated than Ted, bluntly clued-in to his own staggering limitations. "I'd much prefer to sit here and be inactive. Then I wouldn't be dependent on anyone and I wouldn't be critical of my own values," he shared with a reporter. "I'm my own best critic."[764]

Harmon stayed, urging his friend on. When New York called to check on progress, Harmon asked for a little more time. The network needed an answer, but obliged nonetheless. The comeback that seemed imminent within the pages of *Look Magazine* was quickly becoming a very bad idea. The same problems persisted. Vision blurry. Speech: one day booming, the next tired and slurred. Ted's energy level fluctuated, sinking to a chair, relying heavy on his cane. His friends wondered what ever happened to Ted's most attractive attribute, guts. "When we went to dinner, it was difficult for him to walk, and sitting at the table his head would go down and rest on the top of the table," remembered Elyse Knox. "He tried real hard. It was not easy."

Finally the network ran out of patience and officially announced on Feb. 11, 1958, that Husing would no longer be retained as an employee. Cold and typically corporate, CBS contacted Hanna via letter, who broke the news to his client in Pasadena. Ted was crushed, reacting with his usual candor. "I'll starve, that's all,"[765] he told reporters. "I had rather anticipated rolling into something good on radio. Now I'll have to hustle for a buck."[766] Long gone were the days of family atmosphere and contracts sealed with a handshake. A CBS spokesman delicately explained the decision. "We tried to create with him a show that would be usable on the network. We just couldn't come up with anything. Ted was just unable to do it. His voice quality was bad."[767]

Faster than one could say "bad publicity," a firestorm of protest erupted. Angry letters and phone calls bombarded the CBS offices in support of Husing. Columnists questioned the network's poor timing and apparent insensitivity. Nick Kenny of the *New York Mirror* wrote, "The $150 a week they have been paying him isn't a drop in the bucket compared to the millions the network wastes on other things, including some very silly programming."[768] Robert Buark in the *New York Telegraph* blasted CBS, writing, "It seems to me that any industry owes some debt to the people who made it— people who became synonymous in the national life with the art form. And it seems to me that radio certainly owes a decent comfortable old age to Ted Husing, even if it means cutting down on the luncheon table at Toots."[769] Perhaps longtime *New York Daily News* critic Ben Gross, a supporter from the early days of Ted's career, said it best. "Isn't there any sentiment in radio or TV? Sure, when there's and audience on hand to applaud it."[770]

CBS countered with damage control, stating that they would reconsider once the ailing announcer's health improved. In the end, Ted took the high road. "It was all a big mistake," he said. "I wasn't ready. It was nobody's fault."[771] In spite of it all, he remained in demand. Stories continued to circulate about his impending employment, most of it hearsay. One of the more attractive stories had a Hawaii radio station offering a deal, beach house and rainbows not included.[772] Plans remained hot about "Ted Husing Reminisces." Harmon never let go of the idea, in spite of what CBS thought, confident Ted could do the job. Rumors of national syndication deals put certainty at an all-time high.[773]

Various social organizations jumped on the Husing bandwagon throughout the summer as well. In June, the Elks Club threw him a party. Two months later, the L.A. Press Club honored him with a gala affair at the famous Ambassador Hotel. The Lions Club made him honorary chairman of their annual White Cane Days, a charity raising thousands of dollars for blindness research and care.[774] A brief September ceremony on the steps of City Hall commended the radio star for his return to broadcasting, an actual broadcast still pending, of course. During the formalities, Councilwoman Rosalind Wyman read a congratulatory telegram from one of Ted's biggest fans, President Dwight Eisenhower.[775]

More good news arrived by way of agent Mark Hanna. It was not another job offer, nor a reprieve from CBS. Some thought it even better. Iris finally agreed to divorce, settling the matter in a Mexican court. The reclusive town of Ciudad Juarez seemed a smarter choice than Reno or Las Vegas. She had no need for publicity. Her phone still rang from reporters looking for a juicy quote about her ex-husband. Iris usually hung up wanting nothing to do with the man. Ted took the news in stride. Glad the nightmare called "Iris" was finally over. Three swings at marriage and three strikes. Sadly, it would be one of the last phone calls he ever received from Hanna. A stroke took his life in mid-August.

Clearly he stood in front of any mirror a changed man. The trappings of success meant little at this point in life. Ted Husing now woke everyday to a few minutes of prayer, a combative mix of giving thanks to God for the simple life he had and begging for a taste of past glories. A fire and brimstone religious man he never became. That would have been too phony for Husing's unaffected instincts. No one would have believed it anyway. He did, however, welcome a good bible story, one of hope, one of inspiration. He spoke regularly of attending Sunday church services. But, rarely did, too weak, self-conscious, or depressed. Instead, the church came to him. "He lived with his mother and we used to service him as a church," recalled former Messiah Lutheran Church member Carl Bergland. "He was very receptive. I wouldn't call him an outwardly religious man, but I would say inwardly, yes."[776]

Ted might have disagreed. "I am terribly religious and this was not occasioned by my illness," he boldly stated in a 1958 interview. "I always went to church before my programs and prayed for help."[777] Being a spiritual man sounded righteous. Reality was something all together different. Rarely did Ted step inside a church beyond his adolescence. If he ever prayed at the height of his fame, it would be to crush the competition or have his horse win at the track. On more than one occasion, Ted admitted to having "very little idea of who God was."[778] His newfound faith never spread deep roots. It was more a work in progress. His constant mood swings, verbal assaults, and submissive temper gave further proof. Ted himself admitted to a weak inner voice saying, "I want to rise above the difficulties of my illness but sometimes I wonder."[779] Not everyone saw Husing's change of heart as genuine. A mea culpa act typical of celebrities desperate for forgiveness in times of distress. "Even Voltaire had a priest at his deathbed," said a skeptical Stanley Wertheim. "Ted wouldn't have had such regrets and he wouldn't have had a 'religious awakening' if even at the age of sixty, he could have been at Toots Shor's with another blond on his arm."

Ted's spiritual commitment seemed to stir similar feelings of devotion in Bertha. Most California observers saw her as a simple woman of faith. Front and center every Sunday. First to find a pew, taking in every word the minister spoke. Fervent in her beliefs, quiet and stoic. Bergland described her as "a fine lady, a woman of deep religious faith." David Lacey concurred, calling her "quite devout." Those who knew Bertha during her New York days would have never used such adjectives.

Despite his ever-increasing blues, an upbeat vibe around the "Husing story" continued. Movie treatments rattled around Hollywood lots like Jane Russell look-a-likes. Big time stars were said to be interested in playing the lead role, including the Oscar-nominated actor Richard Widmark.[780] But, what seemed more plausible than seeing his story on the silver screen was reading about it in hardcover. The idea of a book surfaced as early as 1957. Several New York publishers would soon make offers to tell the Husing story in book form. One such offer came from Bernard Geis Associates.

Jerry D. Lewis again emerged as a catalyst. His candid series for *Look Magazine* profiling the great Ted Husing captured all the elements of a best seller. And it did not take long before a deal was struck with Geis. Lewis, however, had no interest in ghost writing the longer book version. He was, like Husing, simply interested in profit. "I know about ghosts," he once cynically wrote. "I've been one. Many times."[781] Collaborating with Ted this time was Cy Rice. Writing about celebrities, especially sports figures, was nothing new for Rice. Tennis star Pancho Gonzalez entrusted his life story to him a year earlier. The book sold well. Ted hoped for similar results. "No more charity," he promised. "I'll carry my own weight." The broken down broadcaster was more than ready to earn an honest day's pay.

In time for the Christmas rush, *My Eyes Are in My Heart* was released on November 9, 1959. The title packed a power punch, reminding the public of his impassioned acceptance speech spoken at the Roosevelt Hotel in New York two years earlier. Readers would finally have Husing's full story in his own words to digest for themselves. However, Ted could never escape the addictive world of competition he claimed to have kicked. Bill Stern's autobiography *The Taste of Ashes* was offered to readers three weeks earlier. Even in their weakened state, the two broadcasting giants, were trying to outdo each other. The book received mixed reviews. The radioman always tightroped a love-hate relationship with critics. Some laced their columns with jabs of scorn and cynicism. Bill Dougherty of the *Newark Evening News* wrote, "And again like Stern, Husing claims to have been humbled, to have realized what an incomparable egotist he used to be and that he will be, forever and amen, sorry for it."[782]

Ted's supporters had trouble crowning him a literary genius. Former Mark Hellinger protégé Jim Bishop in one of his columns admitted, "It isn't a great book, but I can remember when I wrote worse ones and Ted Husing would get on his bandstand at WMGM and say, 'You people out there have a treat in store. Jim Bishop has written a new book and it's a beaut.' Please go out and buy his book and tell your friends about it. If you can't do that, drop him a note. He needs a lift."[783]

In the end, most pundits were willing to give the Master his due. "The book is a fascinating one," wrote the *Chicago Tribune*.[784] The *New York Herald Tribune* said, "His is a life story with ups and downs steeper than most men's and he has told it as honestly as any."[785] Even, the aforementioned Bill Dougherty couldn't help but praise Husing. "If it becomes, in sections, overly-theatrical, it can be excused. The man was, it should be remembered, either the best or next to it."[786]

Ted cashed in every chip he earned. Once lying in a hospital, he felt nothing but self-pity and cold indifference. Now he wanted everyone to remember. If nothing else, money was a motivating factor to sell his new book. Anyone who wanted a signed copy got one. Old copies of *Ten Years Before the Mike* surfaced and he signed them, too. He called on his powerful friends in the media to help ring cash registers, doing several radio interviews and telling old stories. [787] Anyone with a by-line, anyone with a microphone received a print, including his old pal Walter Winchell who still punched out his daily column for the *New York Mirror*. The opening of his once famous weekly radio show brought listeners to the edge of their seats quicker than a Ted Husing touchdown call—"Good evening, Mr. & Mrs. America and all ships at sea!" Like Husing, he was from era receding into the pages of history. Ted hoped his friend still possessed some clout. In a letter dated January 18, 1960, he reminded Winchell of their shared past and invited him to plug the book.

> "Dear Walter: My book has been out several weeks. I've tried to put into it all the high spots of the thirty-seven eventful years we've lived through together. My publisher Bernard Geis Associates have probably sent you a review copy of *My Eyes Are in My Heart,* but I wanted you to have a personal autographed copy and I am sending you one under separate cover. If you like it, I know that you will want to tell the people about it. If you don't like it, for God's sake keep still. Cheerful, Ted."[788]

More opportunities came for Ted to sell books and perhaps save a few souls. In the spring of 1960, he shared his story with *Guidepost Magazine*.[789] Not long ago, a niche spiritual periodical seemed the last place one might find Ted Husing discussing his life. Now, it seemed to be a natural. Dr. Norman Vincent Peale, the original motivational speaker and best-selling author of books like *The Power of Positive Thinking*, started *Guidepost* as a way to spread his message of charged faith and enlightened hope. Ted's transformation, both physically and spiritually, represented all of that and more. His picture graced the April issue cover. Inside, he wrote again of his once arrogant attitude. A grand life and successful career destroyed by brain cancer. And how strong willed friends and family helped him find God. Ted sounded hopeful throughout the short article, trying to spread a message of optimism to others. " . . . whatever happens, I am at ease in my heart."[790]

My Eyes Are in My Heart sales put much needed cash in his back pocket. Ted had not seen this much money in over five years. He felt proud. His friends came through to help, of course. But, the gallant effort to promote was vintage Husing. Satisfied, he thanked God, even praying for Iris during his daily devotions. He also gave thanks she was out of his life and unable to mess with his new earnings. He wondered how he ever let her get control of his money in the first place.

Despite what he wrote in *Guidepost*, the positive attitude, the heart at ease, did not last long. No one was surprised. A stretch of apathy took over. He stopped taking his medication, refusing to swallow the tiny pills. He refused, some days to even get out of bed. Ted hated everything about California. It was all wrong, spread out, drifting hills, the peaks high, the valleys low. Roads, stores, and traffic signals stretched as far as the eye could see. In New York, they stopped. By water's edge or building mass, the city ended. The isolation of Los Angeles fed his depression. The contrast of two cities was never more evident. A belief in his own words trapped Ted in a perpetual state of gloom. "You have no idea that the world is such a wonderful place when you can see it, and such a horrible place when you can't."[791]

CHAPTER THIRTY-SEVEN

A DARKNESS BEFORE THE LIGHT

S till Ted someway stayed on his feet to fight. The long awaited show "Ted Husing Reminisces" finally aired on September 27, 1960, on station KFI.[792] The grand plans of syndication lost to set-backs and impatient advertisers. For the first time in more than five years, Ted was back on radio. His voice was rusty. But, the Husing sound remained unmistakable. "Hello everyone. This is Ted Husing." For fifteen minutes Ted spoke clear, slow, and articulate. Tom Harmon sat as his first guest, answering questions, reliving the days of Michigan football glory. Careful editing by Harmon limited mistakes and helped Ted sound his best. No one guessed that the taped interview was nearly two years old. His sit-down with former Light-Heavyweight champ Max Rosenbloom aired a week later. A who's who of yesteryear, Leo Durocher, Joe Louis, and Frank Leahy, agreed to interviews for the weekly show. If listeners weren't into sports, Ted promised the likes of showbiz buddies George Jessel, Pat O'Brien, and Joe E. Brown.

Radio junkies welcomed him back, glad to hear the iconic voice of sports, as if he never left them. *Los Angeles Times* radio columnist Don Page went so far as to name Husing "L.A.'s Best Sportscaster of the Year." Page admitted to honoring Ted more out of sentimentality than anything. But, he defended his claim writing, "Ted's voice is remarkable and clearly the greatest of his contemporaries."[793]

It took three years to put Husing back on radio. After three weeks, he disappeared, off the air once again, succumbing to the usual symptoms, unable to lift a hand much less open his mouth. Harmon sighed in frustration, but stayed positive, "Don't worry about it, Ted. The station loves the show. So do the listeners. The mail's been pouring in. When you're up for more talk we'll bring out the recorder. . . Ted? . . . Ted?" He looked into Husing's eyes, blinking slowly then staring off to a distant, unknown place. Harmon wondered, for the first time, if his mentor and friend heard anything he said.

Bertha could do no more. The tenacious German woman fast approached her eighty-eigth birthday. Pegge gave up long ago, knowing professionals were needed. The loving hands of family were no longer enough. Ted took residence at the Cloisters of Pasadena Convalescent Home in the middle of October. He was their problem now. On November 27, the staff presented him with a cake to celebrate his fifty-ninth birthday, a single candle plunged into a layer of thin white icing. Doctors, nurses, and orderlies sang and wished him well. Ted sat, low on energy, breathing heavy, hardly in the celebratory mood. A nurse blew out the candle for him.

Over the next twenty months, Ted's rickety health sank further. He did his best to stay engaged, listening to the radio and begging staff members to read box scores from the sports section of the newspaper, an uplifting Bible passage, the 38th Psalm or Lazarus rising from the grave. The Husing attitude remained undaunted at first, chewing out male orderlies with a barrage of profanity to chatting up a few of the more talkative nurses. But as the weeks and months past, his appetite decreased, weight began to shed, less movement, less sound. Some days the radio stayed off. "My recollection is that he was not well," recalled Kim Lacey visiting her grandfather as a child. "It was scary to me being five years old. He did not speak much. When he did it was difficult and seemed painful."[794]

Ted's relocation to a convalescent hospital shut off contact with most. Visitors trickled to a few brave souls. Harmon looked in on occasion, staying only a few minutes. He no longer cared about a "resurgence." Pushing, egging, prodding, and pep talks had all but ended. The only thing Harmon thought about was his dear friend's comfort, a once hopeful project well beyond repair. The press also left him alone, tired of the comeback story that seemed doomed to fail.

The facility of care might have changed. Bertha and Pegge's concerns, nonetheless, did not. Together they came, every day, an assortment of gifts in hand, chocolates, mail, a copy of the *New York Journal-American*. Anything to lift his spirits. The load seemed more daunting for Pegge, the daily drive down the L.A. Freeway, picking up Bertha, and dragging daughter Kim along. The only time Pegge did not make the trip to the Cloisters was to give birth to her second child Kate in the fall of 1961. Juggling double, sometimes triple duty, an unyielding desire to care for her ailing father never wavered. "That was her dad and she was his daughter. His one and only," explained Kim Lacey. "Through it all, he remained very special to her."

On January 1, 1962, the staff managed to coax Ted out of bed and in front of a television set. His eyes did not work but he could hear well enough. New Year's Day meant football games, more specifically, the Orange Bowl. Many of the orderlies remembered Husing's stirring broadcasts from Miami as kids. They understood the significance the game had to their famous patient. If only they knew how much. Curt Gowdy and partner Paul Christman called the action over the ABC network. ABC? Had Ted's ears deceived him? Yes, indeed, how things changed. The invalid announcer pondered the contest of '37, his first Orange Bowl, the one that almost got away. Duquesne's late game heroics. Earnie Seiler, the conman who sold him on a broadcast booth made of chicken wire. A tropical ocean breeze. The women. A glowing cabana at the Roney Plaza Hotel. The women. He was glad he decided to stay. Ted listened to the action, enjoying the play-by-play of his old friend Gowdy, even mumbling a positive word or two of encouragement.

The telecast ended after almost three hours. Gowdy signed off, Louisiana State a 25–7 winner over Colorado. "How about da Rose Bowl, Mr. Husing?" a young orderly asked. "Should be a good one, yes sah. Da Grand Daddy of 'em all!" Ted nearly jumped from his wheelchair shouting. "NO! NO!" The staff member insisted, switching the channel. He yelled again. "NO! Take Me Back! Stop! Take Me Back to My Bed. NOW DAMNIT!" Ted broke into a flood of tears. Everyone sat stunned. An emotional outburst from a patient was not uncommon. Yet, it was the most Ted Husing had spoken, the most impassioned energy he had shown in weeks. No one dared ask why. The orderly did as requested. He clicked off the television picture, then pushed Ted, hollow eyes darting, sobbing uncontrollably, back toward his bed.

Loneliness fed his depression once again. But, unlike before, his faculties began to fail. A kidney infection alarmed the medical staff. Some thought he might not survive. Ted battled back. A mystery fever ravaged his body month after month, usually sweating it out until the next attack came. Headaches returned in full force. The pain might have blinded him if he wasn't already without sight. In between, more restless nights, more tormented visits from the demonic microphone in his reoccurring dream. The once trying patient gave over to the daily probing and prodding of nurses and doctors.

His mind, his memories remained strong oddly enough. The Golden Age of Radio consumed his thoughts. "Did anyone listen to radio anymore?" he wondered. Millions of admirers he had before, so it seemed. Millions of dollars earned. Gone. Where did it go, where did they all go? Many of his friends, late night pals, and the only woman he ever really loved were all dead. The buzz of a live microphone, the roar of the crowd was the thing that had pumped life into his body. It kept him up when he was down; it made him wage war when there was nothing left to fight. A comeback seemed so hopeful at one time. Physically, it would be impossible. Ted could no longer live for what was now. Yesterday is where he existed—for they knew him in that place of triumph. Again, Ray Noble's haunting melody spoke the words he could not.

I'm living in a kind of daydream
I'm happy as a king
And foolish though it may seem, to me that's everything.
The mere idea of you. The longing here for you.
You'll never know how slow the moments go 'till I'm near to you . . .[795]

By June, Ted's weight dropped below 125 pounds, light enough now for one petite female nurse to rotate him unaided. Doctors with stethoscopes listened more intently to his lungs for fluid build-up. They ordered hourly turns of the body, side to side, anything to avoid infection. Come July, no one bothered with the routine. Instead they simply propped up pillows, adjusted his legs, checked his weakening pulse.

A pale sun broke the horizon on the morning of August 10. Murky rays, yellow, gray, and soft blue in color leaked into his room, curtains opened slightly, unattended for several days. He might have described it as "vivid" if he could see. Ted's senses had all but shut down. His lungs were soaked with pneumonia. The man coughed repeatedly now, wincing in discomfort. But on this morning, he lay quiet. He had to understand that the end was near. Instincts took over. For the first time in his life, Ted Husing did not try to fight. He accepted with a peaceful resolve. "Here I am Lord, thy will be done."

On cue, his vision opened. A dim light entered, then grew brighter. He felt an unnatural shift, a surging power. A simultaneous sensation had his body falling, his soul rising. Death entered ready to take him. Then, like a hot jolt of lightening, fear brought him back to life. "WAIT! Maybe there's more? One last measure of truth to face?" he asked. Guilt. Pride. Validity. Would it make perfect sense that even on his deathbed, Husing thought of McNamee? "We Americans are a practical people; we still want our romance, will always want it, but prefer it based on fact," Mac once wrote. "And romance growing out of truth is more satisfying and casts a more magic spell."[796]

Ted closed his eyes and everything came into focus. Maybe, just maybe, he stood once again primed, tall and lean before a live microphone that waited to capture every word he spoke. On a wooden stage he looked out to a distance that seemed to stretch for miles. A massive crowd of humanity stood before him, tens of thousands, hundreds of millions. They all gazed upon him cheering in unison, "Speak to us, master. Speak to us. Tell us what you see!" And for the first time what had always been shadowed figures in a dream of darkness, became familiar faces. He saw the welcoming presence of Jack Kriendler applauding. Behind him, the rough mug of confidant Mark Hellinger, with a cigarette in mouth, smiled back.

Located near a tree was Henry Husing, healthy as mountain air, a clear, unscarred complexion and fiery orange hair. Positioned next to him holding his left hand was a young girl of eight. Curled firmly around his other arm, a small boy, a toddler. They lifted their fingers and waved. Of course he knew his father, but for the first time recognized a brother and sister he never had a chance to love. Ted continued to pan his audience and was drawn to a bright young woman with blond, sunbathed hair. Under a street lamp, glowing off the light, alone among the massive throng stood Helen. Never before had he seen her so beautiful. She put a hand to her lips and tossed him a gentle, inviting kiss.

Helen had always been his biggest fan and now urged Ted to address the multitudes one more time. Ted felt the impulse, wanting to seize a moment he had captured and delivered countless times before. He stepped forward one giant leap to approach his supporters. Ted looked down to cup the mike, but it suddenly moved away. On cue, the microphone melted into an animated, sarcastic face.

Once again, it seemed to possess an agenda all to itself. A taunting, belligerent attitude danced like a jack rabbit to keep Ted Husing away—far away from his destiny. The crowd fell silent. A light breeze swept across the ghostly town. Like a manic featherweight boxer, the microphone weaved back and forth, up and down inviting confrontation. "Come and get me you, son of a bitch," the demon-like figure continued. "Come and get me if you can!" In the past, the announcer never could capture his nemesis. Yet, everything—something—about this dream was different.

Ted lifted an eyebrow and studied the wild microphone spirit. He felt strong, able, and confident. Ted lifted his forceful hand and accomplished something he had not been able to do in the dream before. He grabbed the microphone and placed it to his mouth as if to swallow it whole. Squeezing the life from this form, his heart suddenly filled with compassion. He had come to this place not to take life, but so he could live again. Ted loosened his grip and bellowed out the words all had come to hear. "Good afternoon everyone, everywhere, this is Ted Husing speaking." The crowd exploded in praise and adulation. There would be no more nightmares for the radio master. The announcer was back among his people. He had come home.

At ten minutes past 8 o'clock, Ted Husing died. It was Friday. The weather that day in Pasadena was like so many before, hazy, hot with a choking smog index that warned anyone with a respiratory condition to stay inside. The broadcaster would no longer have to worry about that. Back east, the temperature was a cool fifty-four degrees. It would be the coldest day of August New York ever felt.[797] The smell of dry leaves filled the air. No one would have enjoyed, in the middle of summer, an autumnlike day more than Ted, his favorite time of year. For those who knew and loved Ted Husing, clouds of heartache and melancholy rolled in. The greatest sports broadcaster, perhaps the most transforming talent of radio that ever lived was gone. And somehow, the city that reared this rugged yet complex man wished to share the grief of a fallen son. Saturday, the following day, it rained.

A HAUNTING SPIRIT

During his lifetime, Ted Husing not only swayed the profession of sports broadcasting and radio in general, he permeated America's pop culture in a place everyone knew but few noticed. Perhaps the most beloved animated figure of the 1930 and '40s was not Mickey Mouse or Dick Tracey, it was Joe Palooka. The popular syndicated comic strip was about a no-frills, good-natured prize fighter and his many adventures. Palooka, over a forty-year period, spawned a radio show, television series, and numerous films depicting the brawny fighter. Creator Ham Fisher admitted that several of his drawings came from his frequent visits to the 21 Club. "A Mr. Husing was the inspiration for many of the characters who later found their way into the strip," he said. "If any of these bums expect any royalties, they're crazy."[798]

Years after his death, Husing has continued to show a strong presence in movies, primetime TV sitcoms, and various halls of fame. "The Cotton Club," Francis Ford Coppola's depiction of Harlem during the Roaring '20s starred Gregory Hines and Richard Gere. Coppola knew that shooting scenes of the club's heyday would not be complete without a certain CBS radio announcer. But, who could play the part? Coppola knew just the man, casting his newphew Marc, who just happened to be a New York disc jockey, in the role of Husing.[799] Film director Martin Scorsese presented a stark, raw portrayal of boxer Jake LaMotta in his 1980 masterpiece "Raging Bull." He shot the entire picture in black and white, uniquely placing cameras inside the ring to capture the boxer's expressive emotions during fight scenes. Scorsese's recreation of the "St. Valentine's Day Masacure" is art imitating life. As Oscar-winning actor Robert Dinero screams, "You never knocked me down, Ray!" it is the prevailing sound of Husing's actual call of the match that underscores the bloody carnage.[800]

During one memorable episode of the popular 1970s television comedy "The Odd Couple," Oscar Madison, played by Jack Klugman, is given an opportunity to further his sports writing career as a radio sports call-in host. As usual, his roommate and partner in crime Felix Unger gets surreptitiously involved in this airing appropriately entitled "The Big Broadcast." It was an ideal premise for the two veteran actors, especially Tony Randall who began his early showbiz career as a radio performer.[801] While the plot unfolds, Felix makes a visit to the station to check up on his friend. At one point, he turns to Oscar and asks where his announcer is to introduce him. Flippantly, Oscar responds by saying, "I don't need one. I'm not Ted Husing."[802]

But, of course, today no sports announcer, man or woman, can walk into a broadcast booth and not feel the presence of Husing. And the fact that CBS remains on the air might be overstating the importance of his contribution, but it is a testimony nonetheless. Not long ago, CBS was known as the "Tiffany network," the network of class and quality programs, the network of Murrow, Cronkite, and serious news, the network of the Masters golf tournament and big time sports. Over the years, at times, it has struggled to maintain those lofty expectations. But, whether first in the ratings or last, they should also be known as the network of Husing. Gary Stevens, the man Husing called "Talent," perhaps summoned up his legacy best.

"There will never be another guy who had the impact and influence in the broadcast business as Ted. Nobody was that qualified. He was an all-around man, who specialized in one thing— he became an authority and was blessed with a developed voice of an actor, much different than the average screaming announcer."[803]

Ted Husing has been inducted into several Halls of Fame since passing, including the National Association of Broadcasters, American Sportscasters Association, National Sportscasters and Sportswriters. In Pasadena, surrounded by eucalyptus trees and the peaks of the San Gabrilles, is a graveyard called Mountain View Cemetery, Ted's final resting place. Roughly ten miles west, atop the sidewalk of Hollywood Boulevard in Los Angeles, between High-land and Orange Avenue, among retail stores, bus stops, and tourists, is etched a large gold star. The name "Ted Husing" engraved inside, a member of an exclusive club, given the ultimate symbol of status on the Hollywood Walk of Fame. Down the street glows the star of his old friends Bill Stern and the "voice with a smile," Graham McNamee.

THE PRINCIPLE PLAYERS

Jimmie Britt: The San Franciscan boxed his last match in 1909, knocked out by Johnny Summers in the ninth round. Despite the loss, he remained immensely popular. He toured England and the States with various vaudeville shows playing himself. At the breakout of World War I, he signed up with the Australian Army and was stationed in the Gallipoli Peninsula in Turkey. He continued to act in silent films, managed fighters, coached boxing at Stanford while prospering in real estate. Dapper to the end, he was found dead of a heart attack in his San Francisco apartment on January 23, 1940. Like Husing, he was sixty years old.

Charlie Berns: The remaining original owner of the 21 Club continued to be a quiet fixture of efficiency running 21 Brands, Inc. until his death in 1970. The company stayed solvent for nearly two more decades, selling its last bottle of liquor in 1988.

Jimmy Dolan: The "Johnny Irishman" served loyally at CBS until 1967. Along the way, he recruited to the broadcasting towers football players Frank Gifford and Pat Summerall, giving them early exposure to the network. After a series of strokes starting in 1977, his health failed. He moved to Ohio under the care of his daughter Ellen. Dolan died at the age of eighty-three on June 20, 1986.

Fr. Benedict Dudley: He remained chaplain of the New York Giants until 1978, forty years in all, when dementia and Alzheimer's began to poison his mind. Fr. Ben Joe eventually passed away in the summer of 1986, no clue of who he was and the many acts of kindness he bestowed on others.

Bertha Hecht Husing: Bertha outlived all of her children and husband. She died on December 2, 1974. She was 101 years old. As promised, Bertha was buried next to her husband Henry in New York. Their graves remain unmarked.

Tom Harmon: Harmon, over the coming decades, would do preseason NFL games and voice UCLA football during the '60s and '70s. The job took on a new challenge when his son Mark started for the Bruins, referring to him on the air as "the quarterback" in an attempt to sound unbiased. Outside of football, Harmon's favorite passion was golf. Hours after winning a best ball tournament with playing partner Dr. David Boska at the Bel Air Country Club, he dropped dead of a heart attack on March 15, 1990. He was seventy years old.

When Elyse Knox married Lt. Harmon in 1944, stitched into her wedding gown were patches of the parachute he used to bail out of his burning plane over China. The couple had three children. Kristin appeared regularly in the hit TV series "The Adventures of Ozzie and Harriet" and later married one of the show's stars, teen idol Ricky Nelson. Kelly became a highly sought-after model and commercial actress of the 1970s and '80s. She is perhaps best known as the "Tic Tac" girl. Mark Harmon may be the most recognized of all, star of network television series "NCIS," "Chicago Hope," and "St. Elsewhere," among others.

Lennie Hayton: Hayton and Lena Horne married in 1947, choosing to have the ceremony in Paris. Fear of racial intolerance made them keep the news of their weeding under raps for another three years. Hayton went on to make his biggest mark in Hollywood during the heyday of musical films. He was music director for MGM studios from 1940–53. When he died of a heart ailment in Palm Springs, California on April 24, 1971, his marriage to Ms. Horne was in it's twenty-fourth year. He is buried at Forever Hollywood Memorial Cemetery in Los Angeles.

The Husing/Hayton riff never healed. Those who stayed loyal to Husing, namely Jimmy Dolan, stayed true to his sullen heartache. "My father was Irish Catholic. He blamed people for broken marriages," said Dolan's daughter Betty Farrell. "I was a Lena Horne fan. My father, was not!"

David Husing: A graduate of Wellesley College outside of Boston and a veteran of the Vietnam War, Husing did attempt to become a sports announcer. "By the time I got into it, the Husing name was forgotten." He did, however, continue his father's legacy of being expelled from a Boston area sports stadium. In 1966, he was kicked out of the old Boston Arena for calling the owner of the complex an "asshole." Now a Nassau County police officer, he lives on Long Island.

Walter Kennedy: Following the final season of Army football broadcasts, Kennedy became PR director of the Harlem Globetrotters. He then reigned as Commissioner of the National Basketball Association (1963–75), laying important groundwork for the league's future prosperity. He became mayor of Stamford, Connecticut and died in 1977.

Peggemae H. Lacey: Husing's first child and only daughter was killed in an auto accident by a drunk driver. The date was August 9, 1986. Peggemae was sixty-one years old.

<u>Betty Lawford:</u> The actress did decide again to wear a wedding ring, marrying ad executive Barry Buchanan in 1955. She continued to perform on stage and early television shows like "Studio One" and the "Kraft Theater" until her untimely death at age fifty in 1960.

<u>Iris Lemerise:</u> After Husing's death, she returned to CBS as a production staff coordinator. She stayed at the network until her retirement in 1978 and passed away ten years later, January 1, 1988. To the day she died, Iris wished to be recognized as "Mrs. Ted Husing."

<u>Luchow's Restaurant:</u> Luchow's officially closed in 1982. The property on East 14th Street lay dormant for the next fifteen years when it was finally purchased by New York University and leveled to make room for a new modern building. However, the memories linger. In a 1998 New York Magazine poll, Luchow's was voted the city's most missed restaurant.

<u>Les Quailey:</u> He stayed in Philadelphia the rest of his life, working with NW Ayer for more than thirty-five years and made Atlantic Oil one of the biggest sponsors of sports on radio and television. With no children to continue his legacy, he died April 19, 1982. At the time of his death, he was watching sports on television at his home in Wyncote, Pennsylvania.

<u>Celia Ryland:</u> The actress appeared in two movies, but worked primarily on the stage performing in musicals and reviewes in the U.S. and abroad. She later married stage and television producer Montgomery Ford. The two collaborated writing songs and music for various productions and singers, including Les Paul and his wife Mary Ford.

<u>Toots Shor:</u> Toots never grew up. He chased the jocks and money until he had none himself. His restaurants opened and closed, one failure after the other. His life-long dream of a place on Swing Street came true in 1962. Later, Toots moved his operation to East 53rd. In the end, he was a man hanging on to an era long dead. Uncle Sam chased him until the end trying to collect back taxes six figures deep. Bernard "Toots" Shor died broke but a smile on his face in 1977. He and wife Baby were two months short of celebrating their forty-third wedding anniversary.

<u>Sandy Simon:</u> Continueing to surround himself with celebrities, he later co-founded Simon and Flynn Coummunications, a firm specializing in sports media projects. Retiring to Sarasota, Florida, Simon died in 1989 at the age of eighty-four.

<u>Bill Slater:</u> During the '40s and '50s, Slater would turn to less sports-related shows on Mutual like "Luncheon at Sardis" and game show host of "Twenty Questions."

"He was a much better sports announcer than game show host," the late Heywood Hale Broun admitted. Like Husing, sports remained in his blood, calling the first televised World Series on Dumont in 1949. Slater died in 1965, the ravages of Parkinson's Disease no longer able to destroy his body. He is the great uncle of film/television actor Christian Slater.

<u>Bill Stern:</u> As the title of his memorie suggested, Stern did rise from the ashes. Though he did kick his drug habbit, he never regained past glories. Stern worked his way back into local New York radio and eventually as head of the sports department at Mutual in the late '60s. His salacious on-air storytelling influenced many who followed him in radio, none greater than Paul Harvey. Stern defended his style until his death in 1971, saying while others criticized he "laughed all the way to the bank."

Ann St. George: By the late 1930s she is fronting the Ann St. George Dancers. But, her marriage to Alex Thompson did not last long. After their divorce, St. George's life and career fades into obscurity. Little is know about her final whereabouts.

21 Club: Swing Street is gone, but West 52nd remains. Among a forest of tall office buildings, "21" is the only remaining fixture of the old Street.

Major Andrew White: After leaving CBS in 1930, White became a screenwriter briefly before segueing into a career as a doctor of psychology. He lived the remainder of his life in Los Angeles, staying close to broadcasting as guest lecturer and sometimes announcer. On his weekly radio show during the early '50s, he insisted on being introduced as, "The first president of CBS."

Harry Von Zell: After replacing Husing on the Old Gold Hour, he went on to become a radio and television star himself, if not infamous. His on-air gaff, calling President Herbert Hoover "Hoobert Heever" is still laughable even today.

ACKNOWLEDGMENTS

Ah yes, the proverbial thank you page. Most writers hate them, sharing the spotlight, admitting modesty in the face of perceived greatness. Writing a book, at least in my case, has been an epic, monumental task. Wavering, teetering from arduous to exhilarating, impossible to inspiring. When I began this project, I had a wife, no children, 20/20 vision, and two living parents. I now have a daughter and son, growing fast, attending school, participating in sports, and enjoying play dates. My parents, sadly, are no longer among the living—my eyes no longer perfect. As for my wife . . . well, she still remains my wife, nurturing, prodding, pushing. Some habits, I suppose, are hard to break.

In the end, I am quite proud, quite boastful of my accomplishments. But, even at my most vain, egocentric moments, I never think that without the help of others I could have completed this manuscript. Whether through their words, music, or actions, these special people lifted me, taught me, encouraged me, moved me, and, at the risk of sounding melodramatic, saved me. Simply thanking them would be a disservice, underestimating their immeasurable contribution to the Husing story. For the moment, however, this is the best I can do, a public recognition in the hopes that they, too, can share in my joy. Know that I am forever indebted to you all and look forward to returning the many favors and blessings you have bestowed on me. Here is the short list, in no particular order:

Larry Demers, you were a dear friend and will remain always, Columbia University, David Kenny and "Everything Old is New Again." Thanks for playing the vintage stuff. Eddie Trunk, and "Friday & Saturday Night Rocks." Metal still rules. Sophfronia Scott, my editor and publishing guru. Thanks for being so tough and making me a better writer. The entire staff of Langdon Street Press. You were great. Jay Reed, Trudy Ainge and Ralph Lewis (no relation), friends who kept my stomach full and wallet green through out. My family, especially brother Joe and his wife Marian, my sister Mary Ann and her partner Onie, my parents Doc and Ann Lewis, and my various nieces and nephews especially Buddy Jones, who without their support, especially monetary, none of these pages would be possible. The extended Husing and Lemerise families, especially David Husing, Stanley Wertheim and the Lacey family, especially David, Kim, and Kate, who's blind trust and full access gave me the leeway to write an honest, warts and all, story.

Landon Wickham, thanks for the early council and inexpensive repairs on my bike. Kathy Passero, editing advice throughout. Actors Equity, Screen Actors Guild, and the American Federation of Television & Radio Artists, who helped me dig up the dead and locate the living. The New York City Public Library, the only thing they didn't provide was a warm bed and hot shower. A host of talented sports announcers, all Hall of Famers in my opinion, especially: Mike "Doc" Emrick, Chuck Thompson, Ernie Harwell, Fred Cusick, Guy LeBow, Chris Schenkel, Curt Gowdy, and Marty Glickman. Max Schmid and the "Golden Age of Radio," Sunday nights are always exciting. Dan Teachout, research assistant and friend. Gary Stevens, the man who lived through and befriended many stars of radio's heyday and loved to talk about it. Sabine and Heidi Yearwood, German hymn's never sounded better. David Kelly and Paul Hogroian at the Library of Congress, true professionals.

New Jersey State Library, Trenton. Uwe and Muriel Dielewicz, miss you "Moo." You always did like a good story. Jim Stevenson and his vivid tales of the old Westside of Manhattan, Jennifer Stevenson who helped shape my early chapters and kept up my sagging confidence. Lou Schwartz and the American Sportscasters Association. Thanks for promoting the industry of sports announcing with the class and dignity it deserves. David Siegel's radio memorabilia archives. John Miley and "The Miley Collection," hearing those broadcast never gets old. Ben Abel-Bey, the man with the lens. Thanks for the author photo. Franciscan Order of Friars Minor/Diocese of New York. Not everything stays in the confessional. Michael Farmer and Kensico Cemetery who showed me Henry and Bertha Husing's unmarked grave as well as Lou Gehrig's very marked and often visited place of rest. Pastor Heidi Neumark and the congregation of Trinity Lutheran Church of Manhattan. Shine On! Eevin Hartsough and the Museum of Television & Radio. Thanks for the countless hours to comb through your archives. Brooklyn Public Library, the National Archives. David Wheeler for his invaluable input on cover designs.

Fellow sports broadcasting historians Ted Patterson, Curt Smith and David J. Halberstam for their encouragement. Blair and Sylvia White. Thanks for the photos and the stories of CBS's very first president. New Jersey Division of Archives and Records Management. Danny Stiles and the "The Music Museum" along with Chuck Schaden, Steve Parnall and *Nostalgia Digest*. No men ever worked harder at keeping the golden age of radio alive. Michael Henry and the Library of American Broadcasting, University of Maryland, who gave me access to more periodicals, broadcast tapes and photographs about radio than I ever imagined. Judy Channel at the "21" Club for helping me contact Jerry Berns. Dr. Laurence Demers for providing the complex medical explanations. Mary

Ann Reardone and Lee Peters at Friends Academy of Long Island who helped me research Pegge Husing's adolescence. Cindy Nieves and Stuyvesant High School, who told me the history of that great school. Finally, my gorgeous wife, Petra and our two most endearing creations, Edie and Martin. I love you!

I have no doubt there were others who contributed in ways both big and small. If I have forgotten anyone, please forgive me.

John Lewis
March, 2010

NOTES

** The reader should know that every effort was made to source each footnote truthfully and accurately at press. However, in some cases, especially websites, edits and changes in content may have occurred.

PRELUDE
[1] Interview with Curt Gowdy, October 1999

CHAPTER 1 - A NIGHT OF REDEMPTION
[2] "Que Sera, Sera (Whatever Will Be, Will Be)," music by Jay Livingston, lyrics by Ray Evans, 1956
[3] New York City Public Library Milstein Division Microform Room
[4] *On the Air—The Encyclopedia of Old Time Radio* by John Dunning, p.485
[5] *The Lively Ball—Baseball in the Roaring '20s* by James Cox, p.128
[6] *New York Herald Tribune*, Oct. 1, 1941
[7] *New York Daily Mirror*, Sept. 29, 1941
[8] *New York Herald Tribune*, Oct. 1, 1941
[9] *Sports On New York Radio* by David J. Halberstam, p. 392
[10] *New York Daily News*, Oct. 1, 1941
[11] BWAA – Baseball Writers Association of America
[12] *Sports On New York Radio* by David J. Halberstam, p. 392
[13] *Don Dunphy at Ringside* by Don Dunphy, p.139
[14] Ibid
[15] *New York Daily News*, Oct. 4, 1941
[16] *My Eyes Are in My Heart* by Ted Husing, p. 262
[17] Ibid
[18] "This Is Your Life – Ted Husing," originally aired May 8, 1957, NBC-TV
[19] *New York Herald Tribune*, Feb. 4, 1957
[20] Interview with Jim Graham, Sept. 30, 2008
[21] *The Broadcasters* by Red Barber, p.38
[22] *Don Dunphy at Ringside* by Don Dunphy, p.140

CHAPTER 2 - BLACK SHEEP, GERMAN SALOONS
[23] Interview with Uwe Dielewicz, who grew up in Hamburg, Germany, 2005
[24] www.edwardvictor.com/bielefeld
[25] *The History of Lutheranism* by Eric W. Gritsch, p.200
[26] Interview with Stanley Wertheim, July, 2007
[27] New York Public Library, ship logs—passenger manifest
[28] *Out of the House of Judah* by Julius Abrams, p.19
[29] Interview with Kate Lacey, 2002
[30] Interviews with Kim Lacey, 2002
[31] Interview with Andrew R. Heinze, Prof. American History, University of San Fran-

cisco, 2005

[32] *New Map of the Borough of The Bronx, City of New York*, 1900, Colton, Ohman and Co. New York City

[33] www.mcny.org/museum-collections/berenice-abbott/al22.htm

[34] *Luchow's German Cookbook* by Jan Mitchell, p.25.

[35] Ibid, p.24

[36] Ibid, p.27

[37] *My Eyes Are in My Heart* by Ted Huisng, p.30

[38] Ibid, p.185

[39] Ibid, p.29

[40] *Morbidity and Mortality Weekly Report*, Oct. 1, 1999

[41] Husing birth certificate, New York City Public Library, Milstein Division

CHAPTER 3 - SIR EDWARD

[42] www.cyberboxingzone.com

[43] Trading Card Photo, printed by Phillips & Van Orden Co. 1907

[44] *San Francisco Chronicle*, Jan. 22, 1940

[45] www.antekprizering.com/britt

[46] *San Francisco Chronicle,* January 23, 1940

[47] *Perfect in Their Art* ("The Kid's Last Fight"), edited by Robert Hedin and Michael Waters, p. 45

[48] *New York Post,* September 8, 1950

[49] Interview with Kate Lacey, 2002

[50] *My Eyes are in My Heart* by Ted Husing, p.27

[51] Ellis Island Museum exhibits walking tour, Ellis Island, New York, NY. 2002

[52] *Pediatrics Magazine*, Dec. 2000

[53] *My Eyes Are In My Heart* by Ted Husing, p.28

[54] *New York Times,* May 29, 1906

[55] *San Francisco Chronicle*, May 30, 1906

CHAPTER 4 GLOVERSVILLE

[56] *New York Times*, October 21, 2009

[57] Ibid

[58] www.cityofgloversville.com/ContentManager/index. cfm?Step=Display&ContentID=5

[59] *My Eyes Are in My Heart* by Ted Husing, p.34

[60] Ibid p.31

[61] *Ten Years Before the Mike* by Ted Husing, p.8

[62] *My Eyes Are in My Heart* by Ted Husing, p.35

CHAPTER 5 HOME

[63] www.columbia.edu/cu/german/dhaus/

[64] Ibid

[65] *City Journal*, Spring 1999, Vol.9

[66] Interview with Cindy Nieves, Stuyvesant Alumni Director, 2001

[67] Interview with Steven Babin, mechanical contractor, 2004

[68] *Ten Years Before the Mike* by Ted Husing, p.9

CHAPTER 6 – GET THE KRAUT

[69] Interview with Ann Lewis, June 2002

[70] www.columbia.edu/cu/german/dhaus

[71] www.rsdb.org

[72] "Over There," music and lyrics by George M. Cohan, 1917

[73] Husing discharge papers

[74] *My Eyes Are in My Heart* by Ted Husing, p.31

[75] Interview with Jim Stevenson July 2005

[76] *My Enyes Are in My Heart* by Ted Husing, p.30

[77] *When Pride Mattered* by David Maraniss, p.29

[78] Interview with David Husing August 2004

CHAPTER 7 – ON THE LAMB

[79] *My Eyes Are in My Heart* by Ted Husing, p. 58

[80] "This Is Your Life," May 8, 1957

[81] *Radio Guide*, April 15, 1933

[82] *Ten Years Behind the Mike*, by Ted Husing, p.35

[83] *Radio Guide*, April 15, 1933

[84] Interview with Stanley Wertheim, 2007

[85] *New York Herald Tribune*, May 12, 1929

[86] My Eyes Are in My Heart, p.36

CHAPTER 8 – THRILL OF THE CHASE

[87] *My Eyes Are in My Heart* by Ted Husing p.58–59

[88] Ibid, p.38

[89] Ibid, p.38

[90] Ibid, p.38

[91] *My Eyes Are in My Heart* by Ted Husing, p.37

[92] *New York Times*, April 25, 1975

[93] Ibid

[94] Ibid

[95] *New York Times*, May 25, 1997

[96] "Nola," music and lyrics by Felix Arndt, 1915

[97] *Radio Stars*, Oct. 1934

[98] *My Eyes Are in My Heart* by Ted Husing, p. 39

[99] Husing marriage certificate, New York City Department of Records and Information

CHAPTER 9 – WANTED: RADIO ANNOUNCER

[100] *My Eyes Are in My Heart* by Ted Husing, p.144

[101] *Sports On New York Radio* by David J. Halberstam, p.3 - 5

[102] Interview with Blair White, 2003

[103] *As It Happened* by William Paley, p.38

[104] *Ten Years Before the Mike*, by Ted Husing, p.14

[105] Ibid, p.23

[106] Ibid, p. 24

[107] *Radio Guide*, February 1925

[108] Interview with Blair White, May 22, 2002

[109] *My Eyes Are in My Heart* by Ted Husing, p.63
[110] "This Is Your Life—Ted Husing," NBC, June 7, 1957

CHAPTER 10 – PUNCHING IN, GOING OUT AND PAYING DUES
[111] *Radio Retailing*, December, 1926
[112] *St.Petersburg Evening Independent*, December 30, 1926
[113] *American Babel* by Clifford J. Doerksen, p. 123–128
[114] *Ten Years Behind the Mike*, p.24
[115] *Radio Guide*, July 1926
[116] *New York Herald Tribune*, Aug. 27, 1926
[117] *My Eyes Are in My Heart,* p.95
[118] Washington D.C. telephone listing, Altell Co. 1926
[119] *Ten Years Behind the Mike*, p.48
[120] *Radio Mirror*, May, 1949
[121] *Brought to You In Livin' Color, 75 Years of NBC*, p.2
[122] *My Eyes Are in My Heart* by Ted Husing, p.93.
[123] *Radio Guide*, June, 1936.
[124] *Sports Illustrated*, Oct. 12, 1964
[125] *The Broadcasters*, p.29
[126] *Sports On New York Radio*, p.8
[127] *Sports Illustrated*, Oct. 12, 1964
[128] *I Looked and I Listened*, p.90
[129] *You're On the Air*, by Graham McNamee, p.6
[130] *Sports Illustrated*, Oct. 12, 1964
[131] *I Looked and I Listened* by Ben Gross, p. 144
[132] *The Mark Hellinger Story*, p. 88
[133] *Toots* by Bob Considine, p.35.
[134] *Look Magazine*, January 7, 1958
[135] *My Eyes Are In My Heart*, p.94

CHAPTER 11 – THIS GUY HUSING
[136] *The Mark Hellinger Story*, p.77
[137] *Ten Years Before the Mike* by Ted Husing, p.272
[138] Boston phone listings, 1927
[139] *My Eyes Are In My Heart* by Ted Husing, p. 98
[140] *Voices of the Game*, p.21
[141] www.baseball-almanac.com
[142] *Voices On New York Radio*, p.144
[143] *New York Times*, Aug. 27, 1971
[144] *Variety*, May 13, 1942
[145] *As It Happened: A Memoir by William S. Paley*, p.32–38
[146] *Radio Mirror*, May, 1949
[147] *New York Herald Tribune*, Nov. 21, 1927
[148] www.filmreference.com
[149] New York Library for the Performing Arts Photo Archives
[150] *Radio Guide*, April 9, 1933
[151] *As It Happened*, p.34

[152] *Look Magazine*, January 7, 1957

[153] *My Eyes Are in My Heart*, p.108–110

[154] *Sports On New York Radio*, p.391

[155] *CBS Reflections in a Bloodshot Eye* by Robert Metz, p.44

[156] *Now the News: The Story of Broadcast Journalism* by Edward Bliss Jr. p.23

[157] www.cbs.com/specials/cbs_75/timeline.shtml

[158] Interview with Blair White, 2002

[159] *As It Happened*, p. 34

[160] Ibid, p.42

[161] Interview with Gary Stevens, 2003

[162] *As It Happened*, p.39

[163] *Life*, November 23, 1928

[164] *Reminiscing in Tempo: A Portrait of Duke Ellington*, p.67–80

[165] *The Mark Hellinger Story*, p.95

[166] *Time Magazine*, Oct. 2, 1939

[167] *Duke Ellington and His World*, p.155

[168] *Music Is My Mistress* by Duke Ellington, p.79–80

[169] *Reminiscing in Tempo* by Stuart Nicholson, p.77–78

[170] *Music Is My Mistress*, p.79–80

[171] www.freepress.org (*Duke Ellington* by Thomas C. Fleming, August 26, 1998)

[172] *The Encyclodepia of Harlem Renaissance*, Vol. I

[173] Interview with Gary Stevens, 2003

[174] Interview with Blair White, 2002

[175] www.cbsnews.cbs.com/specials/cbs_75/timeline/1920.shtml

CHAPTER 12 – CLYDE VAN HUSING

[176] *Empire – William S. Paley and the Making of CBS* by Lewis J. Paper, p.132

[177] *Ten Years Before the Mike* by Ted Husing, p.121

[178] *New York Times*, May 12, 1929

[179] *Friday's with Red* by Bob Edwards, p.146

[180] *Ten Years Behind the Mike* by Ted Husing, p.121

[181] *Louisville Courier-Journal*, June 5, 1962

[182] Interview with Chick Lang, Nov. 26, 2001

[183] www.sbe35.org (Society of Broadcasting Engineers)

[184] *New York Herald-Tribune*, May 19, 1929

[185] Ibid

[186] *New York Times*, May, 18, 1929.

[187] *Louisville Courier-Journal*, May 8, 1921.

[188] "My Old Kentucky Home" (Poor Uncle Tom, Good Night), music and lyrics by Stephen C. Foster, 1858

[189] www.kentuckyderby.com (article by William F. Reed)

[190] *Ten Years Before the Mike* by Ted Husing, p.122.

[191] *Those Wonderful Days: The Tales of Racing's Golden Era* by Bob Moore, p. 117.

[192] Ibid

[193] *Ten Years Behind the Mike* by Ted Husing, p.122–3.

[194] *Look Magazine*, January 7, 1958

[195] *New York Herald-Tribune* May 19, 1929

[196] *New York Sun*, May 21, 1929

[197] Ibid

[198] *My Eyes Are in My Heart* by Ted Husing, p.121

CHAPTER 13 – OLD GOLD, NEW PALS

[199] *Pops: Paul Whitema, King of Jazz* by Thomas DeLong, p. 28.

[200] *Paul Whiteman: Pioneer in American Music*, Vol. I

[201] *New York Times*, December 30, 1967

[202] *I Looked and I Listened* by Ben Gross, p.143

[203] Ibid

[204] *As It Happened—A Memoir* by William Paley, p.66

[205] Ibid

[206] *The Courier Journal Louisville*, May, 16, 1929

[207] *Paul Whiteman: Pioneer in American Music*, Vol. I by Don Rayno, p.222

[208] *Bing Crosby: A Pocket Full of Dreams*, by Gary Giddins, p.179

[209] *Look Magazine*, January 21, 1958.

[210] "Mississippi Mud," music and lyrics by Harry Barris and James Cavanaugh, 1927

[211] *Look Magazine*, January 21, 1958.

[212] *Paul Whiteman: A Pioneer in American Music*, Vol. I by Don Rayno, p. 225

[213] *New York Daily News*, May 31, 1929

[214] *Paul Whiteman: A Pioneer in American Music*, Vol.I by Don Rayno, p. 237

[215] Ibid, p.234

[216] *My Eyes Are in My Heart* by Ted Husing, p.126.

[217] *Look Magazine*, January 21, 1958.

CHAPTER 14 – HAPPY FEET, STEELY EYES

[218] *Ten Years Before the Mike* by Ted Husing, p.163

[219] *Radio Guide*, June 1934

[220] *Radio Guide*, June, 1936

[221] Interview with Gary Stevens

[222] *Ten Years Before the Mike* by Ted Husing, p.164

[223] *Radioland Magazine*, November, 1933

[224] *The Golden Voices of Football*, p.40

[225] *As It Happened* by William S. Paley, p.119

[226] *Radio Stars*, September, 1936

[227] *Sports On New York Radio*, p.391

[228] *New York Herlad Tribune*, Oct. 13, 1929

[229] www.1847usa.com/identify/YearSets/1929.htm

[230] www.thehenryford.org

[231] *New York Daily News*, Oct. 22, 1929

[232] www.thehenryford.org

[233] *My Eyes Are in My Heart*, p.132

[234] *Ten Years Behind the Mike*, p.127

CHAPTER 15 – TIME MARCHES ON

[235] *The Grand Slam*, p.407

[236] *Popular Science Magazine*, Oct. 1930

[237] Ibid

[238] Ibid

[239] *The Immortal Bobby Jones* by Ron Rapoport, p.155

[240] *The Immortal Bobby Jones*, p.216–217

[241] *The Gran Slam*, p.412

[242] Ibid, p.443

[243] *Radio Guide*, April 9, 1933

[244] *The Visualizers: A Reassessment of Television's News Pioneers* by Michael Conway, p.33

[245] *On the Air*, p.434–437

[246] *News On the Air* by Paul White, p.249

[247] Ibid, p.250.

[248] *On the Air*, p.630

[249] Interview with Bud Collins, Sept. 2005

[250] Interview with Bill Mazer, 2002

[251] *My Eyes Are in My Heart*, p.162

[252] *Literary Digest*, September 21, 1929

[253] *Philadelphia Inquirer*, Sept. 18, 1957

[254] *Duquesne University Magazine*, Spring, 2003

[255] www.old-time.com/ratings

[256] *Brought to You in Living Color*, p.20–23.

[257] *Empire: William Paley and the Making of CBS*, p.359

[258] *As It Happened* by William Paley, p.74

[259] *A Pocket Full of Dreams* by Gary Giddins, p. 7

[260] Ibid, p. 256

[261] Ibid, p. 267

[262] *My Eyes Are in My Heart* by Ted Husing, p.126

[263] Ibid

[264] *Look Magazine*, Jan. 21, 1958

[265] "Dancing in the Dark," music by Arthur Schwartz and lyrics by Howard Dietz, 1931

[266] *Look Magazine*, January 21, 1958

CHAPTER 16 PUTRID

[267] Interview with Will Cloney, 2002

[268] *My Eyes Are in My Heart* by Ted Husing, p.144

[269] *New York Times*, November 13, 1931

[270] *I Looked and I Listened* by Ben Gross, p.90

[271] *Ten Years Before the Mike* by Ted Husing, p.171–72

[272] Ibid p.172

[273] *New York Daily News*, Nov. 8,1931

[274] *Boston Globe*, Nov. 9, 1931

[275] *Ten Years Befor the Mike* by Ted Husing, p.172

[276] *Washington Post*, November 8, 1931

[277] *My Eyes Are in My Heart* by Ted Husing, p.149

[278] *New York Times*, November 14, 1931

[279] *My Eyes Are in My Heart* by Ted Husing, p.145

[280] *Empire, William S. Paley and the Making of CBS* by Lewis J. Paper, p. vii

[281] *New York Times*, November 14, 1931

[282] Ibid

[283] *My Eyes Are in My Heart* by Ted Husing, p.145

[284] *Washington Post*, November 17, 1931

[285] Ibid

[286] Ibid

[287] Ibid

[288] *New York Times*, Nov. 15, 1931

[289] *What Price Football* by Barry Wood, p.136

CHAPTER 17 – MOVE OF THE CENTURY

[290] *F. Scott Fitzgerald: Poems, 1911–1940*

[291] *Radio Guide*, Feb. 1932

[292] *Radio Announcers*, 1933

[293] *Tower Radio*, Novemeber,1934

[294] *Radio Guide*, March 17, 1932

[295] *Radio Stars*, Oct. 1934

[296] *Ten Years Before the Mike*, p.263

[297] *Radio Stars*, Oct. 1934

[298] *Radio Stars*, Sept. 1936

[299] *My Eyes Are in My Heart*, p.137–38

[300] Ibid, p.166

[301] *My Eyes Are in My Heart*, photo flap

[302] *Broadcasting Magazine*, Sept. 15, 1932

[303] www.baseball-almanac.com

[304] *Ten Years Before the Mike*, p.220–21

[305] Ibid, p.206

[306] *The Milers* by Cordner Nelson, p.53–63

[307] Ibid

[308] Interview with Joe Kleinerman January, 2003

[309] *Broadcasting*, Oct. 1, 1932

[310] *Radio Guide*, June, 1936

[311] *Ten Years Before the Mike*, p.165

[312] Ibid, p.297

[313] *On the Air*, p.485

[314] *Los Angeles Times*, August 15, 1962

[315] US Department of Labor consumer price index data

[316] *My Eyes Are in My Heart* by Ted Husing, p. 172

[317] Interview with Stanley Wertheim, 2007

[318] Ibid

[319] Ibid

CHAPTER 18 – THE BOYS IN THE BACKROOM

[320] "The American Experience—Roosevelt" (documentary film)

[321] *The Street that Never Slept* by Arnold Shaw, (inside book cover illustration)

[322] Ibid, p. xi

[323] *Columbia College Today*, Jan/Feb. 2008

[324] *"21" Everyday was New Year's* Eve by H. Peter Kriendler

[325] *"21" The Life and Times of New York's Favorite Club* by Marilyn Kaytor, p.150.

[326] *The Street that Never Slept* by Arnold Shaw, p.14

[327] *"21" Every Day was New Year's Eve*, p.34

[328] www.21club.com

[329] *New York Magazine*, Jan. 18, 1971

[330] Interview with Gary Stevens, 2003

[331] *The Broadcasters* by Red Barber, p.32

[332] *"21" The Life and Times of New York's Favorite Club*, p.146

[333] *"21"Everyday was New Year's Eve* by H. Peter Kriendler, p.270

[334] *The Longest Street* by Louis Sobol, p.72

[335] www.hotel-online.com/News/PR2009_4th/Oct09_BloodyMary.html

[336] Interview with Gary Stevens, 2003

[337] *New York Times*, Jan. 24, 1977

[338] *The Mark Hellinger Story*, p.184–188

CHAPTER 19 – A MOUNTAIN CALLED KENESAW

[339] Interview with Gary Stevens, 2003

[340] *New York Times*, Dec.3, 1933

[341] Interview with Gary Stevens, 2003

[342] *On the Air* by John Dunning, p. 404-409

[343] *The Broadcasters* by Red Barber, p.77

[344] Ibid, p.75

[345] *Friday's with Red* by Bob Edwards, p.73

[346] *The Broadcasters* by Red Barber, p.21

[347] Ibid, p.32

[348] *Radio Stars*, August 1934

[349] *The Sports 100* by Brad Herzog, p.143

[350] *The Golden Voices of Baseball* by Ted Patterson, p.110

[351] *Radio Guide*, November 14, 1931

[352] *Washington Post*, Oct. 9, 1933

[353] Interview with Gary Stevens, 2003

[354] *Voices of the Game* by Curt Smith, p.17

[355] *New York Post*, Oct. 10, 1934

[356] New York Daily News, Oct. 5, 1934

[357] *New York Times*, October 9, 1934

[358] CBS broadcast of 1934 World Series, Miley Collection

[359] *New York Daily News*, October 9, 1934

[360] "Miley Collection," CBS broadcast of 1934 World Series

[361] Ibid

[362] Ibid

[363] Ibid

[364] Ibid

[365] Cardinalhistory.com/1934

[366] *New York Daily News*, Oct. 12, 1934

[367] *New York Daily News*, Oct. 11, 1934

[368] Ibid, p.81

[369] *Washington Post*, July 27, 1935

[370] *The Broadcasters* by Red Barber, p.79

[371] Ibid

[372] *Radioland Magazine*, October 1933

CHAPTER 20 – WAKE UP THE ECHOES

[373] *Notre Dame Victory March*, Michael and John Shea, 1928

[374] *Frantic Francis by Brett Perkins*, 110-120

[375] Ibid, p.2-7

[376] *Woody Hayes and the 100 Yard War* by Jerry Brondfield, p. 77-79

[377] www.und.com/sports/m-footbl/mtt/layden_elmer00.html

[378] *Look Magazine*, January 7, 1958

[379] *Radio Mirror*, April, 1936

[380] *The Broadcasters* by Red Barber, p.35

[381] Ibid

[382] Ibid

[383] *The Golden Voices of Football* by Ted Patterson, p.67

[384] Ibid, p.84

[385] *Chicago Tribune*, Nov.2, 1935

[386] http://ohiostate.scout.com/2/477011.html

[387] *New York Times*, Nov. 3, 1935

[388] *Echoes of Glory – The History of Notre Dame Football*, Warner Home Video, 2006

[389] Interview with Curt Gowdy, 1999

[390] *The Broadcasters* by Red Barber, p.35

[391] *Chicago Tribune*, Nov. 3, 1935

[392] *Echoes of Notre Dame Football* by Joe Gardner, p.27

[393] *New York Times*, Nov. 4, 1935

[394] *Thanks for Listening* by Jack Brickhouse, p72

[395] *Los Angeles Times*, August 15, 1962

[396] Interview with Curt Gowdy, 2000

CHAPTER 21 – THE PRICE TO PAY

[397] *Empire* by Lewis J. Paper, p.247

[398] Interview with Frank Stanton, 2003

[399] *Radio Stars*, Sept. 1936

[400] *Radio Stars*, September, 1936

[401] *Written By Magazine*, June/July 2001

[402] *My Eyes Are in My Heart* by Ted Husing, p. 171

[403] *Friends Academy Yearbook: 1942*

[404] *Radio Stars*, September, 1936

[405] *New York Times*, November 3, 1935

[406] *Boston Transcript*, November 27, 1935

[407] *Boston Transcript*, Nov. 27, 1935

[408] Interview with Ernie Harwell, 1999

[409] *Of Mikes and Men* by Curt Smith, p.47.

[410] *Sports Illustrated*, April, 2, 1990

[411] *Sporting News*, August 21, 1995

[412] *Like It Is* by Howard Cosell, p. 189

[413] Interview with Curt Gowdy, 2000

[414] *Tower Radio Magazine*, November, 1934

CHAPTER 22 – THE MICKEY MOUSE MUSICIAN

[415] *My Eyes Are in My Heart* by Ted Husing, p.180

[416] Ibid, p.181

[417] Interview with Gary Stevens, 2003

[418] *My Eyes Are in My Heart* by Ted Husing, p. 163

[419] *Radio Guide*, December 22, 1933

[420] Ibid

[421] Ibid

[422] *Radio Mirror*, October, 1936

[423] *On the Air* by John Dunning, p. 822

[424] *New York American*, June 17, 1935

[425] *My Eyes Are in My Heart* by Ted Husing, p.167

[426] Interview with Donald Shirley, 2003

[427] Interview with Gary Stevens, 2003

[428] Ibid

[429] *Ten Year Before the Mike* by Ted Husing, p. 297

[430] *Radio Guide*, June 20, 1936.

[431] *How Cities Won the West* by Carl Abbot, p.130

[432] *Radio Mirror*, October, 1936

[433] Ibid

[434] Lennie Hayton and Helen Gelderman marriage record, New Jersey State Vital Records

[435] *Radio Mirror,* October, 1936

[436] *Radio Mirror*, October, 1936

[437] *My Eyes Are in My Heart* by Ted Husing, p. 183

[438] Ibid

[439] *Radio Guide*, July 7, 1934

[440] Interview with Gary Stevens, 2003

[441] Ibid

[442] *New York Daily Mirror*, July 1, 1935

[443] *Radio Guide*, June 20, 1936

CHAPTER 23 – LEMME SLEEP, WILLYA?

[444] *New York Times*, April 28, 1936

[445] *Radio Guide*, June 20, 1936

[446] Ibid

[447] Ibid

[448] *New York Times*, October 5, 1966

[449] *Stork Club* by Ralph Blumenthal, p.16-17

[450] *My Eyes Are in My Heart,* p.195

[451] Ibid

[452] *New York Journal-American*, August 7, 1937

[453] "The Very Thought of You," music and lyrics by Ray Noble, 1934

[454] *New York Evening Post*, April 28, 1936

[455] *Radio Guide*, June 20, 1936

[456] *New York Evening Post*, April 28, 1936

CHAPTER 24 – KEEP YOUR FRIENDS CLOSE AND ENEMIES CLOSER

[457] Interview with Stanley Wertheim, 2006

[458] Interview with Kate Lacey, 2002

[459] *New York Times*, Dec. 21, 1954

[460] *Look Magazine*, Jan. 7, 1958

[461] *This Is Your Life*, June 7, 1957

[462] *Los Angeles Times*, March 30, 2006

[463] *New York Daily News*, Aug. 7, 1936

[464] Interview with Stanley Wertheim, July, 2007

[465] Ibid

[466] Ibid

[467] Ibid

[468] Ibid

[469] Ibid

[470] Interview with Gary Stevens, 2003

[471] Interview with Chuck Thompson, 2000

[472] *Radioland*, November, 1933

[473] Interview with Robert Saam, 2002

[474] Interview with Chris Schenkel, 2002

[475] Interview with Betty Farrell, 2002

[476] *Jimmy Dolan Memoirs*

[477] Interview with Chris Schenkel, 2002

[478] Interview with Gary Stevens, 2003

[479] Interview with Bill Mazer, 2002

CHAPTER 25 – COLOR ME ORANGE

[480] Interview with Gary Stevens, 2004

[481] www.tournamentofroses.com

[482] Interview with Ann Lewis, 2003

[483] *Fifty Years on the Fifty* by Loran Smith, p.10

[484] Ibid

[485] Ibid, p.13

[486] Interview with Pete Seiler, 2003

[487] Interview with Edwin Pope, 2003

[488] *Miami Herald*, Dec. 10, 1935.

[489] Ibid

[490] *New York Daily News*, Jan.1, 1937

[491] *The Broadcasters* by Red Barber, p. 33.

[492] Interview with Dan Magill, 8/2003

[493] Interview with Ernie Harwell September 1999

[494] *Sports on New York Radio* by David J. Halberstam, p.40

[495] Interview with Ernie Harwell, 2001

[496] *Fifty Years on the Fifty* by Loran Smith, p.13

[497] *Fifty Years on the Fifty* by Loran Smith, p.9

[498] *Miami Herald*, Dec. 2, 1936

[499] Ibid

[500] Interview with Pete Seiler, 2002

[501] *New York Times*, December 14, 1930

[502] *Miami Herald*, Dec.29, 1936

[503] *Miami Herald*, Dec.6, 1936

[504] *The Broadcasters* by Red Barber, p.34

[505] Interview with Pete Seiler, 2002

[506] *Jimmy Dolan Memoirs*

[507] *Fifty Years On the Fifty* by Loran Smith, p.5

[508] *Pictorial Review*, August, 1933

[509] *Miami Herald*, December 6, 1936

[510] *Fifty Years on the Fifty* by Loran Smith, p.152

[511] *Miami Herald*, Jan. 2, 1937

[512] *Fifty Years on the Fifty* by Loran Smith, p.

[513] Interview with Pete Seiler, 2002

[514] *The Broadcasters* by Red Barber, p.34

[515] Ibid

[516] *Radio Mirror*, July, 1937

[517] *Miami Herald*, Jan. 3, 1937

CHAPTER 26 – SOCIAL SECURITY

[518] www.socialsecurity.gov/history/history.html

[519] *Radio Guide*, April, 11, 1936

[520] Interview with Ernie Harwell, 2000

[521] *Jimmy Dolan Memories*

[522] *Speaking of Radio*, p.179

[523] Ibid, p.180

[524] *Radio Guide*, March 23, 1935

[525] www.wlshistory.com

[526] New York Public Library for the Performing Arts Photo Archives

[527] *The New Grove Dictionary of Jazz* (Second Edition) Vol II, p.204

[528] Interview with Kate Lacey, 2002

[529] Ibid

[530] Ibid

[531] Interview with Thomas Wagner (writer of documentary film "Finding Lucy"), 2002

[532] *The Saturday Evening Post*, "I Call on Lucy and Desi," May 31, 1958

[533] Ibid

[534] *Look Magazine*, June 21, 1958

[535] Henry Husing certificate of death (NYC Department of Records)

[536] *My Eyes are in My Heart*, p. 185

[537] Interview David Lacey July 10, 2002

[538] *My Eyes Are in My Heart* by Ted Husing, p.231

[539] (The Broadway League) www.ibdb.com

[540] *New York Times*, November 21, 1960

[541] *The Film Encyclopedia*, p.798

[542] *New York Herald Tribune*, Nov. 21, 1960

[543] *New York Journal-American*, August 7, 1937

[544] *My Eyes Are In My Heart*, p.184

CHAPTER 27 – THE LAST OF OUR CLAN

[545] Interview with Gary Stevens, 2003

[546] *The Taste of Ashes* by Bill Stern, p.31

[547] *Sports On New York Radio* by David J. Halberstam, p. 54

[548] Ibid, p. 55

[549] Interview with Bill Mazer, 2002

[550] *On the Air* by John Dunning, p.162-163

[551] *Sports On New York Radio*, p.56

[552] *The Public Calls It Sport*, p. 27

[553] *Sports Illustrated*, Oct. 12, 1964

[554] Ibid

[555] *I Looked and I Listened* by Ben Gross, p.90

[556] *New York Times*, May 9, 1942

[557] *Time*, May 18, 1942

[558] *The Golden Voices of Baseball* by Ted Patterson, p.31

[559] *New York Times*, May 11, 1942

[560] *Sports On New York Radio*, p.59

[561] *The Golden Voices of Football* by Ted Patterson, p.42

[562] *1942 Friends Academy Yearbook*

[563] *Variety*, Aug 9, 1939

[564] Interview with Lena Horne biographer Jim Gavin, 2004

[565] "Nola," music and lyrics by Felix Arndt, 1915

[566] *My Eyes Are in My Heart* by Ted Husing, p.192

[567] Interview with Kay Sedwick, 2005

[568] Interview with Stanley Wertheim, 2006

CHAPTER 28 – RED HAIR, GREENER PASTURES

[569] Interview with Gary Stevens, 2003

[570] Interview with Chris Schenkel, 2003

[571] Interview with Dee Dee Lemerise, 2003

[572] Interveiw with Yvonne Britt December 6, 2003

[573] Interview with David Husing, 2004

[574] *Albany Times Union*, Dec. 30, 1944

[575] Ibid

[576] Interview with Kate Lacey, 2002

[577] Interveiw with Yvonne Britt, 2003

[578] *As It Happened*, p.172–178

[579] *Radio Daily*, January 10, 1946

[580] Interview with Dr. Frank Stanton, 2003

[581] *The Broadcasters* by Red Barber, p.36

[582] Interview with Dr. Frank Stanton, 2003

[583] *Money From Home* by Damon Runyon, p.32

[584] "Ac-cent-tchu-ate the Positive," music by Harold Arlen and lyrics by Johnny Mercer, 1944

[585] *My Eyes Are In My Heart*, p.200
[586] *Look Magazine*, January 21, 1958
[587] Interview with Jerry Cummins, 2002
[588] *Look Magazine*, Jan. 21, 1958
[589] *The Golden Voices of Football* by Ted Paterson, p. 90
[590] Interview with Adam Young, 2002
[591] *Look Magazine*, January 21, 1958
[592] Interview with Goff Lebhar, 2002
[593] *Time Magazine*, Nov. 11, 1946
[594] *New York Herald Tribune*, Oct. 28, 1946
[595] Interview with Dick Barhold, 2001
[596] Interview with Joe Franklin, 2003
[597] Recording of "Ted Husing Bandstand," (Miley Collection)
[598] Interview with Danny Stiles, 2004
[599] *On the Air*, p.429
[600] Interview with Gene Block, 2003
[601] Interview with Joe Franklin, 2003
[602] *Variety*, March 8, 1950
[603] www.jazzplus.gmn.com/artists
[604] Interview with Marty Glickman, 2000
[605] *New York World Telegram and Sun*, Nov. 29, 1956
[606] *Pops: Paul Whiteman, King of Jazz* by Thomas DeLong, p.275
[607] *Philadelphia Daily News*, March 1, 1950
[608] Interview with Gene Block, 2003
[609] *Look Magazine,* January 21, 1958

CHAPTER 29 - IRIS MANAGEMENT CORPORATION

[610] Interview with Chris Schenkel, 2002
[611] Interview with Tim Brundige March 2009
[612] *New York Times*, June 27, 1977
[613] *When Pride Still Mattered* by David Maraniss, p.109
[614] Ibid p.101–102
[615] *Of Mikes and Men* by Curt Smith, p.198–199
[616] Interview with Guy LeBow, 2003
[617] Interview with Eric Carlson, 2007
[618] Interview with Walter Kennedy, 2002
[619] Interview with David Lacey, 2002
[620] Interview with Dee Dee Lemerise, 2004
[621] Interview with Stanley Wertheim, 2007
[622] Interview with Joe Lemerise III, 2004
[623] Interview with Dee Dee Lemerise, 2004
[624] *My Eyes Are in My Heart* by Ted Husing, p.198
[625] Interview with New York City historian Barry Lewis, 2004
[626] Interview with David Husing, 2003
[627] Ibid
[628] WCAU Philadelphia Archives, interview with Powers Gouraud, May 29, 1950
[629] Interview with David Husing, 2003

[630] Ibid

[631] Ibid

[632] Ibid

[633] AP photo archives

[634] Library of Congress broadcast archives

[635] *Look Magazine*, Jan. 21, 1958

[636] Interview with Joe Lemerise, Jr. 2004

[637] Interview with Chris Schenkel, 2002

[638] Interview with David Husing, 2003

[639] Ibid

[640] Interview with Chris Schenkel, 2001

[641] "Call of the Canyon" music and lyrics by Billy Hill, 1940

[642] *Hello Everybody, I'm Lindsey Nelson* by Lindsey Nelson, p. 151

CHAPTER 30 - A FLICKERING CANDLE IN THE WIND

[643] Interview with Kate Lacey, 2002

[644] *New York Times*, Sept. 28, 1950

[645] Interview with Chris Schenkel, 2001

[646] *Watch Your Cleavage, Check Your Zipper* by Guy LeBow, p.267

[647] *New York Herald*, February 15, 1951

[648] *New York Daily News*, February 14, 1951

[649] CBS Television broadcast of Robinson - Lamotta fight

[650] Don Dunphy at Ringside, p.111–112

[651] Ibid

[652] *ESPN Reel Classics* of "Raging Bull," 2002.

[653] *New York Daily News*, Febuary 15, 1951

[654] Interview with Guy LaBow, 2003

[655] Interview with Chris Schenkel, 2002

[656] *Variety*, August 20, 1952

[657] Interview with Herman Masin, 2004

[658] www.nhll.org

[659] Interview with David Lacey, 2002

[660] Ibid

[661] http://showmanshooter.com/html/video.html

[662] *Look Magazine*, January, 21, 1958

[663] Interview with Stanley Wertheim, 2007

[664] www.imdb.com/title/tt0746384/

[665] *New York Daily News*, Oct. 18, 1953

[666] Interview with Bill Giunco, 2009

[667] www.forwhattheygaveonsaturdayafternoon.com/wp-teams/football/1953-football

[668] Interview with Dick Barhold, 2008

[669] Interview with Bill Giunco, March 29, 2009

[670] www.forwhattheygaveonsaturdayafternoon.com/wp-teams/football/1953-football

[671] *New York Dialy News*, Oct. 18, 1953

[672] *My Eyes Are In My Heart*, p. 224

[673] Interview with Dee Dee Lemerise, 2004

CHAPTER 31 – AM I DEAD OR ALIVE

[674] Interview with David Husing, 2003

[675] Ibid

[676] Copy of Husing contract with WMGM

[677] Interview with Gene Block, 2004

[678] www.blockbuster.com/mobile/catalog/movie/details/224662

[679] Interview with David Husing, 2003

[680] Interview with Chris Schenkel, 2002

[681] *Jimmy Dolan Memoirs*

[682] *The Golden Voices of Football*, p. 40–41

[683] Interview with Joe Lemerise, Jr. 2004

[684] Interview with David Husing, 2003

[685] *The Street That Never Slept* by Arnold Shaw, p. 335

[686] Interview with Dr. Laurence Demers, 2004

[687] *Look Magazine*, February 7, 1958

[688] *New York Times*, November 5, 1989

[689] Interview with Gary Stevens, 2003

[690] *Hello Everybody, I'm Lindsey Nelson* by Lindsey Nelson, p.265

[691] *My Eyes Are in My Heart* by Ted Husing, p.237

[692] *Look Magazine*, Jan. 21, 1958

[693] *Coach and Athletic Director*, August, 2002

[694] Interview with Joe Lemerise, Jr. 2003

[695] Interview with Herman Masin, 2004

CHAPTER 32 – DELIVER ME FROM THY HELL

[696] *The Wonderful World of Toots Shor* by John Bainbridge, p.33

[697] *Eastside—Westside, Tales of New York Sporting Life*, p.188

[698] *My Eyes Are in My Heart*, p.117

[699] *My Eyes Are in My Heart* by Ted Husing, p.243

[700] Interview with Dr. Laurence Demers, 2004

[701] Interview with Dorothy "Dee Dee" Lemerise, 2004

[702] Interview with Curt Gowdy, October, 1999

[703] Interview with Franciscan priest Fr. Sullivan, Oct. 2002

[704] Ibid

[705] *New York Times*, July 20, 1986

[706] *Columbia—National Magazine of the Knights of Columbus*, April, 1963

[707] *Beyond the Goal* by Kyle Rote, p. 121

[708] *Columbia*, April, 1963

[709] Interview with Betty Farrell, 2003

[710] www.burke.org/page.cfm?p=73

[711] *The Broadcasters* by Red Barber, p.21

[712] *Look Magazine*, February 7, 1958

[713] *New York World-Telegram & Sun*, Nov. 29, 1956

[714] *Newsweek*, December 10, 1956

[715] *New York Daily News*, January 31, 1957

CHAPTER 33 PASADENA
[716] *New York Enquirer*, April 14, 1957
[717] Kim Lacey interview August 5, 2002
[718] *My Eyes Are in my Heart* by Ted Husing
[719] *New York Journal-American*, December 2, 1957
[720] *My Eyes Are in My Heart* by Ted Husing, p.269.
[721] *Los Angeles Times*, March 17, 1957
[722] *New York Enquirer*, April 14, 1957
[723] Ibid
[724] Interview with Elyse Knox, 2002
[725] Ibid
[726] *Look Magazine*, Feb. 7, 1958

CHAPTER 34 - MAKE SURE YOU WEAR A TIE
[727] www.pimall.com/nais/nl/audiohistory
[728] *Look Magazine*, February 4, 1958
[729] *My Eyes Are in my Heart* by Ted Husing, p.270
[730] *Look Magazine*, February 4, 1958
[731] *The Complete Directory of Prime Time Network TV Shows*, p.788-89
[732] Ibid
[733] *My Eyes Are in My Heart*, p.11
[734] Ibid, p.11-12
[735] Interview with Bob Speck, 2002
[736] "This Is Your Life," May 8, 1957 (NBC)
[737] Ibid
[738] Ibid
[739] Ibid
[740] Ibid
[741] Ibid
[742] Ibid
[743] Ibid
[744] Ibid
[745] Ibid
[746] Ibid
[747] Ibid
[748] Ibid

CHAPTER 35 - HOME AGAIN
[749] *Variety*, June 12, 1957
[750] *L.A. Times*, May 11, 1957
[751] *Look Magazine*, Feb. 7, 1958
[752] Interview with Chris Schenkel, 2002
[753] *Look Magazine*, February 4, 1958
[754] *Variety*, August 7, 1957
[755] *Look Magazine*, February 4, 1958
[756] Interview with Dr. Laurence Demers, 2003
[757] Ibid

[758] *My Eyes Are In MyHeart* by Ted Husing, p. 282

[759] *New York Herald Tribune*, Aug. 11, 1962

[760] Interview with David Husing, 2003

CHAPTER 36 – A LIFE WORTH READING

[761] *Variety*, January 6, 1960

[762] *Look*, "The Look Years," January, 1972

[763] *My Eyes Are in My Heart* by Ted Husing, p.22

[764] *New York Telegraph*, June 20, 1958

[765] *New York Daily News*, Feb. 13, 1958

[766] *New York Herald Tribune*, Feb. 14, 1958

[767] Ibid

[768] *New York Mirror*, February 26, 1958

[769] *New York Herald Telegraph*, Febrary 14, 1958

[770] *New York Daily News*, February 24, 1958

[771] *New York Telegraph*, June 20, 1958

[772] *New York Daily News*, March 20, 1958

[773] *L.A. Times*, May, 18, 1958

[774] *L.A. Times*, Sept. 9, 1958

[775] *L.A. Times*, Sept. 11, 1958

[776] Interview with Carl Bergland, 2002

[777] *New York Telegraph*, June 20, 1958

[778] *Guidepost Magazine*, April, 1960

[779] *NY Telegraph*, June 20, 1958

[780] *Los Angeles Times*, June 22, 1959

[781] *Variety*, Jan. 6, 1960

[782] *The Newark Evening News*, Nov. 8, 1959

[783] *Olean Times Herald*, Jan. 20, 1960

[784] *Chicago Tribune*, Dec. 20, 1959

[785] *New York Herald Tribune*, Feb. 21, 1960

[786] *Newark Evening News*, November 8, 1959

[787] *Variety*, Dec. 2, 1959

[788] Walter Winchell private papers collection

[789] *Guidepost Magazine*, April, 1960

[790] Ibid

[791] *Pasadena Star News*, Aug. 11, 1962

CHAPTER 37 – A DARKNESS BEFORE THE LIGHT

[792] *Variety,* Sept. 28, 1960

[793] *Los Angeles Times*, December 25, 1960

[794] Kim Lacey interview August 5, 2002

[795] "The Very Thought of You," music and lyrics by Ray Noble, 1934

[796] *You're On the Air* by Graham McNamee, p.1

[797] *New York Daily News*, August 11, 1962

EPILOGUE – A HAUNTING SPIRIT

[798] *The Iron Gate of Jack and Charlie's—1950*, p.41

[799] www.imdb.com/title/tt0087089/

[800] www.imdb.com/title/tt0081398/

[801] *Speaking of Radio* by Chuck Schaden, p.304

[802] "The Big Broadcast" ("The Odd Couple" – ABC TV) originally aired Nov. 28, 1974

[803] Interview with Gary Stevens, 2003

BIBLIOGRAPHY

Abrams, Julius, *Out of the House of Judah*, New York, Fleming H. Rvell Company, 1923.

Abbot, Carl, *How Cities Won the West,* Albuquerque, NM, University of New Mexico Press, 2008.

Bainbridge, John, *The Wonderful World of Toots Shor*, Cambridge, MA, The Riverside Press, 1951.

Barber, Red, *The Broadcasters*, New York, The Dial Press, 1970.

Bishop, Jim, *The Mark Hellinger Story*, Appelton–Century–Crofts, New York, 1952.

Blaik, Red, Tim Cohane, *The Red Blaik Story—You Have to Pay the Price*, New Rochelle, NY, Arlington House Publishing, 1973.

Bliss, Edward, Jr., *Now the News: The Story of Broadcast Journalism*, New York, Columbia University Press, 1992.

Blumenthal, Ralph, *The Stork Club: America's Most Famous Night Spot and the Lost World of Café Society*, Boston, Little Brown & Co., 2000

Brickhouse, Jack, Jack Rosenberg, Ned Colletti, *Thanks for Listening*, Diamond Communications, South Bend, Indiana, 1986.

Brookman, Jurg, Bill Harris, *One Thousand New York Buildings*, New York, Black Dog and Leventhal Publishers, 2002.

Brooks, Tim, Earle Marsh, *The Complete Directory to Prime Time Network TV Shows*, New York, Ballantine Books, 1979, 1988.

Bruccoli, Clark, *F. Scott Fitzgerald Poems: 1911–1940*, Columbia, SC, Bruccoli Clark Layman, Inc., 1981.

Buxton, Frank, Bill Owen, *The Big Broadcast 1920–1950*, New York, The Viking Press, 1966, 1972.

Chicago Tribune, various issues 1929–1962.

Coach and Athletic Director, August, 2002.

Columbia College Today, January/February 2008.

Conway, Michael, *The Visualizers: A Reassessment of Television's News Pioneers*, Doctor of Philosphy Dissertation at University of Texas, 2004.

Cosell, Howard, *Like It Is*, Chicago, Playboy Press, 1974.

Cox, James, A., *The Lively Ball—Baseball In the Roaring Twenties*, Alexandria, VA, Refenition Books, 1989.

Davis, Jeff, *Rozelle—Czar of the NFL*, New York, McGraw Hill, 2007.

DeLong, Thomas, *Pops—Paul Whiteman, King of Jazz*, Piscataway, NJ, New Century Publishing, Inc. 1983.

Doerkson, Clifford, J, *American Babel, Rogue Radio Broadcasters of the Jazz Age*, Philadelphia, University of Pennsylvania Press, 2005.

Dunphy, Don, *Don Dunphy at Ringside*, New York, Henry Holt & Co., 1988.

Dunning, John, *On the Air: The Encyclopedia of Old Time Radio*, New York, Oxford University Press, 1998.

Duquesne University Magazine, Spring, 2003.

Ebony Magazine, May 1980.

Edwards, Bob, *Friday's with Red: A Radio Friendship,* New York, Simon and Schuster, 1993.

Ellington, Duke, *Music Is My Mistress*, New York, Da Capo Press, 1976.

Fielding, Raymond, *The American Newsreel: A Complete History 1911–1967*, Norman, OK, University of Oklahoma Press, 1972.

Frost, Mark, *The Gran Slam—Bobby Jones, America and the Story of Golf*, New York, Hyperion, 2004.

Giddins, Gary, *Bing Crosby: A Pocket Full of Dreams—The Early Years 1903–1940*, Boston, Little, Brown and Company, 2001.

Grudens, Richard, *Bing Crosby: Crooner of the Century*, Stony Brook, NY, Celebrity Profiles Pub., 2003.

Halberstam, David J., *Sports On New York Radio*, Chicago, Masters Press, 1999.

Harris, Credo Fitch, *Microphone Memoirs of the Horse and Buggy Days of Radio*, Indianapolis, IN, Bobbs–Merrill Company, 1937.

Hasse, John Edward, *Beyond Category*, New York, Simon and Schuster, 1993.

Harwell, Ernie, *Tuned to Baseball*, South Bend, Indiana, Diamond Communications, 1985.

Hedin, Robert, Michael Waters, *Perfect in their Art: Poems on Boxing from Homer to Ali*, Carbondale, IL, Southern Illinois University Press, 2003.

Heinze, Andrew, *Adapting to Abundance: Jewish Immigrants, Mass Consumption and the Search for American Identity*, New York, Columbia University Press, 1990.

Herzog, Brad, *The Sports 100, The One Hundred Most Important People in American Sports History*, New York, Macmillan, 1995.

Howard, Brett, *Lena: An Unauthorized Biography of A Living Legend—Miss Lena Horne*, Los Angeles, Holloway House Publishing, 1981.

Husing, Ted, Cy Rice, *My Eyes Are in My Heart*, New York, Bernard Geis Associates, 1959.

Husing, Ted, *Ten Years Before the Mike*, New York, Farrar & Rinehart, Inc., 1935.

Galicich, Anne, *The German Americans*, New York, Chelsea House Publishing, 1996.

Gardner, Joe, *Echoes of Notre Dame Football*, Naperville, IL, Sourcebooks Media Fushion, 2001.

Glickman, Marty, Stan Isaacs, *The Fastest Kid on the Block*, Syracuse, NY, Syracuse University Press, 1996.

Gritsch, Eric W, *The History of Lutheranism,* Minneapolis, MN, Augsburg Fortress, 2002.

Gross, Ben, *I Looked and I Listened*, New York, Random House, 1954.

Guidepost, April, 1960.

Kaytor, Marilyn, *"21" The Life and Times of New York's Favorite Club*, New York, Viking Press, 1975.

Kernfeld, Barry (Editor), *The New Grove Dictionary of Jazz*, (Second Edition), New York, Grove's Dictionaries, Inc., 2001.

Kosak, Hadassa, *Cultures of Opposition: Jewish Immigrant Workers, New York, 1881–1905*, Albany, NY, State University of New York Press, 2000.

Kriendler, H. Peter, Paul H. Jeffers, *"21" Everyday Was New Year's Eve*, Dallas, TX, Taylor Publishing, 1999.

Lackmann, Ron, *The Encyclopedia of American Radio*, New York, Checkmark Books, 2000.

Lawrence, A.H., *Duke Ellington and His World*, New York, Routledge, 2001.

LeBow, Guy, *Watch Your Cleavage, Check Your Zipper (Are We On the Air?)*, New York, SPI Books, 1994.

Literary Digest, 1929.

Lomonaco, Michael, Donna Forsman, *The "21" Cookbook*, New York, Doubleday, 1995.

Los Angeles Times, various editions 1957-2006.

Look Magazine, Jan–Feb. 1958.

Luther, Martin, *On the Jews and their Lies*, Translated by Martin H. Bertamn, Philadelphia, PA, Fortress Press, 1971. (1543).

Luther, Martin, *Augsburg Confession (The Confession of Faith)* Translated by F.Bente, W.H.T. Dau, St. Louis, MO, 1921, Concordia Publishing House.

Maraniss, David, *When Pride Still Mattered: A Life of Vincent Lombardi*, New York, Simon and Schuster, 1999.

McNamee, Graham, *You're On the Air*, New York, Harper & Brothers Pub., 1926.

Metz, Robert, *CBS—Reflections in Bloodshot Eyes*, Chicago, Playboy Press, 1975.

Miami Herald, various editions 1934-1938.

Mitchell, Jan, *Luchow's German Cookbook*, Garden City, New York, Doubleday & Company, 1952.

Moore, Bob, *Those Wonderful Days, Tales of Racing Golden Era*, New York, Amerpub Company, 1976.

Muggamin, Howard, *The Jewish Americans*, New York, Chelsea House Publishing, 1996.

Nelson, Cordner, Robert Quercetani,*The Milers*, Los Altos, CA, Tafnews Press, 1985,

Nelson, David M*., Anatomy of a Game, Football, the Rules and the Men Who Made the Game*, Newark, NJ, University of Deleware Press, 1994.

Nelson, Lindsey, *Hello Everybody, I'm Lindsey Nelson*, New York, Beech Tree Books, 1985.

Nicholson, Stuart, *Reminiscing in Temp:, A Portrait of Duke Ellington*, Boston, MA, Northeastern University Press, 1999.

Newark Evening News, November 8, 1959.

New York Daily News, various editions.

New York Herald-Tribune, various editions.

New York Journal-American, various enditons 1957.

New York Post, various editions.

New York Times, various editions

New York World-Telegraph, various editions, 1957 - 1958.

New York Times, various issues 1926–1992.

Olean Times-Herald, January 20, 1960.

Paley, William S., *As It Happened*, New York, Doubleday & Company, 1979.

Paper, Lewis J., *Empire, William S. Paley and the Making of CBS*, New York, St. Martin's Press, 1987.

Pasadena Star-News, August 11, 1960.

Patterson, Ted, *The Golden Voices of Baseball*, 2002.

Patterson, Ted, *The Golden Voices of Football*, 2004.

Perkins, Brett, *Frantic Francis – How One Coache's Madness Changed Football*, Lincoln, NE, University of Nebraska Press, 2009.

Philadelphia Inquierer, 1957.

Popular Science, October, 1930.

Prager, Josh, *The Echoing Green*, New York, Pantheon Books, 2006.

Rapoport, Ron, *The Immortal Bobby Jones—Bobby Jones and the Golden Age of Golf*, Hobboken, NJ, 2005.

Rayno, Don, *Paul Whiteman: A Pioneer in American Music, Vol. I*, Lanham, MD, The Scarecrow Press, 2003.

Radio Announcers—1933, Providence, RI., C. DeWitt Company, 1933.

Radio Mirror Magazine, various issues 1932–36.

Radio Star Magazine, various issues 1931–38.

Radio Retailing, 1926.

Reagan, Ronald, *Ronald Reagan: An American Life*, New York, Simon & Schuster, 1990.

Rote, Kyle, *Beyond the Goal*, New York, Berkley Medallien Books, 1975.

Runyon, Damon, *Money From Home*, New York, Sun Dial Press, 1944.

Schaden, Chuck, *Speaking of Radio*, Morton Grove, IL, Nostalgia Digest Press, 2003.

Schmertz, Fred, *The Wanamaker Millrose Story 1908–1967*, Westchester, Yonkers, NY, Millrose Athletic Assoc., 1967.

Shaw, Arnold, *The Street that Never Slept*, New York, Coward, McCann & Geoghegan, Inc., 1971.

Smith, Curt, *Voices of the Game*, New York, Fireside Books, 1987, 1992.

Smith, Curt, *Of Mikes and Men*, South Bend, Indiana, Diamond Communications, 1998.

Smith, Loran, *Fifty Years on the Fifty*, Charlotte, NC, The East Woods Press, 1983.

Spink, J.G. Taylor, *Judge Landis and Twenty-five Years of Baseball*, New York, Thomas Y. Crowell Company, 1947.

Sports Illustrated Magazine, 1964, 1990

Sobol, Louis, *The Longest Street*, New York, Crown Publishers, Inc., 1968.

Soyer, Daniel, *Jewish Immigration Associations and American Identity in New York 1880–1939*, Cambridge, MA, Harvard Press, 1997.

St. Petersburg Evening Independent, 1926..

Stanley, Dave, *A Treasury of Sports Humor*, New York, Lantern Press, Inc., 1946.

Stern, Bill, Oscar Fraley, *The Taste of Ashes*, New York, Henry Holt & Co., 1959.

The Sporting News, *Cooperstown—Where the Legends Live*, New York, Crescent Books, 1997.

Trager, James, *The New York Chronology*, New York, Harper Collins, 2003.

Variety, various issues 1927–1957.

Washington Post, various issues, 1927–1962.

White, Paul, *News On the Air*, New York, Harcourt, Brace and Co., 1947.

Wintz, Cary D., Paul Finkelman, *Encyclodepia of the Harlem Renaissance*, New York, Routledge, 2004.

Wood, Barry, *What Price Football*, Boston, Houghton Mifflin Co., 1932.

Woog, Adam, *Duke Ellington*, San Diego, CA, Lucent Books, 1996.

INDEX

ABOUT THE AUTHOR

Born in Washington D.C. John is an actor who has played various roles in regional theater productions, independent films, and television shows. He has also written for the stage, creating and performing his one-man show *In the Ballpark*. John has written several articles and essays published in such places as AssociatedContent.com and Themestream.com. He is also host of the Internet radio show "Sportscaster Chronicles." John lives in New York City with his wife and two children. *Radio Master* is his first book.

www.sportscasterchronicles.com
www.tedhusing.net